CONFESSIONS of a BAR BRAT

Confessions of a Bar Brat

Growing up in Rosendale, New York

A Memoir

Judith A. Boggess

Epigraph Books
Rhinebeck, New York

Confessions of a Bar Brat: Growing Up in Rosendale, New York: A Memoir
© 2017 by Judith A. Boggess

All rights reserved. No part of this book may be used or reproduced in any manner without written permission from the author except in reviews and critical articles. Contact the publisher for information.

Author's disclaimer: Some characters, dates and events have been combined in order to bring this memoir to an end. Some names have been changed to protect the guilty along with the innocent. Any factual errors are due to a faulty memory and not meant to cause any personal harm.

Paperback ISBN: 978-1-944037-66-6
Hardcover ISBN: 978-1-944037-67-3
Library of Congress Control Number: 2017941995

Book design by Colin Rolfe

Epigraph Books
22 East Market St., Suite 304
Rhinebeck, NY 12572
(845) 876-4861
www.epigraphps.com

*To my brothers: Eddie, Andy, Mickey, & to Steve,
born after the time of this memoir. This is what you missed.
To my eldest sibling Arlene Morningstar,
once unknown, found, and sadly left unexpectedly.*

Acknowledgments

Thank you Tony Cacchio Sr. and family for operating the Rosendale Theatre, Rosendale, NY, for 61 years, from 1949 to 2010. It was the movies of the '50s that kindled my imagination, enhanced my power of visualization, gave me strong female role models, and planted the seed for this memoir.

Thank you Rosendale Theatre Cooperative for continuing the operation of the theater, keeping Main Street alive, and giving me the opportunity to make popcorn and take tickets of theater goers.

Special thank you, Drew Boggess, my husband for his love, constant patient support and sound advice regarding this memoir.

Thank you Kathryn Gutierrez and Melissa Brenner, my daughters, for patiently waiting for this manuscript to be published.

Thank you Dale and Patrick Brenner, my sons, for having graced my life with your presence for thirty-four and twenty-seven years respectively.

You are never more than a thought away.

Thank you to my grandchildren, and their children. You are a constant reminder that children have better memories than adults realize.

Special thanks to author Fred Poole, Woodstock, NY, and the Authentic Writing Group. Through the safety of his workshops, I found the courage to tell my story the way I lived it.

Thank you to the following for their invaluable insight & support: the Thursday Night Women's Critiquing Group; to Sandra Gardner, author; Lena Adams, PhD & Stage Manager for Performing Arts of Woodstock; Ursula Zorika unflinching final editing & unwavering support.

X-Special thanks to Kathleen Caproni PhD, who helped pick the bar brat up from the barroom floor.

Many, many thanks to my Bestest Friend and Lifelong Sweetheart Harold "Porky" Rosenkranse ~ "Tag. You're it."~

As promised, an "Honorable Mention" to Peter Stein fellow inmate of St. Peter's School.

Never Cry

Learn the secrets of survival.
Observe, listen and don't talk.
Pray to Jesus.
And never cry. At least,
not where they can see or hear you.

Study them. Scrutinize them.
Look for the flick of her eyebrow;
The narrowing of eyes;
Red painted lips pulled into a thin line.

Watch the vertical blue vein, the barometer,
on his forehead turn purple, throb.
Don't wince or jump, as his meaty fist
sledgehammers the tabletop.

Feign innocence, be disinterested but attentive.
Don't speak up, or defend yourself.
Pray to Jesus.
And never cry. At least,
not where they can see or hear you.

Judith A. Boggess

1954

Prologue

Reid's Hotel & Bar
Rosendale, N.Y.

I was born upon thy bank, river,
My blood flows in thy stream,
And thou meanderest forever
At the bottom of my dream.

Henry David Thoreau

It was a muggy night in August 1954, in the cement-manufacturing town of Rosendale, N.Y, which sits on the banks of the Rondout Creek. A rowdy crowd of single women, uniformed soldiers on leave from Korea, and the soon to be unemployed cement mineworkers with girlfriends or wives, were partying hard at Reid's Hotel and Bar. It was "Big Ed's" closing night and he, Big Ed, was holding a blowout going away party. His five-year lease expires at midnight, but he didn't care. He pushed the limits of the lease and said to his wife, Edith, "We're leaving tomorrow, what's the problem?"

The sounds of laughter and the music from the jukebox, comes up through the ceiling of the bar, into my bedroom and helped me to fall asleep.

A little after midnight, Mom burst in my room, switched on the bare overhead light and shouted, "Get up! We're being kicked out!"

Mickey, my five-year-old brother and I, had been dead asleep. I rubbed my eyes in confusion, as I thought Pop had said we were moving tomorrow, and I hadn't packed up my stuff yet.

An expert at age 11, I could tell by the sound of her blubbering voice that Mom had been drinking again. "It's the middle of the night and he's throwing us out in the street," she cried.

"Who, Ma? Who's throwing us out?"

Green frog panic jumped into my belly and hopped up into my throat. Didn't Pop want us any more? Or was Mom getting hysterical because she was drunk?

Grabbing a few clothes of Mickey's and mine, Mom stuffed them into the small suitcase I used when I visited Aunt Helen.

"Are we going to Aunt Helen's?"

She wasn't listening to me.

"Judy!" she snapped, slapping the lid closed. "Get Mickey out of bed and get outside. Now!" She was on a tear. "This is your father's fault. We needed to be out tonight. But *no-o-o-o*, 'Big Ed' wouldn't listen. 'Big Ed' had to have a closing party. One last fling!"

She looked in my mirror and then at my dresser top, and snapped up a tissue lying there. Finding a clean spot on it, she wet it on her tongue, then dabbed at the dribbling brown mascara staining her cheeks.

"Oh *no-o-o-o*, Joe Reid won't put us out. Right! Well, look what's happening now." She continued yammering as she primped herself.

A fat policeman appeared at my bedroom door. "C'mon Edie," he said to my mother. "You need to leave." He smiled at her. He'd been to our bar before when fistfights got out of hand.

The police were from the sheriff's department in Kingston. When we got outside, they said we couldn't stand on the sidewalk in front of the bar because it was Mr. Reid's property, and our lease was up. Mickey and I went and stood in the middle of Main Street, me in shorty p.j.'s and untied sneakers, and Mickey in a T-shirt and underpants, while Mom sniffled and hung onto that suitcase. Where were my older brothers, Andy and Eddie? They made me feel safe when things got bad, like now. My insides shivered.

The policemen tried to empty the bar. Customers came out and stood in the road laughing with drinks in their hands, as red patrol car lights bounced off buildings.

"What are we going to do?" Mom asked Pop, who was arguing with the cops.

The policemen were warning my father. "Cool down now, Mr. Cherny. Mr. Reid has the perfect right to evict you. You were supposed to have vacated the premises by midnight. That's what your lease says right here. Look, I have a copy of it."

"Yeah? And I got kids, for Chrissakes! Who puts kids out in the street at midnight?" Pop asked.

"You should've thought about 'em and not try to use them as pawns," Joe Reid shot back.

"Screw you, you black-Irish Mick and the friggin' horse you rode in on! Ya son-of-a-bitch!" Pop roared, while two burly officers hooked onto his arms.

"Ed, do me a favor," the police chief said; "leave now before I'm forced to arrest you. You know I don't want to do it." He knew Pop from playing illegal poker games set up in the basement under the bar.

Pop threw off the policemen's hands like flicking flies off a pie at a picnic.

"Try and make me!" he shouted, and walked back into the bar, pushing cops out of his way. He cursed Mr. Reid in Slovak and English, loud enough for all Main Street to hear, and added, "I ain't friggin' goin' nowhere!" He waved his customers back inside, and they followed.

Neighbors were hanging out of bedroom windows or standing outside their homes. There was one lady and her husband who lived next door that were standing on their front porch. She was wearing bathroom slippers and a chenille robe wrapped tight around her body, with this frilly dust-cap on her head covering up her bobby pins. I don't remember her name. Our families were never friends. She stared at Mickey and me with a "tsk-tsk" look on her face. Her husband stood next to her in his striped pajama top, work pants, and leather slippers. He shook his head at us. They made me feel like I was at the Academy Awards ceremony, stark naked in a spotlight, getting an Oscar for Worst Actress in the Worst Picture of 1954. My body shook from head to toe, and my face burned.

The news spread rapidly through all the gin mills in town. Mom's friend, Mike Wazelewski, drove down from his place, the pink Astoria Bar and Hotel. He stood by Mom making jokes about cops and offered us rooms to stay in if we needed them.

"Ma? Ma? We gonna stay at Mike's? What's gonna happen to all my stuff? Where's Eddie and Andy?"

"For God sakes, Judy. They're inside. We have bigger problems than worrying about getting your junk?" She dropped the suitcase by her feet, turned away and plastered what Pop called a "come-hither" smile on her face that kept Mike talking to her.

The police chief was telling Mr. Reid, whose hands were waving in the air, to leave and that Pop swore he would be out by tomorrow. Reid's face wasn't happy as he listened to the music and laughter blaring out of the bar.

Snatching up the suitcase with one hand, I hoisted up Mickey with the other. He was scared and about to cry. He wrapped his chubby legs around my skinny waist and clung to my neck with his arms like Tarzan's chimp, Cheetah. Walking past the staring eyes of neighbors, I struggled under his weight as I trudged up Main Street to the Astoria. I ain't going to be gawked at no more. Jeez, I felt like a freak in a sideshow.

"Where we goin'?" Mickey asked. "I gotta pee."

"We're going to Mike's. You pee-pee there. And not on me, or in the bed, or we won't have a place to sleep. You hear?"

"Okay. I wan' my blankie."

"We'll get it tomorrow. I promise."

Mickey laid his head on my shoulder and stuck his thumb in his mouth. The further up Main we went, the quieter and darker it got, until we reached the pink glow from the neon lights of the pink-painted Astoria. I pulled open the screen door and walked into the bar thinking how nice it would be to sleep in a bed with clean, crisp white sheets that had been washed and hung outside to dry by old Ma Wazelewski. I bet they'd smell of fresh air and sunshine. I couldn't wait to bury my nose in them.

"Hi, Ma," I called out to Mike's mother who was tending bar, and dropped the suitcase on the floor. She came out from behind the bar with arms outstretched and hugged us to her pillow-soft chest. It felt so good to be wrapped in her arms.

1949
KINGSTON, N.Y.

"All farewells should be sudden, when forever."
Lord Byron

A FAN WAS BLOWING HOT AIR AROUND THE KITCHEN. I sat at the table with Eddie and Andy eating a peanut butter and jelly sandwich, while Mickey in his high chair, was eating and tossing Cheerios on the floor. We tried to ignore Mom and Pop yelling at each other.

"Look, Edith, you wanted me out of this partnership with my brother. You were right. A partnership's a bad ship to sail. We're going to Rosendale; getting out of Kingston."

"What do you mean . . . ?" Mom asked. "We've invested everything in this grocery store."

Mom slapped the potholder down on the cook stove. Oh, boy, I thought, fur's gonna fly now.

My head felt like a Ping Pong ball as it snapped back and forth, looking from one to the other.

"I signed a five-year lease with Joe and Bridey Reid for their bar and hotel. You know, Reid's Hotel. Reid hurt his back and can't work the bar no more. It's a lawsuit thing."

"But, Ed . . . Reid's? Where did you get the money for a lease?"

A bar? Pop's gonna get a bar?

"My brother Joe and I got an arrangement about the store."

"What about your GI loan? We're just gonna lose it? You can't get another one."

I had lots of questions too, but knew to keep quiet or be told to get lost. Eddie will tell me later about having to move again.

"We're not losing money. Jeezus, Edith. You were just bitchin' and bellyachin' about my brother and his wife getting a salary from the store and you weren't. Aren't you the one who walked out and went back to Hercules' Powder Mill? Now ya can quit."

"And when the five-year lease is up, what then?"

"We'll get another business. Or maybe Reid will sell us his place."

"You never ask what I want," she said.

Pop was the kind of man, Mom said, who couldn't work with or for anyone else. He had to be his own boss because he thought he knew it all. And the only time he'd stay in one place and see something through would be the day he was planted six feet under.

"Well, what d'ya want?" he shouted

My shoulders jerked up. I clapped my hands over my ears and squeezed my eyes closed. Pop's loud voice made me pukey inside, and I couldn't eat anymore. It hurt my stomach. My brothers ate like nothing was happening, except Mickey looked scared when Pop yelled. His bottom lip pushed out and was shaking.

"I don't know. Buy your brother out."

"Jee-zus-H-Kee-rist! There's no pleasin' ya, is there Edith?" Pop stormed out of the kitchen and went back to the grocery store.

Mom narrowed her eyes, and snapped at me. "What are you looking at?"

I gulped down my milk and picked at the bread lying on my plate. I knew she didn't want an answer. She just wanted someone to yell at.

Get outside. Go play under Mrs. Van Etten's porch. Her porch had crisscrossed strips of wood all around it. She called it lattice. I could see out the small square holes, and nobody could see in because of the tall bushes growing in front of the porch. And I could stand straight up underneath without banging my head on the porch floor beams. I like it there. It's cool and dark and quiet. It was my hideout.

Pop said he hated August. It was when the "gawd-damn dog days" hit, when the temperature and humidity both went into the high 90s. The thought of packing and moving in this heat had him and Mom's teeth on edge. We had one week left to move to Rosendale. I was glad I got to finish first grade, but sad to leave my new friends.

While the sun steamed up the garden roses and made the air around the grocery store smell sweet, Mom packed dishes and glasses in cardboard boxes she pulled from the grocery storeroom. We weren't moving too far from Kingston. I knew Rosendale from visiting Grandma and Dad DeWitt, Mom's parents. They once owned a grocery store and a couple of houses there on Main Street. Now they lived a mile outside the village.

Sitting in the wooden rocking chair on the porch, smelling the roses, I thought about having to make new friends. Mom said there were lots of kids in the village, but would any of them be six-years old like me? I rocked and listened to the eek and squeak of the porch and the rocker, and felt like crying. Are we taking the rocker? I liked to sit in it and hold Mama Cat in my lap, pet her silky fur and scratch behind her ears. When I rubbed her belly, she didn't always like it. She squirmed and meowed to get down. I worried about her. Mr. Reid told Pop "no cats," because they peed on everything and you couldn't get rid of the smell. I begged Pop. Mama Cat didn't do that. She never did it here. But Pop said, "No! End of story. Cat's not coming."

I went inside and found Mom folding in the flaps of a box. Hugging my wriggling cat to my body, I asked, "What's gonna happen to Mama Cat?"

A sweaty, red-faced Mom, looking down at the box of glasses, said, "I have to take these to Rosendale. Bring her along. We'll decide on the way. Where's Andy?"

"Dunno," I shrugged.

Mom was crabbing about Andy never being around to help. She put the small boxes, loaded with fancy cut-glass dishes and wineglasses from Czechoslovakia, in the trunk of the car. The glasses had been Pop's mother, Grandma Julianna's. Mom went in the house and changed Mickey's diaper, while I waited on the porch and whispered to Mama Cat petting her. "We're going to see our new home," I said, and kissed the top of her head.

Mom all freshened and smelling like perfume, came out of the house carrying Mickey. She put him in a padded wicker laundry basket in the back seat of the car next to Mama Cat and me, and popped a bottle in his mouth. I was supposed to make sure he didn't choke. He was my real baby doll and I liked taking care of him.

The ride was 15 minutes, and Mom talked all the way. She drove around Rosendale pointing out all the bars and other businesses. When people first came to Rosendale, she said they built right on the banks of the Rondout Creek. They came to work in the cement mines and mushroom caves, and couldn't care less about a sleepy old shallow river that flooded its bank now and then.

Rosendale's claim to fame, she said, was that the Empire State Building, the Brooklyn Bridge, and the base of the Statue of Liberty were built with hydraulic cement mined here. Our cement made the hardest concrete in the U.S.A., maybe even the world. And that sixty percent of all cement in the U.S.A. came from here, and I could be proud of that, she said.

Rosendale was also known for its eight gin mills in a mile strip. You could park your car at one end of town, drink your way up the street, stagger across the road, and drink your way back down to where you left your car parked. And after all that walking you might be sober enough to drive home without ending up in the creek, or killing some innocent person, or yourself, she said.

In the center of the village were four bars. Smack in the middle was Reid's Hotel and Bar. On up the street were the Well, the Astoria Bar and Hotel, and the Valley Inn. The Brookside, Bianco's, The Chalet, the Elms and the Bridge View Inn were outside the village limits, but still an easy walk, depending on how desperate you were for a drink after other bars had kicked you out for being drunk. And there were two churches in the village: Episcopal and Dutch Reformed. The out-of-business Baptist church had been turned into a Grange Hall. The Roman Catholic Church was up on James Street. Mom said that was because Catholics thought they were on "higher moral ground," so they had to build up and away from the heathen churches.

There were a few boarding houses; one called Fielder's, where vacationers stayed and some of the cement and mushroom workers lived year-round. Old Dr. Rymph's office was on Creeklocks Road. (Pop called him a horse doctor.) Grandma DeWitt liked him because he used herbs to make people better. He got replaced by Doc Galvin. (Pop called him a pill-pusher.) And there was a place to get candy, Doc Vaughn's Drugstore and, later on, Gilmartin's Luncheonette. Rosendale had three small grocery stores with different foods: German wursts and potato salad at Hermance's; Jewish blessed-by-a-rabbi foods at Goldwasser's; and just plain American bologna, cheese, and white bread at Roosa's. Rossler's, a big grocery store, opened up and sometime later it was sold to the Tratarios' family and became "The Food Center."

The rest of Main was cram-packed with homes sandwiched in between stores on both sides of the road. Except for a driveway here and there, buildings were planted so tight together there was hardly room for a kid to squeeze through sideways. It looked like the builders had fought for space and weren't giving up an inch of ground for grass to grow, except for a tiny front or back yard here and there.

Reid's sat to the right of a house where Grandma and Dad DeWitt used to live. There was a driveway to the right of Ried's and then a couple more houses. Mom stopped the car in front of the bar and pointed it out.

"Well, that's where we'll be living for the next five years, Reid's Hotel and Bar, Main Street, U.S.A. Aren't you thrilled? I am," she said, grimacing.

She turned in the gravel driveway and parked around in back. It was a plain, ugly, three-story square red brick building with lots of windows.

"Wait with Mickey while I carry these boxes inside," Mom said, turning off the engine.

She went through the back door of the building. Mama Cat wanted out, also.

"Look, Mama Cat. This is where we're gonna live. Maybe you

can stay outside. See? There's a house back there with kids running around. Maybe you could live with them." I held her face to the glass so she could see out the window.

Kids were going in and out of the faded, two-story gray clapboard house. It looked like three boys. One my size, and maybe my age. The other two were older. On their front lawn were catalpa trees, same as the ones in the park in Kingston. By the left side of the house was a big maple tree with a rope-and-board swing tied to a branch. It'd be great to have kids in my backyard to play with. But there wasn't any yard for the hotel. I looked around. Nope. No yard at all back here. Just a gray slab of concrete the length of the building, and a gravel driveway the people who lived behind the hotel used to get to their house. There wasn't even a place for Mom to grow flowers, or mint for iced tea, like she did at the grocery store.

Mama Cat scratched my arm to get free and jumped in the front seat of the car. I went after her and rolled up the front windows while I pinned her to my body. Cat hair floated in the air, stuck on my clothes and was all over the car. Pop was gonna have a hissy fit when he saw it.

Mom returned and said she wanted to show me Saint Peter's, across the creek on James Street. It had the same name as the church and school I'd been going to in Kingston, so I guessed it wouldn't be too different. "Who're those kids over there?" I asked.

"I don't know. When we move in, go find out," she said and turned the key in the ignition.

"Can we give them Mama Cat? Maybe she could sleep in their house. I could feed her outside. And we could give them some cat food in case I forgot or something. Please?"

"No."

"But, you said we'd . . . ."

She gave me a look that said, "Shut up!"

We drove to the opposite end of town without speaking. She turned and crossed the ricketiest bridge. It shuddered, shook and rattled. I was afraid it'd fall apart.

"Am I gonna have to walk across this thing?" I asked.

"Yes, unless you're going to fly over it."

If I'm going to cross it, Eddie will have to hold my hand.

"There's boards missing over where you have to walk," I said, peering out the window.

"Step over the gaps," she said.

On my right was the red brick school. Up a little hill was the red brick church. Catholic schools and churches all looked the same. Red and brick. These were smaller than Kingston's, and just about as far to walk to. Mom turned her car around in the driveway of the church and drove back down the hill and across the bridge again. But, instead of going back the way we came, we went away from the village, passing under "the tallest train trestle in New York State," Mom said. The trestle went high over the road and over the creek and into the treetops, until you couldn't see it no more.

"We gonna see Grandma and Dad DeWitt?" Maybe my grandfather was taking my cat for me.

"No, we haven't got time."

"But this is the way to Grandma's, right? Where we going then?" I asked, trying to hold onto my cat and look out the car window.

"Don't say 'ain't'. It isn't in the dictionary and you're not a hick. We're going to a farm where we can leave Mama Cat."

Her words scared me, and I began to sniffle.

"But Dad has a farm. Why can't we leave her at Dad's? How come we never go see Grandma and Dad DeWitt?"

"Because Dad's got enough cats and he doesn't want any more. And I don't feel like stopping today. Grandma isn't feeling well. I don't want to get stuck visiting and . . . Okay?"

"And I don't want to leave Mama Cat with strangers!" I cried.

"Stop! We'll find a dairy farm with cows. She'll be all right. The farmer will be glad because cats catch mice that eat the cows' feed. He'll give her lots of milk, too." She smiled.

That didn't make me feel better.

When Pop said I couldn't keep Mama Cat, I'd prayed to Jesus that Uncle Joe might want her to catch mice in the store when he moved in. I guess Jesus didn't hear me, or else Uncle Joe didn't like cats neither. Now I prayed to change Mom's mind. Please, please, please, Jesus. Don't let her do this, I begged Him with all my heart.

We came into the town of High Falls, took a left and drove until Mom saw a sign that said Clove Road, where she made a right turn. Later, another sign said we were in Alligerville. Mom slowed the car. I saw her looking at a farm, which had a big old red barn with cows outside it, and a large white farmhouse with green shutters. There was a long driveway, but Mom didn't drive up it. She made a quick U-turn in the road and stopped the car before their mailbox. "Open the door and put the cat out on the grass," she said.

"You said we're gonna leave her at the farm, not on the road!" I howled. "You lied! You lied!" I screamed.

"Put her to hell out on the grass and say good-bye to the damn cat," she snapped. "Damn" and "hell" were the only two bad words Mom ever used. She said them when she was really tired, angry, or both.

She scared me, yelling. I put Mama Cat in the grass at the edge of the road, and was petting her, crying and saying bye; when Mom spat out, "Get in the car so we can get out of here!" She didn't want to get caught dumping my cat.

Mom stomped on the gas, giving me a slim second to close my door. I climbed over the seat into the back of the car. Looking out the rear window, I wailed as loud as I could. Mama Cat was meowing and turning in circles, walking back and forth where the grass met the edge of the road. She didn't know where to go. We drove around a turn in the road and she was gone. My cat was gone! I won't ever see her again! I sat down and started crying harder and louder, kicking my legs up and down, pounding the seat with my fists. My throat was raspy, my face red and sweaty. I screamed inside myself, Liar, liar! I hate you! If Pop was here, he'd smack me up topside my head. But he wouldn't have made me dump my cat neither.

It's all my fault. I should have known she'd do this. She did it to our dog. Spots never got outside unless someone walked him. But nobody ever did. Pop kept him down in the cellar temporarily. Mom said Pop's temporaries were the only things that ever became permanent. She griped about having to clean Spots' crap up off the floor in the cellar. Even though Pop told me, "Never pet a dog that's eating. He'll bite you." I had petted him and he bit me. When he chomped down on me, she said, "That's the last straw. That dog is history!"

Mom took him for a ride, too. Put him out of the car by Island Dock block and lumberyard down on the Strand.

"He's a purebred Dalmatian. Someone will snap him right up," she said, snapping her fingers when I asked what would happen to him. He wasn't bad. If I hadn't petted him, he wouldn't have bit me. Mom wouldn't have gotten rid of him, and she wouldn't have lied to Pop saying he broke away on a walk, and wouldn't come back when she called him. In Catechism class we learned about lies, and was glad Pop didn't ask me any questions about Spots, because I ain't lying.

From now on, I ain't ever going to get any animals ever again. Hey Jesus, you too busy to hear my prayers?

The Sister who taught first grade said Jesus always heard everything. If He did, how come He didn't hear me and help my cat? Maybe He's mad and getting even because I petted Spots when I wasn't supposed to.

"Stop that damn caterwauling; you're going to wake Mickey!" Mom said. She saw my face in the rearview mirror. "Wipe that hateful look right off your puss."

Okay. I wiped my dripping nose onto the front of my shirt.

"Don't do that!"

With all my might I began to sniff snot up my nose, making as much noise as I could.

"Stop that!"

I stopped sniffing and began to lick my top lip. She kept looking at me through the rearview mirror.

"You're disgusting, you know that? A disgusting pig! I don't know where you came from."

I ignored her. And I'd get even with her for dumping my cat. Cross my heart and hope to die. I'm gonna tell Eddie what she did. Ain't telling Andy. He'd just laugh.

Day's End

There are more truths in twenty-four hours of a man's life than in all the philosophies.

Raoul Vaneigem

Back at our grocery store in Kingston, I jumped out of the car and ran to the railroad tracks that crossed East Chester Street, four houses down from ours. Mom screamed at the top of her lungs, "Judith Ann! Get back here, young lady! Or you'll get 'what-for' when you get home!"

When she called me Judith Ann, she was real angry.

"Just wait till I tell your father, young lady."

Yeah and just wait till I tell him what you did with his dog.

She had Mickey in her arms. She wouldn't chase me, and she wouldn't keep yelling because she was always saying, "What will the neighbors think?"

At the railroad tracks, I walked the hot silvery iron rails pretending to be a tightrope walker in a circus. Then I felt it in the rails. The train was coming and I knew I'd let it run over me and let her scrape my body off the tracks with a pancake flipper. I'd look like a dead porcupine splattered on the road. And, when I was dead, Mom would be sorry she got rid of my cat.

The engineer slowed and sounded his steam-whistle warning before the train crossed the road. Then he picked up speed. The rumble in the rails tingled my feet through the soles of my sandals. It was getting harder to keep my balance. The engineer leaned out his window, looked at me, shook his fist and yelled words I couldn't hear over the noise in my ears. He blasted his whistle long and loud, scaring me. My legs wobbled, my knees gave in, and my arms beat the air as I fell backwards onto my butt away from the tracks. The train chugged by throwing hot cinders against my bare legs. The engineer yelled, "Ya friggin' nuts?"

"Oww-ouch!" The cinders burned. "Stupid train! You missed me," I yelled back and cried. I wanted to be squished flatter than a flapjack.

My hands and legs were covered with coal dust and dirt. I was a mess top to bottom, and couldn't care less.

Picking myself up, I crossed the tracks to the one-lane dirt road where the colored families lived in a tight row of houses. I played here almost every day with my friend Alverta Palmer.

Alverta lived in the middle of the row. She was lucky. Her house always smelled of something cooking, and her mom and pop liked children. Kids of all ages were there most of the time. They didn't all belong to the Palmers. Some were take-in kids, some were neighbors, and then there was me, who Alverta called the white sheep of the family. Today it was real quiet. Alverta said her aunt was taking them someplace, probably swimming at Kingston Point in the Hudson River.

Alverta's mom peeked through the curtains of her window, watching me kick up dust in front of her house. She came out wiping her hands on her apron, saying, "Whatcha doing out here? You look a fright. Come sit a spell and tell me what's a matter."

She put her thin, strong black hands under my armpits and lifted me up, carrying me to her rocking chair. The porch boards went eek, eek as she rocked back and forth.

"How'd your face get all sooty?" she asked. "You been playing with those cinders by the tracks?"

Mrs. Palmer smelled sweet, like Lily of the Valley flowers and baked cookies all mixed together. Her arms wrapped round me. I laid my head against her chest and cried and she began to sing in a quiet voice, "On a hi-l-l far a-way. . . ."

Her voice drifted off into a hum as she took the corner of her apron and wiped soot and tears from my face. I told her I wished she was my mom, and she smiled and hugged me real tight and said, "Now that'd be something."

I loved Mrs. Palmer. She reminded me of my colored nanny I had when we lived on the Strand. Pop had joined the Navy and left for the Philippines, and Mom got a job at Hercules Powder Mill soldering wires on detonators for bombs for our warplanes. She worked the night shift because it paid more money. Mom hired old Mrs. Shepherd, a colored lady, to care for us. Mrs. Shepherd fed my brothers sweet potato pie, rocked me in her rocking chair and sang hymns to me, also.

Pop left when I was a baby and didn't come back until I'd turned four. When he got home, he changed everything. He told Mom we didn't need Mrs. Shepherd anymore because Mom was gonna work in the grocery store he was buying. "We're movin' uptown. The store has a three-bedroom house attached to it and you won't need a sitter."

Mom said it was okay, because she was tired of working nights at the powder mill, and too many coloreds were moving in on the Strand. She said they could live wherever they wanted, but she didn't want to be the only white person on the block. "Before long," Mom said, "the whole Strand will be colored."

After we moved I never saw old Mrs. Shepherd again, and I missed her, till I found Mrs. Palmer. When I told Mrs. Palmer I believed old Mrs. Shepherd was my grandma and my pop didn't like it at all, she laughed. Pop couldn't make me understand till I could add and subtract large numbers, that Grandma died in '42, a year before I was born. And she wasn't colored!

It felt good in Mrs. Palmer's arms. Sucking my thumb, I almost fell asleep. When I was quiet, Mrs. Palmer asked, "Now what's got you all in a tizzy?"

"I don't want to move," I said, and told her what Mom did to Mama Cat.

Mrs. Palmer said in a calm voice, "Now, li'l missy, I know Jesus's taking care of your cat. She'll be au-right. When you think about her, you just tell Jesus 'Look in on my cat,' and He'll do it. Yes sir-ee. You bet He will."

Her belief in Jesus made me feel good. Maybe Mama Cat would be all right.

She asked if I wanted something to drink, set me down and went to make a small glass of fresh-squeezed lemon juice and water with sugar in it. She gave me an oatmeal cookie. When I finished, she said, "You best be getting on home now before your brother comes looking for you."

I hugged her really tight and told her I would miss her and Alverta.

"I'll miss you too. You be a good girl now and come back and see me sometime."

Pop asked where I'd been. Before I could answer, Mom, who was fixing supper, said, "Down playing with those niggers again."

It was okay to play with Alverta, just couldn't bring her into the store. Mom said white customers wouldn't buy groceries from us if a nigger kid touched any of the food.

Pop said, "Hey, Edith? Why don't ya join the Ku Klux Klan in Wallkill? I'm sure your uncle could use you."

"What's a Clue-clucks clam?"

Mom shot him an evil, squint-eyed look.

"Pa? What's a Clue-clucks clam?"

Pop turned to me and ordered, "Get upstairs and take a shower. You're filthy. Hurry up. Supper's almost done."

"You look like a nigger as dirty as you are," Mom chimed in. "If you didn't have blonde hair, I'd think you were . . . ."

"Enough, Edith!" Pop demanded.

Mickey fell down in his playpen and started screaming. Andy jumped up from the table and went to play with him, and I ran upstairs to take a shower. I wish I was a nigger. Then I wouldn't live here. I'd live with Mrs. Palmer. I'd have my cat. I'd be one of her take-in kids.

My bedroom was empty except for my cot. My p.j.'s and the clothes for tomorrow were lying at the foot of the bed. All my toys and most of my furniture had disappeared.

"Where's my toys?" I called down from the top of the stairs.

"In the garbage!" Mom yelled up. "You should've stayed home and packed for yourself!"

"For Chrissakes, let up on the kid!" Pop shouted. "Why do ya talk to her like that? What t'hell's the matter with you?"

"You baby her too much, Ed. She's a spoiled brat."

"She's our only daughter and we're lucky to have her."

"You treat her better than the boys. You never lay a hand on her. I think she means more to you than I do!" she snapped.

"For God's sake, Edith. Ya jealous of a friggin' kid?"

Standing at the top of the stairs, I watched as Mom stormed out and slammed the front door behind her, rattling the glass. Mickey began screaming again. This was Mom's last night at work. Pop said, "Dollars-to-donuts she'll go out with her friends and tie on a jag. And God knows what time she'll stagger in."

Eddie came in from the store and we sat down to eat. Pop bowed his head and made the sign of the cross. Touching his fingers to his forehead, he prayed, "In the name of the Father . . . ." Mom once said we should pray thanking her, because she was the one who did all the cooking.

Pop kept both doors open to the storeroom that separated the grocery store from our kitchen. When a shopper came in, the bell on the front door would jingle and Eddie would go wait on them while Pop ate, unless meat had to be cut up. Pop wouldn't let him touch the sharp knives or the slicing machine. He said it'd be hard for Eddie to get a job with no fingers. Pop fed Mickey playing airplane with his food on the spoon. When he was finished, Pop set him in the playpen that had red and green painted wooden balls on a wire, stuck between the wooden slats. Mickey could pull himself up to stand. He looked so dumb trying to bite the balls with his four tiny front teeth, and he'd get angry when the balls wouldn't come off the wire. He'd slap at 'em, making them spin around and around. He often fell down on his rear and rolled over onto his side like a stuffed rag doll. He was cute and chubby with eyes like yellow-brown marbles. I liked to rub his thin blonde hair with a balloon until static made it stand straight up in the air. Then I'd stick the balloon to the wall and he'd laugh.

Pop never thought I was too little for work, and after dinner I stood on a chair and washed the dishes.

"Let me wash 'em. You'll be here all night," Eddie would say if he was in a hurry to get out of the house. "You and Andy dry and put them away."

Eddie was twelve and a half, and he never wanted to be home if he didn't have to. He put Mickey to bed before he took off for his friend Donny Van Etten's house across the street, leaving Andy and me who was ten, to see to Mickey. We listened to stories on the radio like "Inner Sanctum," "The Shadow," and "The Green Hornet." Or else we colored until Pop told us to get to bed. Tonight "The Fat Man" was supposed to be on the radio. He had a really big belly laugh. But the radio station was all staticky and you couldn't hear anything. Andy didn't want to color. He went snooping in the storeroom and found a big empty toilet paper box.

"C'mon upstairs," he said, dragging the box past the living room. "Clean up and turn out the light."

Andy folded in three sides of the top of the box and told me to get inside. He sat down behind me, reached around me, and grabbed onto the loose flap.

"Hold onto this," he said. He bent up the edge of the flap for us to get a good grip. With his fists clenched tight around the flap, he started rocking the box backwards and forwards.

"Hi-yo, Silver!" he yelled.

In our bouncing around, rocking backward and forward, and hollering "Giddyup!" we went over to the top of the stairs. Maybe Andy planned this and maybe he didn't. Next thing, we were bouncing down the flight of stairs while sitting up in the box. Fear kept us leaning backwards, which kept us from tumbling head-over-heels. We leaned and pulled back as hard as we could on the cardboard flap. Boom-bam-bang-bam-bam, down fourteen steps we went on our butts. I counted out loud each new bump on my tailbone. This was fun! We ran up the stairs again, carrying the box. And, bam-bam-bam-bam, we went down again, laughing all the way.

"What t'hell's going on in here?" Pop's voice bellowed through the storeroom, into the kitchen and around the stairs, just as we were getting ready for our third trip.

"Shit!" Andy said. "Get in your room. Hurry up."

Pop's feet pounded the floor like a herd of stampeding elephants, making the kitchen windows rattle.

As fast and quietly as we could, we ran to our bedrooms. The battered cardboard box lay at the bottom of the stairs. I jumped in bed, stuffed my jammies under my pillow and pulled the covers up under my chin to hide my play clothes. Pop thudded up the stairs, looked in my room, and went into Andy's room.

"What t'hell ya doing up here? You trying to wake Mickey and Judy?"

"I was playin'," Andy whined. He sat on the floor with a metal toy car, no doubt praying he wasn't going to get cuffed across the room. Andy was always getting smacked for something, even if he didn't do anything wrong.

"Well, get your friggin' ass in bed and don't let me hear another peep outta ya," Pop warned.

He came in my room and tucked the covers in around the mattress because I fell out of bed every night, and patted my head. He tucked me in so tight it was hard to breathe. As he walked out of the room, I opened my eyes and stared at his broad back. I kicked the covers loose, got up and watched as he stood at the top of the stairs looking like he forgot how to go down them. Then he let out a big sigh, slid his beefy hand along the banister and disappeared down the stairs.

I was in the clear. I tiptoed to Andy's room and peeked around the corner. I let out a, "Nan-na-a-nan-na, you got caught and I didn't." I stuck out my tongue, blew a raspberry, turned and ran. He didn't chase me. He knew I'd scream and then he'd be dead. Instead, he pitched a toy car at my head. He missed.

It was half dark out, getting closer to morning when I awoke with a scare, hearing mad voices coming from downstairs in the kitchen.

"Why t'hell did ya have to go out tonight!"

"It was my last night, Ed, for God sakes."

"Is it the full moon again?" Pop asked, and "argh-ROOOO"ed like a wolf louder than the train whistle. "You'll be friggin' useless with a hangover. Did ya have to get sloshed?"

"I'm not sloshed!" Mom snapped.

"Hold a match to the fumes from your breath and you'd be

a friggin' flamethrower. This the same shit you pulled while I was overseas?"

"You didn't have to enlist. You were exempt. You had kids," she said. "You're the one who took off and stuck me with all the bills. I had to get a job."

"Helen told me," Pop said. "Ya couldn't stay outta the bars."

Mom hated her sister-in-law. She said Aunt Helen couldn't get over Pop and her moving to the Strand apartment where Grandma Juliana had died. It didn't help that Pop's other sister, Aunt Moncie, lived there with them.

Aunt Helen would walk up the three flights of outside stairs and into our backdoor without knocking, any time day or night, as if the place were still her mother's. That was until the day she went into Mom's underwear drawer and took out letters Pop had written from the Fiji Islands. Mom came home early and caught her. I never saw Mom so mad. Aunt Helen was a tumble of high heels, hat and high-pitched screams when she was thrown out the front door and flew ass-over-teacups down the stairs.

"I didn't do a thing to her," Mom had said afterward, with a big fat smile on her face. "Could I help it if she's clumsy? She must've tripped."

Mom was yelling that she hated Pop's whole family. She said that lots, but now she added that she hated Rosendale. It didn't pay for her to get angry, because she always went along with everything Pop wanted to do. He told her if she didn't like it, she could leave. I think she stayed because fighting and making up seemed to be the only thing they enjoyed doing over anything else, because they sure did it a lot.

I lay in bed and wished Mama Cat was here. I missed petting her and listening to her purr. Was she hungry? Did she know to go to the barn to get something to eat? Like Mrs. Palmer told me, I asked Jesus to make sure Mama Cat was okay. And told Him I was sorry for whatever it was I did, even though I didn't know what it was, and if He'd just let me know then I won't do it no more.

I couldn't help it. I started to cry because I missed Mama Cat. I was scared maybe Jesus didn't take care of animals. My mind kept seeing pictures of dead raccoons and possums flattened by car tires on the highway. All those squirrels, rabbits, and smelly skunks lay dead with their guts oozing out on the ground and crows picking at them with their long black beaks. The Sister at school said dead animals don't matter none because they don't have souls, but that doesn't seem right. Thumb in mouth, I rolled over to face the wall. Mom and Pop sounded like our radio in between stations, garbled and staticky. I pulled the pillow around my head and covered my ear to shut out the fighting.

Porky

*God gives us our relatives—
thank God we can choose our friends.*

Ethel Watts Mumford

We were all moved into Reid's. Pop put the porch rocker outside on the concrete patio behind the bar. Mom called it "the patio," but it was a thick gray slab of Rosendale cement where you could have a table and chairs and eat outside if you wanted to. But we never ate outdoors unless we went on a picnic. I tried to find a shady spot to put the old rocker, where I could sit and pretend not to be watching the boys play on the lawn with lots of shade from the Catalpa tree's wide leaves. I wanted to ride on their swing, but was afraid to ask.

Earlier that morning, I'd been walking down Main Street looking for someone to play with, and met a colored girl sitting on the stoop of her apartment building. Her mother, Lillian Wynkoop, let me come inside. She said they were the only colored family in the village and she was moving where there'd be more children for her daughter to play with. I understood what she meant. She said they'd be gone before school started, so I knew not to get too comfortable here and to keep looking for other friends.

Back at home, the chubby boy, about my age, who had dark brown hair and a round face, stood near our driveway. He stared at me a long time before he hollered, "Hey, you! Ya want to play or sumpthin'?"

"Sure!" I hopped out of the rocker and crossed the driveway.

"Where you come from?"

"Kingston."

"What's your name?"

"Judy Cherny. What's yours?"

"Porky Rosenkranse."

"Porky?"

"Yeah."

"Like Porky the Pig?"

"Yeah. So what?"

I didn't want to make him mad, so I asked, "How old are you?"

"Six."

"I'm almost seven. What are you?"

"Whadda ya mean?" he asked.

"You know, Polish, Irish . . . Catholic?"

"German."

"That's it? You ain't Catholic? You won't be going to Catholic school?"

"Nope. I'm going to that school," he said pointing in the direction of a well-worn path with a field of tall weeds growing alongside. I couldn't see any school so I took his word there was one in there somewhere. "My teacher's name is Miss Hornacher," he said. "What are you and where you goin' to school?"

Proud as a peacock, I said, "I'm Hungarian, Czechoslovakian, Holland Dutch, French, and Catholic. I'll be going to that school," I said, pointing in the opposite direction.

Wrinkling up his nose and squinting his eyes he said, "You some kinda mutt or sumthin'?"

"What?" I asked.

"Well, you're a lot of mixed-up stuff."

"Yeah, well maybe I am but I ain't no mutt!" I said. He hadn't taken his eyes off my face all the time we were talking.

"What you staring at?"

"Yer nose."

I put my hand to my face. "What about it?"

"Nuttin', I guess. It jist looks like a pig's nose."

Blushing, I raised my voice at him, "I have a pug nose!"

Porky shrugged his shoulders. "Okay," he said.

His two older brothers burst out laughing and grabbed their sides. They looked a little older than Porky, but not much. Pointing at us, they teased, "Porky's found Petunia. Porky's found Petunia."

What idiots!

Porky jerked his head, and said, "Him, with the white hair, is Myron." With a jerk in the other direction, he said, "Other one's Georgie. My real name's Harold, but nobody calls me that. Everybody just calls me Porky because I was a fat baby. You got any brothers?"

"Yeah, three," I said. "Andy's older than me. Eddie's older than Andy. And Mickey's a baby."

"Got any sisters?"

"Nope."

"I gots two. Bobby Ann and Lina. My oldest brother is, Dicky."

Then he said, "Wanna meet my Ma and then go to the playground? Her name's Millie and my Pa's Mike."

Porky pointed to the big, long tractor-trailer with a Piel's Beer sign on its side. It was parked on the far side of our driveway. He said it belonged to his father. "Sometimes," he said, "my father's gone for days, and when he comes home, he's real tired and has to sleep a lot before deliverin' more beer. We gotta be quiet when we go inside."

We walked up onto the front porch. Porky and I went inside. The screen door banged behind us. We went through the dining room and into the kitchen. Millie Rosenkranse was doing breakfast dishes. She wore a plain dress with a faded flower bib apron, the kind you pulled over your head before tying around your waist. Her hair was dark and it curled under at her ears, and she was short with a soft body. She smiled real warm, and said, "Hi, there. Who we got here?"

"Ma, this is Judy. She lives in the bar. She's got three brothers. We're gonna go play at the school. See ya." Out the kitchen door we went, not waiting for her to say yes we can go or no we can't.

"Does your Ma work?" I asked.

"Nah. She stays home," Porky said.

"You're lucky," I said. "I wish my mom didn't have to work."

As we walked the path alongside the empty lot behind their house, Myron and Georgie saw us.

"Hey! Wait up!" Georgie called. "You going to the schoolyard? We'll go with you."

The path ran through a field of overgrown weeds and came out onto the lawn of the playground where the boys' red brick school was.

"Wow! Look at all this!" There was a great big, silvery slide, a double dipper. And metal monkey bars, red-painted wood seesaws, and a merry-go-round. There were baby swings, and big swings with chain links instead of ropes. And a baseball field.

Georgie looked at me, staring at my wide-open mouth. "Ain't you ever seen a playground before?"

"Yeah, well, in Kingston, but not one in my backyard that I can go to every day. This is gonna be great!" I said, bouncing up and down.

Myron shook his head. Georgie took his index finger and made small circles near the temple of his head.

"I'm not crazy! I know what that means."

"Just ignore 'em," Porky said.

I was stuck going to Catholic school, where they didn't have swings or slides like the public schools did. "Nuns don't like girls acting like boys, or letting a boy get a peek at a girl's underwear."

"Where'd they get them screwy ideas?" Georgie asked.

"Maybe," Myron said, "it's because they're stupid like penguins. They sure look like 'em, all dressed in them black and white faggy dresses."

I knew I was gonna rot in hell, but I laughed.

We slid down the slide, swung on the swings and bounced our butts sore on the seesaws. I hung from my knees and did tricks on the monkey bars, pretending the bar was a trapeze. We took turns running and pushing the merry-go-round in a spin, while the rest lay on their stomachs, dragging their hands in the soft silt. We tried to pick up small stones and twigs from the ground, almost falling off. The one who collected the most was the official "winner." There wasn't nothing to win except the title of "winner."

Porky didn't like going around in circles because it made him pukey. "Hey, I'm getting bored. You want to go to the crick?" he asked.

"Sure, great!"

We turned around, dug our feet in the dirt, and brought the merry-go-round to a stop. Dust coated my sandals, my white socks and the blonde hairs on my legs. My hands and fingernails were grubby from the metal bar I clung to while pushing the merry-go-round, and from dragging my fingers in the dirt.

"Can we play in the water?" I asked, looking at my black hands and dirt packed fingernails.

"Yeah," Myron said. "Water ain't deep. Low right now 'cause it ain't rained. You can walk out to the islands."

I saw the creek when Mom and I crossed the bridge to look at the Catholic Church and school. I knew it ran behind the businesses and homes on our side of the street, but didn't know you could walk along its banks from the public school almost all the way up Main Street.

Georgie said the path we were on ended just before the pink Astoria bar at the other end of town. But halfway up, he said, there was another path on the right that would lead up to the red barn and the end of our driveway where their father parked his beer truck.

New friends, a big playground, a creek, and a barn, all in my backyard! Maybe moving wasn't so bad after all.

We took off our shoes and waded out into the shallowest part of the river and crossed over to one of the islands. I washed the dirt from my legs and used sand to help scrub some of the crud off my hands. The older boys skipped flat stones across the water. Porky tried to show me how, but I couldn't get the hang of it. One, just one, I prayed. Com'on Jesus! Let me skip one stinking stone. I searched the pebbled beach for the perfect flat stone. But all of them seemed to be too heavy. Whizz . . . plunk. Whizz . . . plunk. Again and again I tried.

"You ain't holding it right," Porky said. "Do it this way."

"Yeah," Myron piped in. "Kinda pitch it underhand and snap your wrist more."

Porky skipped a stone. The rotten thing did four blips across the water before it sank.

Nuts. "Let's do something else," I said. I'd practice on my own when no one was watching

Porky and I floated boats made out of leaves with bugs for passengers. Then we sank them with outgoing rock missiles. We tried to catch minnows with our bare hands and put them in puddles we made in the sand. It didn't work. The sand sucked up the water, and we never could catch one of them skittery fish.

A sound caught Myron's ear. He told us to hush up. We heard a voice calling across the creek, "My----run, Georg---eee, Pork----eee!"

"Com----ing!" he shouted back to his mother. He said she was calling from their back porch. I couldn't believe how far voices could go. Myron said it was because of the water. Even on Main Street, he said you could yell at one end and be heard at the other end, a quarter-mile away. "That's how everybody knows your business," he said. "Ya can't even fart without someone smelling it at the other end."

Kingston was noisy with cars and crowded with houses and businesses, and your voice couldn't get through anything. But here it was different. I took a deep breath. Even the air smelled better, till Georgie farted, as we were making our way back home.

"Jeezus, George. What crawled up your ass and died?" Myron asked.

"It weren't me."

"Bullshit, it weren't you. Ya better check your draws because you shit 'em."

"It was somebody up street. Smells drift this way. Just like ya said."

"Don't think so. Wind's blowing the other way, jerk!" I let him know.

Porky grabbed his throat, making gagging noises. I held my nose. Myron found the path to the barn and ran on ahead of us.

Georgie let another fart rip, and then another, and another.

"Man, Georgie, go home an' take a crap, will ya? Or get behind us," Porky begged.

Georgie was smiling really big; like he was super proud he'd made us choke.

We came to the driveway. Porky promised tomorrow he'd show me the rest of the way up the riverbank behind Roosa's grocery store and the Astoria.

"Ya gotta be careful behind Roosa's," Georgie warned. "There ain't much bank left because the river's washing it away. Ya take a chance of falling in and drowning.

"There's a towpath across the street," he said. "A lot safer, and it runs up against the mountain. You can go from The Elms Bar and bus stop down on Route 32 all the way to the Valley Inn Bar across from the Post Office, just past the Astoria. Best part, grownups don't ever use it. If you don't want your folks knowin' where you're at, go that way," Georgie said.

"Yeah, everybody minds every kid's business here," Myron said. "Someone's always saying, 'I saw your kid. They wuz with so-n-so. Nosy freaks."

Porky and I went banging back into his house, and Millie scolded us this time about letting the door slam shut. Porky asked if I could stay for lunch. It was my first time eating a cold boiled potato sandwich on Wonder Bread with salt and brown mustard, washed down with a glass of cool tap water. After lunch, we played out on his lawn. I was getting tired, and said, "See you later," and went home. Halfway across the driveway I yelled back, "Hey, Porky! You want to go to the drugstore and I'll buy some candy later?"

He nodded and waved.

At home, Mom was in the kitchen scouring the oven, and got short-tempered when I asked her for candy money.

"Get upstairs and do something with your room. You and Mickey have to sleep in there tonight," she said.

Pop, Eddie, and Andy were working in the bar. Pop was full of big plans for a grand opening with a band for the weekend. He hired the Marconi Trio: Artie, Harry, Arthur, and Frank. I guess they called themselves a trio because "the Marconi Quad" didn't sound right.

Pop put ads in the *Kingston Freeman*, the local newspaper, and cut them out and showed them to me. All he did was yak about how great these guys were, and how he stole them from The Black Swan bar in Rifton. "We're gonna do a boomin' business," he bragged.

I tried to tell Eddie and Andy about the playground and the baseball field. Eddie shooed me away. "Later, Brat. We got work to do."

Hanging my head, I stuck out my bottom lip and made my way up the flight of stairs to our apartment on the second floor over the bar. The living room was at the front of the building. It looked out onto Main Street and the mountain. The kitchen was down a long hallway where I could see Rosenkranses' yard out the window over the sink. Pop and Mom's bedroom was next to the living room. Mickey and I shared a room next to theirs, across from the bathroom. Eddie and Andy were at the end next to the kitchen.

The living room was being used for storage, except for a short time when Pop put tables in there for playing craps and poker. Lawyers, judges, cops, and other businessmen from Kingston came to gamble. Eventually, Pop had to move everything to the basement because I kept trying to sneak in and see what was going on. And the men didn't like trying to use our john to take a leak and find me sitting on the pot. It was also easier to get rid of the evidence downstairs when a city judge warned Pop in advance of a raid. He could hide the tables and chairs in another part of the cellar, where he removed all the light bulbs. The poker chips, dice, and cards were scooted out the basement door. Sometimes he had less than half an hour to disappear everything. Pop never got caught.

The kitchen in the apartment never got used for cooking, because there was one downstairs where Mom made one meal a day for us, the hotel guests, and people at the bar. We all ate supper in the dining room off the bar. The upstairs kitchen was a place to keep unused dishes, the washing machine and Petey, Mom's yellow canary bird she got at the Woolworth's in Kingston.

I stood in the doorway of my bedroom and looked at the mess. There were boxes on the floor, dresses on hangers lying on my cot, along with pillows, and folded blankets and sheets to make up my bed.

Ewweeee! What a gawd-almighty ugly room.

Pop said there was nothing he could do about the walls. They were made of scratchy hairy brown stuff called beaverboard, which was supposed to look like real wood. It didn't. This beaverboard was made out of spit and wood fibers, or sawdust and glue, all squooshed together.

Pop said because we were leasing the place, he couldn't paint over them.

"No tacks, no tape, and no nails," he warned. "We can't make holes I won't be able to patch up."

My dresser was an old one from the hotel. Double puke yuck! It was the color of a black snake. It was full of dings and scratches, water rings, and spilled red nail polish somebody tried to chip off. One of the dresser drawers fell out if I pulled on it too hard.

"Make do till we get some money coming in," Mom said. "Then you can get something better." I made do, they made money, and I never got a new dresser. I wanted my old one back, but she'd already put Mickey's clothes in it.

"It's a baby dresser and you need a bigger one," she said.

I went through the cartons, shoved Mickey's boxes with toys under his crib, and started opening mine.

"Where're my toys?" I kept pulling clothing out of boxes.

After unpacking and stuffing my clothes in the rickety drawers of the dresser, I found one box with toys.

"Just one? Where are all my things?"

Mom hadn't been kidding. She threw most of my stuff away, again. She threw out clothes, toys, and all my drawings I was proud of. Even the good ones I got "A"s on in first grade. Anything that looked cracked, ripped, chipped, or broken she chucked in the garbage. She did it to me when we moved from the Strand to the grocery store, and now she did it again.

"Your mother's not the sentimental type," Pop said later, when I cried about my pictures.

Mom called Pop and me pack rats.

Damn her! I stamped my feet hard on the bedroom floor.

"Whadda ya doing up there?" Pop yelled.

I stopped stamping, got up on the Army cot and jumped on all my clothes and sheets and blankets. I heard some springs go twang! as they popped off the side rails of the cot's frame. I didn't care.

"Knock it ta' hell off up there!" Pop yelled, again. "Ya hear me?"

"Okay!" I screamed down at him.

My eyes blurred. I jumped off the cot and pouted as I dug around in my toys. I found my black cloth Aunt Jemima doll, which looked like the picture of the colored lady on the maple syrup bottle. She was wrapped in my dingy brown and red plaid baby blanket. Good thing she didn't get rid of her. Shoving empty boxes out of my way, I crawled onto my unmade, sagging bed and laid down. Plopping my thumb in my mouth, I curled my knees to my chest and snuggled in with the dresses, the rumpled blankets and the bent wire hangers. It had been a long, hot day playing with Porky and his brothers, and I was tired. I laid my head on the sweat stained, faded striped ticking of my feather pillow. Aunt Jemima with her black face smiled her stitched-on smile, and looked at me with her black button eyes. I wished she could sing like Mrs. Shepherd, or Mrs. Palmer. I wished I had my Mama Cat.

Clouds Are Real

"Pray look better, Sir . . . those things yonder are no giants, but windmills."

Miguel de Cervantes

A COUPLE OF WEEKS WENT BY and I thought the Rosenkranses' lawn was mine when no one was around, like this morning. Huge puffs of white clouds moved across a sky so blue I wished I could fly up there. I spread my arms wide, ran and twirled in circles till I got dizzy, and dropped onto the lawn. I flopped backward onto the lumpy damp ground and lay like a dead man, spread-eagle, eyes open, staring up at the clouds.

Porky's sister Bobby Ann came out of their house, stood behind and over top of me, looking down in my face, blocking my cloud watching. She was a big girl, maybe two years older than me.

"Oh, hi, Bobby Ann," I said, wishing she'd move the heck out of my way.

"Whadda ya doing?" she asked. "Why are you here so damn early? Don'cha ever sleep past seven?"

"I'm watching clouds and seeing what shapes they make. I always get up early. Want to watch with me?"

"I s'pose," she said, and laid down beside me. "I saw you out the window twirling around, and then you fell down," she said. "Didn't know what happened to you."

This was the first time she bothered to speak to me. Maybe she wanted to be friends.

"I'm okay. Wanna piece of gum?" I asked.

"What kind?"

"Black Jack."

"That black shit? No way," she said, making a face.

"Want some red hots?" I asked, holding out a few candies to her.

"Okay. Got any more?"

"Yeah, sure." I dug deep in my pocket and pulled out another handful of tiny, sticky, lint-covered, cinnamon red hearts.

"These got fuzz all over 'em. How t'hell long you had 'em in your pocket?" She wiped each one between her fingers before popping them in her mouth.

"I dunno," I said. "Couple days, maybe."

The clouds were squooshing together and one began to look like a large, white, charging buffalo.

"Bobby Ann, look! A buffalo."

"Yeah, I see it," she said, without much interest.

Is this what the Indian, Chief John Big Tree, meant in the movies when he said he saw a great white buffalo in the sky, and it talked to him? Do Indians really talk to clouds? Hi, buffalo. Can you say something to me? The buffalo twisted and turned with the breeze, pulled out of shape and disappeared. This is stupid. Maybe this buffalo story's all made up because movies ain't real. They're pretend. I wish someone told me that before I went crying to Mom because Jimmy Cagney got killed in a movie.

"Bobby Ann? You know actors, when they get shot, don't die?"

"Of course. What jerk doesn't? Why'd you ask?"

"Oh, no reason. Just kinda wondering if you knew, because kids like my brother Mickey thinks that stuff's real."

"Well, of course babies think it's real."

Heat rose up in my cheeks. So did I, till last week.

Last Friday, Mom thought it was funny, and ha-ha'd at me being so upset about Jimmy Cagney. "He's not dead. He'll be back in the movies next week or next month," she said.

"But Ma-a-a, there was blood and everything! I saw him die!"

Pop was in the dining room shoving tables together, making a place for everyone to sit down to dinner. I'd asked him one question after another, and got madder and madder at his answers.

"How can actors get killed, then get up and go home?"

"What do you mean, they're faking it?"

"Where'd the blood come from?"

He tried to explain actors were people playing, and didn't die or get hurt, and at the end of the day they went home. It was their job. It was pretend.

"Don't you play 'pretend'?" he asked.

"Yeah, but this is different," I cried.

Pop gave up trying to get me to understand that on the big white screen was made-up stories.

By now, the guests were sitting down to eat. Boy, did I feel dumb looking at the faces of my smirking brothers and grinning hotel guests, sitting around the table. Everybody was laughing at me.

"The blood is *not* just ketchup," I said.

"It ain't funny."

"I'm not crying because he's dead, it's because you're making fun of me. I ain't stupid!" I stomped my feet a couple times.

"Why did you tell her the blood was ketchup, Ed? Now she'll never eat ketchup again." Mom snickered.

"She t'ought Cagney was dead, hah! Good thing them bullets ain't real or that'd be one actor shot all t'hell!" Jerry Mertine said.

Everything started to go out of focus. Loud buzzing noises were in my ears. People's voices sounded far away. I'd thought I'd upchuck. I went charging out of the dining room, through the bar to upstairs.

Pop shouted for me to get back to the table.

"No! I don't want supper. I ain't hungry!" I yelled back.

Behind me, I heard everyone in the dining room laugh all the harder. Even Pop joined in.

Upstairs, I flopped on my bed. Movies were . . . magic. Pop let me go every night the theater was open, as long as I took Mickey. "Cheap babysitter," he'd said. Something inside me changed. It was a scary feeling, like a big chunk of me disappeared. It was nothing I could see when I looked at my body, my hands or my face, but I knew the movies would never be the same. The magic was gone, I wailed.

The movie program lay on my floor. I hung off the bed and read the coming week's shows. James Cagney was going to be in another movie with Edward G. Robinson. I always thought he made these movies before he died, because in some of them he got away. If all these actors were pretending, Errol Flynn or Kirk Douglas . . . Agggghhh! I won't ever go back to the Rosendale Theatre, ever again. Movies lie. Grownups lie!

Why do people make movies anyway? Pop said they weren't any different from reading a book, except most people were too lazy to read anymore, and that's what makes movies popular. Some books, like some movies, were about real people but, Pop warned, "believe part of what you read, none of what you hear, and half of what you see," or something like that.

Mom said the real reason movies were popular was they were meant to be cheap entertainment during the Depression and the War, when there wasn't any money to do anything else. It gave people something other than the War or being hungry to think about. Besides, you could see a whole story in a couple hours, where a book could take you a couple weeks to read.

... I KNEW CLOUDS CAME FROM GOD. They're real. Just like the puffy sterile cotton that comes wrapped in dark blue paper that I found in the medicine cabinet. "Look, Bobby Ann! An angel!"

Angels. Sister Dorothea said I had a guardian angel that watched over me. The angel sat on my right shoulder, she said, and whispered good things in my ear to keep me safe. The devil's helpers, she said, sat on my left shoulder and told me to do bad stuff. Sister said angels are in the Bible and the Bible never lies. But Pop had said not to believe all someone tells me, or what's in books, because people lie in books all the time. The problem was, you had to figure out who was the liar and what was the lie. And I ain't ever seen an angel. Could the Bible be making this up? What if Sister didn't know for sure, and I didn't have no guardian angel? Boy, that would stink!

"Do you have a guardian angel, Bobby Ann?"

"I guess so."

I couldn't believe she didn't know much about guardian angels. She knew the prayer. So I explained. But just like my mom, she didn't believe in all the stuff the nuns taught me. Now I see why Protestants aren't going to Heaven, like Sister said.

This cloud looks like a German helmet. Pop also says you never know who is a Nazi, or a filthy no-good Commie son-of-a-bitch. They could be living right next door to you and you wouldn't know, because they look just like everybody else. Even Walter Winchell in the newspaper says so. Mom says she doesn't know no Nazis or Commies, but her uncle knows some Ku Klux Klan members, which she corrected me and said were people, not clams. Pop says her uncle is one of them, which is no better than being a Nazi, or a filthy no-good Commie son-of-a-bitch. And her uncle is no doubt running around with a bed sheet over his head, burning crosses on colored people's lawns in Wallkill.

Sometimes Pop makes up stories so people laugh, or to make Mom mad. I never knew which, or knew if he was full of baloney about the bed sheets. Why would men run around looking like Casper the Friendly Ghost and burn crosses on people's lawns? That would be so stupid. No Catholic would do that. They must all be Protestants.

The clouds began to thin out and disappear. The sky turned lighter blue. I rolled over on my stomach and pinched off several clover buds and put them in my mouth.

"Whadda ya doing?" Bobby Ann asked, wrinkling up her face like a prune.

"I'm eating. Flowers have honey in them. My Grandma De-Witt showed me once when I was at her house. Want some?"

"You're weird. Clover's rabbit's food. And I ain't no rabbit."

"Want to go to Vaughn's to get some candy?" I asked.

"What are you gonna get?"

"Maybe some watermelon-slices and malt balls. Some licorice. What do you like?" I asked.

"Sugar dots and candy cigarettes," Bobby Ann said. "I wet the red on the cigarette tips and use it for lipstick. Do you do that?"

"Nope. I just get the red wax lips, but we can get the cigarettes."

"Come get me when you go," she said.

All this talk about food made my belly growl. Maybe I should go inside get a Coke and some Cheese Doodles. And some Fig Newtons, if Pop's got any left. Mom eats those dried-up Lorna Doones. Yuck! Tastes like sand. I wonder if anybody is out of bed yet? Better go see if Mickey's awake and get him some breakfast.

PETEY THE CANARY

God is Love," we are taught as children to believe.
But when we first begin to get some inkling of how
He loves us; we are repelled; it seems so cold,
indeed, not love at all as we understand the word.

W. H. Auden

Petey died. He didn't last long after our move from Kingston. Mom didn't fuss over him no more, and I don't think he liked being left alone with nobody talking to him. I don't blame him for just up and croaking.

When I remembered, I fed him, cleaned his poopy cage, and hooked the plastic birdbath onto his door. I even tried to help him take a bath by catching him and shoving him into his birdbath. When he ran out of grit to help chew up his seeds, I put Pop's sandpaper in the bottom of the cage till Mom could remember to get what he needed.

Petey liked to listen to fancy piano music and sing. Sometimes I turned the radio on for him, but some idiot was always turning it off when I went out to play.

"Ah, gee, Petey. I tried. Didn't I do a good enough job?"

He was stiff as a board lying on the bottom of his cage on his back. Both feet were sticking up in the air curled into circles. His body felt like an empty eggshell coated with tiny yellow feathers. I was afraid if I squeezed him, he'd crunch into a million pieces. So I stuck a pencil through the circles of his feet and carried him down to the bar to show Mom. "For gawdsakes!" she yelped. "Get that dead bird out of here! Go bury it."

"You think it's funny to see Petey upside down swinging back and forth on that pencil?" she said. Pop thought so. He roared with laughter.

PETEY HAD A NICE FUNERAL. I asked Porky and Bobby Ann to help bury him and say some prayers. I grabbed a roll of toilet tissue from the ladies room of the bar. Bobby Ann said I shouldn't have. "Pop'll think some woman stuck it in her pocketbook and stole it." I wasn't worried.

We wrapped Petey in wads of toilet tissue like a mummy. Then we stuffed him in an empty cigar box I got from Pop. Bobby Ann and I tied the box closed with lots of string from the ball that Pop kept in the kitchen table drawer. I didn't want the worms getting Petey too soon.

Petey liked to be warm. We buried him in the sandbank by the creek, in the late afternoon sun and where nobody would step on his grave, and where the violets grew. Silently, Bobby Ann led the way down to the creek carrying some Queen Anne's lace, black-eyed Suzie's and white daisies. I carried Petey in his cigar box, and Porky carried a cross made of Popsicle sticks with Petey's name written on it.

If God can do all things then why does He let everything die? Tears wet my cheeks as I stood looking down at the tiny grave, and then up to heaven. "Why'd Petey die?" I sniffed.

"I dunno," Porky answered.

"I know you don't!"

"Then why'd ya axed me?"

"I didn't ask you. I was thinking out loud."

"If we didn't die, it'd get real crowded here," Bobby Ann said.

"Yeah," Porky chimed in. "And my house's crowded 'nough."

"What? Jeez, shut up and say some prayers."

Porky and I knelt down by the little grave, closing our eyes and folding our hands together in prayer.

"Judy, hey psssttt, hey, pssttt . . ." Porky whispered.

"*Wh-aa-tt!*" I yelled. "Can't ya see I'm praying? Whadda you want?"

"I don't know no prayers except 'lay me down to sleep'."

"Then say it!"

"Now I lay me down . . ."

"To yourself! Ah, crap," I muttered.

The sad mood was gone. I couldn't even cry anymore. "Rest in Peace, Petey. I'll bring you some flowers tomorrow. Bye."

"Bye-bye, Petey. See ya t'morrow," Porky said. "Poor old bird."

Porky jumped up smiling. "Wanna go play Tarzan in the barn? Go swing on the rope?"

Bobby Ann looked at me and shrugged her shoulders.

"Why not?" I said.

"I want to be Tarzan dis time," Porky demanded.

"Ya look like Tarzan's chimp," his sister said.

"Yeah? And ya look like a big fat, ugly, drool'n g'rilla."

"Take that back!"

"King Kong. Oooff, oooff," Porky teased, jumping up and down and scratching his sides like a monkey.

"Take it back!" Bobby Ann yelled again and chased Porky up the path and into our barn. I followed at a walk, and knew I wasn't playing no stupid tee-heeing Jane. She acted so dumb and got all googly-eyed when "Me, Tarzan" swung with her on the grapevines. I didn't need nobody to help me swing on a rope.

Over the Jukebox

*Precisely because we do not communicate by singing,
a song can be out of place but not out of character;
it is just as credible that a stupid person should sing
beautifully as that a clever person should do so.*

W. H. Auden

I slept over the jukebox. My bedroom floor had nothing between it and the ceiling of the barroom. Hearing the same songs night after night, I memorized the music, and would sing them for fun and play.

Aunt Helen said, "You have a 'rep-er-twaa' of songs to sing, not a 'whole bunch,' for gawdsakes." Later, I learned you spelled it "repertoire."

So I had this whole bunch of songs I could sing when Bobby Ann and I played Fred and Ginger, or Marge and Gower Champion. Bobby Ann had to play the guy because I couldn't hold her in a dip or bend her backwards over my knee; she was kinda bigger than me. But she could dance! We'd swirl around in long skirts, poofed out with crinolines begged from Eddie's girlfriend, or Bobby Ann's sister, Lina. We pretended to be the professional dancers and singers we knew we'd be someday. We practiced songs and dance routines in the dining room of the bar after school and on weekends. My "rep-er-twaa" grew from seeing musicals at the theater.

After seeing a musical, Pop bought the sheet music I begged for, because if a customer asked, "Hey Ed, d'ya know, 'Indian Love Call,' or 'Be My Love' from the movie …?" He didn't like ever saying no. After school, I had fun taking out the sheet music and memorizing the words. Listening to Pop sing the songs taught me the melody. Gill Kelder, a customer who played our piano when he came in for a drink, showed me how to read notes and find some of them on the piano. I heard music in my head all the time, but it was hard to figure out how to play.

There were times when I was playing alone and business was slow that Pop would come in the dining room and dance with me. He'd put one of my 45-rpm records on the record player and say, "C'mere. Lemme show ya how to move."

At first I had to stand on his feet. Later he had me stand on my tiptoes to dance. "Never drop your heels on the floor. Stay up on the balls of your feet." He took a piece of chalk and colored in the heels of my shoes. "Now, I don't want to see any chalk scuffed off. Ya' hear me?" He said that's what the judges did at the dances where he and Aunt Helen won prizes when they were teenagers.

"Ya wait till I signal with a push from the heel of my hand," he said. I felt a gentle push and then we glided across the floor. "Pay attention," he said over and over. "What are my fingers tell'n ya to do?"

"Come forward?"

"Right. And this?" he asked, and I'd feel the nudge in my ribs in a different direction.

"Go back?"

"Don't be like your mother. Let the man lead. And lay your right hand loose in my palm, like a lady."

Dancing with Pop was fun. He taught me to waltz, to fox trot, how to dip, bend over backwards, and how to twirl under his arm. He even knew how to do the Charleston, and swing dancing. I felt all goose bumpy inside when I did the steps right and he said for a kid I was a great dancer.

Pop asked me to sing a couple of times in the bar. Customers said I sounded like Teresa Brewer when I sang, "Put another nickel in, in the nickelodeon" . . . but I didn't like it when they laughed. Pop said customers laughed because I was a ham and I should stop being a Sarah Bernhardt. I heard about her, and I didn't think I was anything like her at all!

"And," he said, "if you want to sing, ya gotta do it right or don't do it at all! Here let me show ya." His "Let me show ya" drove me nuts. "Ya gotta fill your lungs up with air and then push the words up and out so people can hear ya. And open your mouth bigger so the sound can get out."

When I did what he said, singing wasn't fun no more. He made me mad. Mom called him, "Mr. Perfect" behind his back and said no one could live up to his ideals. She said, "There's a right way, a wrong way, the Navy's way, and then there's your father's way. Just do what he says and it'll make your life easier." Great for her, but I didn't like him taking over everything I did. I didn't like having to be perfect. It made me think I couldn't do anything right.

I quit singing where Pop could hear me because I didn't want to be doing it wrong. But I didn't quit dancing because he never picked on me for that. And I didn't quit listening to the music coming up into my room with my ear plastered against the floor. It felt like I was floating invisible over the jukebox, or where Pop was singing. I sang with him in my head, so Andy wouldn't yell at me again for "squawking like a strangled chicken" and waking him up. Besides he threatened to wring my neck like Pop did to the live hens he brought home, if I didn't shut up. Pop kept wondering, when he checked on me after closing the bar, why I was sleeping on the floor, because he knew he had tucked me in each night at nine. He never asked and I never told him.

Sometimes I'd wake up because of loud voices coming from the bar. I thought I had fallen asleep in the movies, till I got wide-awake and knew the moon was shining in my room and Pop and Mom were yelling. All I could think was, Gawd! Not again! Still arguing about the same old crap. Rehash, rehash, Pop would say at some point. As their voices grew louder, I often worried if one might kill the other.

"When the moon's up, drunks drink more, nut cases get nuttier, and your mother gets meaner," Pop would say. He put an extra bartender on full moon or new moon nights, because he once worked as a guard at the state nut-house in Poughkeepsie, and inmates went off their rockers at those times, and bar brawls seemed to happen then also.

Pop and Mom didn't need a full or a new moon to fight. Maybe it was because both of them were drinking more now. Mom bragged she could down a bottle of scotch and still walk. Pop said she had a hollow leg. He drank Canadian Club and ginger ale, but not too much, because he had to sing at church the next day. Plus he did all the ordering for the bar and the kitchen, and couldn't afford to have his head in a fog like some people he knew, he said.

Pop never threw up in the bathroom. Mom puked and called it, "Paying homage to the porcelain god." Pop said it was throwing hard-earned money down the toilet. She drank a bottle of ale the next morning for her hangover. He didn't. And I can't remember him ever saying he got a headache from drinking. He said Mom was his biggest headache and aspirin couldn't reach the place where she pained him the most.

No fighting in front of the customers ever, though. After he'd locked the front door and turned off the lights, all bets were off.

Tonight's fight sounded real bad. I ran to get Eddie, but he wasn't in his room. There was a loud crash, like glass smashing against a wall.

Pop yelled a curse.

I ran downstairs and pushed open the swinging door to the bar. Looked like Mom must've thrown a glass beer pitcher. There was broken glass lying on the barroom floor by the front door. Pop and Mom were standing toe-to-toe screaming at each other. Mom was as red-faced as him.

Eddie sat on a barstool watching like a referee. "Get outta here, Brat," he said, looking down at me. "Gowan, get upstairs."

Pop gave Mom a shove. She hit the jukebox with her back, and then her head bounced off the hard plastic like a rubber ball. Eddie jumped off the barstool and yelled, "Pop!"

Before Eddie reached them, I ran barefoot through the broken glass, yelling at the top of my lungs, "Get away from my mommy! Get away from my mommy!"

Pop froze, looked at me, then up at the ceiling, hooking his fingers behind his head. I swung my fists at him. Eddie grabbed me, scooped me into his arms. I was swinging and kicking.

"I hate you!" I screamed at Pop.

"Stop, Brat. Stop it," Eddie begged in a whisper as he carried me out of the bar trying to clamp his hand over my mouth as I twisted my head side to side and attempted to bite his hand.

"Put me down," I demanded. I wanted to go back and hit my father some more.

"No way, you little shit." Eddie had me tucked under his arm, slung over his hip, and carried me up to my bedroom. The fight between Pop and Mom was over.

Eddie sat by me after pulling the covers up around me. I was too riled up to sleep. "When you get pissed, that temper vein you got right here," he drew a line down the center of my forehead from my hairline to my eyebrow with his finger, "bulges out just like his, you know."

"Does not!" I yelled. "I ain't nothing like him . . . or her! I hate 'em both!" I turned my back to him. I wished Aunt Helen, ugh! was my real mother, and Uncle Howard who got killed in the war was my real father. Even if he was dead, he still would've been a good father.

Sucking my thumb, I hugged Aunt Jemima doll. Eddie wouldn't go away unless he thought I was asleep. I closed my eyes. He brushed my hair with his hand, kissed me on the cheek and left to go to his bedroom. Soon after, I heard Mom in the bathroom puking as usual, and the springs squeaking as Pop got in his bed.

IT WASN'T ALL BAD SLEEPING OVER THE JUKEBOX. Jack, the man who changed the records, liked me. He came on a Saturday, once a month to open the jukebox, take out the metal box full of change, and dump all the coins onto the bar. He tipped back his hat, order a whiskey and water, or a coffee with a shot, light a cigarette, and leave it hanging out of the corner of his mouth. The smoke curled up in his left eye. He squinted and blinked and water dripped down his cheek. But Jack kept counting his money. We sat together at the bar and separated the quarters, dimes, and nickels into large piles. Songs were a nickel apiece or six for a quarter. I watched Jack's cigarette ash grow longer. He smoked it right down to a butt without ever taking it out of his mouth. The ash stuck on until he stubbed the butt out in the ashtray. After we counted the coins and stacked them in neat rows, he put them in paper sleeves. He added up everything and wrote the total down on a pad he kept in his coat pocket, and then Pop got his cut.

Jack knew how many times each song played because each record had a "counter." Ones that weren't making any money were pulled. I asked if I could have them seeing they weren't any good, and Jack gave them to me if I knew most of the words to the songs. No other kid had the pile of 45s that I had. Even if I was just getting the Mills Brothers, or the Ink Spots, they belonged to me. Sleeping over the jukebox wasn't all that bad.

I'll Drink To That

*The taproom in many cases is the poor man's only parlour . . .
Reformers will never get rid of the drink shop until they can
outbid it in the subsidiary attractions which it offers to its customers.*

William Booth

It was early Tuesday evening, the movie theater was closed, and the bar was crowded. Mom was tending bar and Pop was off singing at the Mendelssohn Glee Club rehearsal in Kingston. Mickey and Andy were upstairs. Tonight was joke night. Remembering the jokes that rang out one after the other, as I sat at the end of the bar pretending to read my Little Lulu comic book, was difficult.

Mom threw her head backwards, opened her mouth wide, and laughed. Heads turned. I looked up from my comic book. Customers said she had a great laugh, a beautiful smile, and loved how happy she always was.

"She's loud, improper, and uncouth," Aunt Moncie, Pop's younger sister said within my earshot. Aunt Moncie said ladies weren't supposed to laugh at dirty jokes. But Mom did. And I know Aunt Helen Evans, Pop's oldest sister did. Seemed like all the aunts in Pop's family talked mostly about Mom because she either couldn't hear what they were saying, or because they never invited her to anything where they had to talk to her, like Cherny cookouts. Though I don't remember Aunt Beatty, who wasn't a real Cherny, ever chiming in on the gossip. She was a Cherny only by marrying Uncle Joe Cherny.

When gossip got back to Mom, she said, "Aunt Moncie has no room to talk. She belts back quite a few rye Presbyterians and laughs right along with the rest of us. And Aunt Helen can't talk. She has more marriages under her belt than a gunslinger has notches on the handle of his gun."

But Aunt Helen didn't think those marriages counted because she got them wiped out by annullin' them. I'd asked Mom what "annullin'" meant, and she said, "It's a stupid Catholic church law that says if you pay their lawyers, they'll tell you your marriage stank and you can get a divorce. If you don't pay them, you're told you'll rot in hell when you die if you ever get married again."

"What . . .?" I stammered.

"That's right," Mom said. "And after Aunt Helen gives them hundreds of dollars, the church lawyers say it's okay, dump your husband. And poof! No longer married. Just like that," she said, snapping her fingers. "It's a way for people like your aunt to feel better for having made so many stupid marriage mistakes."

Mom was still laughing when Leo Trandle turned and asked, "What's so funny, Edie?"

"Paul The Pollock" Danashevski leaned over to Leo and whispered the joke to him. Leo chuckled. I saw his eyes narrow. He asked, "You got that joke, huh Edie?"

"Of course." Mom had this puzzled look on her face. "Why do you ask?"

Leo, who always stood at the bar while he drank, pushed back the side of his suit jacket and shoved his hand in his pants pocket and jingled some coins.

"Nothing. It's just . . . most women, jokes go right over their heads like a B-52 bomber," he said as he brushed his free hand over the top of his thinning hair and whistled. "Even if they did get them, they pucker up their pusses and say, 'Ooohhh, that's disgusting, or 'Why don't you men grow up?'" He said, in a sissy voice. Leo took a long drag on his cigarette and blew the smoke out both nostrils and out the side of his mouth at the same time. He reminded me of a dragon.

"I have to have a sense of humor. How do you think I stayed married this long?" Mom laughed.

The other men sniggered. Paul slapped Leo easy on his back.

"Do you think I should titter like sweet Debbie Reynolds?" my mother said. "Wasn't raised in a convent, you know!"

"I'll drink to that," Uncle Everett, mom's baby brother said. He raised his beer glass in a pretend toast to her.

"Most women, like my wife, God bless her, don't have the sense of humor God gave to a goose. Hell, that's why us guys are here and not home." Leo laughed.

"I'll drink to that," Uncle Everett called out. He was on leave from the Navy and he'd be drunk day and night till he had to go back. Then Pop would have to put him in a taxi to New York City where his boat was docked. The bar top was propping Uncle Everett up from his forearms to his elbows. Each time he raised his glass, beer would slosh over his hand, while he lost his balance and almost fell down.

"I'll drink to that!" he'd call out even when no one said anything.

"No shit, Everett!" Georgie Winters shouted. Georgie, who needed a shave, looked like a sleepy grizzly bear. His chin was about to hit the bar while his fanny kept sliding backwards off the barstool.

"I'll drink to that, too," Uncle Everett answered Georgie.

Paul broke in with a whiskey-slurred voice, "Edie's gotta have humor, Leo, she gotta deal with drunks like us, heh?" Paul smiled a squinty-eyed, big gap-tooth grin. He looked like the actor Glenn Ford. A kinda drunk, beat-up Glenn Ford.

Mom sat behind the bar, her fanny spilling over the red vinyl padded stool with the chrome legs. She sat with her thighs spread apart, her high heels over the rung of the stool. She bent forward with her chin in her hand leaning on her elbow, her boobs laying on the bar. The crack between them was what Pop called "a furtive feast for a drunks' eye." As long as it sold booze, he said, he didn't care how many men looked at Mom. They just couldn't touch her or Pop would pulverize them like Popeye did to Bluto protecting Olive Oyl. Mom bent over further and said to Paul, "What did one drag queen say to the other drag queen when they looked in the window of a bar full of queers?"

Paul shrugged his shoulders and took a swig of his beer.

"Look, Alan, smorgasbord!"

Paul snorted his drink out his nose. Tears started to roll down his face as he laughed and coughed and choked all at the same time. He put his cigarette in the ashtray, stood up, then bent over and put his hands on his thighs while trying to clear his throat. Leo slapped him on his back. Paul pulled a handkerchief from his trouser pocket and wiped his nose and water from his eyes. "Die already, will ya!" Uncle Everett yelled out.

"I'll even buy a round of drinks if you do," said Jerry DeFelicis, the florist's son.

Paul pulled himself together and took another sip of beer. His face was beet red. "Damn Edie, ya 'most kilt me. Lemme swallow 'fore ya make a joke. Damn."

Some men inched in closer to Mom. None of them wanted to be left out. They sat across from her sucking in the smell of her Chanel #5 perfume, all smiling like Dopey in the movie *Snow White*, while they sneaked a peek at her soft boobs whose nips pressed bumps into the front of her tight black dress.

Paul broke the silence, "I buy ya drink for dat one, Edie. Hell, I buy everyone drink. Round's on me."

Customer's gulped their drinks down and shoved their glasses forward for the refill. Mom poured everyone a drink, and one for herself. She put a shot of whiskey on the bar next to Paul's bottle of beer, took his money and rang up the bill.

Mom raised her glass and toasted Paul, "Through the teeth, over the tongue, look out stomach, here it comes."

"*Naz-droh-vee-ay*," Paul said as they clacked their glasses together. He downed the shot of whiskey, made a shuddering motion with his shoulders and then took a long swig of beer. I giggled at the wiggle dance he did and the homely face he made.

Different toasts rang out along the bar. I'd heard them a bunch of times.

"Cheers," red-faced Kitty Dutcher said.

"Down the hatch," handsome Bob Hueben said.

"*Skøl*," rugged Chris Raisner called out, raising his glass up above his head.

"Here's looking at ya," said swaying Floyd Swehla while he turned and clinked glasses with Chris's wife, Ceebee, as she said,

"L'chayim."

"May the hinges of friendship never rust, or the wings of love lose a feather," John Boyle added.

"May ye soul get to heaven, before the dee-vil knows your dead," Isabelle, John's wife said, sitting there with her cloche hat tilted and her flowered silky dress pulled tight across her round body.

And not to be outdone, Veikko Jalante, the masseur for Williams Lake Hotel, had combed his hair flat and to the side and put the comb under his nose for a mustache. He stood up, raised his right arm up in the air and call out, "*Sieg, Heil!*" and clicked his heels. He looked like the Hitler in the movie newsreels. Everyone laughed.

"I'll drink to that," said Uncle Everett, raising his glass and spinning around in a half-circle.

"Gawddamn, Everett! Ya'd drink to anything," brawny Johnny Plonski shouted.

"Amen!" many voices piped up.

Bottles and glasses click-clacked together and after long swallows, they thunked them down onto thick, round paper coasters.

Customers sat still, frozen in a holy moment of perfect silence I once felt in church, only to have it broken by Leo singing out, "Hit me again, Edie!"

"Uncork one for me too," Ben Barbato added.

Mom turned towards the cooler to pull out a bottle of beer and noticed me.

"Don't you have school tomorrow? Get to bed," she said. "Now. And make sure Mickey's tucked in."

Nuts! I jumped down from the barstool, and ran upstairs.

WHEN LEAVES FALL

What moistens the lip and what brightens the eye?
What calls back the past, like the rich Pumpkin pie?

John Greenleaf Whittier

The alarm clock went off at eight. I jumped out of bed and ran into Andy and Eddie's room. "C'mon, guys! Geddup! We gotta be at school by nine! It's our first day!"

They moaned and groaned, rolled over in their double bed and paid me no attention. I picked up Eddie's clock and saw that he forgot to set it, so I did. I put it on his dresser and it began to ring.

"Shut that freakin' thing up," Andy growled.

"What the hell?" Eddie sat up in bed rubbing his eyes. He threw his pillow at the clock, which bounced on the floor and turned in circles on its face on the linoleum still ringing.

Andy turned out of bed and put his feet on the floor. "Get up," Andy said and poked at Ed. "And shut that friggin' clock off, will ya?"

"Fuck off," Eddie answered. He stole Andy's pillow, lay back down, and buried his head.

"Whadda you want?" Andy snapped at me. "Get the frig outta here, ya annoyin' little turd."

I ran to my room to get dressed.

At our new school there were two grades to a classroom. In

Kingston, Andy brought me to school and home every day, and he always made sure I made it to my first grade class before he went to his. Today, he'd walk me too. "But tomorrow on," he said, "you're on your own, because I want to be with guys my age, and not with a snot-nose booger brain like you."

Good. Because I was four months and eighteen days short of being seven, and I didn't need anybody to hold my hand. I wasn't a baby no more.

Besides, one day at this new school and it felt just like the old one, and I began to live for the holidays.

When the leaves changed color and started to fall I knew it meant Halloween was coming. After all the leaves fell, that meant Christmas was coming with lots of snow for sleigh riding.

The night before our first Thanksgiving in Rosendale we got a light snow. Pop and my brothers were smiling and happy about it. They were going deer hunting with Dad DeWitt and Mom's brother, Uncle Ernie, and snow made it easier to track deer. They were leaving by five-thirty in the morning and wouldn't get back till dark, right in time for turkey dinner.

Mom said sharing is what Thanksgiving was about. "Wouldn't it be nice if, after a long day in the woods, I could come home thumping my chest and sit down to a big meal that someone else cooked?" A scowl crossed her face. "Wouldn't that be a novel idea?" she asked, and took a gulp of her scotch.

She crabbed about it, but she cooked the turkey and made the pumpkin and apple pies. I tried to help, but was told to get out of her way, that it was easier to do by herself.

"Set the tables and stay out from under my feet," she said, while she slammed things around in the kitchen and took another sip of her drink.

The giblets were always Pop's to eat. When Mom was mad at him for some reason like today, she diced them up and put them in the gravy. He said when she did that to leave them in the gravy boat for him. It was a treat if a slice of gizzard or liver dropped by accident onto our stuffing or mashed potatoes while ladling on the gravy. Pop often traded us pieces of heart for pieces of gizzard.

My brothers didn't sit next to Pop at the dinner table because of the noises he made eating. Pop had blocked sinuses that made him breathe real loud when he ate. He snorted, woofed, burped, and sometimes farted. It always made Mom say, "For gawdsakes, Ed, do you have to do that at the dinner table?"

"Where would you like me to do it? It sneaked out." He'd grin like Oliver Hardy. "In Australia, burpin' and fartin's a compliment to the hostess' cookin'."

Well, then, go to Australia. Maybe he was a hillbilly. I knew what hillbillies were because of the movies, and I wondered if my father's parents were not really from Europe.

I sipped the rose-colored wine Mom and Pop gave my brothers and me to have on holidays. It tasted awful. They thought a few sips during special times would make us grow up knowing how to handle our booze and not become drunks. I'd rather have a Seven-Up and grenadine, and a maraschino cherry. At least that didn't send fumes up the back of my nose and have a taste like vinegar.

My brothers were dumb. They sat away from Pop, which meant I got to sit next to him at dinnertime, and that was good because I just had to hear him eat. My idiot brothers had to hear him and see him shovel his cheeks full like a squirrel and watch juice drip down his chin. Pop ate like one of the starving refugees he was always telling us about. "I saw 'em eat outta garbage cans. Food with maggots, and flies buzzin' all over 'em. Be thankful you got a roof over your head and food in your stomach," he said. "Ya don't know how lucky you are."

Knowing when to keep my mouth shut, I said, "Please pass the cranberries."

I liked cranberry sauce. It tickled the hinges of my jaw. Mom opened both ends of the can with the opener and used a lid to push the jelly out and onto a plate. Then she sliced it up. It looked nice, but was hard to carry to the table and was even harder to serve. Pop and Mom ate the whole berries with skins and seeds. It looked like the dog had eaten it first and upchucked it in the bowl.

Pop said, when he was a kid, his stepfather ate first and the kids got whatever was left over in order of age. That meant he didn't get much because he was next to last in the line and he'd always give some of his food to his little sister, Aunt Moncie.

"How come there's no corn?" Pop asked.

I always had a shoulders-up-to-my-ears feeling at the dinner table even on holidays. No talking was allowed, and everyone's elbows had to be off the table. And, if you didn't have anything to say, you wouldn't get accused of having hoof-in-mouth disease, saying the wrong thing at the wrong time.

We could tell when Pop was spoiling for a fight by the way he bit down and chewed his food, kinda like an English bulldog ripping apart a raw steak. Another sign was the vein that ran straight up his forehead, between his eyebrows. It swelled up, turned purple, and thumped. It reminded me of a thermometer with the red mercury in the glass pushing up the hotter it got.

"Potatoes are lumpy," he said.

Pop's jaws were chewing up and down even though he didn't have food in his mouth. He slammed his fist down on the table making glasses slosh over and silverware jump up and fall to the floor. When he did that, I stopped chewing and choked my food down in a lump, held my breath and waited. Waited for his words to burn holes in my soul. He glared at me. "Clean your plate. Ya took it, you eat it."

"Gravy's cold," he said, looking over at Mom.

"Could we please make it through one meal without you bitching and bellyaching?" Mom said. "If you don't like the way I do things, do them yourself!"

She pushed away from the table and left for the bar followed by his, "Jeezus-H-Ke-rist! Can't ever say a friggin' thing to you without you bustin' into a crying jag."

Mom poured another scotch. We took our dinner plates to the sink and cleaned up the kitchen. Pop sat by himself, stuffing turkey or potatoes or turnips into his face. Even the hotel guests left for the bar or their room. Mom and he kept taking little potshots at each other. Neither knew when to zip their lips. As we cleared the table, Pop tried to drag us kids into the argument. "Ya think I'm wrong, don't ya? Y'all come and piss on my grave when I'm dead. A guy can't even take a day off and go hunting without getting a ration of shit when he walks in the door."

"Late! You were an hour late!" she screamed back at him. "And I didn't say anything to you!"

"Piss on my grave, that's what ya'll all do . . ."
"When's my day off?" she asked.
" . . .every one of you. Piss on my grave . . . ."

They didn't hear each other. It was like a movie script they kept rehearsing and couldn't get right so "The End" could flash across the screen.

"Your face said everything. It told me you were pissed," he said. "I'm gonna get outta these hunting clothes and take a shower. Put the coffee on. I'll have my pie when I come back."

"Do it yourself," Mom mumbled.

We held our breath. The more she drank, the braver she got.

Pop turned. Looked at her. The vein went from neon blue to dark purple and looked like it'd blow any minute. Grabbing Mickey, we ducked under the shuffleboard. Andy and Eddie stood with clenched fists by the kitchen, waiting.

He didn't give more warning. No narrowing eyes. No gritting his teeth. Pop flew into a rage. He pounded the bar top with the pinky side of his fist. A fierce thud spilled Jerry Mertine's beer, the only renter that hadn't beeline it upstairs earlier. Jerry sopped up the mess with a cocktail napkins and kept drinking.

Pop cursed stuff that made me hold my hands over Mickey's ears. My eyes went from Jerry, who was pretending nothing was happening, but whose hand was shaking as he took a sip of his drink, back to my father and mother.

Mom smirked. She didn't flicker an eyelash, turned her back on Pop, and grabbed her bottle again.

"Leave some for the customers, will ya!" Pop snapped, as he stormed out of the bar. Mom took her drink and went to make coffee.

THE HOT SUDSY DISHWATER IN THE KITCHEN felt good on my hands. It was nice to have something to do even if it was washing dirty dishes. I wasn't too happy or thankful, but I bet I could come up with something to be grateful for. Let's see. I was thankful Pop didn't hit Mom; my brothers had to help clean up; I didn't have to eat out of maggoty garbage cans, and I had a roof over my head and food in my stomach. Also, I was thankful for the giblets that fell onto my stuffing and I got two slices of cranberry sauce before my brothers hogged the rest up.

Mom put on her coat and her hat. Bet she's gonna go to the Astoria. "Watch the coffee," she said to Eddie. "Tell your father I gave the pies to the starving refugees. If he wants some, he knows where he can find it."

I would've been real thankful for a piece of pie, I thought as I watched Mom turn the pies upside-down, and smash them into the garbage, pie plates and all.

Breaking The Mold

It's what you do, unthinking,
That makes the quick tear start;
The tear may be forgotten—
But the hurt stays in the heart.

Ella Higginson

December's late afternoon sunlight was shining through the plate glass window blotting out the red neon beer sign. The sun's glare made Mom look like a dark shadow. I sat at the end of the bar doing homework, and watched while she bent over the bar sink washing glasses. The top of her arms hung like a raglan sleeve, and jiggled when she pushed narrow-waisted beer glasses onto a brush in the hot soapy water. She rinsed the glasses and put them in neat rows on a white linen towel to drip-dry before being put away.

When finished, Mom lifted the top of the red Coca-Cola cooler. From deep inside she took out a little bottle of dark brown bock beer and popped off the metal cap.

Mom once gave me a taste. "Bock" means "goat" in German, Jerry Mertine told me. It tasted like beer gone rotten. I didn't like the taste of the yellow-colored beer neither. I once watched Andy take a leak in the john. It was yellow and foamy, and it smelled and looked like what was in beer bottles. Ugh!

Mickey and I saved bottle caps. We pried out the cork lining, put the caps on the outside of our shirts, and pushed the cork in from behind, trapping our shirt in between. Andy and Eddie did the same thing to their baseball caps. The nuns didn't think it was a good idea to advertise beer in a Catholic school, and they got told, "No baseball hats with bottle caps allowed."

"Ahhhh!" Mom sighed and smacked her lips. "That sure hits the spot." She checked her looks in the bar mirror, reached around the side of the cash register for her lipstick, and put some on. She fluffed her bleached-blonde hair.

Mom started talking with Bill Bender.

"Mom?" I called politely. I was antsy.

Bill Bender, a regular customer took a long swig of his drink. His large wrinkly hand set the wet glass in the center of the cardboard Schlitz beer coaster. He reminded me of Dad DeWitt, kinda Spencer Tracy looking. Both were about the same size and wore the same type of clothes. The window light played tricks with the color of his suit coat, hat, and trousers, even his plaid shirt. They looked tarnished-gray. It felt like looking at a faded black-and-white newsreel. The only thing missing was the flickery light spots and streaky lines running over his face.

"MOM!" I said, louder.

Two dusty cement miners came in and sat on stools near the front door. They asked if they could eat their lunch at the bar as long as they bought a couple of beers. Mom didn't care. One guy got up and dropped a quarter into the jukebox and Hank Williams began to sing "Lovesick Blues." Mom gave the miners their drinks and then came back to Bill.

Mom and Bill talked about dancing. If Bill heard polka music, he'd lift up and slide off the stool. He'd push back the sides of his suit coat, hook his thumbs over the waist of his pants, let his belly flop out, and start slap-tapping his leather shoes on the barroom floor. He called it clogging. He said kids doing the jitterbug, "look like drunken cockroaches in a hot frying pan." Bill taught me how to play the spoons, holding them back-to-back and slapping them between my hand and my thigh. He showed me how to play a hair comb with a piece of waxed paper folded over it. The noise made my lips tickle.

"MOM-ME-E-E-E!" I shouted.

Grownups in the bar were fun to watch, I thought while waiting for Mom to answer me. Some nights, ladies danced on our bar and did stripteases, folks sang dirty songs and told dirty jokes, and men started fistfights. Once there was a farting contest. Someone got the bright idea everyone should drink lots of ale or bock beer, eat peanuts, and eat all of Pop's pickled Polish sausages, pig's feet, pig's knuckles, and hard-boiled eggs. Then they waited. One after the other they began to fart, trying to outdo each other. Even the women got in on it, except for Mom. She didn't eat anything. There were long farts, short farts, squeaky ones, juicy-sounding ones, and bad smelly ones. People were busting their guts laughing. It made me hold my breath and leave for my room. It smelled worse than Mom's Limburger cheese in the 'frigerator.

"MOM-ME-E-E-E!" I shouted again.

Her smile fell off her face when she looked at me.

"Can I have a dime so I can go over to Bobby Ann's and we can get some candy?"

"Go ask your father," she said, and turned away.

"He's taking a nap. Can I have a nickel instead?" If I woke Pop up asking for money, he'd get mad, swear, and say, "Go ask your mother." I didn't want to play the "Go ask your father, go ask your mother" game. They'd keep it up till I got tired of running back and forth and stopped asking.

"Kids are always wanting," Mom complained to Bill. "Gimme this. Gimme that. Buy me this. Buy me that. They think money grows on trees."

"Ain't that the truth," Bill said.

I jumped down from my stool, looked at her and waited a few minutes. She didn't care if I left or not, but Pop had said to tell someone where I was going or to wait for permission. I was tired of trying that with her. After a long time of waiting and begging, "Can I go? Can I go? Ple-e-ease." She'd turned and said, "Why are you still here? I thought you already left." When Pop asks later where I am, she'll say, "I don't know. She didn't tell me where she was going."

Explaining to Pop that she doesn't give me a yes or no, I got,

"Then you sit there till she does." Baloney. I could tune Pop out in my head by singing the "Star-Spangled Banner" like Kate Smith when he gets lecturing. In time, he gives up. Maybe he figured out I wasn't lying because I always told him where I was going and always asked when to be back.

"Yeah," Mom said to Bill. "When we had her we broke the mold. I'd take ten boys to one girl." She took another swig of beer.

Mom started telling him the story I heard so many times, I had it memorized. What she told him made me feel bad. I walked behind the bar and began to stuff my pockets full of sticky bottle caps.

"I had whooping cough when I was carrying her," she said. "That's why she's nuts today. Jangled her brains loose with all that coughing I did." Together they laughed. "Maybe that's why she can't sit still for two-seconds. Walked when she was eight months old. Never crawled. Wasn't like having a baby at all. She was born up and running." They ha-ha'd some more.

Then her voice turned very serious and she added the part that always made me squirmy inside. "Did you know that the Catholic hospital saves a baby's life over the mother's if there's a problem? Well, when I found that out I told Dr. Shea no way was I going to the Benedictine Hospital. It was the Kingston Hospital or nothing." She made her hand into a fist and with her pointer finger poked at the bar several times. "If it's a choice between me or an unborn kid, Doc had better look like saving me," she said. "Who'd take care of Ed and my boys if I weren't around? And, you know what that's like, having lost your wife, right?"

"That's for sure," Bill said.

She got Bill's nod that meant she was right, and that earned him a drink. "Here, have one on me," Mom said drawing him another glass of beer from a tap.

"Would you want to die and leave your kids with no mother?" She had once asked me.

"No, I wouldn't," I said. But I wasn't sure. I guess Mom was right. Who'd have taken care of my brothers and Pop if something had happened to her when I was being born? If I died there wouldn't have been a problem. But if she died . . . .

I guess Mom would never be like Maureen O'Hara, the actress who got shot in the chest with an arrow protecting her kid when the Indians were circling the wagons. Mom wasn't the heroine type. With pockets full of bottle caps, I made my way outside, out of the dark cool of the gray newsreel barroom, out into the bright warm sunshine. I took deep swallows of air and pushed down the large lump sticking in my throat. Running to Bobby Ann's house, with bottle caps bouncing around in my jean pockets, I thought, We'll clean these up and sell them to the kids at the playground for a penny apiece. Chocolate-covered peppermints. That's what I want. Lots of them. They always made my stomach feel better.

O Christmas Tree

"A lovely thing about Christmas is that it's compulsory, like a thunderstorm, and we all go through it together."

Garrison Keillor

We got to visit Grandma Sarah and Dad DeWitt at Christmas. Gram's house was small with low ceilings, which she might not have noticed because she was little, and wore a size four shoe, same as me. Her wood-stove in the kitchen always had a pot roast and biscuit smell coming from it. Cooking odors mixed with the smoke coming out of the stove when she lifted the metal plate to shove in more kindling.

Gram had pretty tree decorations that Aunt Joan DeWitt helped put on the tree. Clipped to branches of her tree were silver birds with pointed beaks and stiff white tails sticking up in the air spread out like a fan. She called them peacocks even though they didn't have those funny eyes on their tails. Grandma strung shiny glass beads; tiny ones round as peas, and long hollow tubes of bright red, dark green, and silver onto darning thread and pulled them together into a shape of a diamond. Glass beads hung from bent wire hooks and dingle-dangled with Santa Claus balls with red and white painted hats and real faces pressed into the glass. Strings of cranberries and popcorn were draped along the branches and cellophane-wrapped candies were fastened on hooks and hung not too high.

The bubbling, colored glass lights in shapes of candles were my favorites. They were filled with oil and got very hot. Gram warned me not to touch them, but I did and got a blister on my finger. I didn't cry or tell Mom and Pop because I knew I'd hear, "I told you so." The glass candles were tall and mixed in with almond-sized light bulbs of orange, blue, white, red and green. The long, crinkled, thin strips of lead tinsel sparkled. Gram hung them on one neat strand at a time, with several pieces to a branch. They shimmered like a rainbow from the lights, and moved as you walked by.

On the very top of the tree was a color print of an angel pressed into a piece of flat cardboard. She had white wings and hair made of fine spun glass, waved like the hairdo of a '20s flapper girl in the movies. The light from the bulbs made her hair and wings shine. Grandma's tree was magic, like the ones I read about in books.

This might be the last Christmas I could come to Grandma's house to look at her decorations. She was very sick. I heard grownups talking about her having "The Big C-A." Those initials that scared grownups. I could see it on their faces, so it must be bad. I sat on the floor and stared at the angel for a long time, waiting, wanting, and willing her to move her wings, even if it was just a tiny bit. I wanted to believe angels were real and miracles would happen if you believed and wished and prayed hard enough to Jesus. I wished and prayed Gram would have lots and lots of Christmases, but I wasn't sure I believed she would.

Christmas at the bar was different from what it was like at Grandma's. The dining room walls were twelve feet high and the top of our tree almost touched the ceiling. Pop had to make a special stand from two-by-fours and a washtub filled with sand. He strung guide wires from the trunk to fat hooks he screwed into the wall. He wasn't taking any chances of it toppling over and landing on a customer. Pop hand-drilled holes around the trunk and stuck in extra branches. He kept at it until it was full and very round, just the way Mom wanted it. "Anything to make you happy, dear," he said, shaking his head. "Just like it grows in nature." When he finished, he whispered to me on his way out to the bar, "Stay outta her way till she gets done or she'll be chewing your ass out for nothing."

"But I want to help." I pouted.

"Don't say you weren't warned."

Mom brought out strands of multicolored lights and handed them to Pop, who came back with a beer in his hand and was halfway up the ladder. She told him where she wanted the lights. "Change this bulb. Ed, you can't have two reds together. Now you have two greens. Oh, for Pete's sake. Here." She held her hand up to him. "Change it with this blue one."

All he kept saying in a sugary voice was, "Yes, dear," rolling his eyes up to look at the ceiling. When he was finished, he went back to tend to customers at the bar.

Staring at the top, Mom climbed the ladder and removed the glass spire Pop put up there. It came from his mother. Mom bought a new top from Woolworth's, a doll with a head and arms, but no legs under her dress. She looked like an angel with real white feather wings, white hair, and a gold wire halo stuck in the back of her head. She also had a white light shoved up her rump to make her glow and look like she just came down from heaven and landed on top of our tree. She was pretty, but I still liked Grandma Sarah's old-fashioned paper one better.

"Hand me the boxes of balls," Mom said.

"Can I put some on?"

"No. They have to go in order of size. Besides, you might drop one," she said.

She had me climb partway up the ladder and hand her the box of tiniest ornaments, the size of the rubber ball in my set of jacks. They got bigger and bigger as Mom moved down the tree. There were ones like golf balls, tennis balls, hardballs, and softballs. Some were solid colors, some were striped and some had flowers with glitter on them. There were a few of those clip-on birds like peacocks, a few short fat Santa's and a few bells with clappers in them from Grandma Sarah.

Mom went up and down the ladder. She stepped back and looked hard from all sides of the room. Sometimes she moved a ball to a better spot. I watched her, looked for what she was seeing, and began to tell where a bare spot was, and sure enough, Mom put a Christmas ball right in that spot.

When she was sure that nothing else had to be changed, she went up the ladder once more. This time it was to spread a thin layer of angel hair over everything, but not on the angel sitting on top.

Pop said he'd be itching to-hell-and-back if he touched that stuff. "No sense, no feeling," he said as he looked at the spun glass draped over Mom's arm. She put it on so no one would steal the balls, he said. Mom said she did it because it made a halo around the lights and softened the look. I think she did it to keep me from playing with the balls. Like Pop, I got a rash if I touched it. What she didn't know was I could lie on my back, shimmy under the tree and touch the bell ornaments and make them tinkle. I did it when her and Pop were busy in the bar.

Mom didn't need me. I looked at her and said, "I'm going to Rosenkranses'."

"Ask your father," she warned.

I went out to the bar.

"Mom said she don't need me no more and I can go over to Rosenkranses'."

"If it's okay with her," he said.

I left. Millie said she'd be baking and decorating with her kids and I could help. At least there I could do something.

It felt like I lived in Rosendale a long time and knew Bobby Ann forever. She was like the sister I'd always wanted. We played in the woods or by the creek, swung on the swings, or hung from our knees on the monkey bars at the playground. We roller skated or played hopscotch, danced and sang, or went to Vaughn's to buy lots of candy and ice cream. She told me secrets about girl stuff her big sister Lina had told her. Stuff I was sure she made up. Because it was near Christmas, we were always looking in the "Monkey" Montgomery Wards catalog at toys we wanted. I wondered what she was going to ask for.

Lina, Bobby Ann, and their brothers were sitting at the dining room table busy making garlands with red and green construction paper. Millie was baking in the kitchen. The house smelled like pine needles and baked sugar and cinnamon.

"Can I help cut some paper for you?" I asked Bobby Ann,

"I s'pose. Why aren't you doing your own?" she asked.

"Cause it's all done. My mother did it all." I said, and whispered, "Do you get to put the balls on?"

"Of course, dummy. Don't you?"

"Not allowed to. I might put one in the wrong place."

"Well maybe you shouldn't touch our stuff neither." She snorted at me.

Wow! She sure has a bug up her butt.

"Bobby Ann," Millie scolded from the kitchen doorway. "That's no way to be so close to Christmas, now, is it?"

"Sorry."

"Tell Judy. Not me," her mother said.

"*Sor---rreee,*" Bobby Ann said, making a face, crossing her eyes and sticking out her tongue.

We all took turns placing balls on the branches and I stepped back once in a while to look at our work. Wherever there was an open spot, I put a ball. I tried to move one of Bobby Ann's into an empty spot like I saw Mom do.

"Hey! What the freak you doing!" she shouted.

"You got two on the same branch," I pointed to show her.

"So? Freakin' leave your mitts off it. I'll put them wherever I want. Leave my balls alone."

"Yeah!" Dickey said, trying not to laugh. "Leave my balls alone, too."

Georgie jumped in, "That goes for me, too."

"Me too." Porky said, not wanting to be left out of the fun of teasing me.

"Okay. Okay," I said, blushing from ear to ear.

My eyes stung. I blinked several times, stood away from them, and let them finish. I wouldn't touch another ball if they'd paid me a hundred dollars. I should have stayed home.

Their tree was loaded with balls, colored lights, handmade ornaments, and paper garlands. It looked good. I joined them sitting on the floor, admiring their work, and sucked in all the colors. The paper garland and the other handmade ornaments made this tree just for kids. I felt good inside because I got to help.

"You got two orange lights right next to each other," I said to anyone who listened. But no one paid any attention. I tried again. "Right there," I pointed.

"So?" Myron said.

"Yeah," said Porky. "It's because you're sitting there you notice it. Sit over here by me if it bothers you."

"Why's everything got to be so perfect with you?" Bobby Ann asked.

I shrugged. Maybe it was because Mom was so fussy, and because Pop had said a thousand times, there's a right way and a wrong way to do things, and if something was worth doing, then do it right or don't do it at all.

I didn't think Mom would like their tree, but then she wouldn't say so because she taught if you can't say something nice, then don't say nothing at all.

I sat having second thoughts. Bobby Ann was right. Why was it so important to have all the bulbs a different color and why did the balls have to be put on in order of size? It looked okay once I moved over and sat down next to Porky. Besides, one of those orange bulbs was bound to burn out and they'd have to replace it, and it'd be a different color anyway. But there sure was a big orange glow to my right.

"This sure is one pretty tree," I said to Porky as I turned my back to the bright orange area. "I think it looks better than mine."

Mrs. Pettybone's Perfect House

If I were asked to name the chief benefit of the house,
I should say: the house shelters daydreaming,
the house protects the dreamer,
the house allows one to dream in peace.

Gaston Bachelard

THE TOY BABY IS IN THE CRIB. The Mommy is wearing a dress and is in the kitchen cooking. Its Daddy is in a suit and tie. He is in the living room watching television and waiting for supper.

I took the tiny pink rubbery baby from its crib and looked at it. Its stiff arms stuck out in the air, like it always wanted to be picked up. Its knees were bent, so it could sit in its high chair. I popped baby in my mouth, chewed on its tiny hands, and squashed them flat.

The small dolls were part of the painted metal dollhouse I got for Christmas, which came flat in a box and had to be put together. Metal tabs held the first and second floor to the walls and the walls to the roof, but not for long. It wiggled and wobbled and the tabs eventually broke and the dollhouse had to be thrown away.

But while it held together, it was fun. Each room was painted a different color. Everything was painted in the dollhouse even the pictures and rugs. The furniture was hard plastic in solid colors, and could be moved around the house. Beds were always made and the couch cushions were always in place. It was a perfect house, for a perfect family. Except for the baby. I chewed its feet flat, too.

What would it be like to live in a house with no business in it? A home where the mommy made breakfast for the kids before they went to school, and the daddy came home from work and watched television at night? It'd be nice to have white lace curtains with shades underneath. When I get a house, it's gonna look like a movie star's house, with a maid to clean up and do the dirty dishes. I put the baby back in its crib. It looked like it had pink fans for hands and pink frog flippers for feet.

"Judy!" Mom called to me from her bed. "Where's Mickey?"

"Over at Pettybone's!"

"Get him and give him some breakfast," she said.

"He already ate at Doc Vaughn's with Jerry Mertine. Besides, Mrs. Pettybone feeds him, too."

"Go get him and bring him home!" she said, a little louder.

"He's watching her television."

"Go get him!"

"I will! Later. I'm playing . . . ."

"GO, GAWD DAMN IT!" Pop yelled from their bedroom. "Move your ass now before I get outta bed and move it for you."

Mickey's lucky. Mrs. Pettybone saw him outside by himself one morning and she asked if he wanted to come inside. Then she asked if he was hungry and he said yes, and she fed him. Now, he goes there every day and she makes him something different. I wish he didn't tell me about the pancakes, waffles, and the French toast, with butter and syrup. The lucky duck also gets to watch cartoons and Hopalong Cassidy while she cleans her apartment and her husband goes downstairs and opens up his plumbing store.

Mrs. Pettybone asked if I could wait till Mickey finished watching a puppet show.

"Sure." I said. I kept peeking around the corner of her kitchen to look at the television. I didn't want to seem too nosy because then she'd know I didn't know much about television. Aunt Helen said it's okay to be stupid, just don't show it. And Pop said I could learn a lot by keeping my mouth shut, ears open, and watching instead of always asking 'why,' which pissed him off.

The television looked like someone put the movie newsreels into an old stand-up radio. The pictures were spotty, black and white. I wondered how they did that. Eddie said the pictures came through the air and went down the antennas on their roof. What a bunch of baloney!

Mrs. Pettybone's apartment was spotless. Everything was in its place. She had Mickey sit on the floor so he wouldn't dirty her couch. His shoes and boots were by the kitchen door.

"Take your boots off," Mrs. Pettybone said, "and go sit on the floor by your brother. It's all right."

"Nah, that's okay," I said as I stood with snow dripping onto the braided rag rug by her door. "I gotta get back." I didn't want to take my boots off because my shoes would come off, and I didn't want her to see the holes in my socks.

"What's that?" I said, as I turned to watch her ironing.

That was the first time I ever saw a mangler. Mrs. Pettybone explained it was what professional laundries used to press clothes. She pulled the handle of the mangler down and hot steam seeped out of its edges. She pressed sheets and put creases into Mr. Pettybone's pants. It was quicker, she said, than using a hand iron.

"Mr. Pettybone ordered it for me out of a catalog he has downstairs in the plumbing store."

"My mom has the laundry guy do the towels for our bar," I said. "But Mom does the sheets. She irons just the tops where the hems are and the same with the pillowcases, because that's what shows. She doesn't iron us kids' sheets because we don't need no ironed sheets."

Without knowing why, I began to brag about my chores. "My pop showed me how to iron his shirts and pants just like the Navy does. I do his boxers and hankies, too. He's a stick-in-the-mud about wrinkles. Pop doesn't want me to do his white shirts because I might burn them, so old Ollie Moore, who lives by the lumber yard, comes gets them with her red wagon with the laundry basket in it. She washes and starches and irons them. He pays her. She's a widow and has a kid."

"Yes, I know," she said.

Mrs. Pettybone was a good listener, so I told her, "Pop showed me how to use the wringer washer, too. I put hot water in the tub, soap and bleach, and then I wash the white clothes first and then the colored. Pop said I gotta know this stuff because people ain't gonna do for me all my life." I smiled. "If I need clean clothes for school, I ain't got no excuses now because I know how to wash and iron." I grinned real big. "And," I added, "I ain't ever got my fingers pinched in the wringer. Sometimes I put in too much and the wringer pops apart. But Pop showed me how to fix it."

"My, my," she said. "And how old are you?"

"I'll be seven in a couple of months."

I could tell she was surprised.

"I even hang clothes on the line out my brothers' window."

I do other work, too" I figured she'd like to know that also.

"Really now?"

"Yeah. I sweep the hall stairs down and wash them. All twenty-four of them."

"Oh-h-h?"

"And I sort beer bottles in the cellar. All by myself. Cases of them."

"You do-o-o?" She sounded very surprised. "Well, you're quite the helper. I hope your parents know how lucky they are to have such a special little girl like you."

I shrugged and blushed. Nobody never called me special before. Mrs. Pettybone made me feel important. I figured I better say something nice to her, too.

"You got a swell apartment. Nicer than ours."

"Why, thank you."

"It's perfect."

"Perfect?"

"Yeah." I pointed and said, "You got them crocheted doilies like my grandma, and pictures on your walls, and a couch, and lacy curtains, and a television . . . it looks like the dollhouse I just got for Christmas. I wish our apartment looked like this," I said. "But Mom's got all her good stuff packed in boxes in our living room that we ain't using. It don't matter, because we ain't staying in Rosendale that long."

Mickey's show was over and it was time to leave. Mrs. Pettybone helped him with his coat and rubber boots, and reminded him to wear his hat and gloves. She took a tissue and had Mickey blow his nose. "Tell your mother," she said, "I think Mickey might be getting a cold."

Mrs. Pettybone walked us down the stairs, and as she let us out she said, "Come back again. Be careful. Look for cars . . ."

Not waiting, we ran up and over the snowbank. I gave a quick look up and down the street. No cars. I held onto Mickey's hand, pulled him across the road to our slushy driveway, and asked, "Did you say thank you?"

He shook his head no.

"Turn around and say it, right now." I spun him in her direction. "Or she won't ever let you come back."

"T'ank you Miz Peta-bone!" Mickey called out and waved to her. "See you 'morrow!"

She smiled, and returned his wave.

1950
ORCHIDS ARE FOR EASTER

*To me the meanest flower that blows can give
thoughts that do often lie too deep for tears.*

William Wordsworth

IT WAS EASTER SUNDAY AND, like every other Sunday, Pop was gonna be late for church. "You'll be late for your own funeral," Mom said. We were all dressed and ready to go to the eleven o'clock Mass. I was standing outside their bedroom door, waiting, while Pop was fussing and fuming.

"Ed, how you can curse and swear like that and then go to church? You say, 'Where's my effing shirt? Get my G. D. shoes. Where's my S. O. B'ing socks?' And then curse more because I'm not handing you what you want. From now on get your own damn clothes!" Mom snapped.

Pop standing in his striped boxer shorts, bowed at the waist. Like a swami, he brought his right hand up, touched his fingertips to his heart, his lips, and his forehead, saying, "Allah-h-h, your royal majesty." Standing upright, he added, "Get me up earlier."

"What?" she said, in disbelief.

"If you laid my clothes out the night before ..."

"You should've married a maid," she cut him off.

"I did. I married you." He chuckled.

"Fire me!" she shouted.

Pop would lie in bed till ten-thirty, no matter how many times you called him, and then make a beeline to the bathroom to shower and shave. Thirty minutes later he'd be back in the bedroom, smelling of Old Spice After-Shave Lotion, and start yelling for his clothes and shoes.

"This is the last Sunday you'll ever see me in church! The last time!" she said in her "I mean it" voice.

That worried Pop because he thought since Mom changed her religion for them to get married in the Catholic church, it was his job to get her to Sunday Mass and Confession once a week. If she didn't and keeled over, and if she went to hell, it would be all his fault. He didn't want that on his record when he met Saint Peter at the Pearly Gates. Catholics didn't want to get sent down to hell with all those Protestants, Jews, Negroes and atheists. Mom said the priest tried to make her believe that. "But," she said, "it's a lot of crap."

Mom said she changed religions because Grandma Julianna forced her. She was nineteen and Pop was twenty-one when they ran away and got married. They didn't go far, just across the Hudson River to Poughkeepsie. They didn't know each other very long before Mom got pregnant, which I wasn't supposed to know, but I heard them arguing about it once. When they told Grandma Julianna Cherny that a Baptist minister married them and Mom was pregnant, Grandma Cherny "Puh-too!"ed on the kitchen-floor, the spit just missing Mom's feet, and said, "Married? Naa-na-na-na-nah. You not married," Grandma Cherny said. "Not in God's eyes. Not in my eyes. Not till you marry in the Catholic Church! In this house, your child will be bastard till then."

Mom said one religion was just as good as another, "But Catholics think they've got the only way to God, which leaves a helluva lot of good people going to hell, which makes me think hell isn't such a bad place to go." Catholics, she thought were a bunch of hypocrites, "like your father's family the Cherny's," she said, "they never practice what they preach, and then treat me as though I have a scarlet letter on my chest." I didn't know what she meant and I didn't ask.

The only one Mom got along with was Aunt Beatty, because she was an outsider that married into the Cherny family like Mom did. Aunt Beatty was Irish Catholic, not Protestant, so she met with the approval of the Cherny's, according to Mom.

On the day before Easter, Pop sent me to Mr. DeFelicis' florist shop to pick up corsages. Mr. DeFelicis was a nice man with slicked-back black hair and a nose like an eagle's beak. His florist shop was up the street from Doc Vaughn's and sandwiched in between the homes of Bobby Fisher, a tap dancer whose father drove a Trailways bus and the Reverend Sneider and his daughter Charlotte's house. Mr. DeFelicis' Rosendale Florist had a glassed-in showroom that stuck out from the front of his house. Everybody who had a business on Main Street lived in a house or an apartment built onto it or above it. Later, Mr. DeFelicis moved his family across the creek to James Street, the ritzy side of Rosendale, because people were always bugging him after closing hours. He got tired of that.

Pop had standing orders for a corsage of red rosebuds for my birthday in February and one of gardenias for Mom on her birthday in March. Also, a dozen long-stem red roses for their wedding anniversary in April, and always orchids at Easter, along with some strange potted plant that came from the African jungles. And there were always poinsettias for Christmas. Sometimes Pop surprised Mom during the week with a bouquet of carnations or lilies, especially when he was trying to make up for something stupid he did or said.

Pop paid extra money to get Mom the biggest orchid that Mr. DeFelicis could get. I got a baby one with freckles and thicker petals. My orchid reminded me of Peggy McGlocklin's face, all creamy white with rusty spots, and it lasted longer than Mom's. I got to wear it to school till it died. Then I pressed it in the altar Bible. Big John Batira, a pock-faced, squinty-eyed, New York City gangster type who gambled at our place, gave Mom the Bible. He made Edward G. Robinson, the cigar-chomping actor, look like a sissy.

Pop must've thought that if Mom had the biggest and bestest orchid, she'd be happy to show it off in church. She went. But he wasn't able to make her go to Confession and Communion.

"Catholics," Mom said, "confess their sins, come out and do

the same things all over again. So, why go? I may be a sinner, but I'm not a phony. Besides, what would I confess to a priest who wears a long black dress? His advice won't come from the experience of being married, will it? Unless of course," she said, "you take in consideration the homo-goings-on in seminary, or when they take off their collars and hit the bars. Or, the pregnant nuns . . . ." She sounded like a broken record with the needle stuck in a groove.

When Mom got an idea like priests being fags, or Confession being a waste of time, or anything else for that matter, Pop would say, "Changing her mind'd be like busting up Rosendale cement. I'd need ten cases of dynamite." Or, "No use being Dutch, Edith, unless you can be thick-headed."

Mom knew the church said you had to go to Confession and Communion once a year or be excommunicated. The last day to do this was Easter Sunday. She didn't care. "I'll take my chances in hell with the rest of my friends," she said. I tried to tell Mom that Sister said receiving the wafers was like putting money in a piggy bank. The more you put in, the greater your reward in heaven. Mom said that was just more made-up Catholic crap. "No one's counting," she said. Not for her soul, but to save on arguments, she had agreed to go to church only on Easter, Christmas, and for funerals of family or friends she liked.

Andy and Eddie walked to church. Lucky them. I got to stay home, hang onto Mickey and listen to fights, except when Mom said to take Mickey over to Millie's house. Mickey liked Millie, called her Ma just like I did. Her house was our second home.

Pop stuffed himself in the front seat of the car, started it and zoomed out of the driveway. He dropped us at the front door of the church and drove off looking for a place to park. Huffing and puffing, he came in wiping sweat from his brow onto a handkerchief with a fancy initial "E" embroidered in blue on one corner. He handed Mom money for the collection and went upstairs to the choir loft.

Mom and I walked to the pew where Andy and Eddie were sitting. It felt like everyone's eyes were on us because we were late, but I held my head up and walked with a straight back like Mom. Besides I looked good in my pink jacket with a matching skirt and my corsage. My hat was white straw with a darker pink band of velvet ribbon. It had a bunch of teeny flowers pinned to the band. I wore white gloves and carried a black patent leather pocketbook that matched my black patent leather shoes. I even a remembered to put the white linen hanky that Grandma Sarah had embroidered for me into my pocketbook. Mom put perfume behind my ears and a tiny bit of pink lipstick on my lips. I couldn't see it, but I knew it was there.

I slid across the pew next to my brothers. Andy's stomach growled real loud. Eddie play-punched him in the arm. Catholics weren't allowed to eat before receiving Communion and my brothers had been fasting since midnight. I hadn't made my first Communion yet, and had a full stomach.

Andy's stomach gurgled like a stopped-up drain coming unplugged. Eddie and him snickered. It was hard not to giggle. Mom squeezed in next to me, leaned forward, and gave them a warning look. She dug into her pocket book, pulled out a Lifesaver candy, and handed it to Andy. "Here," she said, very quietly. "It's not food. Eat it." She didn't have to tell him twice.

Father Mulry was walking toward the pulpit. Boy, were we late. Any later and we would have missed the Gospel reading and that would have been considered missing Mass, a mortal sin.

Father Mulry spoke very low. Even with a microphone, I couldn't understand one word he said. His bee-hum voice made me yawn. A couple of men in the back pews were reading the Sunday newspaper. Mr. Boyle was asleep and snorted a couple of times. His wife elbowed him awake.

After the sermon, came the time to receive Communion. This was the kneeling part of the Mass that lasted too long. My knees got sore and I wiggled, squirmed and got scolded for it. Older people in front of me rested their fat behinds on the seat of their pew. Sister would've had a stroke if she saw that. We were supposed to kneel with our backs straight and our butts off the seat. It didn't help that the church was too warm and smelled of ladies' perfume, and the fifty potted Easter lilies - I counted them - and dozens of burning beeswax candles.

And then, Oh, no. Here goes Father Mulry with the freakin'

frankincense. He waved the gold smoking container of incense from a long chain. He twirled it up high as his shoulder. Up and down, clink-clank. He censed the altar and the altar boys. They disappeared in the fog. He turned, walked up and down all three aisles, and censed us all. I held my gloved hands together like I was praying and pinched my nose with the tips of my fingers. It was hard to breathe. Smoke filled the church and Father Mulry disappeared. I bet this was how he got even with the people who only came to church once a year. Or else he was trying to kill off the spiders hidden in the cracks of the wall.

People coughed and sneezed while the choir was singing something in Latin. The force of Pop's voice, I believed, pushed the incense up to the ceiling, up the wall behind the altar, to the round stained glass window of God holding the world in the palm of His hand like a toy blue ball.

Father Mulry appeared at the altar. I looked around at the people shooing away the incense. Mr. Boyle was wiping his eyes and crying. Not from the incense, but from Pop singing the "Our Father." Mr. Boyle cried whenever Pop sang that, or the "Ave Maria," or any Irish song at our bar. His wife looked straight ahead and ignored him.

I once asked Mr. Boyle why he cried when Pop sang. He said Pop was better than Lanza and Caruso all wrapped into one, and added, "Your Pop's singing tickles de marrow of me bones and wiggles de water right outta me eyes."

His wife, Isabelle, said, "It doesn't take much to make an Irishman cry."

Pop's rich tenor voice stopped flooding the sanctuary. He left the choir loft to receive Communion. He was dressed to the nines in a brown pin stripe suit, starched white shirt, and striped wide tie with its double loop knot. The light from the stained-glass windows danced on his spit-shined, brown wingtips. He looked handsome, all five foot eleven and 250 pounds of him. His black-brown, Brylcremed hair was combed straight back, showing his widow's peak. Brown eyes with gold glints stared out from his serious face as he walked straight up the center aisle and knelt at the altar railing. He never looked down at Mom as he went by.

Mom stared out in front of her, smiling like a store mannequin as families paraded their Easter wear up to the altar. "Mom, you can receive now and always promise Jesus you'll go to Confession later on. C'mon, Mom. C'mon," I whispered.

"No!" she said, through clenched teeth and smiley lips.

I clambered over her legs and left the pew. I wedged myself between Pop and Kay Sullivan Werber, a flaming redhead on his left. She was stacked like Jane Russell. She looked down at me with eyes that said, "Whadda ya want, kid?" I stared back. She was Mom's age and had three boys who went to St. Peter's school. She sang at our bar with Pop and made Mom jealous. Kay was a "widow looking for a husband" according to Mom. Mom liked Kay, but didn't trust her around Pop.

As beautiful as a magazine make-up model, Mom sat ignoring the stares of others. She held her head up like a queen. She liked what she was wearing, a dusty-pink suit with the large purple orchid pinned to her lapel. The veil from her matching hat came over her Clairol champagne-beige hair, her ice-blue eyes, and stopped at the top of her hot-pink Max Factor lips. The corners of Mom's mouth turned up as if she had a joke going on inside her head.

Mass ended, and Father Mulry waddled down the center aisle to the front door. The crowd slowly filed out, row-by-row. Father Mumbles Mulry, as I thought of him, stood outside church shaking hands. He told some adults not to be strangers and it was good to see them again. People would come for the next couple of Sundays after Easter and wouldn't show up again until next year. Pop told Father Mulry the road t'hell was paved with part-time Catholics. Then he took the old priest's hand and pressed a hundred dollar bill into it.

"There he goes again," Mom said, "trying to buy his way out of hell."

We stood together as women walked by. No one said a nice thing to Mom about her outfit, or her orchid, like they did to the other women. The men who got drunk at our bar gave Mom a slight nod, a bare tip of the hat, or a whispered, "Hi, Edie," from a bowed head, like they were afraid to get caught talking to her. She tugged on my wrist to leave. Without a peep, I let her drag me to the car.

"They can't even look me in the face," she mumbled. Her eyes were sad and watery-looking. I knew she was feeling bad, but wouldn't cry here.

Mom opened the car door, pulled her seat forward and pushed me into the back. She dropped into the front seat and fumed. Pop hurried after us. As he pulled the car away from the curb and headed down the hill toward Main Street, Mom started, "Pious, sanctimonious..."

"Give it a rest, will ya, Edith? You could've gone to Communion, but no-o-o-o-o. Ya sit in church actin' like a prima donna and ya wonder why no one talks to you."

Mom smirked.

We drove across the bridge.

"No faggot Pope in a dunce cap has the right to tell me I'll go to hell...,"

"The Pope's not a faggot, Edith." Pop cut her off.

I couldn't believe she said that! She's gonna rot in hell. Jesus, don't let my mother die without confessing what she just said, I begged.

Pop braked for the stop sign at the end of the bridge, turned right onto Main Street. His face was serious.

Mom started to say something and Pop bellowed, "Just shut t' hell up!" He slammed the steering wheel with the side of his closed fist and the hard plastic, which was molded over a steel wire ring, cracked and bent. "Ah, Jesus Christ! See what ya made me do!" he shouted.

She smiled.

It was a brand-new car.

Dead silence filled the air. I took my hands off my ears. Andy and Eddie walked home from church and probably stopped for soda and to play pinball. Mickey was at Millie Rosenkranses'. Why did I have to get stuck with my parents?

Pop pulled the car into the driveway and stomped on the brakes, making Mom put her hand up on the metal dashboard to stop herself from going into the windshield. My body flew forward and banged into the back of her seat, bending a petal on my orchid. Tears came to my eyes.

I prayed, just let it be, Mom, please. Without a word, she got out of the car, and with all her might, slammed the car door shut and rattled all the windows.

Pop looked at me in the back seat. Our brown eyes locked. He looked sad, but then grinned. "Gowan'," he said. "Wipe your nose and go get Mickey. When ya get back, we'll see what the Easter Bunny left. Thank Millie for me and give her this money for watchin' Mickey," he said, handing me a ten dollar bill.

I shook my head okay and wondered, Why can't Pop be like Randolph Scott or Gary Cooper? Why can't Mom be nice like Betty Grable or Ginger Rogers?

Feeling queasy, I walked on shaky legs to the Rosenkranses', fingering the crease in the petal on my orchid. Don't cry, I told myself. Or the boys will call you a baby for blatting over a broken petal on a dumb flower. I wish I never got this stupid thing. I'm gonna throw it away when I get home. I didn't want to dirty it, but I pulled my hanky from my pocket book and blew my nose before I reached Millie's front door. Maybe the Easter Bunny made a mistake and left my basket with her. I stepped into Millie's house and called out, "Hey, Ma, whatcha doing? Did the Easter Bunny come yet?"

Where Babies Come From

*Everyone is ignorant,
only on different subjects.*

Will Rogers

THE NEIGHBORHOOD BOYS WERE STANDING AROUND in a half-circle with their backs to the path leading to the public school, staring down into the weeds. Two of the guys were my brothers.

"Hey, Eddie, whatcha doing?" I asked, trying to peer between his long legs.

"Go 'way, Brat. There's nothing to see," he said, and pushed my head away with his hand.

But there was. Porky was lying on the ground on top of a sister of one of the big boys in the group. Porky looked like he was trying to push all the air outta her. She was making "oof-oof" noises.

"What's Porky doing? Why's he wrestling with her?"

Eddie laughed. The rest of the guys were rooting Porky to move faster.

"Well, at least he can't get her pregnant," Kenny Post said.

"What's he mean, Eddie?" I jerked on his pant leg.

"He shoots blanks," Andy said.

All the boys chuckled.

Figuring they weren't gonna tell me anything, I went to find Bobby Ann who was alone on a swing at the playground.

"Did you see 'em?" I asked, pointing back to the path.

"Yeah," she nodded. "Bunch of friggin' slobs."

We doubled up on her swing. Bobby Ann sat and I stood on the seat facing her, my feet on either side of her hips.

"What'd the guys think was so funny?" I asked.

Bobby Ann pushed off and got us swinging. Bending my knees, I pumped up and down to get us as high in the air as we could go.

"What were Porky an' her doing?"

"He's fuckin' her, or trying to," she said.

"Wha--at?"

Bobby Ann looked up at me and said, "Ya got that glassy-eyed look. Don't you know anything?"

I didn't know what she meant. And I couldn't ask because I didn't want to look stupid. I knew how to spell "fuck" and use it in a sentence. But I guess that didn't count.

"Don't you remember anything I told ya?" she asked.

I shrugged. I didn't bother remembering because I thought she was making up things. Andy was always telling me stuff that wasn't true and he even said, "Honest to God. I swear on the Bible." But he lied, and he was going to hell.

Bobby Ann went on to tell me where babies came from and how they got here.

"You gotta be a teenager 'fore you can make a baby," she said. "That's why those idiots were laughing because Porky's dick don't squirt anything yet, and that girl ain't a teenager."

"You're making shit up," I said.

"Yeah? Well, just ask Lina. Where'd ya think you came from, the stork, or 'the pelican, because its mouth can hold more than its belly can?'," she sang the old rhyme.

"You're disgusting, ya know that? My father never put his dick in my mother."

"Has so."

"Has not!"

"Did so."

"Did NOT!"
"At least four times."
"DID NOT!"
"Man, ya are so-o-o-o-o stupid."
"Yeah?"
"YEAH!"
"Your sister don't know everything," I said.
"Lina knows because she can have babies, because she gets her monthly."
"Her what?"
"Jeez Louise. Her friend!"
Our swinging had slowed.
"What friend? Who . . . whadda ya talking about?"
"Ya gotta to be the dumbest, shittenist kid on the block. Ain't your mother ever told you anything?" she asked. "You go to Doc's and get her rags when she bleeds, right?"
"I don't get her rags."
"Kotex, dummy. Pads?" Bobby Ann sounded angry.
"Oh, them."
"A-a-ah! What did you think they were for? You seen them in the garbage can didn't you?"
"Yeah." But I didn't know . . .
"They're for when you get your bloody friend."
So what if I didn't know what they were? When I asked Mom, she said I'd find out soon enough. It couldn't be that important, or she would've told me.
"Look. I'll spell it out for you. Now, pay attention," she said, as we came to a full stop, "and don't forget. You get to bleed once a month from down there." She pointed at my privates, which were at her eye level as I still stood in front of her on the swing seat.
"It lasts about five days," she said. "It washes out old dead baby eggs. And then you get new eggs that you keep up inside you till you want to make a kid. Then the man has to squirt his jism juice inside you because it's, well . . . it's like putting water on a seed that you planted in the ground. If you want it to sprout, ya gotta water it. And if you wan' a baby, ya gotta let a man stick his dick in you, screw you and juice up your eggs. That's sex. And if you don't get

your friend the next month, you're gonna get a baby in nine months. That's how it works." Bobby Ann slid off the seat as I jumped down to the ground. My privates felt like they were on fire and needed to be washed after she pointed her finger there.

"Well I ain't getting' no bloody monthly, and I ain't letting no boy stick his dick in me!" I yelled at her. "And I ain't having no babies if that's what you gotta do to get 'em!" I ran to the path and prayed the boys had left to find other things to do.

"You can't not get your monthly!" Bobby Ann shouted after me. "You hare brain! It comes when it wants too! MORON!"

My head was all swarmy like bees were inside using it for a hive. My mother wouldn't let my father put his dick into her. Mom said us kids were surprises and you never knew when you were gonna get one. Bobby Ann is lying. I just know she is.

At dinner, I couldn't look at my mother and father . . .yuck! Bobby Ann had to tell me this crap. Even my food didn't taste good. Maybe I'll ask Mom again what she does with them Kotex things. Maybe I'll ask Eddie's girlfriend about making babies. But what if it's true and Eddie and her are . . . and she tells me . . . . This is just too yucky to think about.

I hummed while I was chewing my food to fill my mind with something other than pictures of Porky pumping up and down on that girl. "Humm-hum."

"Judy!" Pop called.

"Humm-hum-a-humm."

"Judy!" He called louder.

"Hum-a-hum."

"Judy!" he shouted.

"Wha-a-at!"

"Stop humming while you eat, ya damn crazy kid."

I managed to put what Bobby Ann said out of my mind till a couple of weeks later, when I lay in bed asleep and was woke up by strange sounds. What were they? It sounded like Dad DeWitt's pigs in the pigpen when they were rooting around, their noses stuck in the mud, looking for food. And what was that "ahh-ahh" over and over again. It was coming from Mom and Pop's room.

I sat up and pressed my ear to the wall. I got out of bed and sneaked down the hallway toward their bedroom. The closer I got, the louder the noises got. Peeking into their bedroom, I could see by the streetlight shining in the window on my father's hairy back as he moved up and down on the bed. I couldn't see Mom, but she must have been under him because that's where the "ahh-ahh" noises were coming from. The sounds were scarier than Boris Karloff as the Mummy. I woke up Eddie.

"Eddie. Eddie," I whispered near his ear. "Ya gotta wake up."

"Wha. . .? Whadda ya wan'?" he asked.

"Shhhhh, Eddie. Pop is doing something to Mom. C'mon. Get up," I said, and pulled on his arm.

"What else is new? Go way. Lemme sleep."

"Eddie. He's killing her. He's squooshing the air outta her."

Eddie propped his head up on his hand and listened. "I don't hear anything," he said and lay back down.

Eddie was used to me waking him up late at night telling him that Mom and Pop were downstairs arguing after the bar closed.

"Ya gotta come down by their bedroom," I begged. "I think he's choking her to death. She's going agh-hh, agh-hh, and he's bouncing on top of her."

"Shit. Ya woke me up for that? Gowan back to bed. It's nothing."

"But Eddie, I can't sleep. I hear it through my wall. He's killing her. I just know it."

"Will you two shut up," Andy said, pulling his face up out of his pillow. "He's just porkin' her."

"What's porkin'?"

"They're making bacon." Andy chuckled and added, "he's dickin' her, ya jerk."

Eddie smacked Andy hard on his back. "Shut your trap."

"Fuck you! Ya guys woke me up," Andy complained, trying to rub his back where Eddie slapped him.

"What's he mean, Eddie? I want to know."

"They're doing this," Andy said. In the dim light in their room, I saw Andy roll over onto his back. He held his arms up and with his thumb and forefinger of one hand he made a circle. He took the pointer finger of his other hand and stuck it in the center of the circle with quick jabbing motions, the symbol the older boys used for fucking.

"You're a lying sack of crap, Andy!" It was hard to keep my voice to a whisper. Everything Bobby Ann had told me about fucking came crashing together in my brain. Mom and Pop couldn't be fucking like . . . Porky and . . .! No way!

Eddie gave Andy a shove with his foot and Andy fell halfway out of bed. "Why you telling her that shit? You're a real asshole."

"You're sick, Andy," I added.

"Oh, Jeezus Chrissakes. Go back to bed," Eddie scolded me. "I'll talk to you tomorrow."

Pop coughed two or three times, real hard. Was that a warning, meaning he heard us, or was he having a hacking fit from those Pall Malls he smoked? He called it a cigarette cough. His bedsprings squeaked. He was getting up.

"Get to bed," Eddie said. "Quick, before he goes to the john."

"I hope ya get caught," Andy whispered.

I stepped into the dark hallway, pressed myself up against the wall into the black shadows and held my breath. In the light from his bedroom doorway, I saw Pop all hairy and naked, like King Kong. Holy shit! His dick hung down swinging between his legs like the wanger on Dad DeWitt's horse. His coughing made it and his balls bounce up and down, and when he stopped hacking, everything hung to his knees. Sweet baby Jesus! As Pop came down the hallway, it looked like his dick was waving Hi! to me, this long rubber salami saying, "I see you." Pop hacked his way into the bathroom, closed the door, and snapped on the light.

On tiptoe, I ran to my room. I was shaking like a leaf, thinking about what would've happened if I got caught. I didn't know whether to say an Act of Contrition because I stared at Pop's dick, or to say a prayer of thanks to Jesus for not getting caught. I climbed into bed. I couldn't get rid of the picture in my mind of my father's big thing going in and out of my mother. Yuck, gag, puke. I kept rubbing the pictures out of my eyes. Oh God, this has to be those impure thoughts Sister taught us about in Catechism class. I better pray them right outta my head or I am never gonna be able to make First Holy Communion next month. I grabbed my glow-in-the-dark rosary beads from my metal headboard and began to say Hail Marys. No way will I tell the priest in my first Confession that I saw my father's dick.

Repeating the Hail Marys made me sleepy, and I started to doze off. Wait till I see Bobby Ann! She won't believe it when I tell her how big Pop's dick is. She'll want proof. When he takes a nap and the covers fall off him, I'll get her so she can see for herself. Before, I was too embarrassed to look into his room when he was napping naked, but now I'd seen everything! So I can look all I want to! Some things I got to keep to myself, though. I ain't ever letting Bobby Ann know that Mom and Pop were fucking. No way. She'd want details. My body shuddered from head to toe.

First Communion

*... if only one good memory is left in our hearts,
it may also be the instrument of our salvation one day.*
Feodor Dostoyevsky

Making my First Communion was scary. First I had to go to Confession and tell the priest all the bad things I'd done. I said to the priest, "Bless me Father, for I have sinned. This is my first Confession. I told a lie to my friend. I disobeyed my mother. How many times? Oh, at least five times. I say bad words. What ones? Let's see, shit; piss; ummmmh fuck; aaahhhhh, mother-fucker; cock-saa ..."

"Stop, stop, stop, stop! That's enough," Father Gafney said. "Just tell me how many times you used bad words." I was glad I got him and not Father Mulry, and I was glad he told me to stop. It didn't feel right telling him those words I only used with Porky or Bobby Ann.

"Look," Father said, "just forget about it. How many times did you think bad things about anyone, and how many times have you ever said bad things about someone?"

This was hard. Next time, I'll come prepared. I'll figure it out first and come with a list, because I run out of fingers counting. Sister said Confession makes you feel good. She tells fish tales.

Father Gaffney told me to pray one Our Father and two Hail

Marys before I left the church, and promise to stop swearing. "If you don't stop swearing," he said, "God won't like you anymore and He'll punish you. He doesn't like little girls that swear. It's not nice."

The longer someone stayed in church and prayed, the worse we thought their sins must be. I prayed real fast, because my knees were getting sore, and, besides, everyone, even the grownups who went to Confession after me, were getting up and leaving.

For First Communion Sunday, the second-grade boys had to wear white suits and girls had to wear a white dress, shoes, and veil. Mom had to buy me a slip to go underneath the dress she bought because it was see-through. She thought we could make do with the one in my drawer, but it was too small. We went to Nugent's Department Store where the saleslady put your dollar bills in a little can that would shoot upstairs through a bunch of tubes to another lady. That lady made change and shot the tube with the change back down to our sales lady.

My dress had poofy short sleeves and a ruffle that ran around the bottom. It wasn't as pretty as the ones with stiff, stick-out taffeta skirts and crinolines underneath. Mom said she wasn't gonna waste money on something so fancy, and I didn't need any crinolines, either, because I didn't have those kinds of dresses. It was the same with the veil. Some girls got the double-layer fancy veils and others rented the cheap, plain ones from the nuns. That's what I had to do. "You're only going to wear the veil and dress once," Mom said.

I wanted a pair of white patent leather shoes from Yallums in Kingston, and a white pair of socks with lace trim. "I have to have them," I pleaded. "Please, plea-zzzzze," I begged, but Mom didn't give in.

"Plain white socks with white sandals will do," she said. "Besides, summer is coming and you need the sandals more than you need white patent leather that won't last, and won't go with anything you wear."

"I'm gonna look like a jerk," I mumbled.

All the pleading in the world would not change her mind. "Go tell your problems to Jesus," she said. "Sandals were good enough for Him."

After First Communion, most families went out to eat and

celebrate. Italian families went to Bianco's. The Polish families ate at the Valley Inn or the Astoria, and Irish families went to the Bridgeview Inn. Other families went to The Well, The Chalet, or the Brookside Inn. Some kids stayed home, where their parents had a party with their relatives. The kids got cards with money in them. They couldn't spend any of it. It had to be saved in the bank for when the boys went away to college or the girls got married.

After church, Mom and Pop went back and opened their bar. Mom got busy checking on dinner that was slow-cooking in the oven. She made a ham with pineapple on it for the hotel guests and whoever else wanted to eat with us. Pop never turned anyone away, even if they couldn't pay.

One of our hotel guests was a man who had worked the oil fields in a place called Saudi Arabia. He made lots of money there. He stayed with us every time he came home on a break. He was sitting at the bar drinking. "C'mere," he said to me. "Got something for ya." I looked up at his dark tan face and sun-bleached brown hair. "This is for being a good kid and for making your First Communion," he said, and handed me a small box with a ribbon tied around it. I blushed. I felt funny taking a gift from a guest. I opened it. My fingers were shaking. Inside was a gold crucifix on a thin gold chain he bought up the street from Emcee Lewis, the jeweler.

"Here, let me hook it on for ya," he said. I thanked him and told my mother I was going to show Ma Rosenkranse my necklace and my dress. I ran out of the bar before I started to cry.

Nobody was home at the Rosenkranses'. I went to the barn instead of going back home, climbed the ladder to the second floor, being careful not to catch my dress on the splintery wood. I spread my arms out for balance, stepped across one open rafter after another, and made my way to the window. I pushed open the wood door that shuttered the window. From here, I could see Rosenkranses' lawn, their front porch, the swing tied in the maple tree. I could see behind their house, the path to the schoolyard that ran alongside the field of tall weeds soon to turn green, and to the woods that went down to the river. If I looked over to my left, I could see the kitchen door of our hotel, my brothers' bedroom window, the kitchen window, and the guest window to room number seven. I fingered my gold cross.

The Rosenkranses, my brothers, and I played here after school, on the weekends, and during the summer. It was our fort, but, when I was alone, it was my secret hideout. No other kids except us were allowed in. We told the rest to go away.

The wooden floor below was covered with dry loose hay. I liked to lie in the hay mound and look up at the open window where the hay bales used to be brought through to the second story. That's where half the floorboards were missing. Older people sneaked in and stole the planks instead of going across the street to the lumberyard and buying them.

We kids broke apart all the old dry hay bales and heaped the hay into a pile, and Eddie and Dickey got a rope and tied it to an open rafter. We'd grab hold of the rope, swing over the hay pile, and let go. Dust would rise up and make us sneeze. I played Tarzan, and daydreamed if nobody bothered me.

A cool breeze blew through the window, and I smelled the stink of my permed hair. Mom asked Helen Dittmar, the town's beautician, to perm my hair so it wouldn't hang down into my eyes.

"I don't want you looking like a sheepdog at your Communion," Mom said.

Two Saturdays before First Communion Sunday, I spent almost four hours at Mrs. Dittmar's house in her beauty parlor. Boy! Did this perm stink! I tried hard not to breathe. It's a good thing for Mrs. Dittmar I didn't like to puke.

By the time she was done, my skin burned and my head itched like I had cooties. My head felt like a fried egg from the chemicals and being under the dryer so long, and I smelled like a dead skunk. Then she said I couldn't wash my hair for a week! I ain't ever coming back here! Mrs. Dittmar held up a mirror so I could see the front and back of my hair. God! I looked like . . . Harpo Marx! I paid a smiling Mrs. Dittmar her money and left fast. I ran up the street to our bar, stomped upstairs to the bathroom of our apartment, jumped up and sat on the edge of the sink, and stared in horror in the mirror.

"It looks like a bird's nest!" I shouted at the mirror, as I put

Vaseline on the cherry-redness around my hairline and the back of my neck, like Mrs. Dittmar told me to do.

"I ain't going to Communion," I said aloud. "I'm a freak. Everybody's gonna laugh at me." I yowled loud and long.

After a week of stink and another week of washing my hair every day, I decided I better go to Communion. God was already getting even with me for swearing, so He'd probably zap me with lightning for not making Communion. Besides it's gotta be a mortal sin not to show up.

A LOUD, sharp sound snapped me out of my daydreaming and back to the barn. It was Pop. He was whistling out the kitchen door for my brothers and me to come home to eat. He timed us. If we didn't get in the door in five minutes, he'd bug us about where we were, who we were with, and what we were doing. It wasn't worth being late. Eating on time was important to him.

"Your mother cooks one meal a day, if we're lucky," he said. "Ya can be here on time so the guests aren't kept waiting either."

Besides I was supposed to set the table.

"Oh, shit! Oh, piss! Oh, frig! I'm dead now!" I said, as I leaned back from the window, and looked down at the front of my dress.

The owner had painted the outside of the barn last week. He was thinking of selling it. The red lead paint had leaked into the cracks of the siding and was still wet! I got paint on the front of my dress. There wasn't anything to do but go home and face the music.

Pop tried to get the paint out with kerosene, gasoline, turpentine, and nail polish remover in the upstairs kitchen sink. Nothing would take the redness all the way out.

"What t'hell were ya doin' in the barn?" he crabbed. "Don't ya use your head for anything besides a friggin' hatrack?"

Mom looked at me with mean eyes. "Give me that necklace," she said. "Next thing you know you'll lose it. You don't know how to take care of anything."

"I want to keep it on my dresser," I told her.

"No," she said, and unhooked it from around my neck.

"You can wear it on Sundays. Otherwise, it stays in my jewelry box, you understand? Don't look at me like that," she said. "Take that nastiness right out of your eyes."

I knew I would never see that cross again.

Mom said she was going to hang the dress in my closet with its dull pink stain on it forever, to remind me of how I'd ruined it. And maybe I'd learn a lesson from it.

"Now young lady, you see why I didn't waste hard-earned money buying you a fancy dress from London's?" she snapped.

The useless dress stayed in my closet for months, making me feel bad and stupid. One day, tired of looking at it, I ripped it off the hanger, stomped on it, and kicked it into the back of the closet, where it stayed, a rumpled-up mess, until the day we moved out of the hotel, and Mom threw it away.

Lady Kerry

*Seven to eleven is a huge chunk of life, full of dulling and forgetting.
It is fabled that we slowly lose the gift of speech with animals,
that birds no longer visit out windowsills to converse.
As our eyes grow accustomed to sight
they armour themselves against wonder.*
Leonard Cohen

SITTING OUT ON THE PATIO IN FRONT OF THE BAR, I was watching the cars drive by, while soaking up some summer sun. My dream was that in one of them was the actor Glenn Ford. He was hurrying home to his wife, June Allyson, who was waiting with their five clean little kids, to say, "Hi, Daddy! Did ya have a nice day?" He worked hard driving a garbage truck, or maybe he worked in the cement mines, or for the town, repairing roads. He'd be tired and glad to see his wife, who would give him a smooch and tell him how much she missed him. Glenn Ford would hug and kiss his kids, then wash up to eat supper. June Allyson would have a dinner of roast chicken, mashed potatoes with lots of gravy, corn on the cob, hot and dripping with butter, waiting to be salted and eaten.

It was after six and I was told at least three times by Mom to get inside and eat supper. I was waiting to be adopted by Glen Ford and June Allyson. I was waiting for chicken, and mashed potatoes, gravy and corn. I didn't want to eat fatty kielbasa, slimy sauerkraut, and boiled potatoes with gray spots where the eyes had been. I ignored Mom. Besides, Pop wasn't home.

I looked up and thought I saw Andy walking toward me with a dog. We didn't have a dog. Not many kids did.

The dog I liked was Doodles, an old beagle hound that belonged to my grandfather, Dad DeWitt. Doodles would talk; you'd talk and he'd yowl. But he was dead now. Dad DeWitt said one day Doodles would have to go to heaven because he was getting old. And Dad sent him there after the frost went out of the ground. He brought Doodles down from his farm to see me before he sent him to doggy heaven. We sat together on the blue stone stairs that led up to Mrs. Pettybone's apartment.

"Dad, how is Doodles gonna get to heaven?" I asked. I didn't care what the nuns said. I knew dogs went to heaven.

Dad took a pill out of his pocket and said, "I'm gonna put this in his food." He had a little bit of ground meat in a paper bag. He put the pill in the meat and rolled it into a ball. "When Doodles eats this," he said, "he'll go to sleep, and when he wakes up he'll be in doggy heaven."

I didn't want Doodles to go, but Dad said he wouldn't be sick or blind or deaf or have fleas any more. I said my good-bye and Dad fed him the meat with the pill in it. Doodles swallowed it in one gulp, his eyes closed and he went to sleep in Dad's arms. His head hung over loose and limp and his tongue slid out the side of his mouth. I petted his soft ears and sniffled. Dad stood up and asked me to bring along the shovel from the back of his pickup truck. We walked the towpath behind the businesses on Main Street to some property Dad still owned a couple of doors down from Pettybone's. He dug Doodles a hole, laid him down and covered him with dirt. Dad said this was the way for Doodles's soul to get out of his body and go to doggy heaven. Bodies were no good to us in heaven. I knew that from the Sisters. Dad DeWitt buried a lot of animals, so I guess he knew all about it, too, even though he wasn't Catholic. Jesus died and he went to heaven after the soldier put stuff in his mouth. I wondered if it was the same stuff Dad gave to Doodles. I wondered if it was the same stuff movie actresses like Bette Davis or Joan Crawford, or was it Marlene Dietrich, kept in their rings to poison the drinks of guys they didn't like.

Andy got closer and I saw he was with a long-legged skinny dog with long red hair more beautiful than Rita Hayworth's or Rhonda Flemming's!

"Oh, Andy, she's so beautiful!" I cried, as I went running toward them. "Where'd you get her?" I patted the dog's head and stroked her beautiful shiny red coat. "Look how long the hair on her tail is. Her ears are silky!" The dog licked my face when I played with her long ears.

Just then, Pop pulled his car into the driveway, parked and came over to see what we were doing. He jumped on Andy right away, wanting to know where he stole the dog. He didn't believe Andy's story about how the dog just came up to him while he was fishing at the creek. Andy said the dog wouldn't leave him after he fed him half his sandwich. Pop checked the dog's collar. There was no name tag. He lifted her leg and said she was a female.

"Well, we'll keep her till we find out who owns her," Pop said. He said she was a purebred Irish setter, a bird dog, with a large knowledge bump toward the back of her head. He said she was worth hundreds of dollars and someone was bound to be looking for her.

"Don't get attached," he warned. "She's gotta go back where she belongs."

We went inside and Pop told the dog to sleep on the old Army blanket he placed underneath the shuffleboard for her. But at night she wouldn't stay there after Andy went to bed. She banged her rump on the self-closing door by the stairs till it came open. She was quick to stick her nose in the crack and force her body through. Up the staircase she went and stood scratching on the apartment door till we let her in. She wasn't gonna sleep on the floor here either. She jumped up on my brother's bed, forced her way between Eddie and Andy, crawled under their covers, turned around and put her head up on Andy's pillow. Pop later said she thought she was people. No matter how much he scolded her and made her get off the bed, she didn't listen to him. As soon as he walked out of the boys' room, she jumped back up on the bed.

Andy named her Lady because she was so pretty. Lady would follow us to school in the morning and then turn around and go back to the bar, or run in the woods hunting. When Mickey took his noontime nap, and Lady was there, he slept half on her blanket and half on Lady. She wouldn't move till he woke up. And it was like she could tell time. She would wait for us by the bridge at three o'clock and walk back home with us from school. She was smart enough not to walk across that rickety old bridge.

A couple of months after Andy found her, Lady's owner showed up. The man told Pop he lived in Rifton, eight miles away, and he raised Irish setters to sell.

"And this one," he said, "is always getting out and I never know where I might find her. Once it was in Kingston. Another time it was in New Paltz. And now she's here in Rosendale." He looked at us kids and looked at his dog. "Lady Kerry. Come," he called. "Sit."

Obediently, she came to him and sat by him. Andy, Mickey and I put on our saddest faces when we heard him say, "I believe you have my dog."

"We call her Lady. It's why she came to you," Andy said and hugged her. Lady licked the tears running down Andy's face.

"Well," said the man. You named her Lady, huh? Look at these papers," he said, as he reached inside his suit jacket and pull them out to show Andy. "Her name is Lady Kerry."

"Look, Pop!" Andy said. "She's got a birth certificate!"

The man smiled. He took out a pen from inside his pocket, signed his name on the paper and gave it to Andy.

"Here you go, fella. As long as you have these papers, she's all yours. Now take good care of her." He got up to leave.

Andy was so happy he couldn't even say thanks. He just stared at the paper, then at Lady, then at the man.

"I've been looking for her for weeks. Someone said they thought she was here." The man looked at Pop and said, "You can have her. After playing with kids, and because she keeps running away . . . hell, she's ruined. She'll never make a good hunting dog."

"Hunting dog, huh?" Pop played real stupid. "What kind you say she was?"

"Irish setter. Bird dog," the man replied. "Hunts pheasants, partridge."

"Oh. Uh huh," Pop said, like he wasn't interested.

The man shook his head and finished his beer. He must have thought he was giving his dog to some local yokels, and, if the dog liked us, she couldn't have been much to start with. But he was wrong.

Pop was a hunter, and he already had Lady out in the fields. Without doing much more than pointing or whistling, Lady flushed birds and brought them back after Pop shot them. Pop said a dog is only as smart as its owner. And Pop, even though he quit school in eighth-grade, thought he was pretty smart, because we now had the most intelligent and expensive dog we would ever own, and we got her for free.

Irish setters are intelligent dogs, but they are also very stubborn. Lady wouldn't eat peas, and because she wouldn't eat them, I wouldn't eat them. If they weren't good enough for her, then they weren't good enough for me. Pop tried making our peas all kinds of ways. Nothing worked. When Pop scraped my cold peas into Lady's dog dish, she'd pick them out one at a time with her front teeth, never breaking the skin, and put them in a neat pile on the floor by her bowl.

Pop tried to trick Lady by smashing the peas up and mixing gravy into her food. She sniffed her dog food and looked at him. "Gowan," he said, "eat." Lady looked at her food, looked up at him again and walked away. She went to her blanket, scuffed it up with her paws, circled round and round about ten times, and dropped down with a loud "thud". She snorted air out her nostrils and it made her lips flap like a wild horse. She held her head up and shoulders high, like a queen. When Pop talked to her she turned her head away and looked at the wall. I thought it was funny and giggled. Even Pop grinned. Lady gave him the cold shoulder.

Pop once left the same food for her for two days. It was a test. He said if she got hungry enough, she'd eat it. He tried giving me peas for two days in a row, also. I piled them up on the side of my plate and left them. Just like Lady. And, just like her, I wouldn't talk to Pop when he said, "Eat them damn peas, now!" If Lady wasn't afraid of him, why should I be? Pop told me I wouldn't get anything to eat till I ate them. If it didn't bother Lady none, it didn't bother me none. Besides no one got up with us in the mornings. They didn't see Lady eating big bowls of corn flakes for breakfast along with me, and getting half of my peanut butter and jelly sandwich from lunch that I would save for her. We weren't hungry at suppertime.

Pop gave in before Lady or I did. I was so happy when he told us we never had to eat peas again that I grabbed a butter knife from the kitchen and ran upstairs to my bedroom. I slid some money out of the slot in the lid of the can sitting on my dresser for collecting coins for the poor refugees. Rushing back downstairs, I grabbed Lady and we ran to Doc Vaughn's Drugstore where I bought us both a chocolate ice cream cone. I held a cone in each hand as we sat side-by-side on Doc's stairs, licking them. The ice cream dripped out of the soggy ends of the cones, down my elbows and onto Doc's red brick steps.

"Get off my steps!" Doc yelled, as he came storming out of the store carrying a bucket and a broom. "Go home and make a mess!" I stood halfway up when he threw hot soapy water on the mess Lady and I made. Doc took a broom and brushed away the drowned black ants crawling all over the drips of ice cream. If he waited a minute, Lady would have licked the bricks clean for him.

Goin' Fishin'

We may say of angling, as Dr. Boteler said of strawberries,
"Doubtless God could have made a better berry, but doubtless God never did";
and so, if I might be judge, God never did make a more calm, quiet,
innocent recreation than angling.

Izaak Walton

Andy was in the backyard where we burned garbage in an old rusty 55-gallon drum. He was hunched over, making a small fire on the ground with sticks and wadded-up newspapers.

"Whatcha doing, Andge?" I asked my brother.

"Nothin'. Get lost."

"What's that metal thing?"

"A mold."

"What's a mold?"

"It's for making sinkers, stupid!" he said, his face getting all red.

"How d'ya make sinkers?"

"Shut up and watch if you have to know."

"Can I help?"

"No."

Andy brushed his hair off his face as he bent over making a spit from two small forked tree branches he stuck in the ground. He laid a piece of metal coat hanger across them. He broke chunks of soft lead into small pieces and put them into an empty soup can he pulled from the garbage before it got burned. He punched two holes near the top edge of the can and ran another piece of coat hanger through.

"What's the wire for, Andge?"

"It's to hang the can over the fire."

"Why d'ya do that?"

"'Cause I gotta melt the lead and pour it in the mold to make sinkers. Got any more questions?" He glared at me. His blue eyes looked liked frozen marbles. Cold and hard.

In a few minutes, the lead was bubbling in the can. Andy piled up some sand, which he got from the river bank, and flattened down the top of the pile.

"What's the sand for, Andge?"

"Shut your hole and watch."

I zipped my lips and watched his every move.

Andy took the two pieces of the mold and screwed them together and turned it on edge.

"Why are there holes in it?" I asked.

"It's where you pour the lead in."

Andy forced the mold into the sand. With Pop's pliers, he grabbed the edge of the tin can and poured the melted lead into the holes until each one was filled.

"Whatcha ya gotta do now, Andge?"

"Wait."

"For what?"

"For the lead to cool off and get hard."

A few minutes later, using the pliers again, he pulled the mold from the sand and dropped it into a bucket of water. When the mold stopped sizzling and smoking, he reached in and picked it up, unscrewed it, taking the two halves apart. Inside were teardrop sinkers with a ring on top to put fishing line through. Each sinker was a bit bigger than the next, with a raised number printed on it.

"Wow! Whadda you gonna do now, Andge?"

"I'm gonna catch me some eels and sell 'em to Goldwasser. Then I'm gonna buy some new fishin' stuff."

Mr. Goldwasser owned a grocery store up past the Post Office on the way to school. We never went in there because we weren't Jews. He only sold food that Jews could eat.

"What's Goldwasser gonna do with eels?" I asked.

"Eat'm, stupid. He pickles them and eats them with sour cream and crackers. They call it gelt-a-fish."

"Eeewwweee!" I said, scrunching up my face. "How could you eat them creepy things?"

Andy ignored me and continued the sinker-making till he ran out of lead.

"Where you going, Andge?" I asked, as he stomped out the fire and headed back to the bar to get his fishing gear.

"Goin' fishin', but first I gotta put the old man's tools back."

"Can I go, too? I'll help carry stuff." Besides I thought he was lying about Mr. Goldwasser and I wanted to go see for myself.

"Oh, gawd! I s'pose so." He sighed.

We went up Main Street carrying three sturdy branches he cut earlier. Andy wrapped fishing string around the end of each one, enough to reach the bottom of the creek where the eels lay. He got the line out of the basement where Pop kept his fishing tackle for fishing in Canada. Andy wasn't supposed to touch Pop's stuff but figured he'd never find out. Andy should've known by now Pop notices everything.

"Here," Andy said, "carry the sinkers. If you fall in the river, you'll sink to the bottom and become bullhead bait." He laughed. Ha, ha, real funny, I thought.

As we came around the turn by the Post Office, we could see Mr. Goldwasser and his wife sitting on chairs in front of their store. They looked so much alike that people thought they were brother and sister. They were short and round, with faces like gnomes.

Mr. Goldwasser saw Andy carrying the fishing poles and called out, "Hey, boy! Ya vont make mone-ey? Ya get eels. I pay ya," he said, as he held up one hand, rubbing his fingers against his thumb.

Holy mackerel! Goldwasser does eat them things!

No one in their right mind tried to catch an eel, especially with a regular fishing pole. Eels looked like the fattest, blackest rubber hose with a mouth full of needles for teeth. If they hooked your line, they fought hard. They could break your good pole right in half. You had to play them out till they got tired. If they ever got tired. And if you got them to shore, you whopped them on the head with a club, cut your line and kissed your hook goodbye. No way could you get it out of their mouth. Selling eels to Goldwasser was a way Andy could go to Rossler's Hardware to replace stuff he needed for bass and trout fishing.

We climbed down the loose dirt embankment and sat on some rocks at the edge of the creek underneath the rickety bridge. Andy rigged up his poles with old rusty hooks, the new lead sinkers and bits of Pop's steak.

"Where d'ya get the meat, Andge?"

"The 'frigerator."

"You idiot! Pop's gonna kill you!"

"He'll never miss it." Andy waved me off.

"Oh, yes, he will. He always misses food. You're gonna get your ass kicked again."

"Fuck'm. You want to fish or go home?" he threatened.

We sat quiet for a while watching the sun go down. Andy said that Jerry Mertine told him that he used to fish in a rowboat at night with a lantern and a net. The fish thought the lantern light was the sun and they'd jump out of the water right into his fishing net. Sometime soon, Jerry had told Andy, he was gonna take him night fishing. But first Jerry would have to buy a boat.

It was quiet by the water except for footsteps of people, and the cars crossing the bridge. When a truck drove overhead, the bridge shook bits of gravel and dirt down on us. I got afraid the rotten thing was gonna fall on top of me. The planks on the walkway that had rotted away a long time ago had never gotten replaced. On the way to school one day, Andy said if I pissed him off again he was gonna shove my skinny ass between the rotted-out boards and watch me fall into the river and drown. When we were going to school or coming home, the Sisters said to stay put and wait if a truck was coming across, just in case. The bridge shook like my great-grandfather Struber, who died of Parkinson's disease. If I was in the middle when a car came across, I grabbed hold of the shaky rusty iron railing, and prayed, "Jesus, don't let this railing break loose."

Mom said the bridge was there when she was a kid. She liked to tell how she would roller skate down the hill from behind the Catholic church, roll down past the school, cross over the bridge, make a sharp right turn onto Main Street, and run out of speed somewhere past the Astoria Hotel.

"I'm moving, Andy. This piece of clap-trap shit above us is gonna fall and I ain't getting killed. Besides you ain't catching anything. Even the eels won't swim here."

"Ya know . . . ya . . . ah, forget it," he said. He moved all his stuff down about twenty feet. Right after everything got rigged up and we sat down, two of the three poles started to move and looked like they were gonna jump free of the rocks Andy piled around them.

"See? See? I told ya so! I told ya so!" I yelled at him.

"Quick!" he yelled. "Grab hold of that pole and don't let go while I grab the other."

It must be a huge eel, I thought as I felt my feet sliding on the loose sand and stones.

"Sit down!" he shouted. "Lean back and pull. Push your feet up against the big rock." I did what he said. Crap. This eel fishing ain't fun. It's scary. They're freakin' strong!

Andy pulled in his eel. It fought and squirmed and bounced and wriggled and tangled itself all up in his line.

"Motherfucker!" he yelled, and smashed the eel over the head a lot of times with a club like branch of a tree. "Don't let go!" he shouted to me and ran over to where I was dug in. He began to pull on my line with his bare hands. "This is a big mother! Pull!" he yelled.

He got it to shore and clubbed this eel to death even harder than the first one. It made my stomach turn to watch him beat it until its head was a bloody mess and it died. How can he do this and call it fun? I ain't ever coming again. The look on Andy's face scared me. He reminded me of Pop when he got angry.

"Andge? I want to go home." I saw his hand was cut, and asked, "You all right?" He was bleeding where the fishing line bit into his skin. Blood was splattered on his T-shirt and jeans from whacking the hell out of the eels. He looked like he'd been in a fight.

Andy looked at his hand. "I'm fine," he said, jutting out his chin with the dimple in it like Kirk Douglas. He was trying to act brave like Kirk would've. His friends even called him "Kirk."

"This ain't nothing," he said.

"You didn't bring a bucket," I said. "And I ain't carrying these ugly fuckers."

He took off one high-top sneaker and pulled the sock off his foot. He wrapped the sock around his bloody hand and put his shoe back on. He wrapped the line hanging out of the eels' battered mouths around his bandaged hand, swished the fish in the water to wash them off, and said, "Let's go."

"What about the poles?"

"Leave'm."

He carried the eels down the street, slung over his shoulder because they were so long. The one on my line was so big, he said, he'd get Goldwasser to pay him more for it.

"How much you gonna give me?" I asked. "I helped."

"I'll buy you a red and white plastic bobber for your fishing pole," he said.

"Can I have candy instead?"

"No, you eat too much of that shit."

Before Goldwassers' was Kelder's tavern where Mom liked to drink. The men at our bar made jokes about guys called faggots going in there. They said no real men would ever get caught dead drinking there where all the women were lezzies. Pop said that's why Mom went—because you weren't supposed to.

As we got closer to Kelder's bar, the door opened and out came Mom. "Aw, shit," Andy whispered, and shoved me in between two buildings so close together I felt like jelly in the middle of a sandwich.

We stood with our noses and butts to the bricks. Andy warned me to be quiet. He kept peeking out into the street. "Okay, she's in the car. She's pulling away. Stop pushing me, ya jerk!" he snapped. "She's around the corner. Okay. We're clear."

"She looking for us?" I asked him.

"Yeah, she's looking for us in a queer bar."

"You think she's going home to make supper?"

"She's probably going to Mike's to finish getting drunk," he said, meaning the Astoria Bar.

Andy peeked through the window of Kelder's to look at the clock on the back bar. "It's 4:30. We gotta get going."

Andy got a lot of change from Mr. Goldwasser. At first, Goldwasser didn't want to pay extra, but Andy said he'd throw the eels back in the creek. Both of them. Andy was real proud. I could see it in his face. He was even happier when he came out of Rossler's with a paper bag of fishing supplies. And I got my red and white bobber with the pushbutton line-hook. I could pinch my skin by the side of my fingernail and let the bobber dangle there.

When we got home and inside the kitchen, Pop came storming out from behind the bar and grabbed Andy. He scrunched up Andy's grimy T-shirt in his fist and slammed his back against the refrigerator door. I was afraid Andy was gonna eat a knuckle sandwich.

"Do ya know anything about the porterhouse steak with a great big chunk taken out of it?" Pop said, real close to Andy's face.

Before he could answer, the flat of Pop's free hand came smashing down across Andy's face.

"Don't even think of lying to me! Used it for fishin', didn't ya?" Wham! He slammed him again. "Get outta my sight before I kill ya, ya son of a bitch!" He shoved Andy toward the doorway of the bar.

Andy tripped over his own feet, tore out of the kitchen and ran upstairs with his paper bag of fishing goodies still clutched in his hand.

I stared at Pop.

"Ya gotta problem with your damn eyes?" he snapped.

I put my hands on my hips, glared at him, and didn't answer. *You don't scare me, you bully!*

"Don't look at me with that tone of voice in your eyes. I know what you're thinking."

Good. Then I won't need to say anything. I'm just gonna stare him down like Randolph Scott in a gunfight in the movies. I ain't gonna be the first one to flinch.

"Ya see your mother up the street?"

He was trying to change the subject.

Hah! Like I'd tell you? You want her, go find her.

"Aw, gawd-damn kids," he mumbled, as he brushed by me and went back to tending bar.

"Hey, Ed. Have a drink. Cool off," Johnny Thorpe said.

"Think I will." Pop looked over at me standing in the kitchen beaming out all the hate I could muster up.

"She's putting an evil eye on ya, Ed." Johnny laughed. "She's a pisser."

Pop poured himself a CC and ginger ale. "Anybody hungry?" he asked the men at the bar. "Just sandwiches or pizza tonight. The cook's off duty."

I won! Pop flinched first.

Bleach is Next to Godliness

*Man does not live by soap alone; and hygiene, or even health,
is not much good unless you can take a healthy view of it
—or, better still, feel a healthy indifference to it.*

G. K. Chesterton

Eddie started Kingston High School in September, and got the job of waking Andy and me up every morning before he caught the school bus. Pop told Eddie to make sure that my feet were on the floor, that he led me into the bathroom to go pee, and I was wide awake when I came out. Otherwise, I'd "yes" him to death in my sleep, lie back down, and be late for class.

Andy never waited for me anymore. By the time I dressed, he was gone. I got myself ready because Mom and Pop slept in. They worked until three or so in the morning. Even Mickey was gone with Jerry Mertine to Doc Vaughn's for tea and toast, or he was over at Mrs. Pettybone's having pancakes.

Mom didn't do much washing and ironing anymore. And, even though Pop showed me how, I didn't always remember to do my clothes because I was busy playing, doing homework, or other chores. Pop said my memory would get better if I had to go bare-ass naked to school one day. I knew I was running low on clean clothes and this morning I'd have to dig out whatever I could find hanging in the closet. But there wasn't anything. Nuts! I picked through the heap of dirty stuff lying in the back of my closet and pulled out the cleanest, least wrinkled dress. It smelled okay, except the hem was torn out in the back. The last time I wore this dress my hem got caught on the heel of my shoe while I was jumping rope on the playground. I'd have to use the straight pins from Pop's new dress shirts that I saved in a Band-Aid tin. I once tried to fix a hem with cellophane tape, but it didn't stick very good, and I used yards of it. Pop blew a gasket and said, "Tape don't grow on trees, ya know! Don't do that again!"

Bobby Ann said I should go to 4-H class and have Mrs. Fiedler show me how to sew. But it was where the Protestant kids went, and the priest said Catholics couldn't hang around with them because they weren't saved like us. I ignored the priest when it came to having friends, but Mrs. Fiedler held her classes in the Dutch Reformed Church, and I was afraid of being found out.

My socks all seemed to have holes in them, too. I kinda knew how to darn them because I watched Grandma DeWitt weaving thread in and out of the heel of one of Dad DeWitt's socks, but there was no darning needle or thread in our sewing box. I stretched my sock so the hole got pulled underneath my toes. Sometimes I had to do the same thing to the heel because it wore out there, too. It stayed in place a short time, then hurt like the dickens when the shoe rubbed against my skin and made a blister. Band-Aids didn't help blisters much because they didn't stay stuck when my feet got sweaty. In school, a kid asked if my parents were too poor to buy me new socks. My parents weren't poor. They just didn't shop unless it was your birthday, Christmas, or Easter, which for me, left eight months in between. If you ruined something, you lived with it because money didn't grow on trees, along with cellophane tape. I decided I was going to Mrs. Fiedler's sewing class, Protestant or not!

On the way home from school, I stopped in Johnny Rossler's dry goods store and checked out the price on a darning needle and heavy thread. Johnny was a lady with a man's name. Her real name was Patience. I told her I was looking for darnin' thread. She said if I didn't get candy for a couple of days, I'd have the money to buy what I needed. I couldn't afford the wood darning egg with the handle and figured I'd just use a dead light bulb instead. Johnny showed me how to put in a hem. Between her and Mrs. Fiedler's class, I couldn't wait to get started fixing my clothes.

Holes in the bottoms of my shoes were different. Pop said he never saw a kid who had to have a new pair of shoes every three months. He took me to what he thought was the best store down on the Strand, Yallum's. Mr. Yallum fitted me with lace-up, leather shoes with leather soles. They felt like Army boots till they got broken in. But even they got holes in the soles. Mr. Yallum shrugged his shoulders when Pop complained, and said, "What's a parent s'posed to do? All kids need shoes."

From the movie *The Grapes of Wrath*, with Henry Fonda, I learned to cut cardboard and stick it in my shoe to cover the hole that was wearing through the sole. I thought if I did this I could make my shoes last longer. The tops never wore out. And Pop would be happy not having to spend his money on me. The problem was, Henry Fonda never stepped in a mud puddle or had to walk in the rain, because they were in a drought. Gene Kelly, in *Singin' in the Rain*, got his feet wet tap-dancing in puddles, and didn't seem to care. Stepping in water is how I learned cardboard doesn't work too good. It left a big wet brown stain on the bottom of my sock that never washed out.

After getting dressed, my breakfast was now a small bag of curly orange Cheetos and a bottle of Coca-Cola. Pop didn't like me drinking Coke because, he said, it ate into his profits. But, if I put the bottle in the wooden soda case under the bar sink, he never knew I had one. If I had time, I sometimes ate Niagara Shredded Wheat, or Corn Flakes that came in a small box that had to be cut open and filled with milk. The box was lined with waxed paper, but it always got soggy and leaked making a mess on the table.

Sister insisted I bring lunch to school. I made the same sandwich every day, Peter Pan peanut butter with Welch's grape jelly, on Wonder bread, wrapped in Cut Rite wax paper and taped shut because it unwrapped and would be stale by noontime. She also made me buy milk in school and said I had to drink it to keep my bones strong. She held up pictures of starving African babies with bent bony legs, stick arms, big fat basketball bellies, and sunk black eyes.

She told us we'd look like this if we didn't drink our milk. I hated it. The milk was always warm and tasted awful. At home, I drank it with Hershey's chocolate syrup, which we couldn't get at school. I gagged the white milk down through a paper straw that got soggy and unraveled before I could finish. Sister said if I didn't wait so long to drink it, the straw wouldn't fall apart. Now I gulped the milk down and stuffed my sandwich in my mouth to kill the taste.

There were places in the bar that I looked for loose change to pay for my milk. I climbed up on the back bar by the cash register, stood on tiptoe, and reached over the shelf's trim holding the fancy whiskey bottles on the top shelf. Customers pitched coins up there just to see who could do it. The loser had to buy a round of drinks. Before Eddie started high school, he'd put me up on his shoulders to reach the shelf. We split the money we found. Other places he taught me to look were in the cup of the pay phone and under the floor racks behind the bar.

Sister got tired of me sometimes paying her and sometimes not. She sent a note home telling Pop to send in money for the whole week. He said he didn't know I needed money and why didn't I tell him. Now each Monday morning, I found an envelope at the end of the bar with milk money for the week. All the change I found in the bar became sewing supplies and candy money.

During recess, Father Mulry picked on me about my grubby fingernails. Talking very quietly, like his teeth were stuck together with taffy, he said to me, "Ya have ta use a shrub braash on your hanz ta get your nailzs clean. Cleanlinez is next to Godlinez," he said. He used his middle finger to push his glasses back up on his nose. He stuck out his very white hands with the bulging blue veins. Then he held up of one of my grimy mitts and asked, "Whadda ya thin' Gawd would say if my nailzs looked like yers?"

God wouldn't like it, I guessed. There didn't seem like there was much God did like. Getting dirty sure wasn't one of them.

Father Mulry's skin and nails were as white as the nuns' were. I wondered what nationality he and the Sisters were. You could tell if someone was Irish or Italian or Gypsy, or if they were colored. I ain't ever seen a colored nun or priest. You couldn't tell with the regular nuns and priests. They didn't have any accent when they spoke. It was like they all went to a special school and had accents taught out of them.

Maybe they used bleach when they washed. In third grade, Sister said sins were like stains on the soul. She cut her fingertips with a razor blade and let the blood stain a white piece of paper to show us what she meant. Yeah, I'm sure they use bleach. That's how Ollie Moore got the dirt rings off the collars of Pop's white shirts when she washed them on the scrub board.

What Father Mulry said about my nails and my hands made me feel crummy. I had to do something, or he'd keep picking on me. In our upstairs kitchen, I found an old floor scrub brush and a Clorox bottle in the cabinet under the sink. I put the plug in the drain and poured in lots of bleach. This stuff stank and made my eyes water and my nose and throat burn. Jeez, I tried holding my breath as I dipped the brush in the bleach and began to scrub my nails and the backs of my hands. Cleanliness is next to godliness, I kept repeating. Yow! The bristles splashed bleach on my face and arms. Shit! My hands turned bright pink and burned worse than my eyes and throat. T'hell with this crap. I pulled the plug and washed my hands with a bar of Ivory soap and water till they looked like prunes before being boiled and eaten for constipation. I smelled my hands. They still stank. Mom had hand cream on her dresser. Wiping cold cream up and down my arms and over my hands, I saw the front of my plaid dress in her mirror. It had lots of tan polka dots on it, big ones and small ones down the front that weren't supposed to be there. Ah, nuts! I'm gonna get killed. I ruined another dress, not one I liked, but it wasn't even an old one.

From now on, I'm gonna chew my nails to stubs so they can't get dirty. Then Father Mulry won't be able to say anything. It's lots better than having to wash with Clorox. No wonder the nuns and priests never smiled. They always had bleach up their noses.

Gypsies and Violets

Ah, good taste! What a dreadful thing!
Taste is the enemy of creativeness.

Pablo Picasso

THE GYPSIES WERE HERE! They came to town in the hottest part of the summer every year, looking for work. They went door to door, asking who wanted their leaky roofs tarred. They got jobs for several days, and when done, they drove to the next town and did the same thing.

I watched the Gypsies as they worked on the homes on Main Street. Nobody let them into their houses because of old wives' tales, Pop said, about how they were thieves, stealing kids and killing people, just for the heck of it. They didn't look scary to me. Besides, some of them wore gold crucifixes around their necks, which meant they believed in Jesus and were probably good Catholics.

They smiled at me but never talked unless it was to tell me to get out from under their feet. They had dark skin, dark hair, and dark eyes, which made them stick out in snow-white Rosendale.

Their last job before moving on was to tar the roof of the Grange Hall, two doors down from our bar. The Grange used to be a Baptist Church, which Grandma Sarah belonged to when she and Dad lived in town right next door. Now they used the building as a place where groups could hold meetings. It was also rented out on Saturdays to the dance teachers, Blossom and Blanche from Kingston, and sometimes to a person who came around once a year to take family photographs.

Watching the Gypsies, I wondered how they got the dried gooky tar out of their clothes and off their skin. It must be great to be able to get this filthy, and ruin your clothes, and your mother can't say anything to you because you're being paid to be a mess!

Two of the biggest men in their group heaved a huge block of tar down from the back of their dump truck and dropped it on the lawn in front of the Grange. They chopped it up with an ax and a hatchet. Each swing of the ax threw tar chips into the air. They looked like splinters of black glass from a shattered jar. The Gypsies put chunks into a trough and built a fire underneath it. The same man put a metal mop bucket with a rope tied to its handle into the hot, melted, ooze. He hauled the black slop to the roof top by a pulley. Up there, men poured the goo onto the roof and spread it around with push brooms and what looked like mops.

While they were busy working and not watching me, I scooped up tar chips into my pocket, and shoved a piece into my mouth. At first, it was hard to chew and it had a fumey taste, but quickly lost its smell. After chomping on it, it felt more like the stiff bubble gum left for weeks on the head rail of my cot. My jaws ached.

The Gypsies worked hard all day and took turns stopping to eat and taking drinks from jars of water. I watched from the time they started in the morning until early afternoon, until one of the oldest Gypsies caught me and scolded me for chewing the tar.

"Don't chew that," he said. "Ya want to gum up your insides? Spit it out, now! Get away from the tar buckets 'fore ya git burnt." Or at least it's what I thought he said. They talked funny and had their own language. But this guy could speak some English.

In a snit, I spit the lump of tar at his feet, ducked between the Grange and Grandma's old house next door, and went to lay on Rosenkranses' lawn.

The blades of grass made my legs itchier than they already were from the poison ivy rash I got from picking blackcaps last week. I sat up and rubbed my legs with the heels of my hands.

"Don't scratch. It'll make it spread," Mom said. It was all over my whole body already. Where else could it go?

The scab on my knee from when I fell roller-skating, looked like it was ready to peel off. Nope. Why didn't I leave it alone? Now it's bleeding. Nuts. I should get peroxide and a Band-Aid. But if I do, Pop'll find work for me or tell me, "Don't pick your scabs. Whadda ya want, a big, fat, nasty scar? Ya want to get infected and get gangrene? Ya want to have your leg cut off at the knee so ya can go hobbling around like a cripple with everybody laughing at ya?"

I wiped blood with the bottom of my T-shirt, and I scratched my red blotchy rash on my leg with the other hand. This morning I had smeared it with pink Calamine lotion, but it didn't do any good.

The Gypsies finished and packed up to leave. Since there wasn't anybody around to play with, I went to the creek and sat on top of the metal drainpipe sticking out from the bank. It hung over the creek, dripping sludgy water. It didn't always smell great because, Eddie said, the storm drains and bathrooms emptied out here.

I wished I could crawl inside this pipe and see if I could make it all the way to the metal grate in the road in front of the hotel. But I worried what'd happen if somebody flushed their toilet. I didn't know whether to believe Eddie or not. I knew the storm drains emptied here, but I wasn't too sure about the toilets. He teased me and made up stories like Andy did. Best to stay right where I was, watching the long skinny snakes making S's in the water under the pipe.

Eddie said the snakes were water moccasins and they could kill you with one bite, because they got poisonous from eating everybody's shit that dropped in the water. And it gave them an evil temper, too. Some chased him when he was wading across the creek to the island and almost got him, he said. He also told me it was how he won the medal for swimming the fastest across Williams Lake and back without stopping. He thought he saw a water moccasin and was scared it'd bite him. Pop said the water moccasins here weren't poisonous. I didn't know who to believe.

The bank near the drainpipe and the pathway was sandy, and not far from where we'd buried Petey. I couldn't remember where Petey was. His Popsicle marker was gone. I prayed he was happy, singing and flying around in heaven, glad he wasn't stuck in no cage.

Violets grew by the creek in the grassy area next to the path and sandy bank. In the spring I picked them to sell and put on Grandma Sarah's grave. And I ate some, too. They tasted better than chewing on a squeaky rubber band, or sucking on a copper penny, and a whole lot better than tar. I don't remember anyone telling me I couldn't eat violets. Mom said I got my taste buds from her mother. She said Grandma Sarah put violets in her salads (that must be where I got it from) and picked herbs to dry. Grandma wouldn't go to the drugstore for anything and that was why she liked Dr. Rymph. He used herbs, too. Mom said when she was a little girl and got a cold or sore throat, Grandma had a cure. In the middle of the night when she was asleep, Grandma would come in her room, hold Mom's nose, and make her take a teaspoon of warm skunk's grease with sugar sprinkled on it. Mom said if Grandma Sarah and I lived in Salem, Massachusetts in the old days, we would've been burned at the stake as witches.

I ate almost anything. Except peas. And anchovies, because they looked liked skinned worms hammered flat, sprinkled with salt. And I wouldn't try chocolate-covered ants and grasshoppers or slimy frog's legs that after they were cooked were supposed to taste like chicken. The thought made me gag. Mom, though, was always willing to try something new. She said chocolate-covered ants and grasshoppers crunched like Rice Krispies. That killed it for me ever eating that cereal again. The snap, crackle, pop noise it made when you poured on milk made me think of bug guts popping out after being fried in hot oil, before being dipped in chocolate.

Maybe Mom ate those things because it's what the French eat. Mom was Dutch but she was also part-French. Pop said that made her half a stubborn Frog, and the Dutch part of her made up the other stubborn half, making her one full-bred stubborn broad. Mom also ate Limburger cheese from Germany that smelled worse than ten dead bloated skunks rotting on the side of the road in the hot summer sun with no breeze blowing. And she wasn't even German. She ate the Limburger with a slice of raw Bermuda onion, smeared with her homemade hot mustard on pumpernickel bread. Pop and I both agreed, double yuck!

In April, when the violets came out, I saw a strange group of green-and-white-striped flowers near them. They looked like the Calla lilies I had to draw in school for an art and science project. This flower had a thing in its center Sister called a pistol. And it had one big petal curled around like a Calla lily. I picked a few and gave them to Mom and she put them on the back bar in a beer glass filled with water. She was real happy.

Later in the day, something began to smell very bad in the bar. Pop and Mom checked everywhere. They thought a rat died in the wall, or maybe the sewer was backing up. It smelled worse than the refrigerator with Mom's cheese in it. It wasn't a rat, it wasn't the sewer, and it wasn't the cheese. It was the flowers. A man came in for a beer and said he knew a lot about plants, and told Mom the flowers were called skunk cabbage and for a very good reason. Pop, with a grin on his face, threw them out in the fire barrel, while Mom yelled at me to never pick them again.

I went back to picking violets and picked them every day until they were all gone. Like the Gypsies and orphan kids in the movies, I went knocking on doors up and down Main Street, selling my flowers. Mrs. Russell told me I looked like a dirty, rumpled-up Shirley Temple in beggar's clothes. I hated Shirley Temple. I hated people telling me I looked like her because Mom made me get a stupid perm each year. Shirley Temple looked like a jerk wearing dumb white dresses with big polka dots and big stupid bows in her hair. She never got dirty and I guess she didn't swear. And I could sing better than she could. Besides it was good to look like a beggar. It sold lots of flowers.

"Would ya like to buy some violets?" I asked, trying to look like a sad-faced kid actress in need of money.

Some neighbors paid me a nickel for my violets, and some stingy ones gave me two pennies. If they gave me a nickel, I gave them a fistful of violets, while the others got half a fistful. I charged Mom for flowers, because I could get a quarter from her.

I tied ribbons from old presents around some bouquets. I tried rubber bands, but they broke the stems off. I put those broken violets in a bowl of water because their stems were gone. They drowned. There wasn't anything to hold them up. The next day, they were all soggy and at the bottom of the bowl. After a couple of days, I had to throw them away because Mom started yelling, "Where's my vegetable bowl?" and I better never dare use it again, yakkety-yak....

Most of the money I made I spent buying chocolate Highland Ice Cream and chocolate-covered raspberry jelly candies and chocolate cookies with sugar sprinkle and chocolate Drakes cakes. All the money I made was supposed to go into the missionary can, a small tin can the nuns gave. The money was to come from jobs we did at home, but Pop didn't pay for chores. Mom said he was a tightwad. But she didn't pay either. The money was to buy food and clothing for starving refugees and poor people in Appalachia and Africa.

Not wanting to go to school with the can half-full, I sat on the sidewalk, rattled my can and asked people for "money for the poor." Kid actors did it in the movies all the time. It didn't make me much money, so, I went door-to-door. Some dirty rat-fink neighbor squealed on me. The next day in school, Sister said I had to stop begging and to use my own money. She said some kids filled two, three, or four cans from what they made from chores. I told Sister that my mom and pop didn't believe in paying kids to do what they're told to do. Besides, they said they donated enough money to the poor.

"Well," Sister said, "other children went to their neighbors, picked weeds and raked lawns. It helped their neighbors and made money for the poor," she said. "They didn't beg for it. Perhaps you could try that."

Well, after she chewed the crap outta me, I cashed in any nickels or dimes I got for pennies and I stuffed the can up full. It filled up fast and the rest of my money I spent on myself. Sister noticed the penny trick, as she called it. "Do you think you could spare a nickel for a starving child?" she asked, and handed me another can to fill.

I heard Pop whistle. Supper must be ready and I had to go do my 'free' chores. But first, if nobody cleaned up real good around the Grange, maybe I could find more tar chips. Then I could give some to Bobby Ann and Porky later, and take some to school. I wondered if Ma Rosenkranse would get mad at me for giving tar to Bobby Ann and Porky.

Sometimes it seemed like nothing I did was right. Big people and kids don't think the same. Grownups made everything you did, or wanted to do, or anything you tried to do, wrong. Just like God, they had too many "can't do's" and not enough "could do's." God, you maybe made tar, but I betcha you never chewed it, I thought, and popped a sliver into my mouth.

WHO'S A THIEF?

Commit a crime, and the earth is made of glass.
Ralph Waldo Emerson

WHAT'S WORSE THAN GETTING CAUGHT STEALING? It's where you get caught that can scare the crap out of you! Eddie once had a light-fingered girlfriend with big boobs. I nicknamed her "Tits." She couldn't walk into a store without stealing something. She'd say, "Just takin' my stepdad's advice: Why pay for it if ya can get it for free?"

Tits asked Mom if she could bring me shopping in Kingston. Mom gave me two quarters for the Trailways bus. She said she knew I was safe with Tits and glad to have me being watched, instead of running the streets or hanging out in the bar. I got an extra fifty cents from Mom, by saying I would bring her some peanut brittle from Fanny Farmer's. I put my quarters in my sneakers so I wouldn't lose them, and off we went.

Tits was eighteen, a year older than Eddie. She was kinda pretty with dark eyes and black hair almost to her shoulders. She said she was Italian, Irish, Spanish, and Indian. A mutt, like me. Tits said anytime Mom wouldn't give me money, she'd pay my way to Kingston because she always had money. She was stealing it from her stepparents, she said, to buy packs of Chesterfield cigarettes. To pay her back, I had to steal lipsticks or nail polish for her. The store clerks didn't watch me at the display racks the way they did her.

"The trick to stealin' is to carry a shopping bag by one handle. Keep it open. Hold it close to the counter and when no one is looking, drop whatever you want into the bag. Act normal," she said, "and keep looking at things. And whatever you do, don't leave the minute you put something in your bag, because that's what all dumb thieves do."

Tits made sure we didn't leave Kingston till her shopping bag was almost full. Tits stole clothes. She'd put the store's clothes on in the dressing room and then put her clothes on top and walk out. Then she'd find a public bathroom, take off the clothes and price tags and put them in the bag. I didn't do that because it was too scary and I was too skinny and it would've shown. When Tits stole clothes for me, I told Mom or Pop she bought them.

I took all colors of lipstick for Tits. And for myself, I took baby bibs, doll clothes, toys, and barrettes for my hair. She said I could say I was borrowing them from a friend. Or I could say she bought them for me. But Mom and Pop never asked where the new stuff came from. I don't think they noticed because they were always too busy. This was a great way to get what no one would buy for me.

Tits told me to keep my mouth shut and not tell anybody what we were doing, or she'd break my neck. I had to tell Bobby Ann. She was willing to take things too, but said I had to pay her bus fare. In the morning, while everyone was still sleeping, and Tits wasn't around, I climbed up on the counter by the cash register. I reached up over the ledge of the back bar and found the best haul I ever made. Bobby Ann and I ran up to Meyer's bus garage and caught the 9:25 to Kingston. We planned to take the 12:10 back and be home in time for lunch. Nobody would even know we left Rosendale.

Having to hurry so we wouldn't miss the bus didn't give us enough time to get dressed up, or to comb our hair back into neat ponytails like Tits made me do, which was a big mistake. It was a bigger mistake trying to take something from Monkey Ward's. And the biggest mistake was taking Bobby Ann with me.

Bobby Ann and I went into Ward's and split up. Tits said

to always go in two different directions. That way, it'd be harder to catch what we were doing. Bobby Ann and I wasn't in Ward's fifteen minutes when a big fat hand clapped down on my shoulder. A floorwalker caught me stealing a pair of baby socks for my doll. Luckily my bag didn't have anything else in it. The man made me feel like the ground was crumbling and falling out from under my feet and I was either gonna faint or puke, I thought.

"Whatta ya got in that bag, young lady?" he asked in a deep voice, as he took the shopping bag from me. "Do ya have money to pay for these?" He waved those tiny baby socks in his fingers.

I shook my head no because my voice was stuck in my throat under a lump that was bigger than a peach pit. I tried to swallow and couldn't. I had to go pee. My shoulders were scrunched up to my ears, my legs were like cooked spaghetti, and my eyes were open as wide as they could go.

The man, who must have been a son of Mighty Joe Young, said, "I think you'd better come upstairs and speak to my boss. Your friend is up there waiting for ya."

Oh, gawd!

Bobby Ann and I sat side-by-side in the office as the boss man asked us questions. He wasn't as scary looking as the other guy.

Tits told me if I ever got caught, "Don't say anything. Pretend you're too scared to talk. Just nod your head." I didn't have to pretend. Bobby Ann kept saying, "Yes sir, yes sir," to whatever the man was saying. It was all getting blurry. The room went from normal to looking wavy.

The boss man was telling us never to come into Ward's again unless we were with a parent. He said he was going to let us go with a warning this time. And then, out of nowhere, big-mouth Bobby Ann said, "Judy, doesn't your Uncle Andrew work here?"

Oh, fuck me! She didn't say that! Yes she did! Why did she say that? I shot her a glance that said, "Jackass!" And she grinned at me!

The big boss put his hands on his desk, pushed up and stood staring down at me, "You're that Cherny? Your uncle is Andrew Cherny, the manager of our furniture department?" I nodded yes. Yup! That was him. My uncle. Manager of the furniture department. My father's big, mean brother. Sweet Jesus! I'm dead now.

The man made phone calls, and Aunt Helen showed up. She was not happy. She told the men she'd take us home to get punished. I had to go pee really, really bad.

Good thing the nuns didn't let us go to the bathroom whenever we wanted because all that holding it in was coming in handy right now. I hoped I wouldn't wet Aunt Helen's car seat.

Aunt Helen went yakkety yak, all the way home. "Ya know what it'll be like for Uncle Andrew to go to work on Monday? Total humiliation. Serve you right if he never spends another penny on you. What'll people think? You haven't the sense God gave a goose. Hoodlums. Both of ya. Your whole family," she said looking at me. "Poor Uncle Andrew." Bobby Ann sat in the back seat, kept her mouth shut for once and stared out the side window. Good thing, too, because I was ready to sock her. Aunt Helen was quiet for about half a minute when she started up again. "Tell me what Jesus thinks about you right now."

I didn't care what He thought. I was more worried about what Pop would think, till she said, "Wait till you go to Confession and have to tell the priest. Stealing is a mortal sin. If you died right now, you'd go t'hell. What did you learn in Catechism class? Nothing?"

Shit, why did she have to remind me about Confession? I ain't been telling the priest about taking stuff. Tits said it was a venial sin because we only took little stuff. We didn't rob banks.

"You know what the priest will do? Make you pray a whole rosary. And you'll be lucky if God ever forgives you. You're just like your brother Andy." That hurt. There wasn't anything wrong with Andy. So what if he took some of Mom's jewelry to give his girlfriend. He didn't steal it out of a store.

"You could be arrested, put in a reform school," Aunt Helen said. "They'd beat you with a willow stick till you bled. And make you scrub the bathroom tiles with a toothbrush till you could see your face in the shine of the floor." She was just like Pop. She never came up for air.

She went on for the entire ride home. Reform school sounded better than having to listen to her. When we parked in the driveway alongside the bar, Bobby Ann jumped out, saying, "See ya," and took off for home. Pissed me off she was getting away scot-free and now I had to listen to Pop bark the same things Aunt Helen just yapped at me. And then Andy would tease me for getting caught, call me stupid and a bunch of other names, and Tits wouldn't ever take me shopping again.

Pop sat on a chair and had me stand in front of him so he could look me in the eye. He said the eyes were a mirror into your soul. I guess that meant he could tell if I was lying or not. So I stared at him while he glared back at me. He didn't look all that mad. Maybe disappointed. Ashamed or embarrassed by me, but he wasn't mad or else the vein in his forehead would be thumping and his jaw would be moving when he wasn't talking. "Well, whadda ya got to say for yerself?"

Nothing. I kept my mouth shut. I didn't want to make things worse.

"Huh? I can't hear you," he said, cupping his hand around his ear. "Would ya like to speak a little louder? Seems ya want to get your name in the paper, huh? Let all the people in Rosendale know you're a thief; can't be trusted?"

I still didn't say anything. That got him mad.

"What t'hell were ya in Ward's for, for Chrissakes?" he asked. "Ya know better. I expect more of ya. Every time something's missing, I'm gonna think it's you." He poked his finger into my breastbone. It hurt.

"What should I do to ya? Hold your hands over a fire? Chop them fingers off like they do in those A-rab countries?" He shook his head from side to side. "Where'd ya learn this shit? Andy? You and him been stealin'? Is that where ya learned this crap?"

Andy can get into trouble on his own. I didn't want him getting beat because of me.

"She taught me," I blurted out. "Ask her," I said, pointing over to the bar.

Tits was sitting by Eddie listening to everything. "What? I never stole anything in my life." Tits said, glaring at me through squinty eyes.

"Apologize to her for what ya said," Pop said.

"No. I won't. She's the liar. And Andy didn't teach me anything. She did!" I pointed my finger again at Tits.

"I don't believe ya," Pop said. "Stand in the corner till ya say you're sorry."

"No, I won't! And you can't make me!"

"What?" He pushed his chair back and stood towering over me.

"I ain't apologizin' to her because she's a freakin' big fat liar!"

"Ya little shit. Get your ass over in the corner. Right now. Stand there till I tell ya to come out!"

I stood, and stood, and stood. My legs ached. I shifted from one foot to the other, with my arms folded across my chest. At church, I could stand through the longest, boring Gospel in the whole Bible. I knew I could stand here until hell froze over. I ain't saying I'm sorry to Tits even if God Himself threatened to turn me into a pillar of salt. Nobody's gonna make me say I'm sorry when I didn't lie.

Being mad made me strong. I stood facing that wall for a very long time. Pop caved in when I started to wiggle and jiggle and squirm. He knew I'd stand there and piss my pants to spite him. He sent me to my room without lunch. Good! I wouldn't have eaten anyway.

I thought my guts would bust before I could get my jeans unzipped. I peed. I cried. I blew my nose on the toilet tissue. I sat there and cried some more. Pop said I couldn't go to the movies for a week. He just should've killed me on the spot. Shot me dead. Nothing was worse than that, not even going to Confession was worse than missing a movie. And, it was all her fault.

Stuck in my room, I sat in my open window, which was large and had a wide sill. I sat with my back resting against the frame, my knees pulled to my chest and watched cars and people on Main Street go by.

Tits came into my room. I ignored her. She grabbed the front of my shirt, turned my body to face her and tried to push me out the open window. She forced me to hang over the sill backwards. All she had to do was let go and I would fall two stories and land on the roof of Pop's car. I'd get hurt bad, but if I dented Pop's car, I'd wish I was really dead.

"Tell on me ya little bitch, will ya? I should drop ya on your friggin' head," she hissed.

A man walking down the sidewalk hollered up, "Hey, you! What's going on up there?"

Tits jerked me in really fast and let me drop to the floor. She leaned out the window and said, "It's nothing. She was washin' the window and almost fell. I caught her just in time." The stranger shook his head and went into the bar. Tits slammed the window closed.

I sat on the floor, hugging my knees to my chest, shaking. She pulled back her foot and kicked me really hard several times in the back and ribs with her new, probably stolen, penny loafers.

"That's for trying to get me in trouble, bitch. I should kill ya." She grabbed me by the hair, slapped my face real hard, and gave me one more swift kick, and stormed out of my room.

Who could I tell? Pop didn't believe me. No one would believe she just tried to kill me. She'll tell Pop I apologized. I just know it. I crawled over to my closet, went inside and closed the door. Curling up in a ball, I stared into the dark. I wished for Tits to drop dead with a bag full of stolen stuff, and plastered all over the newspapers would be, "Big Titted Thief Drops Dead In Street After Stealing Clothes."

Thinking Tits wouldn't come back and hurt me some more, I crawled out of the closet and up onto my cot. Andy came in my room and said dinner was ready. The food would stick in my throat. I refused to go downstairs.

"Tell them I'm sleeping, Andy. Please?"

For once Andy didn't tease me or call me names. He walked out, not saying anything.

Lina came by later to ask what happened at Monkey Ward's. Bobby Ann told her I got caught stealing, but she didn't do anything. Lina said she didn't believe her and wanted my side of the story. She believed that Tits was lying about teaching me to steal and believed it about her trying to kill me.

"I know she steals," Lina said. "I seen her snitch jewelry outta Emcee Lewis' jewelry store. And I know she's got one helluva mean streak. Don't know why Eddie likes her. Must be good in bed." Lina put her arm around my shoulder and we giggled. "Ya gotta forget about it," she said. "C'mon. Let's go to the movies. My treat."

I wanted to see White Heat with Cagney and Virginia Mayo. But I had to tell her Pop said I was grounded for a week. "T'hell with 'em," she said. "We're going. Ya sit in the back row with me. Nobody's gonna know you're there." Lina was big for her age, and tough. She was two years older than Eddie and was his size. Sometimes she tended bar for Pop. She could badmouth the smart alecks right back. She had no problem sneaking me out the hotel lobby door and up the street to the theater.

We sat in the last row. Lina sat me on her lap so I could see the screen over the heads in front of me. She pulled her sweater over my body and buttoned it up. "There," she said. "Nobody can see ya now."

Her big boobs were soft as pillows filled with warm water. I lay my head against her. I could've stayed that way all night, it felt so good. The lights went dim and a few more people came in looking for seats. The theater was almost filled. The cartoons came on and Lina whispered, "Yer Ma and Pa just came in. Stay down. They can't see ya, it's too dark. They're going down the aisle."

Lina said we'd sneak out when the screen flashed "The End," and they wouldn't see her or me. People applauded the ending as we scrammed out the theater, and down the street to the hotel, laughing that we put one over on Pop. She helped me undress and get my jammies on. She covered me up, tucked me in, gave me a kiss, and said to pretend to be asleep. "I'll go downstairs to the bar and play stupid when your folks come in. If they ask where ya are, I'll say asleep."

Pop came in to check on me not knowing I just climbed into bed. Tonight I'd fall asleep hearing "Cherry Pink and Apple Blossom White" playing on the jukebox and dreaming about James Cagney and Virginia Mayo and feeling glad I got to see the movie. "Jesus," I prayed. "I'm sorry for stealing. But it ain't fair that ya let Big you-know-what's get off Scot-free. Whadda you gonna do to her? Huh, Jesus? Whadda you gonna do about that mean, lying thief? Can you please let her get caught, just once, to prove me right? I won't even say, 'I told you so'."

Going Backasswards

No other man-made device since the shields and lances of the ancient knights fulfills a man's ego like an automobile.
Sir William Rootes

It was almost suppertime. I set the dining table and went outside to watch the cars go by and wait for Mom to finish cooking. The sun was shining through the yellow and red leaves of the trees. I liked this time of year because of tree colors, the sun was still hot, and the breeze was warm. Exhaust fumes blew up my nose as people drove by. Main Street sometimes shrunk to one lane wide when cars parked on both sides of the road. Cars tried to squeeze past each other and one would always chicken out if they could go up over the curb onto the sidewalk, rather than risk getting their driver's door scraped. Someone could be forced into backing up into an empty parking space to let the cars go through, too. And then there were the times they got so jammed up going both ways, and the lead drivers would stare at each other through their dirty windshields trying to out-shout each other into backing up. To give an inch would be losing. What? I never knew. And it wasn't only the lead car that lost, the whole line waiting behind the lead lost by having to go into reverse. Mom called the pig-headed-drivers, "King of the Jungle" types, chest-beaters, guys who couldn't stand to lose face. Lina said, "They have testicles, right?" Idiots, I thought.

Today, Morris Crookstan cranked his window down, stuck his head out and yelled, "For Chrissakes! Back your gawddamn ass up so I can get through, will ya?"

"Ya back your ass up, Morris, ya gawddamn nitwit. Can't ya see I'm more through here than ya are," an angrier, louder voice shouted back. I couldn't see who it was because I was looking into the sun.

Car horns began to blow. Someone yelled, "For Jeez-us Chrissakes! One of ya damn fools back up and git the hell outta the way. For cryin' out loud."

This was a show I liked. I hated to think of missing it once the clock time changed next week and it'd be too dark to watch.

The traffic jams happened most evenings in front of Pop's bar because the road seemed narrowest here with cars parked on both sides. When Pop was tending bar, and the horn blowing and name calling got too much, he took care of things. He came out and eyeballed the mess. If he said, "Back up," guys asked how far. Nobody gave him any lip. They backed up because they were afraid he'd back their car up for them, which Pop did once to a New York City guy who didn't know the rules to this game. And when the city guy said he was gonna call a cop, Pop stuffed him back in his car through the open window he pulled him out of in the first place. Never did see any cops come that day.

Guys said they backed up because "Big Ed" asked, and they were doing it as a favor and of course, if it weren't for "Big Ed," they wouldn't be doing it at all. And, make no bones about it, this'd be the only time they'd be putting their car in reverse because of a nincompoop who must have bought his driver's license at Monkey Ward's.

But sometimes, like today, Pop wasn't around and Warnecke would be forced into backing up. He was in front of Mr. Pettybone's, the plumbers building. I could see him thinking about putting his Packard in reverse or having to explain to his wife why he was late for dinner. Keeping his old lady happy meant being able to go out for a beer tonight and see if his favorite Rheingold girl won the beauty contest. You had to buy a Rheingold beer to vote, but, if your girl won, all those bucks for beers were worth it, he told Mom.

"Hell," he said later, "I'd back up five miles just think'n' my redhead was com'n' in first place."

Sitting at the far end of the bar that same night, Floyd Swehla, a guy who drove stock cars, took a sip of his Ballantine beer and shouted, "Hey, Warnecke! Saw ya had to back yer car up t'day. Hell! Ya had to back it all-l-l the way past Edie's bar here and all-l-l the way past the Grange. And those ten cars behind ya, had to backup all-l-l-l-l the way too. Shame. Just a cry'n' shame." He shook his head left to right and then lifted his wet beer glass and took a sip.

"Weren't no ten cars behind me," Warnecke said. He looked down at the foam in his glass of Rheingold beer. He looked like he was watching the tiny bubbles go pop, and I bet he must have been wishing to God that he could pop Floydy in his mouth. Warnecke didn't say anything, though. He drank his beer and said to Mom, "This beer is bitter tonight, Edie. And my girl didn't win."

"What's a matter, Warnecke." Floydy started in again. "Got no 'scuses for backin' up?"

"Sun was in my eyes, asshole. Windshield was one big freakin' glare from cigarette smoke and the sun." Warnecke said.

"Aw, shit, Warnecke. No settin' sun ever bothered ya before. Maybe youse just getting old and youse in need of some 'spectacles'."

Everybody at the bar started laughing.

"Yeah," said Warnecke, "and maybe ya just need to shut your freakin' trap." He put his beer glass down with a bang, turned and looked at Floydy. Then he looked at Mom and said, "He ain't worth it, Edie." He slugged the rest of his beer down and walked out.

"A might touchy fella he is t'night. Wonder what's up his craw?" Floydy said. "Hey Edie, gimme another brewski." He strutted over to the jukebox and dropped in a coin.

I sneaked through the bar and out the front door behind Warnecke, wondering what he was gonna do. Some guys, when they got mad, punched car windshields. I sat in one of the bouncy metal lawn chairs Pop had put out front, watched and hummed to Patti Page singing the "Tennessee Waltz," and wished I had a sweater on.

There wasn't any traffic tonight, but Warnecke looked up and down the street before he stepped off the sidewalk. Maybe he thought with his luck, he might get run over. Fog was coming in off the creek. The street lamps and the neon lights from The Well looked like Christmas tree lights through angel hair. Warnecke had his head down and his hands were jammed into his pockets as he crossed over to his car. "Damn dome light blew out again," he said real loud. He waited a minute and looked up at the sky. I looked up, too. He stared like he was trying to find something. To the stars he said, "Why, damn it, couldn't Ya have let her win? Why'd that bleached-blonde bitch have to win?" He sat down in his car and yanked the door shut. The Rheingold beer beauty contest was over. He often said he was gonna meet his "raven hair beauty" after she won. "I'm gonna tell her about all the beers I drunk just so she could win." And, he always added, "Her being so grateful, she'll ask me to leave my wife." Mom told him he was living in a fantasy land. "Ya gotta have dreams, Edie. Or ya don't get nowhere," he said. "And I'd sure as hell like to get outta Rosendale."

I watched as he leaned over and put his key in the ignition. He had his window rolled down. "No dreams come true in Rosendale!" he shouted out the window to nobody. "The only way to go in this town is backasswards." I giggled.

Warnecke tried to back up his Packard from behind the Studebaker that was up against his front bumper. "Always going backasswards!" he cried out. He revved the engine and put his car into reverse. It made a lot of grinding noises. The car wouldn't budge. He tried again. Still wouldn't budge.

"Ain't this hot shit," he wailed. "I can't even go freakin' backasswards!" I giggled some more, but not loudly. Opening the driver's-side door, he stuck his foot out onto the pavement and pushed until his car rolled back and tapped the front bumper of Floydy's pickup truck.

"Ain't this freakin' hot shit. No reverse means I ain't got no first gear neither," he said, slamming his door once more. Warnecke ground the gears, shoved the shift lever back and forth until it grabbed hold and let him drive off.

I listened to the grinding sounds as his car jerked up the street and disappeared into the fog by the Astoria Hotel. Then it became very quiet.

Bored, I bounded out of my seat, slipped the front door open and went inside. Theresa Brewer was singing "Music! Music! Music!" and it was coming to an end.

"Get upstairs," Mom said, as she caught me slinking in. "Check on Mickey."

Summers At Aunt Helen's

*Family ... the home of all social evil,
a charitable institution for comfortable women,
an anchorage for housefathers,
and a hell for children.*

J. August Strindberg

After I got caught stealing, Aunt Helen said it'd be a good idea to stay with her in Kingston during my summer vacations. "You have too much freedom and the devil makes use of idle hands," she said. Plus, she promised to take me shopping, so I wouldn't have to swipe anything.

She said appearances were everything. "People judge you first by the color of your skin, and then by how you look. You can be poor, but don't have to look like it. Keep your head up, like you're balancing a book up here," she said, pointing to the top of her head. "Work," she said, "and save your money, and read. You can do and be anything, if you read. You don't have to go around being a stupid hick all your life."

While I practiced walking around the house keeping a large book from falling off my head, she stood in front of the bedroom mirror posing like a photographer was taking her picture. She fluffed up her bleach-blonde hair and lowered her eyelids, making herself look sleepy. We both had big brown eyes shaped liked almonds. "Sloe eyes," she called them, "just like the Orientals. Exotic. They're not Chinky eyes, damnit!" She made kissy sounds at herself, puckering up her loose, puffy lips. "I have pouty lips, they're not puffy, for Chrissakes!"

Aunt Helen and her sister, Aunt Moncie, were once married, but Aunt Moncie got divorced, and Aunt Helen's husband, Howard Evans, got killed at the Battle of the Bulge in France in '44. Mom said Aunt Helen had other husbands, but everybody lost count, and nobody talked about them where she could hear.

Uncle Howard and Aunt Helen hadn't been married very long when he got shot dead. She said he was buried in a mass grave, and it was hard to believe he wasn't running around having a good time in Europe.

I liked to look at the picture of Uncle Howard in his lieutenant uniform with me on his lap when I was a baby. He had a mustache, and was more handsome than Errol Flynn. I asked Aunt Helen if I was her daughter because everyone said how much we looked alike. And did my parents adopt me after Uncle Howard died. She laughed, and said no. I never believed her. Why did she have a baby picture of me and him before he went away? If Aunt Helen was my mother, I wouldn't mind I got her Chinky eyes. I was just glad I didn't get her big puffy lips. Mine looked perfect, like Uncle Howard's, or maybe Pop's, if Pop was my real father.

After Uncle Howard died, Aunt Helen bought a house with his insurance money, and then she got a little old rich widower-man, Bill Whitmore, for a boyfriend. When we went shopping, she made old man Whitmore buy me dresses, and, once, he even bought me a baby doll. He took us to dinner at the best restaurants because Aunt Helen would insist on eating in places like Kellor's in Albany, or the Ship's Lantern in Millbrook, where they had five waiters to each table, and poor old Bill had to tip each one. She taught me how to eat using three different forks, spoons, and knives, all at the same meal! If Bill wasn't around, we went to places with one waitress, and ate with one fork, knife, and spoon, and she got to shortchange the waitress' tip.

Aunt Helen learned fancy eating in magazines she bought with the pictures of big houses, pretty flower arrangements, table settings, and recipes for foods with French names like hors d'œuvres, which Pop called "whore's ovaries."

Widowers like old man Whitmore and, after he died, Louie Hasa, a rich architect from New York City, stayed at Aunt Helen's house, sometimes for a week or more. I don't know where she found them. They gave her anything she wanted, and she was meaner than the Wicked Green Witch of Oz. She cursed at them and wouldn't even give them a goodnight kiss. She made them sleep in my bedroom with the door closed, and I had to sleep on the couch. I don't think they ever got up to go pee at night. I felt sorry for them. When they died they left her all their money, and she became a rich widow lady that didn't have to work anymore.

Over the summers Aunt Helen corrected my English and made me look up crossword puzzle definitions in the dictionary for her so I learned new words at the same time. "Your name should be Eliza Doolittle for as little as you know about grammar and manners. It's about time," she said, "you learn some etiquette," which was her fancy word for knowing which fork to eat with. "Staying here, you might become a respectable young lady instead of the foul-mouth, smart-ass friggin' bar brat you're turning into," she said.

She's kidding, I thought, when she said, "Emily Post says, women with class always tap the salt shaker, they never shake it. And you don't scrape the knife across the top of the butter leaving it covered with toast crumbs," she said. "You cut a pat off the end with the small knife, put it on your bread plate and then pick up your other knife to butter your bread." The toast got cold and the butter wouldn't spread! This was so dumb and who was Emily Post? "Wouldn't you like to have known what a finger-bowl was instead of yelling at the waiter, 'What kind of dessert is this?' Gawd! I was mortified!" Aunt Helen said.

The first summer with Aunt Helen was a short stay. We went to Schenectady to look at cocktail dresses for a wedding she got invited to. When we got back to Kingston, we stopped to see Aunt Moncie and show off her new dress. She also wanted to ask if it would be okay for me to stay with Colleen and Nancy on the day of the wedding. Aunt Moncie wasn't too happy about it, but she gave in.

They started talking about weddings and annulments, and how neither one of them never wanted another husband. Since my cousins weren't around to play, I was bored and decided to join in their talk. I asked, "What's a 'nulment?" I'd learned it was okay to listen as long as I kept my mouth shut, but today I ignored the rule.

"An annulment," Aunt Moncie said, in a teacher's voice, "is something you get after a divorce if you want to get married again."

"You gonna get married again?"

"No...."

"But if you ain't getting married again, why do you need this 'nulment thing?"

"Because the church says you have to get the annulment to say you've never been married. Divorce is a sin. And stop saying 'ain't'."

"Why did ya get a divorce, then?"

"It's too hard to explain," she said.

Not satisfied, I asked again, "Why do you gotta get a 'nulment?"

I was confused. How can ya get married, get divorced, and not be able to get married again because you're divorced, then get this 'nulment thing, which says you've never been married, then ya could get married again, but she doesn't want to get married again?

"The Pope says it's a mortal sin to get a divorce and get remarried, unless you get one first."

Oh-h-h-h. The mortal sin, dying and going-to-hell thing again. But this left another question. "If you did get one, does that mean that Uncle Ray wouldn't be Colleen and Nancy's father no more?"

"No, he's still their father."

"If the Pope says you was never married, won't that make Colleen and Nancy bastards?"

Aunt Moncie's face lit up red and then purple. Her eyes bugged out. She jumped up from her chair, almost overturning it, sucked in lots of air and spat out, "No, it does not, you... you ...guttersnipe!"

I tried to say Bobby Ann said a bastard was a kid who had parents but they weren't married, and it seemed to me my cousins would be bastards.

"I don't care what your white trash friend tells you. Don't you ever use that word about my daughters again, do you hear me!"

"Yeah, but the Pope is the one that said . . . ."

"Get out of my house. Now!" She screeched and stamped her foot hard on the kitchen floor and pointed to the door.

Can't even ask a freakin' question without getting my head chopped off. I bet the whole city heard her screaming. I left to go outside with Aunt Helen behind me and Aunt Moncie almost stepping on her heels. I ran to the car, jumped in the front seat and listened. I could make out Aunt Moncie saying in Slovak to get me out of her sight. Then she used some Slovak curses, and Aunt Helen got in the car and roared out of the driveway.

"What am I gonna do now? For Chrissakes!" Aunt Helen shouted. "When are ya gonna learn to keep your friggin' trap shut?" she crabbed. "Who the hell's gonna watch you now? I'm not missing that wedding after all the money I spent on this dress. You bet your sweet ass I'm not." She went on, "You're going t'hell home till I feel like coming and get you again. Fuckin' son-of-a-bitch," she mumbled. When she got mad she swore like a foot soldier. She was the Queen of Swear. I learned lots of new curses from her and added them to my list. "As soon as we get to the house, you pack up. Do you hear? Gawddamn miserable freakin' brat!"

A week later, Aunt Helen came and got me again.

It was boring at her house. Until she got rich, she worked at the Crown Street diner from early morning till mid-afternoon. Even though I could stay in bed as late as I wanted, it felt like I was in Aunt Helen's Reform School. She kept the shades down and the curtains closed so no one could see she left me alone. And I couldn't answer the door, talk on the phone, go outside unless the dog had to go, or unless I was dying and needed help. When Aunt Helen was at work and wanted to talk to me, she'd ring the phone once and hang up. Then I'd call her right back or she'd get all pissy and want to know if I was snooping in her stuff. I know she called during the day not using our secret code, to see if I'd answer the phone, or to see if the line was busy. Once when she let me call home, I tried whispering to Mom I wanted to leave. Aunt Helen had ears like a bat. She got all in a flap about it, and Mom told me to find something to keep me busy.

Aunt Helen never trusted me. If something was missing, she

went into a screaming, cursing fit, calling me names, and saying things like, "What'd you do with it? I put it right here, gawddamnit . . . and now it's gone . . . You must have taken it . . .gawddamn son-of-a-bitch no good thief . . . ." Most of the time what she wanted had been mislaid. She never admitted she found what she was looking for, and she never said she was sorry for yelling. If I saw her with the missing thing, she'd say, "You must've put it back where you took it from."

"Once you're tarred with a brush, all people see is the tar," Pop said. And I was tarred in her eyes. She made me feel bad more times than she ever made me feel good.

There were more rules. She told me, "Don't eat anything in the refrigerator except what I made for you." And, "Never turn on the electric stove. You could burn my house down." Then there was a list of chores she said I didn't have to do, but would bitch when everything wasn't done. I had to make her bed with hospital corners "like the maids for the wealthy," and so you could bounce a quarter on tight sheets. I scrubbed floors and washed dishes. Even though she was a pack rat and had piles of clothes on chairs, couch, and dressers, she inspected the beds to see if I made them with hospital corners.

She checked the dishes for food specks, the floors for dirt in the corners, looked for cobwebs on the ceiling, and checked the toilet for rings. Everything had to be spotless. Like Pop, she never said, "Thank you," and would look for what I'd missed, and say, "You could do better if you weren't so lazy, or tried harder."

Whenever she was scared and couldn't sleep at night, I had to sleep with her. Sometimes she peed the bed and she blamed me for it. She accused me of sleeping like a log and that I didn't realize I peed. But I never wet the bed. She was a liar. But I got stuck changing the sheets and putting them in the washer in the basement the next day.

In between cleaning I played with the doll with green eyes that blinked and had eyelashes and whose skin was cracked and whose body was made of cloth and packed with cotton. Aunt Helen got her at the Salvation Army for me. I played with Penny, her droopy-ear dog, combed her with a fine-tooth baby comb and caught fleas to crunch with my thumbnail against the flat side of the comb. I painted her toenails with bright red nail polish. Sometimes I cried. But I guess I was lucky. Reform schools didn't have dogs.

I felt sorry for Penny. Aunt Helen didn't care for dogs. All she wanted was something that barked and that would let her know it was safe to come inside after being out all day. Sometimes she screamed and hit Penny for laying on the floor, getting in her way, or having to go pee when she was praying her rosary.

When we left the house, Aunt Helen made a big fuss over Penny. "Oh! Penny's going to be so-o-o-o sad when we go," she said, so close to the dog's face I thought she was gonna kiss her. "Judy, say bye to her."

I nodded, okay, said bye and went outside to wait. I could hear her talking. "You gonna miss your mommy? Yes, you are, Sweetums. I'm sorry, I have to go." It took her almost ten minutes of blathering to the dog before she'd leave. "Now you be a good girl. I'll bring you back a doggy bag," she said, petting Penny and shoving a handful of dog yummies at her.

We drove out the driveway with her tooting the horn. Inside, the dog barked and jumped up and down, trying to see us out the kitchen window. Aunt Helen rolled down her car window, waved, tooted some more, and called out, "Bye-bye, Penny! Judy, wave bye-bye to Penny!" she demanded. I waved. This was the dumbest thing I've ever had to do, I thought. She drove around the block, coming back to the house, stopped in the middle of the street, and tapped her horn several times. The neighbors must have thought she was crackers.

"There she is at the window," she said. "Wave, Judy or she'll be upset. Say bye-bye to Penny."

The dog was going berserk, yapping and jumping. "Bye-bye, Penny," I said, and waved to the dog. Oh, gawd, I'm so glad Bobby Ann ain't here to see me do this. Only good thing was she made Aunt Moncie, my cousins, and anybody else who rode in her car wave to the dog, too.

When we were inside, Aunt Helen locked the doors with regular locks, slide bolts, plus chain locks. She was afraid someone would get in, rob her, or do worse to her. Shades were always pulled down over locked windows, some were nailed shut, and draperies were pinned closed so no light could get out to let anyone know she was home.

"It keeps Peeping Tom's from seeing in. What if a man were outside looking in and saw you?" she said.

"What do you mean?" I asked

She told me scary stories about men who stood in the shadows and watched women undress at night. Then she said, "They'd break down your door, grab you, and put their thing inside you." She said men were animals and didn't care how old you were, how fat, or even how much a dogface you were. That, and her stories about lightning, scared the be-Jeezus out of me.

"Lightning hit my front door," she said, "and almost killed me."

She was sitting in the living room making up her mind whether to pray with her rosary beads when a bad storm kicked up. There was a boom of thunder, a flash of light, a loud crack, and steam and smoke poured out of a split in her front door, she said, right alongside the chair she was sitting in. And, ever since, she prayed her rosary every night.

A lady friend of hers, she said, had lightning come through her electric socket and start her rug on fire, and another friend's television blew up while she was watching it during a storm. Then there was a man who got killed when the lightning came through the telephone he was talking on. It struck him in his left ear, came out his right, and fried his brains like bacon in hot oil. She snapped her fingers to show me how quick it happened.

I never used to be afraid of anything till spending summers with her. Lightning was just something scary-exciting if it mixed with thunder. I used to run in the rain and hide in the shadows playing hide-'n-seek. Now, at home, the rain and games weren't fun any more. She had me afraid of lightning, along with those bad men hiding in the dark outside my window, or in the dark corners of my room, or in my closet.

If the radio said rain, we didn't go anywhere, we stayed home. We once got caught out in a surprise thunderstorm and Aunt Helen pulled her car off of the road. "Don't touch anything metal!" she cried. "Keep your hands on your lap. Don't touch the door!" We sat sweating and fogging up the windows with our breath till we couldn't see out. We drove off when she said she couldn't "hold it" any more. She prayed to Jesus all the way.

At home, when she heard thunder rumble in the distance, we'd go sit in the cellar. But first she made me pull out the plugs to the clocks, the toaster, the refrigerator, and the electric stove. Then she turned off all the lights in the house. If I set her hair in pin curls, with the bobby pins making perfect X's across each curl just the way she liked them, she said, "Take them all out. Hurry! They're metal! I'm not gonna be a walking lightning rod." She didn't care how long it took to set her hair. She figured, later, I could do it all over again.

I had to lead the way into the dark cellar, she said, because my eyes were better than hers. She unhooked the chain and unlocked the kitchen door to the basement and followed behind me, lighting the stairs with her flashlight. I carried the empty Hills Brother's coffee can and the toilet paper in case she had to go pee. She lit a candle on top of an old dresser used for storage. She was afraid of fire, but she was more afraid of killing the batteries in her flashlight.

Aunt Helen wore rubber boots on her feet and rubber gloves on her hands. She sat in a faded, flowered slipcovered armchair pushed against the wall, far away from the basement windows that she had covered with heavy oilcloth. She sat stuffed in between rows of old clothes hanging on metal hangers on a metal bar over her head, which I thought was plain stupid. What if the lightning sneaked in and hit the pole? It would fry her clothes and flames would drop on her.

She would take down the rosary beads from a nail in the wall next to her chair and roll the beads between her fingers. The crucified Jesus dangled on the end. She'd start to pray the fifty Hail Marys and five Our Fathers. Each time there was a clap of thunder, her puffy lips would flap like a roller shade that was released by accident. "If I pray the rosary," she often said, "maybe God will stop the thunder and lightning." In the light of the candle, I'd watch as she mumbled, "HailMary fullofgrace theLordiswiththee. Blessedartthou..." BOOM-CRACK...! "Aghhhh...! amongstwomen andblessedisthefruitofthywomb..." BOOM-CRACK...! "Aghhhh . . . ! *Jesus!* HolymaryMotherofGod, prayforussinners, now andatthehour ofourdeath. Amen." On and on she went, praying and yelping at each clap of thunder.

My nerves were jumpy from all the screeching. I'd sit on a small footstool watching her from the corner of the makeshift clothes closet, searching the black areas of basement where the light didn't reach. The candlelight on her face gave her black circles where her eyes should be and black hollows in her cheeks. She looked like the Bride of Frankenstein. Her arms were wrapped around her knees that were pulled to her chest. Every once in a while she'd look at me and snap, "Pray, gawddamnit!"

I'd finger the tiny black rosary beads she'd given me and fake moving my fingers along the beads. I made my lips move, blah-blah-blah. With my eyes almost closed, I'd watch her as she prayed and waited out the storm. And I'd pray, Please Jesus, don't send me back here again.

Gotta Go Confess

*No blame should attach to telling the truth.
But it does, it does.*

Anita Brookner

My palms were sweaty and I kept wiping them on my pants. My legs felt weak as I opened the heavy wooden door of the church, and my insides were all in a gumbo from thinking about what was gonna happen when I told Father Mulry I'd been stealing. I couldn't blame it on Tits, Pop had said. "Even if she did teach ya, she didn't twist your arm to do it. Ya knew stealin' was wrong." At Aunt Helen's, she didn't make any big deal about going to Confession and Communion. But she didn't know I hadn't gone since getting caught. I worried all summer about what would happen if I got killed with a mortal sin on my soul. Hell is where I'll go. Unlike Mom, I didn't have any friends there yet, and wasn't keen on going.

When I got back from Aunt Helen's, I went swimming and almost drowned by going down the rapids on my butt without a tube. Bruce Temple, Eddie's friend, saved me, and I figured God was giving me a big warning. I promised right then and there, while I was plastered up against a big rock with the water trying to suck me under, I'd get my tail to Confession.

It was late Saturday afternoon, as late as you could get to

church and be guaranteed a priest was still hearing Confession. I waited in the vestibule afraid to go through the second set of double doors. I looked through the racks of pamphlets telling you how to be a good Catholic. You could buy a booklet for a dime. I saw the list of forbidden movies and books banned by the Pope. I'd seen so many movies there was bound to be one I shouldn't have gone to. But, if I didn't read the list, I wouldn't know. Besides, I had enough to tell him. I'll check later if I ever need a sin to confess.

Like John Wayne, I had to bite the bullet, confess and take my medicine. Wiping sweat from my palms onto my jeans again, I took a deep breath and pushed the doors open like a saloon door in a Western movie.

The church was always cool and silent inside. People knelt in pews and at the altar railing praying. Some said their rosary like Aunt Helen, their lips moving without any sound coming out. They all looked gray. My heart did a skip. Rosary beads? Did I remember to bring them? I patted my pants pockets. Phew! I put them around my neck so I wouldn't lose them. My heart slowed down. I could feel sweat starting on my forehead. Forgetting my rosary beads would be like forgetting my gun at a showdown with the bad guys.

No nuns had come from the convent to turn on the lights. Candles lit by sorry sinners put a yellow shine on the statues, making them look like zombies standing on high shelves. Spooky shadows bounced around on the walls and ceilings like in a haunted castle.

There was a rack of blue glass votive candles in front of the statue of Mary and red ones in front of the statue of the Sacred Heart of Jesus. He stood there with His Heart wrapped up with thorns and dripping blood, which I didn't like.

The flames of the little candles were like tongues of fire I believed licked and burnt up our sins as we prayed. I knelt before Mary and watched the candlelight give a magic look to her lips and her closed eyes. She didn't look creepy. She seemed real, and like she didn't want to look at me. I prayed to her. Mary, Mother of Jesus, help me be brave as you were brave at your Son's Cross. With your help, I can go to Confession. And, please tell your Son, Jesus, I'm real sorry I got caught stealing. I won't ever do it again. I hope.

I mean, I promise.

I dropped a nickel in the slot of the box attached to the rack of candles. Lighting one, I prayed some more, May this candle fire burn away my sins. And, oh, Mary, when I get some more money I promise to put it in here for this candle, but right now, all I got is a nickel. Amen. I tried to not look at Jesus. Him standing there, pointing to His bloody Heart in His Chest. Sister said each time we sinned we pushed another thick thorn from the crown down very deep into Jesus's Heart. I didn't want to think about that.

Looking around, I saw five or six people waiting in line to confess. Two people were kneeling at the rail beside me, and a young couple in a pew praying their rosary. Oh boy, I shouldn't have waited this long. Father Mulry will get finished and I'll still be here doing penance. He'll come out, see me, and know it's me who confessed to stealing. I gotta go pee. Nuts.

I stood in line behind the grownups. I jiggled up and down. I jiggled so much I bugged the lady in front of me, "Will you please stand still?" she asked. "You're distracting me from my contemplation."

"I can't."

"Why not?"

"'Cause, I gotta go pee."

She went to the head of the line and asked if I could be next, since I had to go to the bathroom. The man in front turned, saw me doing a knocked-kneed chicken dance and nodded, yes.

I knelt and squeezed my legs together, crossing one over the other so I wouldn't pee my pants. I hung on to the little shelf in front of me to keep my balance. The darkness of the box was nice, and for a while I forgot I had to pee. I went over the words to say to Father Mulry. My palms were sweaty again. The wooden door behind the black screen window in front of me slid open with a bang. It made my mouth start to ramble. "Bless me Father for I have sinned, it's been all summer since my last Confession. I haven't received Communion all summer neither, and I lied to my father and told him I was going to Communion so he'd think I went to Confession because I didn't want to get in no trouble, but I didn't go to Confession because I was staying at my aunt's house."

Father Mulry mumbled something.

"Huh? Father, I didn't hear ya."

Father Mulry said the first few letters of each word while the last half of the word went into Never-Never Land. It took practice to understand him.

"I said, were yo -way for the sum-er?"

"Yes Father."

"Well then chi--d, why didn't yo go ta con-fes-yon where yo were?"

"My aunt said I didn't need to if I wasn't doing anything bad. And I wasn't, at her house, that's a guarantee!" I said.

"Gowancha," Father said.

I didn't know what "gowancha" meant so I started, "Well, I got caught stealing something in a store with my friend Bobby Ann. Well, she got caught and ratted me out so I got caught too."

"Yezz?"

What didn't he understand?

"Well, I knew I committed this mortal sin, right?"

"Yezz. Why were- yo- -fraid to com- an- confess?"

"I dunno. Guess I was scared you'd get mad at me like my father and Aunt Helen did and I'd have to say hundreds of Hail Marys and Our Fathers. And, I was real ashamed because I did such a bad thing. And, I was afraid all summer I was gonna die, and I almost died, well not really, but I almost drowned I mean, but I didn't, and I was afraid if I did I'd go to hell for all eternity and then I told Jesus I'd come and tell you… well, not right then, but when I almost drowned I figured He was warning me or something and how many chances was He gonna give me? So, I said I'd take whatever punishment you handed out." There, I said it. I felt proud of myself. It wasn't so bad.

There was a long pause and I heard a deep sigh.

I wondered how many prayers he was adding up behind the window. Or did he have a book telling him how many to dish out for each type of sin. Did he have a kids' list and a grownups' list? I bet he's gonna give me hundreds for stealing. I just knew it'd be hundreds.

Another deep sigh came out from behind the screen. He said, "O- yo- silly, silly, chi-d. Zay two Hail Ma--s n one Our Fa---rs. Promizz never to steal again."

"Is that all? I mean that's okay. You don't have to give me more. I…, I promise I ain't ever gonna steal again cross my heart and hope t'die, stick a needle in my mother's eye."

"Juzz make 'n Act of Contrition and don't ever mizz Confezion fo such a silly rezson again, yo- hear?

"Yes, Father." I bowed my head and prayed.

"Such a silly child," he said. He blessed me in mumbled Latin and slid the door closed with a bang.

That's it? I'm done? Two stinking Hail Marys and one stinking Our Father? I was stumped. It felt like I had been on death row, ready to go to the electric chair, and the warden said I was free. It didn't seem stiff enough punishment for breaking of one of God's Big Ten Sins. Shame and heat crept up my neck, over my chin, over my face and up over my eyebrows. I looked at the black screen. Why did he call me silly? I'm not silly!

Oh, God! Don't let me start blubbering now. I have to walk out of here and see all those people still waiting their turn. I pushed back my tears, parted the velvet curtain, and held it open for the next person. I wondered if Father Mulry told adults they were silly when they confessed to a mortal sin. Feeling all mixed up in my head, I made a beeline up the aisle to the altar rail, knelt down and blessed myself with the Sign of the Cross. I couldn't pray the prayers Father gave me. All I could do was stare at the candle I lit earlier and wonder what made him call me a silly child?

The Astoria Hotel

It takes that je ne sais quoi which we call sophistication for a woman to be magnificent in a drawing room when her faculties have departed but she herself has not yet gone home.
James Thurber

I WAS MAD. Mom made me miss a movie last night. I went stomping my feet all the way up street past Doc Vaughn's and the DeFelicis', singing, "Step on a crack, you break ya mother's back." And I wasn't even going home to see if Mom was lying on the floor wriggling in pain. I didn't care. I stomped passed The Well and Meyer's Garage, and waved to Henry Dittmar standing outside his barbershop. I stomped to death every big black mother-father ant I could, because Aunt Helen said stepping on ants made it rain. If it rained, Mom wouldn't walk to the Astoria to drink. And if she didn't drink, I wouldn't have to go get her and miss any more of my movies.

I kept stomping on past Rossler's dry goods store, Emcee Lewis' jewelry store, and Roosa's grocery store, all the way to the Astoria. The bottoms of my feet stung. My toenails hurt from being smashed into the front of my shoes. By the Astoria, I double-stomped on cracks and sang till my throat and feet were so sore I had to stop.

The Astoria was, Pop called it, the watering hole where Mom

did her drinking when he was out and Eddie was left tending our bar. Mike Wazelewski and his mother Julia owned it. Mike's mom was short and round with white hair. Her eyeglasses were always sliding down her nose, and she was always tying up her apron. She didn't speak good English. Ma Wazelewski cooked chicken paprikash, stuffed cabbage, and kielbasa, just like Mom did for hotel guests. She cleaned rooms and drank scotch like Mom, too. Mike looked like the movie star Stewart Granger but heavier and shorter, and I couldn't imagine him swinging on a rope or fighting with a sword in a swashbuckling movie. Mom said Mike reminded her of Cary Grant. Pop said, "After a few drinks everyone looks better than they are." Mike's hair was slicked straight back with something shiny and he wore black plastic-rimmed glasses. He drank, tended bar, flirted with all the women and drank some more.

Pop didn't like Mike. He said Mike had eyes for Mom and, "He's nothing but a gawd-damn-skirt chasing-drunken-Polack."

"Takes one to know one," Mom had said.

MOM DECIDED TO GO TIE ONE ON LAST NIGHT, to celebrate the holidays. When Pop came home, he ordered, "Go find your mother. If she's at the Astoria, tell her to get ta' hell home. And don't ya come back without her. Ya hear me?"

When I whined "Why me?" I was told, "Do what you're told!"

Sitting at the Astoria bar with Mom, waiting for her to come home, made me feel like Harry Snyder's old hound dog, that sat at his feet in our bar while Harry got drunk. If the Astoria was busy, I couldn't sit on a stool because they were for paying customers. I had to sit on the dirty footrest along with the crushed-out, stinking Lucky Strikes, Camels, and other cigarettes butts, plastic whiskey stirrers, and dirty black chewing gum squooshed flat on the floor. Every few minutes, I pulled on Mom's dress and begged, "Let's go-o-o-o-o. Pop's mad. Let's go-o-o." She never left before she felt like it.

"Inna minute," she said, and handed me money to put in the red pistachio machine at the end of the bar, or to go play the jukebox. I stared at the dirty linoleum footrest with its worn silver metal trim, nailed down with tiny brads. Men rested their feet on it when they stood at the bar. They forgot I was sitting below them and I leaned back and watched them scratch their balls and pick at the cracks of their butts. The women sitting on the padded swivel stools were always reaching under their dresses, straightening the seams of their stockings so the rhinestones going up the back were in a straight line. I watched a man's hand slide up the side of a lady's leg and go under her dress. It made her wiggle for a time. I keep peeking to see what happened next. The lady stopped squirming, then unzipped the man's pants and put her hand inside them. I could see great from down here. Her hand moved really, really fast on his dick like Andy once showed me. I made Andy's dick grow big and hard, and she was making the man's dick hard, too. The man's boner made his underpants push out his fly, and it looked funny. He had to quick zip up when another guy came over and squeezed in between them to get drinks. The guy with the drinks went and found a table. The lady got up and went to play the jukebox. The man put his hand in his pocket, leaned over, put his head down on his arm that was resting on the bar. He was looking down at the floor. I had to be careful he didn't catch me watching him. I know what he was doing. Andy called it pocket pool. A few seconds later, the lump in his pants was gone and he went to the men's room.

Reaching down from the footrest, I picked up cellophane bands ripped from cigarette packs and burnt matches from the barroom floor. I pulled the matches into four strips making them into stick figures. I made whole families. To make little children, I tore the cardboard legs in half.

The barroom buzzed around me like honeybees with voices. Every once in a while Mom's laughter cracked through the buzzing and drowned out the words of the music from the jukebox. The cigarette and cigar smoke, and the sour smell of whiskey and stale beer stung my nose. I made more cardboard people, dressed them in cellophane scarves and belts and made them dance to the music in the dirt on the footrest.

It was better when Mom drank at Nell and Jack Daley's, The Well. Their chef was a little Italian man, Mr. DeFiore, who cooked Chinese food in the basement. When he closed the kitchen and went to the bar for a beer, his daughter Mary and I would take turns riding up and down in the dumbwaiter they used to send up the food to the dining room.

Finally, Mom decided to leave. I held her hand when we went out the door and guided her as she staggered her way down Main Street. She swayed too close to the telephone poles and the curb and I made her switch sides with me. What would Pop say if she walked into a pole or fell off the curb, and landed on her face in the street?

Mom didn't talk to me because it took all her concentration to aim her feet straight down the sidewalk. The cool night air perked her up by the time we got to The Well. She wanted a nightcap, but I said no, we're going home. She pulled herself up and let out a loud huff of air through her nostrils like one of Dad's mares. She said, "Fine."

Our building had three front doors--one for the dining room, one for the bar, and one in the middle, that led upstairs to the hotel rooms. Only the barroom door got left unlocked. Like Aunt Helen, Pop didn't trust people. He wanted to know who was coming and going. Mom used her key to open the middle door. She didn't want to see Pop. She took off her high heels and tried to tiptoe up the stairs, hanging onto the banister to keep from falling over backward. I walked behind her with my hands out in front of me, just in case. As soon as she got in bed I let Pop know, and I went to bed too. A little later, Mom was in the bathroom, paying homage to the "porcelain god." The first time I woke up and heard her retching I thought she was dying, and I ran downstairs to tell Pop. He looked in the bathroom and said to her, "It doesn't take a lotta brains to flush hard-earned money down the crapper, does it? To me he said, "Get used to it. This ain't the first time and it won't be her last."

The Créche

*Singing has always seemed to me the most
perfect means of expression. It is so spontaneous.*

Georgia O'Keeffe

"Sleigh bells ring, are you lis'nin'? ... I don't care if you r-r-r-r, because I don't know the words to this song." I went right into "Frosty the Snowman was a jolly happy soul, with a corncob pipe and a stupid nose and two eyeballs made outta dead moles." I sang and skipped up the snowy sidewalk. Pop thought I was going to Bobby Ann's to spend the night. But I wasn't. When I go back home, I'll tell him she and I had a fight and I didn't want to stay.

I wanted to go to church, and Pop would never give me permission to go at nine o'clock at night, and Bobby Ann didn't want to come with me.

Pop packed me into my heavy winter snowsuit, while I complained.

"I'm only going over to Bobby Ann's!"

"What would happen if ya fell down on the way over?" he said. "Ya'll lie there and freeze to death, or get frostbite and have all your fingers and toes cut off when they turn black."

My toes were going numb from being jammed into my shoes with two pairs of socks on, and stuffed into Andy's old crappy black galoshes with the metal clasps he outgrew. My stocking cap was half falling off my head and my woolen mittens were itchy. I kicked the powdery snow. I sniffed the cold air. It made my nose drip.

The Well, the Astoria, and the Valley Inn closed early. Never any business on Christmas night because most people stayed home with their family. Pop and Mom stayed open only to catch stragglers coming through town, looking for a nightcap.

Four things made me stay awake and go to midnight Mass last night. One, to receive Communion, two, to see Baby Jesus put in the crèche, three, to sing, and number four, the best, to hear Pop sing. He made chills run up and down my spine when he sang. I wish I could do that to people. I'm sure God in heaven and all the angels up above could hear him sing.

I wanted to see Baby Jesus up close when no one else was around. The school principal put Him into the crèche during last night's service, and I didn't get a good look when we were allowed to truck past Him. I liked the word "crèche." Aunt Helen said it sounded better than "manger," a place where dirty animals chowed down and slobbered all over the hay. "It's the word educated people use," she said.

I stamped the snow off my boots, climbed the stone stairs to the church, and opened the door. Taking off my gloves, I went into the sanctuary, and dipped my fingers into the holy water font and blessed myself. Sniffing, I smelled melting beeswax and leftover incense. My wet boots made squeaking sounds against the polished floor. The sounds and smells felt comfortable-scary.

I made my way up the far right-hand side aisle past the plaques of Jesus carrying His Cross and falling down, and getting up and stuff. Votive candles lighted up the crèche and the faces of the Holy Family. Jesus was now here on earth and He'd stay here till He got Himself nailed to the cross and died again on Good Friday. Then He'd go to heaven on Easter and stay there looking over us till next Christmas, when the principal would take Him out of His box and He'd be born again.

Kneeling at the altar rail before the crèche, I looked long and hard at Baby Jesus. So, I guess I didn't have it so bad. At least I wasn't born in a barn with only cow's breath to keep me warm, and

I didn't have to sleep on itchy straw. My grandma was really sick. Nobody would tell me what was wrong with her, and Pop said I can't go walking up to her house to visit anymore. It must be bad, whatever she got.

I looked at Mary and Joseph's face and got sad. They all had the same look ... Mary, Joseph, the shepherds, and the Wise Men. They had this closed eyed, dopey smile on their faces. They looked drunk. I tried to smile that way to see what it felt like, and I felt goofy.

Jesus looked normal, like He knew what the heck was going on. His eyes were wide open, staring at me. I began to quietly sing "Silent Night," and kept looking around, afraid someone could sneak in church like I did.

I was gonna do it, the thing the nuns told us we were forbidden to do. My heart pounded as I slid around the end of the railing, reached out and stroked His Hair and Face and sang Silent Night very low.

Then I sang, "Yes, Jesus Loves Me," a song I learned at Bobby Ann's Sunday School class that I wasn't supposed to go to, but I did anyway. The hair on my arms stood up as I touched Baby Jesus and my body shuddered. "He loves you, Grandma," I whispered. "He won't let anything happen to you. I just know it. It doesn't matter that you're a Protestant. He loves everybody. He said so."

1951

GRANDMA SARAH

No motion has she now, no force;
She neither hears nor sees;
Rolled around in earth's diurnal course,
With rocks, and stones, and trees.

William Wordsworth

GRAM DIED. My Grammy Sarah died. "Gram-e-e-e-e!" I wailed, pushing my face into my pillow. It was safe to cry and scream in my bedroom as long as my face was stuffed in the pillow so no one could hear me.

I pounded and pounded my mattress with my fists, kicked my legs and wailed some more. I'm never going see her again. Mom said it was better Grandma wasn't suffering no more. Don't tell me that. All I wanted is my grandma back. Every time I came up for air, I felt sadder. Pop, poked his head through my doorway on his way to the bathroom and asked, "Ya alright?"

"Yeah." What else could I say? When he left my room, I bawled till I couldn't breathe out of both sides of my nose, and my eyes were all puffed up. Bobby Ann came over and I told her to leave. Lina, her sister, came over too. She went into the bathroom and got a cold wet washcloth for my face. It felt good against my skin. She put her arm around me and asked if she should tell Bobby Ann to come back. I didn't want that. I wanted Lina to keep holding me, but I couldn't ask her, because I didn't want her to think I was a baby. She left after a little while.

Grandma had the big "C-A." Nobody said the word "cancer." If they did, they whispered it. It was like they thought they could catch it by saying it, and if they used the initials, they wouldn't. The doctor told Mom and Pop he didn't know where cancer came from. They thought it was a bug called a virus. They didn't know how to get rid of it, neither. They gave Grandma all kinds of poisons called chemotherapy and radiation, which made her puke and get really weak. Pop said cancer was like rust on a car. Once the doctors opened you up and air got inside of you, it ate you up faster than if they left you alone.

Mom wouldn't let me go see Grandma when she was in the hospital because she said she didn't look like herself no more. And then my grandpa Dad DeWitt said enough with all those damn treatments that weren't working, and he took Grandma home to die. And I still didn't get to see her. Mom said grandma was out of her mind most of the time because of the morphine Dad was giving her for pain. I wondered why he didn't give her the same medicine he gave Doodles the dog if she was dying anyway. Why did he let her suffer and not the dog?

Aunt Joan and Uncle Ernie DeWitt helped Dad take care of Grandma and told Mom how she was doing because Mom couldn't make herself go look at her.

"Better to remember her just the way you do now," she said.

But I wanted to see her, and I didn't care what she looked like, but no one listened to me. I wanted to crawl up on her big feather bed and wrap my arms around her and give her hugs and sing to her and make her laugh.

"Ya don't understand," Pop had said. "She won't know who you are."

"But she'll know it's me," I had insisted.

And now she was dead and I ain't ever gonna see her again. They ain't even going to let me go to her funeral.

At the bar, I heard things like, "Ate her insides up. Went into her brain."

"Radiation?"

"Didn't work."

"Incredible pain. Morphine . . . drugged up. Outta her mind."

"Skinny as a rail. Wouldn't recognize her."

"Coma. Dead."

I begged to know what was going on.

"Get out!" Pop yelled. "Go outside and play."

I didn't want to go play!

There were more whispered words, "Funeral, wake, visiting hours. Plains Cemetery, family plot."

My Grammy, who gave me her old lace-up high heels and taught me what flowers I could eat, was going to be buried in a couple of days.

Grandma put violets in her salad. She had Dad kill a skunk every year for the grease that she used for a cold remedy.

"I'll close the bar," Pop said.

"Don't. I need to be busy," Mom said.

It was Saturday, February 17th, six days before my birthday. I'm never going to have another happy birthday again, I thought, as somebody from the bar asked, "How old was she, Edie?"

"Fifty-two," Pop answered. "Nice lady. She used to walk up to Maple Hill to see the Gypsies once a year at their camp. Her only vice, having her fortune told."

"She Catholic?"

"No. Baptist," Mom said.

"How's Morris doing?" It sounded strange hearing Dad De-Witt being called Morris. "I bet he's glad it's over."

Dad DeWitt told us once that Grandma was asleep and woke up to smell cigarette smoke. She hopped out of bed, came storming into her kitchen, and found Dad and his brothers playing cards. She scooped up the deck of cards and the cigarettes and threw them into the wood stove. She grabbed the homemade hooch and poured it down the sink drain. Then she picked up the straw broom and started smacking Dad and his brothers. She chased them out into the snow and locked the door. They had to sleep in the barn with the cow, the pig, and the chickens. Wish I had seen that.

"She was tiny but she was a tough old bird," Pop said.

"How long was she sick?"

"Got colon cancer in '49. But it was in her female parts, I guess. It spread to the rest of her. Doc must've missed it. Or else she didn't tell nobody about it."

"Can I go to the funeral?" I asked for the tenth time.

"No," Mom said. "It's no place for you."

"Why? I want to see Grammy."

"Ed!" Mom yelled.

Pop looked at me and shouted, "Out!"

"Why?"

"Out! Damn it! Now!" He stood up.

I ran.

Pop and Mom went to the wake. I was told to stay home and to stay out of trouble, and watch Mickey. This was the first time someone I knew died. I asked Pop about the wake. He explained as much as he could. It wasn't fair that Eddie could go. Andy said he wouldn't even if he could and I was stupid for wanting to and I should stop being a pain in the ass about it.

After everybody left for the wake, I went out and sat in front of the bar. It was freezing. People I knew were dressed up in their Sunday best, heading up to the funeral parlor on foot. You could drive, but then there was no place to park close by, except for family, and you'd end up having to walk anyway. I couldn't sit here any more, and sent Mickey over to Rosenkranses'. I had to see what was going on at Moylan's Funeral Parlor, where they had my Grandma.

When I got to Henry Dittmar's barbershop, a narrow shotgun building that sat across the street from the funeral parlor, I sat on his stoop and stared at Moylan's front door. Shivering in the cold, I watched people come out. Some were sniffing, blowing their noses and leaving in a hurry to get back home, or to the nearest bar. Other people lit up cigarettes and stood outside, joking and laughing like there was a party going on inside, and then they left. Mom and Pop came out, got into their car and drove off. Then Dad DeWitt and all my uncles and Aunt Joan. They weren't smiling. No one saw me sitting across the street watching them.

Henry Dittmar, leaving for the evening, came out and locked

the barbershop door. He pulled up the collar of his coat. "Hey, it's Judy, right? Ain't ya cold?" he asked.

"Nope."

"That your grandma Sarah that died?"

"Yup."

"Won't let ya go see her, huh?"

"Nope."

"Don't know why not," he said.

"Me neither."

"Well, don't sit here too long. I don't want to find ya frozen to my doorstep t'morrow mornin'." He grinned.

"I won't," I answered.

Henry jiggled the door handle, checking he locked up tight, gave my head a rub, and walked down towards The Well bar. My fingertips were cold right through my mittens and my feet felt frozen, but I couldn't take my eyes off Moylan's.

I waited five minutes more, got up, crossed the street, and tried peeking in the front window, but the blinds were closed and I couldn't see anything.

A car drove by, and I turned the doorknob to the funeral parlor. In the movies when they did this, the noise of the car would hide the sounds of the door opening. Inside was dark. All lights were turned off and it was hard to see. Grandma's casket was in front of the window with the closed blinds. I stood real quiet to let my eyes get used to the dimness, and listened for Mr. Moylan.

Everything looked blurry, like a camera out of focus at the movies. The flower smell made my stomach curl. My mouth began to water and I thought I might upchuck. I couldn't puke in the funeral home. What would Grandma think? I had to get closer and tiptoed down the center aisle and up to the coffin. Mom was right. This doesn't look like Grandma. Nope. This doesn't look like her at all. I stepped up on the kneeling pad and stared down at her face. Grandma looked like an old rag doll somebody spilled the stuffing out of. Her face was sunk in. Her hands looked bony, with blue veins sticking up through her skin. Nope. This wasn't my grandma. I took off my mitten and touched her hand with my pointer finger. Her skin felt strange, loose and papery, but hard underneath and cold to touch. I stared at her face and hands for a long time, and felt nothing. Could she be pretending to be asleep? I nudged her shoulder. Did she just move? Was that her coffin creaking? I put my face closer to hers.

Silently, George Moylan walked up behind me and tapped me on the shoulder. Somebody let out a very loud, long, blood-curdling scream! Me! George scared the hell out of me, and my ear-piercing scream scared the hell out of him, too. He jumped backwards, spilling his drink down the front of his tie and shirt

"Jumpin' Jeezus Christ! What t'hell ya doing in here, anyway!" he yelled, brushing the liquor off the front of his suit. "Get the hell outta here! Ya goddamn idiot kid!"

I smelled his whiskey breath blowing at me, and I shut my screaming mouth and ran. My legs felt like they were made of Jell-O and I was moving in slow-motion.

"Don't come back, or I'll tell your father!" George yelled, as I slammed out of the front door.

I ran until a fiery stitch in my side made me stop outside of Gilmartin's Luncheonette, next to the theater. Only then did I turn around to see if I was being chased. I wasn't. Jackie, the Gilmartins' mongoloid daughter, was standing outside saying hello to people as they walked by. "Whadda ya doing?" she asked me, as I bent over gasping for air and trying to stop the pain in my side. I couldn't speak. "Whadda ya doing?" she shouted louder. And before I could say, she said, "Fuck you," and went back inside mumbling to herself.

I felt something trickling down my pant legs. Ah, gee! My face grew hot. I held my side, like a Calvary man shot in the gut by an Indian's arrow, and limped home. I could feel pee making its way down into my socks.

Serves you right, stupid. Piss your pants. Shouldn't have gone in Moylan's. Plain dumb-ass thing to do. I wondered if George was phoning Pop right now. God got me big-time and now I have to face Pop. I opened the front door to the bar.

"How many times have I told ya to use the back door when ya come in?" Pop asked. "And where've ya been?"

I went over to the stairwell door, pulled it open, looked at his face and smiled. He doesn't know.

"Out," I said.

"No shit, Dick Tracy!" he shouted, as the door swung closed behind me. "Smart-ass! Just like her friggin' mother!" I heard him say to Mazie Smith.

I ran upstairs to take a shower. Mom was lying on her bed, her back to the door. I could see her face in her vanity mirror, eyes closed, and watched her breathe in and out. I wondered what she'd look like when she died.

I'm glad I went to Moylan's because now I know that Grammy isn't "sleeping peacefully." Maybe Baptists were smarter than Catholics and got the heck out of here as fast as they could. That's why it didn't look like her . . . bet her soul's already gone. Grandma wasn't hanging around for two weeks like the priest said we do. Bet she's playing with Doodles the dog in heaven. I bet she's eating violets, too. I'll come visit you at the cemetery, Grandma, in the spring. And I'll bring lots of violets.

Doc Vaughn's Drugstore

When you're growing up in a small town
You know you'll grow down in a small town
There is only one good use for a small town
You hate it and you know you'll have to leave.

Lou Reed

Since our bar was right smack in the middle of town, I thought the village was either up or down from my front door. We lived on the sunny side of Main Street, the same side as Doc Vaughn's drugstore. Doc's is three doors up and was the only place where you could get a prescription filled, or buy Mom Chanel #5 perfume, or her favorite hair color, Clairol Champagne Beige. It was the place to buy hot pink, or bright tomato red Max Factor lipstick. And Doc had this magazine rack running up the wall with two rows of Dell comic books, one row of rock n' roll music with the words to Johnny Ray songs like, "Please, Mr. Sun," and there were true romance magazines for teenage girls, and *Look* magazine for grownups.

Doc had a rule: You couldn't look at comics unless you bought it. It was hard to know what I wanted just looking at the cover. Grownups could take magazines from the top of the rack, look at them and then put them back whenever they wanted. It wasn't fair!

If I took too long, Doc would say in a gruff voice, "Hurry up.

I haven't got all day to watch you make up your mind." It was like there was just so much air I could breathe in his store for free, and then I had to buy something or get out.

The drugstore had a soda fountain with swivel stools and three booths. Kids weren't allowed to sit at the booths unless with a grownup who was buying lunch or ice cream. We could sit on a stool to give in an order if no grownup needed the seat. If we ordered and it didn't need to be eaten with a fork or spoon or sipped through a straw, we were told to get outside and not hang out on the front steps. Doc was a grouch. It was, "Get what you came for and get out!" We listened because we didn't want to be told not to come back anymore.

Eddie and Andy hung out at Doc's till he closed for the night. Doc hired teenage girls to watch the soda fountain, like Eleanor Post's two sisters. Guys and girls Andy and Eddie's age always had money for burgers and French fries, which they ate in slow motion so they could sit talking for a long time. They ordered an ice cream soda and the ice cream would melt before they polished it off. My brothers and a bunch of other kids started going to Gilmartin's by the movie house when it opened, because they were tired of Doc's rules. At Gilmartin's they could play pinball even if they couldn't sit in a booth unless they bought a soda or food. Mae and Jack Gilmartin had two daughters. One was around Eddie's age, Agnes, and the other girl was Jackie. Jackie was really short, wore glasses, and sometimes talked a little funny. She had a round flat face and Chinky eyes. She didn't go to school. I didn't know how old she was, Eddie said she was fourteen. Jackie acted younger. She sat out in front of the store talking to herself. Everybody said hi to her. She liked to wear cowboy clothes and shoot her toy gun at you. If you made her mad asking her stupid questions, she'd curse at you using the "f" word. I liked her.

Gilmartin didn't check for chewing gum like Doc Vaughn did. Whenever we left the drugstore after a soda or ice cream, he'd look under the counter and the tables to see if any bubblegum got stuck there. If he found some, and he knew who put it there, he'd kick you out the next time you tried to come into the store. He didn't care if you were there to pick up a prescription. Your foot would almost step through the front door and he'd say, "Out!" He wouldn't say why. "Out! Out!" he'd snap, as he walked toward you, pointing his finger to the door.

Doc threw me out and I had to go home and tell Pop.

"Whadda ya mean he wouldn't let ya in?" he roared. "Whadda ya do now? For crying out loud! Now *I* have to go up there! If I wanted to walk there this morning I would've!" Pop went on. "What ta' hell good is having kids if ya can't do what you're asked?" He yammered on, saying I had younger legs than his, and my brothers and I were supposed to be his "go-for's."

When he finished talking to Doc, he told me I had to scrape the underside of Doc's counter and all the tables with a putty knife. Pop told Doc as he headed for the front door, "Keep her here till she finishes."

"But . . . I didn't stick any gum under there," I sassed back.

"Then don't hang out with kids who do," were Pop's last words as he turned and left me standing there feeling ashamed, holding the stupid putty knife in my hand, in front of kids I knew.

I had to scrape off every piece of disgusting dirty pink and gray gum and sweep it all up in a dustpan, and bet Doc let this gum build up all week just for me. He probably asked people to put gum under there. I ain't ever buying anything in here again. I'm gonna go to Gilmartin's. Mom can come and get her own rags, and hair coloring, and rubber girdles.

I just wished Gilmartin's had greeting cards because Pop would still make me buy them. He was romantic like Ronald Coleman, an actor Mom always talked about.

"Hey, Babe!" it's what Pop called me sometimes. Eddie called me Brat, Andy called me anything he could think of, and Mom . . . she didn't call me anything. "Get up street," Pop said, "an' get the flowers I ordered from DeFelicis', and get a birthday card, and a box of Whitman's Chocolates, or those thin peppermint patties in the long green box. Hurry up. Make sure Mom doesn't see ya coming back in. She'll be outta bed by then."

Pop stuffed his hand into his pants pocket and pulled out a three-inch-thick, roll of bills wrapped with a rubber band. He took off the band, and wet his thumb and pointer finger on his tongue.

He liked to rub his fingers on the bills to be sure they weren't stuck together. Then he'd snap out dollar bills one at a time like Lash La Rue cracking his whip. Pop carried only brand new bills from the bank. Each had to be facing the same way and never upside-down. And all his money had to be in order from the ones to the hundreds.

"Hey, Babe!" he called, as I went for the kitchen door. "Tell Doc to wrap the candy!"

Pop wanted me back in fifteen minutes. So first I got the flowers, laid them in front of Doc—he moved them aside—and then I picked out the candy.

"Pop said wrap it up in flowery paper, not stripes, and put some pink ribbon on it, and curl it, too." I lied, but Doc didn't know it.

Besides it was my way to get even for the gum-scraping thing, that, and taking my old slow-pokey time looking at cards. I had to buy a card with just the right amount of mush in it. Too bad it wasn't next year and I could buy this pretty Happy 35th Birthday card for Mom.

Peeking over his glasses, Doc, his thin white hair combed back very neat, stood in his starched white shirt and pressed pants and asked, "Did you wash your hands? You get a card dirty or bent, you bought it." Now he was trying to bug me. For spite I put down the card I was looking at, went into his restroom with the sign, "For Patrons' Only," which should of said, "No Kids Allowed," and washed my hands. This made Doc upset, but he couldn't say anything because I was a "Patron." I came out and he went in behind me to make sure I didn't leave the sink a mess. According to Doc's clock, I had three more minutes. I picked up, read, and then put back one card after another, with Doc watching me all the time.

I walked over to him with my choice and he warned, "Sure this is the card you want? Once it leaves, you're not bringing it back like last time."

I narrowed my eyes to a squint and said, "Yeah, I'm sure." Sometimes I hated big people. They never forget when you make a mistake. I couldn't help it if Pop was being pickier than usual, and didn't like the card and wanted a different one.

I took my time counting out the money Doc asked for. I asked for a receipt, looked at it and checked my change twice like Pop taught me. Time was up. I took my good old time walking out and down the steps. When I was out of Doc's sight, I raced to the bar, sneaked in the kitchen, and put everything on the table. Pop looked up at the bar clock then at the kitchen doorway. He saw me and said to Mom, who was at the bar reading the newspaper, "I'm gonna get some coffee. Wan' anything?" She shook her head no.

In the kitchen he quick-read and signed the card. On it he wrote, "Dear Edith, All my love, all my life. Forever and ever, Love, Ed," and he made a bunch of X's and O's on the bottom. I poured him a cup of coffee from the pot and added the cream. He checked the receipt, counted his change and gave me whatever loose coins came back. Then he put lots of money in the card and sealed it.

Out to the bar he went with the flowers and card in one hand, candy tucked under his arm and a coffee cup in the other hand. Mom read the mushy verse and he wished her a happy birthday. She gave him a kiss and a hug. Pop winked at me and made an okay sign with his thumb and forefinger behind her back. I did a good job.

I did such a good job I got to do it on their anniversary, Easter, Christmas, and her birthday. It didn't take long to learn if I bought a smaller, cheaper card I got to keep more of the change. I also learned there was small and too small.

Sometimes it was hard to know what to get. I hoped bigger cards would make the words inside mean more. It didn't matter, though. Big cards or little cards, lots of mush or just a little, they still got into fights at least one night a week, and more lately.

Our Vacations

"It is better to have loafed and lost than never to have loafed at all."

James Thurber

It was mid-afternoon, and no one was at the bar except Mom who was busy cleaning behind the bar.

"Ma?" I was sitting reading a Wonder Woman comic book.

"What," she didn't look up from scouring the stainless steel sinks.

"When are we going to take a vacation?"

"Kids are always on vacation," she snorted.

"C'mon, Ma. How come we don't go anywhere like other families do?"

"Just your father goes. And when he's gone, it's my vacation. Make it yours, too."

Why doesn't she ever give me straight answers? "Pop gets to go fishing in Canada. When do we get to go somewhere?"

She looked up and asked, "Where would you like to go?"

"I dunno. Anyplace. Criminey sakes." I turned the page of my comic book.

"We don't have the money," she said.

"Well, Pop does. He bought all the fishing junk and the food he took with him."

"Wise up," she said, leaning toward me. "He does what he

damn well pleases. If it's for him, there's money; if it's for us, well, you might as well go whistle 'Dixie.'"

Mom dried her hands, took down her scotch and poured a healthy shot. She reached for the ceramic water pitcher sitting near the beer taps and poured a splash into her glass. She twirled the ice cubes, water, and scotch with her finger, licked her finger and took a drink. It was one o'clock in the afternoon. I could hear Pop calling her "Lushwell" or "Guzzlin' Gertie." She could drink whenever and whatever she wanted with him away. And when he wasn't around she drank often and it usually was Cutty Sark instead of White Label.

"Well, you got to go to Canada," I muttered.

"Yeah, and I had the bad luck to catch the largest pike. The men at camp never let your father forget it neither. Have I ever gone again?" She frowned. "He said the guys bet among themselves, and I spoiled it for everybody. Like I knew I'd hook the biggest fish in the whole damn lake and win the bet?" She smiled.

"Why can't he do something with us?"

Her eyes seemed sad. I could smell the stink of scotch on her breath. "I'd like to get away from here, too. But I'm stuck. You're stuck. Your father's the big spender. Mr. High and Mighty. If there's anything left over, then we get to do. But there's never anything left over except more bills to pay." She stood up taller, stretched her arms over her head and yawned. "You'll be going to Aunt Helen's soon for the summer," she said. "Stop complaining." She finished her drink and filled the shiny sinks with hot water.

"Oh, whoopee!" I said. "All summer I sit locked up in her dungeon with the shades pulled down and pick fleas off her dog. Then she comes home, eats, and watches TV. Then she prays her rosary beads and I get to put pin curls in her stupid hair and paint her stupid fingernails for the next day, like I'm a slave, while she crabs I ain't doing it right."

"It's not that bad." Mom laughed at me. "Look at all the stuff she buys you and all those fancy restaurants she takes you to. And stop saying ain't!"

"Yeah! Well, I'd just like to have a plain hot dog. And not her chili con carne she's always making because it's cheap and looks like the dog puked in the bowl. Besides she doesn't pay for anything when we're with one of her boyfriends. They pay for everything," I said. "If they ain't around, we don't go nowhere."

"Be grateful you're getting anything. She could be taking one of your cousins," she said, wiping her hands on a towel. "Why don't you just pretend you're a rich movie star and enjoy yourself? And I said stop saying 'ain't'."

"I do pretend. How do ya think I get through all those boring dinners? Another thing, I miss all the good movies by going to her house."

"No, you don't. By the time you come back the new movies are just coming to the Rosendale. Tony doesn't get them until they've finished running in Kingston. You don't miss a thing."

Mom must've got on Pop when he came back from Canada about doing something with us, because he said we were going to go to the Ashokan Reservoir for picnics. He could fish, Mom could lie out on the beach, and Mickey and I could wade in the water.

Sundays were a good day for a picnic. The law doesn't allow Pop to open the bar until one o'clock, and most drinkers come out in the evening after their big Sunday dinners. But then there were some who came and knocked on our kitchen door at eight on Sunday mornings. Mom let them in and made them sit at the dark end of the bar where they couldn't be seen from the street. She served them their usual drinks and made change from an open register, never ringing up the money they left as a "tip." If she rang the register and got caught by the alcoholic beverage control, they could take away Pop's liquor license. Mom joined the guys, popped the top off a beer, and took a swig, often saying, "Here's to biting the dog that bit ya."

Mom made food for our picnic, while Pop and I went to nine o'clock Mass. I liked it when we went together because I could sit with him and not with the nuns. The nine o'clock Mass lasted an hour, but, as usual, Pop was not on time. We got to church when the priest was ready to read the gospel. Once communion was served, we left. Going fishing was very important to Pop.

"Why do you bother going?" Mom said. "You're back in a half-hour, quicker than it took you to get ready to go." He ignored her and loaded the car with bags of food and his fishing stuff. Mom made a jug of Tom Collinses for them and brought soda for Mickey and me.

"Judy!" Pop called. "Wake up Eddie. Tell him we're leaving and get up for church. And get the blanket for the beach."

I ran up the stairs and did what he said. "Eddie! Eddie! Pop wants you to get up for church. We're leaving. C'mon!" I pushed and pulled on his hairy shoulder. My brother was as hairy as Pop. His back, his arms, and his legs were covered with hair, and his chest looked like a fur rug.

"Tell him I'm up and get the frig outta here." He rolled over on his stomach and pulled the covers up over his head.

Back downstairs I ran with the blanket.

"Is he up?" Pop wanted to know.

"Uh-huh."

I didn't like lying and an "uh-huh" didn't feel like a lie because "uh-huh" ain't a word, and, if it ain't a word, how could it be a lie?

"Are ya sure?" he asked again.

"Uh-huh."

Pop didn't believe me. I could tell.

"Go make sure he's up!"

"But he said he was getting up."

"Were his feet on the floor? I want his feet on the floor and ya tell him that."

Back up the stairs I stomped. I wanted to get out of here before something spoiled our trip and we didn't get to go.

"I'm gonna give ya something to stomp about!" He yelled after me.

"Eddie, Pop wants your feet on the floor. Come on, Eddie. I want to go swimming and we can't till you get up!" I said louder and tugged and pulled on his covers.

Eddie rolled onto his back and turned sideways in his bed. One hairy leg dropped over the side of the bed, and then the other. With legs bent at the knees, both feet on the floor, and the rest of him lying on the bed under the covers, he let out a rip-roaring fart and said, "Tell him this's from me."

I ran back downstairs. I said, "Let's go, his feet's on the floor." I ran out the door to the car. Andy sat at the table eating a bowl of cereal. He said he was going to eleven o'clock Mass and then going fishing with Jackie Regan in the creek. Pop said okay. Who was he kidding? He ain't going to church and Eddie wasn't neither. They'd pay me a quarter apiece later to find out what the sermon and gospel was about because they knew Pop would ask them.

Eventually we got to the reservoir. Mickey liked playing in the cold water. He stood on the slimy stones in his baggy underwear, with his fat little belly hanging over the waistband. He'd go into the water up to his ankles. Getting him to sit was hard. He wanted to be in the water but didn't want to get wet. Mickey would sit down and stand up really fast. His wet underwear sagged to his knees, almost falling off his butt. It was my job to keep him happy and see that he didn't get hurt. Pop and Mom read the newspaper and napped on their blanket in the sun. Pop had a fishing pole propped up in the rocks and said to let him know if he got a bite.

Next year the reservoir rules got stricter and we couldn't wade in the water anymore. Pop found a different day to go fishing, and Sundays were now a time for picnics only. The day was spent at the park area by the aerators where huge fan-shaped sprays of water shot up into the air, making rainbows. Pop said they used to turn colored lights on the water at night and he'd watch the water spraying up for hours. It probably was with an old girlfriend, because Mom glared at him, and he said it was in the old days before he married Mom.

The mist from the water made it feel cool as we lay out under the tall pine trees. Pop said when he was 19, he planted some of these trees when he belonged to Civil Conservation Corps during the Depression. It was a way to make money for his family.

Mickey and I were sitting around after eating, doing nothing. We got the idea to climb the low-branched pine trees. As we headed for the trees, Mom knew what to expect. She leaned on her elbow and nudged Pop awake. "Tell them to stay out of the trees. They'll get pine pitch on their clothes."

Without opening his eyes or lifting his head up off the blanket, Pop yelled up to the sky, "Stay out of those trees; your mother said so!"

"Oh, thanks a lot!" Mom spat "Like they're going to listen to that!" She threw herself down on the blanket, turned on her side away from him, and fell asleep.

But we stayed out of the trees. Instead, Mickey and I collected pine cones to play war. We each hid behind a large tree, lobbed them like grenades at each other, and made whiz-bang war sounds. I kept score. Direct body hits counted. Mickey always lost because he couldn't throw very far. If he started to cry, I told him he won. Sometimes it was hard to throw the pine cones because the gooey sap on them made them stick to our fingers. Then our fingers got stuck together. The pine sap stuck to our hair worse than bubble-gum when one of us got hit in the head. Mom squawked about having to go home and take lighter fluid on a cotton ball to our hair and hands.

When he'd heard enough, Pop said, "Vacation's over. Let's go. This is the last friggin' time . . . ." And it was.

The Cooler

Nowadays most people die of a sort of creeping common sense, and discover when it is too late that the only things one never regrets are one's mistakes.

Oscar Wilde

It wasn't bad enough that I had to scrape the crappy gum from underneath Doc's counter, now I was stuck doing freakin' beer bottles again. Grumbling, I wondered why I had to sort these smelly things. Because everybody else is too lazy, that's why, I said to myself. His Royal Highness ain't gonna do it. Mom ain't gonna chip her nailpolish, and Eddie's got a job. You can't ever find Andy because him and Carole Beesmer are always out riding horses. Andy lies and says he's working for Fred Pelham cleaning stables. It ain't fair!

Dead bottles got dropped into an empty wood beer case under the sink. When the case was full it went down to the cellar to be sorted by brand, and their cases were stacked against the basement wall. Deliverymen wouldn't search around to find what was theirs. Pop had to have everything ready for them because he got a refund for each case of empties he gave back.

I flipped a wooden beer case over on its end and sat down to a half-circle of empty cases around me, after getting the slop bucket to pour leftover beer and cigarette butts into. Pop got pissed when someone put butts into a bottle. So did I because sometimes it meant running upstairs to wash them out. Then I got the idea to take the bottles over to the big metal fish tank in the basement that was chest-high to me, and two times bigger than a bathtub. Pop stocked about a thousand hundred million minnows and sold them to fishermen. It was easier to take a little cold water from the tank, put my thumb over the top of the bottle and shake it. The soggy cigarette butts plopped into the bucket when I whacked on the bottom of the bottle. Sometimes I had to get more water. Sometimes the minnows got to eat small bits of tobacco. Sometimes they died and Pop couldn't figure out why.

It was hot outside and it was muggy in the basement. Sweat rolled down my armpits, and I wished I had a fan. The next best thing would be to go inside the beer cooler. The thick door was made of wood and stainless steel and it took all my strength to open it. Pop kept cases of beer like Piels, Ballantine, Schlitz, and specialty ones in there to chill down before they got brought up to the smaller cooler. And this was where the four big kegs of beer, Budweiser, Miller High Life, Schaefer, and Rheingold, got kept cold for the beer taps upstairs. I was warned never to play in here because Pop said he didn't want the temperature fuckshuatin', which I guess meant going up and down, like in sex.

The only time I got to go in there was to get beer or soda to restock the upstairs cooler, but I had to leave the door open. If I didn't, he warned, and the door closed, I wouldn't be able to push in the plunger to open it from the inside. But I knew I could open it, if I was ever stupid enough to lock myself inside.

The light switch on the outside of the door had a tiny red bulb smaller than a maraschino cherry with a wire basket protecting it so it wouldn't get broken. If this light was on you knew either the inside light was left on, or someone was inside. I turned on the light, went inside, and closed the door till it almost latched, just in case I couldn't get it open. I sat down on a case of beer and closed my eyes. Ah! the cool air felt great!

A few minutes later, the door clicked shut. My eyes flew open as the light went out. Shit! Oh my gawd!

Pop must've come to check up on me. When he didn't see me,

he probably thought I skipped out of my bottle-sorting job. When he saw the red light on, the door not closed all the way, he must've flipped the light off and shut the door.

Oh, fuck me! This is like being in that above-ground tomb I sneaked into in the cemetery. Only it's blacker in here. No one could hear me if I screamed, the walls and door were as thick as my forearm was long from my elbow to my fingertips. Wait, I thought. Wait for my eyes to adjust to the dark like they did at night in my bedroom, but it didn't happen. There wasn't any light coming in from anywhere. I worried how much air I had to breathe before I'd pass out and then die from the cold. Maybe even die from the cold before I ran out of air. You'll still be dead, you moron!

I could see it now, my father opening the door and there I was, lying face down, dead as a doornail on the cement floor, all blue and stiff. They wouldn't be able to put me in a casket without breaking my arms and legs. Stop it! I yelled at myself. Think. Get your ass out of here. The pukes came up in my throat and stayed. I've never been in anything so black in all my life. Not even the culvert under the road up on James Street when I was playing Army, and I crawled through it on my belly to get to the other side of the road. I didn't shake like this even when the truck drove over the culvert and I was in the middle of it and thought I was going to be crushed to death. Think, stupid! Stop scaring yourself! Which way is out? I couldn't remember which direction I was sitting when the light went off.

On the inside of the door, there was a black steel plunger to push to open the latch. I needed to find it and avoid the plastic hoses that ran out of the ceiling down to the kegs of beer. Every few months, Pop, who only drank bottled beer, had to wash out the beer lines because they built up a green slime so thick the beer only trickled out the tap. The Health people would fine Pop if he didn't keep them clean. If I banged into one of those kegs, it could pull out a hose. The kegs were under pressure and I could have beer shooting all over the place. Sometimes that happened on its own if a keg was bad or not filled with the right amount of gas. It was tricky tapping a keg. Pop let out a string of "fuck this's" and "fuck that's" when a keg blew and he came out sopped in beer.

What should I do? It was probably safer for me to get down on my hands and knees and crawl in search of the door. Then I could feel for the bottoms of the beer kegs. God, I hope none of those creepy thousand-leggers was in here. The concrete floor scraped my bare knees as I prayed to please don't let me touch a thousand-legger. Pretty please with sugar on it.

There was a beer keg on my left, and then another, and then another. Bam! My head found the door before my hands did. Sliding my hands up the door, I stood and groped around for the plunger, which would set me free. I found it and pushed and pushed. Nothing happened. Ah, shit! With all the strength I could bring up I threw my body against my hands and against the plunger. The latch clicked. I pushed with all my might and the heavy door creaked its way open. Oh, gawd, don't let Pop be in the basement.

The basement air, stinking of stale beer, never smelt so good. As I closed the door, I suddenly remembered that Pop had put a live, humongous snapping turtle, bigger than our largest iron skillet, in the cooler last night! He found it when he went fishing. He was savin' it to give to Dad DeWitt to make turtle soup. Chills ran up and down my spine. I could feel prickles in my scalp. Holy shit! If I bumped into that thing while I was crawling around in there, it could've bit my fingers off! Thank you, Jesus!

God's Fools

The great God endows His children variously.
To some He gives intellect....
To some He allots heart.....
But to some He gives only a soul, without intelligence—
and these, who never grow up, but remain always His children,
are God's fools....

Mary Roberts Rinehart

Christine and I were watching a funeral procession forming across the street by the Dutch Reformed Church. Mr. Ott died. He weighed about four hundred pounds or more. Maybe more. Moylan had to order a special extra-large casket. The doors had to be taken off the Reformed church to get him in and out, and it took a whole bunch of big guys with red faces to carry him up and then back down the stairs of the church. The whole town, I think, came out to watch.

"If they drop the casket, would Mr. Ott go rolling down the street?" Christine asked.

"I don't know," I shook my head wondering where she gets her ideas from. But then her whole family was kinda kooky. Christine once told me it was okay to play at her home as long as we stayed outside. Her mother's rules. I didn't think much of it because most mothers didn't want their own kids in the house when they were cleaning. But her mother wasn't cleaning. She stood behind the curtain at the window watching us like an espionage agent in a Nazi movie. I pretended I didn't see her.

Then one day I had to take a pee. "Can I use your toilet?"

"Ya gotta go home an' pee," Christine said.

"How come?"

"My Ma's scared ya come inside ya gonna steal sumpthin'."

"Why does she think that?"

Christine shrugged her shoulders, looked away from me and fiddled with her doll's dress.

"I gotta go bad. You want to come with me, then we can play in my bedroom?"

"Can't," she said.

"Why?"

"Can't go inna bar."

I felt like she just told me she had seen cooties running in my hair.

"Lots of people got their businesses and houses together. You go in them. You think you'll catch something?"

"I just can't, that's all. My Ma said so."

That was the dumbest, stupidest thing I ever heard.

The next time we played when Bobby Ann wasn't around, Christine and I went to the woods behind the school. At least there I could pee behind a tree. We found branches to use like brooms and made clean dirt squares on the ground, pretending they were rooms of a house. Then the older boys spoiled it. They heard us and came to see what we were doing. They told me to leave because Christine was gonna dance for them and it was a guys-only show. After a few minutes of riding the merry-go-round by myself, I decided to look and see what they were doing. Since they told me to stay out of the woods, I climbed up on the slide and stood on my tiptoes. From there, I could see the boys over the shrubs and in between the trees. They were standing around in a circle. Christine was in the middle doing a bump and grind like Gypsy Rose Lee. It looked like the boys had their hands down by their crotches. Holy mackerel! Were they pulling on their dicks? How could they be so disgusting? I got to ask Christine why she dances for them.

Hearing a noise, I turned and looked toward the school lane. Christine's father came around the corner of the building carrying his wide black leather belt folded up in his hand. Holy shit! I froze and couldn't say anything. She did this before and he's come looking for her again. I scrunched down on the top of the slide, hoping he didn't see me. He went into the woods. There was hollering and yelling and out came the boys going every which-what-way. They were trying to run and zip up their pants. Some of them couldn't because they had boners.

Dickey Rosenkranse was screaming, "I got my pecker caught in my zipper!" He tried to run but stopped and hopped on one foot then the other. "Ouch! Wait up, ya guys," he yelled, as he fumbled with his pants. Then he ran some more and hopped some more. "Oh Shit! Oh, Fuck! My prick's getting' ripped off!" he cried.

Andy came out of the woods hooting to the others, "I gotta get laid! I'm dying! I got blue balls!" The boys' laughed as they ran crashing through the high weeds and disappeared.

I heard the leather belt slapping and Christine's cries. Each time her dad's belt cracked, I scooted further down on the top of the slide into a tighter ball and buried my face further into my knees. I covered my ears to block out the sounds of the beating and my friend begging, "Don't hit me, Paw! Don't hit me! I ain't never dancin' again!" I started to cry. He came out of the woods dragging her by the arm. She stumbled, tripped, and fell, and he kept dragging her till she was able to pick herself up. They went around the front of the school, while she stumbled and cried and begged.

I climbed down the ladder of the slide, afraid to make any noise. Afraid he might come back after me. Maybe he'd hit me, too. I ran from the slide to the path, ran like the devil was chasing me. I sneaked in our back door, went through the kitchen to the dining room, and used the door that went upstairs to our apartment, which was supposed to stay locked. No one in the bar saw me. I wanted to hide, get away from everybody. Really quiet, I opened and closed the door to the apartment. I knew which floorboards squeaked, and walked around them and made my way to my bedroom. Pop was taking a nap and snoring really loud. I unhooked my closet door and went inside, closing the door behind me. There was a secret way

I could latch the outside hook-and-eye lock from inside the closet using a coat hanger. With the door locked, no one would look in here for me. I crawled into the back of the closet, curled up in my dirty clothes pile. Andy's gonna blame me for them getting caught. It'd be my fault, too, if Dickey's pecker got infected with gangrene, rotted, and fell off. I should've warned them. Grandma used to say if you had problems, sleep on them because they don't seem so bad when you wake up. I closed my eyes.

After supper, Mom was talking with Jerry Mertine. She told him what she'd heard about Christine and how she got beat for dancing for the boys.

Jeez, even she know's!

"I know my boys were involved," Mom said. "If I asked, they'd deny it. Stupid kids." She laughed. "What will they do next?"

"It's hard having a kid like her. Never know when she'll get herself in trouble. Ain't right beatin' on a slow kid," Jerry said. "They just don't know that they's doing wrong."

"Nothing anybody can do about it," Mom said. "She's not stupid enough to be sent away. But . . . I guess it's nobody's business what goes on in somebody else's house. There but for the grace of God . . . . In this town you mind your own business and be glad they're not gossiping about you."

"I'll drink to dat," said Jerry and they clicked their glasses together.

Being Defined

*In the animal kingdom, the rule is, eat or be eaten;
in the human kingdom, define or be defined.*
Thomas Szasz

Andy said Christine was sexy because she was French, and that the French were horny toads and that's why they were called Frogs, and not because they eat frog legs. He said he could buy pictures of naked girls on any street corner in France.

"You're full of crap, Andy. Right up to your eyeballs," I said.

"Yeah? Well, come look at Eddie's girlie magazines and you'll see I ain't lying."

We sat on his bedroom floor and looked at the magazines that had been hid under the mattress. Andy got a boner and he showed me that too. He told me to touch it. It felt awful, like Grandma's dead finger, or like a dead chicken neck—loose skin with a bone in the middle. "No," I told him. "I ain't stupid, and you can't trick me. You want to play with it, go ahead. But I'll leave." Andy stuffed his boner back into his jeans and we kept looking at the magazines.

Andy said Italian girls, like Ann Marie, were hot stuff, too.

"But," he said, "Italian girls get fat when they get old, and they smell like burnt olive oil and garlic because they eat too much of it. Only good thing about them is their tits are big as cows."

Andy pointed out the Italian girls with their dark hair and dark skin. He was right. They did have tits bigger than Dad's cow when she needed milking. I wonder how they could stand up and walk without falling over on their faces. Maybe that's why they were lying on their backs in all the pictures. Andy said, "I want to marry a French girl because they stay skinny and smell of perfume and they like to screw."

"How do you know that?"

"I got it from these books," he said. "I read, you know."

When Christine got grounded and Bobby Ann wasn't wanting to play, I tried to hang out with Ann Marie to see if she really did smell of olive oil and garlic. I never got close enough to find out. It was hard to be friends with her because some days she was nice and other days she acted like she didn't know me.

The first time I went to her house to ask if she wanted to come out and play her mother said, "Get off my porch. Stand on the sidewalk and wait."

After a long time of me dancing from one foot to the other, Ann Marie still didn't come out. I wondered what was taking her so long. It was hot and I was sweaty. It took a while, but I got it. She wasn't ever coming out. I felt like such an idiot for waiting all that time. I should've known better.

At school, Ann Marie told me her mother was just in a bad mood, and I should come to play again.

"Why don't you come to my place instead?" I suggested.

"Not allowed to."

"Why?"

"Not allowed to be in your bar."

"We won't be in the bar," I said. "My mother won't let us. We gotta play upstairs."

"Nope." She shook her head. "My mom don't want me around the drunks that hang out at your place."

"You kiddin'? Your dad comes there for a beer."

"Yeah, well, my mother don't even want him going there."

I never knew why she and her family thought they were so great and my family and I wasn't. Her father got drunk at our bar. Mom said he was a mean drunk. And later it got him divorced. I heard it said that after one of their fights, Ann Marie's mom really looked bad and wouldn't come out of the house. Because I was nosy,

I went to see. When her mom opened the door she looked wrecked. Her nose was puffy and her face had black and blue spots. Even Pop never hit Mom like that. Holy Moley. I felt sorry for her until she slammed the door in my face.

"Is Ann Marie home?" I asked.

"No!" she spat through the closed door. "Get out of here and don't come back."

"Wha . . . ?"

"You heard me. Get off my porch," she hissed. "You're nothing but white trash! You and your whole damn family!" she yelled.

Ann Marie and her sisters were home and their faces was pressed against the living room window, staring out at me. They had big grins on their pusses. I didn't know what white trash was, but knew it must be something evil. The way she said it made me feel ashamed of being me.

A song my mother taught me rang through my ears, "Oh you dirty little devil, does your Mama know you're out, with a hole in your britches and your hiney sticking out." I don't know why the song kept swirling in the space behind my eyes, but it was making them sting. I tore off to home.

I sat outside on the bar patio watching the sun go down and held back tears. Couldn't plain words be a sin? I wondered. Do they have to be curse words? What Ann Marie's mother said sucked the air out of me. I couldn't let what people did or say make me cry. Besides, I was tired of crying.

The sun was low in the sky, making the windows on the houses and the businesses look like colored stained glass. It kept changing from shades of yellow to orange. I liked the way the sun tinted everything . . . tangerine. Yeah. It was like a tangerine-left-out-in-the-sun kind of color.

The sun went down behind the buildings and I wondered how artists painted what they saw. When I grow up I want to be an artist and a dress designer and a ballerina.

One day I'd figure out all these beautiful colors. I'd paint great big pictures, like Sister showed us in school, by famous artists. I stood up, dusted my butt off. Maybe I could make this tangerine color. The color sank with the sun. The air picked up a chill. No traffic jams tonight. Nobody driving up and over the curb onto the sidewalk or backing up fifteen feet. Time to go upstairs and pull out my crayons and some paper.

I lay on my bedroom floor a long time playing with orange and yellow colors. Someday they'd have to make more colors. When they did, I was going to buy them. I looked at my clock. Pop would soon whistle for us to come for dinner, which was late tonight. Mom decided to go grocery shopping, and got waylaid at a bar. I could see in my mind, Pop pulling his lips back tight and putting the tip of his tongue behind his teeth. He let rip a whistle anyone could hear up past the movie house, down past the schoolyard and even out to the islands in the creek.

Pop whistled, but I ignored him. I was still busy trying to figure out how to make tangerine with my crayons. I wanted to use this color for a new gown I was drawing for my paper doll. I was going be a dress designer like Edith Head who did the best gowns for movie stars. Her name was always on the credits at the end of the movies. Bobby Ann said I was a nut case, because nobody stayed and read the credits, but I had to know her name.

Mom said to try water paints instead of crayons because it's what she liked to paint with. But the brush hairs fell out, or the bristles got all bent up from sitting too long in the glass of water. Water paints soaked my drawing paper. When the paper dried, it curled up. Then I had to iron it. Then I burned it. So I just used crayons. And I didn't heat my crayon drawings up with the iron no more neither. It stank and made a mess. Mom had to pin another old sheet on the ironing board before she could use it again.

Crap! Someone was opening the apartment door and coming down the hall. I laid my head down on the bedroom floor and pretended to be asleep.

"Hey, Miss Prim!" Eddie called to me. "Ya better get your butt downstairs so we can eat. Pronto! The old man wants to know where you are."

"I'm not hungry." I rolled over on my back, stretched and gave a big, pretend yawn. I rubbed my eyes like Ida Lupino would do. "Tell him I'm sleeping."

"C'mon, faker. He won't buy that crap," Eddie said. "Get

downstairs. The old lady finally got home and made some food. Guests are waiting." He turned to go down the hallway.

"Eddie, wait!" I called. "What's white trash?"

"What?" He scrunched his eyebrows down and stared at me. "Where'd ya hear that?"

"Umm, in a movie."

"Well," he came back into my room, sat on the edge of my bed, pushing aside my covers. "It's like this. We got coloreds and we got niggers. Coloreds are good and niggers ain't. White trash is like being a nigger."

"White people are niggers?"

"Can be," he said.

"I don't get it. What's white trash?"

"They're white people who don't work, or drunks, who steal, beat their wives and their kids, and they live like slobs in filthy houses."

"Is that why coloreds don't like being called niggers?"

"Yeah. Now let's get down to supper before the bull starts bellowin' for both of us."

I giggled at the picture of my father bellowing like a bull.

"Eddie!" I called, as he got up to leave. "Pop beats Mom and Andy, right?"

"Yeah, sometimes."

"And Andy stole some of Mom's jewelry once, and Mom and Pop drink a lot."

"Yeah. So?"

"And Mom says I'm a slob."

"Yeah. What in hell are you getting at?"

"Well . . . are we white trash?"

Eddie's face wrinkled like he had a sudden gas pain. His eyes looked sad. He said, "You should stay outta those friggin' movies, ya know that? You learn too much."

"Well, are we, Eddie?" I just had to know if Ann Marie's mother was right.

"No, Brat. We ain't. Besides, we umm . . ." he stopped a minute, "we go to church and white trash don't go to church."

"There ain't no white trash Catholics?"

"Yes, no. Jesus Christ!" he snapped. "It's too hard to explain. Wait till you get older. Then ya'll understand."

Jeez, Louise. I didn't want to wait for answers. I had other ways to find out. I'd look in the huge dictionary at school.

My stomach growled when I got up. "Okay, Eddie. I'm hungry. Let's go eat." I reached up for his hand and we went downstairs to dinner. Halfway down, I asked, "Eddie, do niggers go to colored people's churches?"

"Good Christ, Judy! Shut up already, will ya?" He ran down the rest of the stairs alone. "I answered all the questions I'm gonna answer tonight." He shoved the door open to the bar. Holding it for me, I ran past him, through the bar and into the dinning room. I bounced up into my seat. Pop began to say grace. "Bless us . . . ." I looked over at Eddie and thought that he ain't telling me everything. If I can't find "white trash" in the dictionary, I'll ask Lina, or Bobby Ann. And I'll keep asking till I know for sure what it really means.

Because God Made Thee Mine!

*The suspicious mind believes more than it doubts.
It believes in a formidable and ineradicable evil lurking in every person.*

Eric Hoffer

The cigarette and cigar smoke circled and dipped around the heads of people sitting at tables and at the bar. Pop decided to take the shuffleboard out of the barroom and put it in the dining room to make space for some tables and chairs. Everybody wanted to play the pinball machine or darts. There was now a dartboard on the wall by the kitchen and Pop held contests to see who was the best dart thrower. He had the jukebox guy bring out a pinball machine, too. He also rolled the piano out of the dining room into the bar for local musicians to use, or whoever dropped in. Mom and he stopped serving dinners and instead sold huge roast beef, or ham sandwiches on hard rolls, and for a while, they even made pizzas. That made Mom real happy. Now, she only had to make Sunday dinner because Pop insisted on having 'one decent meal a week.'

The bar was packed tonight and it wasn't even a full moon. The gray-white cigarette smoke went zipping out through the open door as three soldiers on leave came in for drinks. One soldier asked, "Hey Ed? You sing, right? D'ya know "Because?" It was my mom's favorite."

Only too willing to comply, Pop asked Gil Kelder, who was sitting at the bar to accompany him on the piano. Gil was glad to oblige and ran through a couple of lines of the sheet music, getting in the right scale for Pop's tenor voice. Chris and Ceebee Raisner got up to dance once it looked like Pop was ready to sing. The Raisner's once were silver cup dancing partners, and moved like ice skaters across the floor when they danced. I wanted to move like they did, which is why I once got Ceebee to teach me some steps.

Pop sprinkled leftover shuffleboard wax around their feet. It helped them slide on the floor, and then he began to sing, *"Be-cause you come to me—with naught save love, —And hold my hand and lift mine eyes above . . . ."* Pop turned up the volume on his voice and drowned out all the talking at the bar. Everyone's attention was on him as he went for the high notes, *"Be-cause you come to m-e . . !"* The bottles on the back bar vibrated.

Ceebee was as skinny as a rail. Even her hair was skinny. She wore a piece of material around her head like old-time flappers did. It held the wispy sweat-soaked strands of hair in place as she danced. She looked like a rich lady when she glided across the floor, even though her faded cotton flowered dress hung like a bag on her bony body. She stood tall, staying up on the balls of her feet, never losing her balance, and was in perfect timing with her husband. How she could move in those canvas sling-back wedges' with the crepe soles to a waltz, or to do the Peabody was a miracle.

Everybody knew her husband Chris used to be a boxer. He had muscles like knotted-up ropes, a large head, thick eyebrows, a bent nose, big knotty knuckles on thick fists, and broad shoulders. You wouldn't think he could move and dance like he did. Ceebee and Chris looked young, like Marge and Gower Champion, when they danced.

Pop could out-sing Mario Lanza any day, and he competed with Caruso from the records I heard. He either entertained or annoyed our neighbors, depending on how early they went to bed, or how close they lived. In the summertime, he could be heard singing five houses up or down either side of Main Street. Some neighbors sat on their porches and listened. More than once someone called the bar and asked if "Big Ed" would sing, "When Irish Eyes Are

Smiling," or some other song, and he did, sometimes going outside on the front patio.

Marge and Bill Russell were sitting at the bar tonight. They lived two houses up from us. They gave up listening from their porch and became regular customers. "Why sit in the back row," Bill said, "when you can have a ringside seat and a cold beer to boot?"

"Be-cause you speak to me in ac-cents sweet," Pop sang, smiled and winked at Kay Werber, which she took as an invitation to add her soprano voice to his. She was the flaming redhead who plopped her butt next to Pop at the Communion rail last Easter Sunday. Bill Kelly said she was built like a brick shit house, and that he'd love to lay some bricks.

Tonight Kay wore her Irish green satin suit with green suede platform shoes buckled around her ankle looking like a movie star. With half-closed eyes and bright red kissy lips, Kay joined Pop and sang to him, *"I find the rose-es wak-ing round my feet...."* They stood side-by-side singing together, staring into each other's eyes.

They continued, *"And I am led through tears and joy to thee, Be-cause you speak to me...!"*

"Speak to him," Mom muttered, "anything else and I'll wrap roses on your grave."

I giggled.

Pop's arm went around Kay's shoulder and her arm went around his waist. They looked at their audience and continued, *"Be-cause God made thee mine, I'll cher-ish the-ee—...*

"And if God makes them a pair, they won't be cherishing anything," Mom said, to no one in particular.

Uncle Ernie, her brother who sat next to Georgie Claus said, "Now, Edie, just take it easy. Ya don't want to start anything. They're just singing. Entertainin' us. That's all."

"Well, it's the idea of them entertaining each other that's lighting my fire," she snipped at her brother.

Oh, boy! She's pouring herself another drink. I bet there's an argument after the bar closes, if she doesn't get drunk enough to forget. Maybe Big Jim Mehan the cowboy guitar player will stop in and give her special attention like he always does, and she'll forget about Kay.

Pop and Kay turned to face each other, clasping hands. They held them chest-high, like movie actors in a musical. Looking into each other's eyes, they finished the last lines of the song, *"And pray His love may make our love di-vine,"* their voices rose together to high G for the finale, *"Be-cause God made thee mine!"*

Ceebee and Chris twirled around and around in front of Pop and Kay. Chris bent all ninety-five pounds of Ceebee into a backward dip two inches from the floor. All four bowed, smiled, curtsied to applause, hoots, and whistles.

It was so exciting! Better than Kathryn Grayson. Better than Howard Keel. Better than Betty Grable, or Ann Miller, or Judy Garland and Fred Astaire! Everyone clapped or whistled their approval. I clapped till my hands were red and stinging.

Pop caught the squint-eyed, tight-lipped look on Mom's face. He knew he better get his butt back behind the bar and take care of business. He took his handkerchief, mopped sweat from his brow and Kay's lipstick from his lips. She had planted one on him by surprise at the end of the song.

Pop went behind the bar and behind Mom, letting his hand slide across her girdled ass. He grabbed the Canadian Club whiskey bottle, poured a shot over ice and walked over to the cooler to pull out a cold ginger ale to top off his shot. He looked at his watch, lifted the plastic stirrer from his drink, and sucked off the liquor, then looked at me in that way that said, "Show's over." It was time to jump off the bar stool, squeeze through the people, and get my tail up to bed.

On Being Invisible

*"Starlight, star bright, first star I see tonight
I wish I may, I wish I might,
become invisible tonight."*

Judith A. Boggess

To be invisible and a spy is what I wanted. The spy part was easy. It was the invisible part I had a hard time with. I wished on the first star of the evening, looked for four-leaf clovers in the Rosenkranses' lawn, prayed to Jesus and promised not to swear. Nothing turned me invisible. Not even being good for one whole day.

For weeks I practiced sneaking up on Mom in her bedroom while she was putting on her girdle and makeup. She gained thirty pounds over the last couple of years, and would send me to Doc's to buy Ayds. They came in a candy box and looked like chocolate candies. Once I sneaked some and had the runs for several days. Mom told me to stay outta her stuff. These "candies" were for losing weight.

When her candies didn't work Mom had me go buy a Playtex rubber girdle at Doc's. She was too embarrassed to do it and be seen. It was something to see her wriggle into one. The girdle looked like a piece cut out of a thick white inner tube with pinholes punched all over. It was so tight she couldn't wear underpants underneath. Besides once you had this thing on, you weren't gonna take it off to go pee.

Mom couldn't get it pulled up unless she used cornstarch to powder herself first and then powder the girdle second. Next, she rolled the girdle down like the top of her stocking before putting her foot into it. Rolled, it looked like a fat circle of white pastry. Being very careful, she stepped into the center of the circle of rubber with both feet. She grabbed hold of it and wiggled it up past her knees before unrolling it. Halfway up her thighs she poured on more corn starch. It looked like the girdle was going to crush her thighbones. But this last bit of powdering did the trick. I couldn't believe how she had to jiggle around, push and pull at her skin on her stomach and her fanny, as the girdle slowly unrolled up over her privates. Beads of sweat were on her face from trying to force all of herself into this not-too-stretchy tube. I felt out of breath watching. She looked like an overcooked bratwurst ready to explode. For all her hard work Mom got a flat stomach, but it also made her butt look like a board, which was how you could tell she had a girdle on.

When business was slow she went upstairs, peeled the girdle off, and laid it inside-out on the towel bar in the bathroom because it was wet with sweat. Red lines marked her stomach and fanny, and white streaks of corn starch stuck in the creases of her skin, which was all pinched in from being stuck in the rubber girdle. She always said, "Ahhhh!" when she pulled it off.

When she caught my reflection in her mirror, she told me to get lost and don't watch her ever again. That's when I started looking into a hand mirror, over my shoulder. It was a trick for seeing around corners I saw in a G-man movie.

It got boring spying on Mom, so I decided to follow Eddie. He was in the bathroom putting butch wax on his hair to make it stick up like a bristle scrub brush. The bathroom stank of Aqua Velva, which Eddie bought because Pop told him to stop taking a bath in his Old Spice and to leave some for him.

I knew I had to follow Eddie when he left the bar carrying a big empty mayonnaise jar over to Dickey Rosenkranse's house. About three minutes they both came out laughing and punching each other in the arm. Eddie was still carrying the jar. What are they gonna do with it?

They headed out to Main Street. I hid behind the catalpa tree until I couldn't see them any more. No good spy gets too close. It was so easy to follow them. I scooted behind hedges and ducked between cars. At Doc Vaughn's, Eddie got a few more of his friends to go with him to Gilmartin's. They crossed the street and stood in the driveway between the luncheonette and the Reformed Church. Eddie went inside and came out with four more guys.

It was getting dark. How was I gonna watch them from the street? If I think invisible, I'll become invisible. Even though I could see me, maybe Eddie and his friends wouldn't be able to. Pressing my back up against the brick of the church, I flattened my body as tight to it as I could. Moving in teeny steps, I came around the side of the church. Most of the boys were facing away from my direction.

They were making a circle. Some were smoking cigarettes. I recognized all of them.

If I could make it to the side alcove of the church and up a couple of stairs, I'd be in total blackness. Breathing real shallow, I moved as if I was in slow motion. I'm invisible. No one can see me. I'm a spy, the Mata Hari of Rosendale. I'll never get caught. To get caught is death, I thought. I hid in the shadows of the stairway. Hot diggity dog, I did it! They don't see me!

Just in time, too, because Dickey left the circle and walked toward Main Street. He looked up and down and came back. "Coast is clear," he told Eddie.

This was some sort of signal because all the boys unzipped their pants and took out their peckers.

Shit! Holy Shit! I clamped my hand over my mouth. Oh, my gawd. Bobby Ann ain't gonna believe this!

It was pretty dark, but I could see Eddie. He pulled out a tape measure he must've stole from Mom's sewing box. Wait till she finds out what he's doing with it!

Someone else had a pencil and paper. Each guy measured his limp dick and wrote down the number. Then they began pumping them up. They grew bigger and stiffer. They were giving themselves hard-ons! Is watching a sin? Am I gonna have to tell this in Confession? Each guy measured himself once more and wrote on the paper.

"What we gonna do with these, Ed?" someone asked, shaking his hard-on at Eddie.

"That's what this jar is for, stupid!" Eddie laughed.

They squeezed into a tighter circle. Moaning, groaning, rooting for themselves, they jerked off, passing the jug from one jerking-off guy to the other.

Oh, yuck! Double yuck! I'm gonna be sick! Boys are so disgusting!

Soon they were finished, laughing, slapping, and punching at each other. All but Kenny Post, who was now stuck holding the jar. He said he couldn't do it with everybody watching. I was so glad when the rest of the guys zipped up their jeans and went into Gilmartin's to have Cokes, or whatever, leaving Kenny to do what he had to do. Now I wished Kenny would hurry up and get done. It took thirty-seconds or so for the other guys. But you could see by the look on Kenny's face this was gonna take until Doomsday.

He finally finished, or else he gave up, left the jar by the side of the building and went inside to join the others. I was glad he was done and came out of the shadows, sneaked over and examined the jar. Afraid to touch it, but curious, I picked it up. It felt warm. I looked into it. It smelled awful. Phewy! It had cigarette butts floating on some goopy-looking white glop. Eeeeewwwww!

The back door of the luncheonette opened and slammed shut. Jack Gilmartin was dumping trash into a large garbage pail when he spotted me.

"Who's there? Hey Cherny, whadda you doing out here? You with your brother?"

"Yes, Mr. Gilmartin. He has to come home soon. Pop said so."

"Okay. Well, get on now. Hey! Don't put that jar there. You take it with you."

"But it ain't mine. It was here. I was just looking at it."

"Yeah. Well just look at it some more. Get and take your garbage with you before I call your father."

Oh, shit! Now what am I gonna do? Oh, screw me!

I scrunched up my face and carried the jar as far away from my body as I could. How do I get invisible and stay that way? Everything I do gets all messed up. Maybe God's smart not making me invisible. What am I supposed to do with this stinking jar? I mumbled to myself all the way down the street to the bar. Ah! T'hell with it, I thought and hugged the jar to me. When I got to our driveway, I put it next to the chimney. Right next to Pop's car! Right where he'd see it tomorrow. Ha! Double ha! Let Pop figure out what's in it, and let Eddie figure out how it got there. Ha! Ha! Ha! Mata Hari strikes again!

Bowling Lies

A little inaccuracy sometimes saves tons of explanation.
Saki

Mom and Pop bowled on leagues and took turns having a night out at Gene and Harriet Mulligan's place, The Chalet. It was a large building that housed a bar, a reception hall, a chef's kitchen, plus the bowling alley of six lanes.

Pop and Mom never hurried home after their league finished playing. Mom bowled on Tuesday, and Pop bowled on Wednesday. It didn't matter if they were on the early shift, or the late shift. Whenever either of them came home, it was always after our bar closed for the night. It sometimes felt like they tried to outdo each other each week. Mom came home at one in the morning and Pop came in at two. The next week she came in at three and he came in at four. The morning Pop came in at six was not good.

After closing our bar, Mom sat drinking with "Tiny" Ray Williams, who got his name as a joke because he was six feet four or more, and weighed over two hundred pounds.

The sun was lighting up the morning sky when Pop's car pulled into the driveway. The crunch of gravel under his tires beneath my window woke me up. I looked out my window, saw it was Pop, and looked at my clock. This was a really late bowling night for him. I tiptoed down the hall. Mom wasn't in bed. Uh, oh. I bet she was lying in wait for him downstairs. I opened the apartment door a crack and saw Pop closing the middle outside door. He put his keys in his pocket and reached for the banister. He made it up the first step, when the swinging door to the bar opened and Mom came into the foyer.

With Pop I could never tell if he was drunk unless he punched a hole in the wall when it got in his way. Sometimes he got Red Skelton's goofy Clem Kadiddlehopper look on his face. Most times, he was in a good mood.

Mom, on the other hand, who would down a bottle of scotch when she was pissed, would get really nasty, have a crying jag, or both. Pop said when she drank it was like priming a muzzleloader. You never knew where the lead ball would hit. This morning she was in a fighting mood. Pop kept climbing the stairs.

"Who was she tonight?" Mom asked.

No answer.

"Do you know what it's like having one of your filthy whores call up and say, 'D'ya know where Ed is tonight? *I* do,' and then she hangs up?"

In Rosendale, no one was beyond lies. Lying was a way of life. There are many types of lies: white lies, slight untruths, fish stories, bullshit stories, and "lies of omission," which were Catholic lies.

You either got rewarded or you got punished, depending on who was judging and who was doing the lying. Most lies, I thought, were a little bit of each type. Like when Floydy said he drove between the sycamores so he wouldn't crash his car and that's how he ended up in the river. Everyone in the bar laughed and he got rewarded with a shot of Wild Turkey. Floydy's lie was part white lie and part bullshit story. But because nobody was hurt, he got rewarded.

Pop told lies by omission and bold-faced lies. When Mom asked him what he was doing out till six in the morning, he said, "Bowling."

Boy, he sure knew how to wind her up.

Pop turned around when he got to the top of the stairs. He saw Tiny standing beside Mom.

"Where were you?" Mom yelled, and charged part-way up the stairs.

Tiny reached out and grabbed her wrist trying to pull her back. "Edie, don't," Tiny said. "Yer just askin' for trouble."

"Get your hands off me, Ray!" Mom shouted. She twisted and jerked his thumb off her wrist.

"Shit, Edie!" Tiny yelled. "Ya just broke my fuckin' thumb!"

"I did not."

"Ya fuckin' did too! He yelped. "It snapped. Ya bent it backwards. It's broken," he cried.

I poked my face out the door some more. Tiny had turned white and was hurting.

Pop smirked. He stepped inside the apartment, leaving Mom and Tiny standing on the stairs looking at the broke thumb. Pop saw me scrunched up against the wall. "Ya miss anything?" he asked.

I shook my head no.

"Shhh," he said, putting a finger to his lips. "Let's listen."

He left the door ajar so I could see and hear as I stood in front of him.

"Shit, Edie." Tiny said, "what am I gonna do now. My thumb's broke. Look at it."

Pop looked at me, made a face, and mouthed, "Poor baby."

I stifled a giggle.

"Oh, stop your bawling and let's put some ice on it," Mom said, heading back down to the bar. "I'll drive you up to Doc Galvin."

Pop closed the door. "Okay. Get in bed. I'll tuck you in, in a minute."

He walked me down to my room, turned and went into the bathroom.

Didn't seem much sense going back to bed since I have to get up again in an hour for school, but being tucked in by Pop was something I liked and he liked to do.

But first, I ran to my window to watch Mom and Tiny getting into our Chevy. When they backed out of the driveway, I heard Pop flush the toilet, and I jumped into bed.

It was good Mom broke Tiny's thumb and couldn't argue with Pop all morning and make my stomach sick. I hope when she comes back I'm gone for school. If not, I hope Pop is asleep.

The Red Coat

"Buy not what you want, but what you have need of..."

Cato

Mom came out of the kitchen carrying coffee for Pop. Before she got to the bar she said to his back, "I need money." She set the cup on the bar next to where he was reading the newspaper. He didn't look up. He turned the page of the *Daily Mirror* like he didn't hear, looked at the photos and read a little more before flipping the page. He slid the coffee across the worn mahogany bar top, shifted his butt on the stool, and took a sip.

"I need money," Mom said again a little louder. She made it sound like a demand.

I watched from my seat next to Pop when he turned to the horoscopes. He ran his finger down the column mumbling, "Scorpio... Scorpio..." until he reached his sign. "How much ya need?" he asked. He wet the end of his finger to turn the page to the horse racing section to see if the numbers he bet on had won. He played the same numbers every day with his bookie. The first few numbers of the total money taken in on the horse race the day before was the winning number for the next day.

"Shit," he muttered. He didn't win. He flipped back and read Mom's horoscope. "Pisces... Pisces... have fun tonight."

"Ho, boy," he said.

"I don't know how much I need," Mom said.

"Well, whadda ya buying?"

"Snowsuits. Boots. Gloves for Mickey and Judy."

"For Chrissakes!" he grumbled. "Can't it wait a few weeks? It's almost Christmas."

"It's snowing now. They need them."

"What's wrong with the ones from last year?"

"Kids grow."

"Ya gonna drive on slushy roads? It's gonna freeze."

Mom glared at him. She went through this begging stuff every time she wanted to go shopping. "Getting money out of your father is like pulling hen's teeth," she often said. Today she said she had cabin fever and needed to get out for the day. Winter came too soon this year. There was snow on the ground before Thanksgiving, and the only ones happy about it were deer hunters and kids. She was in a bad mood. I could tell by her face, but she never said what was on her mind, at least not to Pop. He always said she stuffed anger and waited till she was drunk to throw the brickbats.

He looked her up and down. "Yer pretty dressed up for shoppin' in that slop out there, ain't ya?"

She didn't answer.

Pop peeled off crisp ten and twenty-dollar bills from the roll he pulled from his pants pocket. He snapped the new bills out one by one onto the bar top. Older bills would tear in half. He re-rolled his wad and wrapped it with his wide rubber band.

Pop fast figured how much money Mom would need and gave her five extra dollars. "Put some gas in the car. I don't want to drive to church on fumes tomorrow. And bring back receipts."

Mom snatched up the bills from the bar, counted them and walked to the kitchen. "Can you afford it?" she mumbled.

Pop ignored her, grabbed a second newspaper the *Daily News*, and looked up the weather forecast. He put his elbows on the bar, ran the palms of his hands up and over his face, and buried his fingers in his hair.

"Oh, gawd," he moaned in a hushed voice, "full moon tonight. No friggin' way she'll be back sober."

Mickey finished eating cinnamon toast and drinking his Hershey's chocolate milk at the kitchen table. Mom picked up her beige cashmere coat with the blonde fluffy fox collar.

Pop called to me. He handed me a dollar and said to buy myself something at Fanny Farmer's candy store. "And," he added, "make sure your mother doesn't get tied up in no bar."

I shook my head and ran to grab my coat and boots. Mom was heading out when Pop asked her, "How the hell ya gonna buy 'em snowsuits if the kids ain't with ya?"

"I know their sizes," she snapped.

"Yeah?" he said, getting up from the bar. He took several steps toward the kitchen. His body blocked the doorway. "I don't mind watchin' him," he said, pointing to Mickey, "but you're takin' her." He jerked his head in my direction.

She glared at me. "Get your coat, now!"

I shoved my feet into my galoshes, grabbed my coat and hat and started to hurry out the door behind her. Mickey's eyes were wide. He looked like he was about to cry because I was leaving. "Don't cry, Spud. I be back. Want me buy you candy?" He said okay, but his face wasn't happy.

Mom was gunning the engine of the car like Pop told her never to do on cold days. I barely closed the car door when she slammed the shifter into reverse and backed up real fast out into Main Street. Pop told her not to do that neither, because you can't see cars coming with the snow banks in the way.

"Who the hell does he think he is, King Tut?" Mom griped. "Moylan will have to sew extra pockets on his pants when he dies so he can take his money with him."

She backed up, turning the steering wheel hard right, and the car squished and slid its way around in the direction of Kingston. She hit the brake hard. Still sliding backwards on soupy slush, she shoved the shifter into first gear with a horrible grinding sound. She stomped the gas pedal when Pop came out the front door of the bar, yelling curses and waving his fist in the air.

"Go to hell!" she yelled at him, which I'm sure he couldn't hear because the windows were rolled up and the heater was blowing.

Mom sped off throwing slush up under the fenders, while the

rear end slipped side-to-side. I grabbed the armrest and hung on, as her driving was scary.

In Kingston, Mom parked on the steep hill beside Montgomery Wards department store. Inside Wards, she went right for the sale rack. There wasn't much to choose from. All the best outfits went by Thanksgiving. Mom pushed and shoved around the coats, snow-pants, and snowsuits hanging on hangers. She grabbed one in Mickey's size and handed me another. "Here," she said. "Go try this on while I grab some gloves and hats. Don't worry if it's a little large. You can get two seasons out of it."

"I hate it," I said. It was an ugly, shiny, copper penny color. Yuck! Puke! I wanted the red wool coat with the shiny black buttons and black velvet trim and skinny waist. It had a muff with fur inside of it, red leggings, and a bonnet-type hat.

"Good, hate it. It's good enough to go sleigh riding in. Besides, it's all your cheap father can afford. Try it on."

I sat on the dressing room floor and took my good old time unsnapping the buckles on each boot. She asked what I was doing. Then I took my old sweet time putting the snowsuit on. Ugh! I thought as I looked in the mirror. My legs and arms looked like puffed-up sick hot dogs that floated in a pot of greasy water overnight and got all blown up.

Mom stuck her head in and said, "It looks great. Try these boots on."

Brown rubber pull-on boots, phooey! I was happy they were pull-ons, but I wanted red ones.

"Okay," she said. "Take everything off. Let's go." And before I could say anything she added, "If you don't take everything, you'll get nothing."

"All right." I pouted. "But I hate all of it. I look like a toasted marshmallow." And, I thought, this dumb snowsuit can rot in my closet for all I care.

In an hour, she got what she came for; boots, snowsuits, hats, and gloves for Mickey and me. All on sale. She asked for and got Uncle Andrew's discount. She had the clerk leave the original price tags on the clothing, crumpled up the paper receipt with the sale price and put it in a tissue in her pocket book.

She saw me staring at her. "What?" She asked. "Look, what he doesn't know won't give him indigestion. Now we have money to get lunch."

I didn't want to lie to Pop. Most of the time I didn't have to because he didn't ask me the right questions. I hoped he'll show me the tags on the snowsuit and say, "Is this what the snowsuit cost?" And I'll shake my head yes, because he didn't ask if it was what she paid.

We left the store with our bundles. "We'll go eat after we put the bags in the trunk," she said.

The bundles got locked in the trunk. She took my hand and we walked up the hill to North Front Street. She had to watch where she was going to miss the puddles of melted snow. She wore thin zip-up rubber boots over her high heels, but her toes must be freezing because she wore nylons and no socks. We walked to a cut-out in a snow bank and into the road. A car slowed and the driver waved us across. Mom flashed a toothy smile. He tipped his hat. We got up on the sidewalk in front of Fanny Farmer's. I liked looking at all the boxes of candy stacked up in rows across the window. I wanted to spend my dollar and get Mickey and me something.

"Later, after lunch," Mom said.

We argued. I knew if she got her way, later wouldn't never come.

She won.

We walked to Artie's Bar & Grill. Mom reached for the door handle. The smell of stale beer and cigarette smoke hit us as she pulled open the front door.

"You said we were gonna go eat." I said. I planted my feet and pulled backward on her arm.

"We can eat here." She jerked my hand and pulled me into the stinking bar. My eyes had trouble seeing in the dark. This place was gloomy. I wondered if it was a dive like in the movies where gangsters hung out. On the juke box Nat King Cole sang, "Too Young."

A voice boomed out from some guy sitting on a barstool. "Hey, Edie! How the hell ya been, Babe? Long time no see. Where ya been hiding, gorgeous? Hey! Artie? Give Edie a drink, will ya?"

He looked familiar, but I didn't remember his name. Mom sat

on a barstool beside this strange guy and he put his arm around her shoulder and planted a sloppy kiss on her lips. Oh, gag, gag! Then he took her coat and hung it up on a hook.

This skinny creep stuck his nose in Mom's neck and said, "Gawd, Edie, you smell good. I could eat you right here." Mom giggled like a kid and play-shoved him away. My stomach knotted up.

Kids weren't supposed to sit at a bar, so I stood looking up at her and this man slobbering all over her. I wasn't going to sit on the footrest in the dirt from the street like at the Astoria.

"What'll it be, Edie?" Artie asked. "The usual . . . Cutty and water?"

Mom nodded. She always said all she needed was a couple of bucks admission fee to buy one drink, and then guys would buy for her all night. Today she didn't even need that. This guy was real glad to be setting her up.

Artie poured the scotch over the ice in the glass and stopped when he felt it was one shot. He picked up a pitcher of water and filled the glass to the top. The strange man paid Artie for her drink.

I yanked on Mom's dress. "I'm hungry."

"Artie, make her a ham sandwich and give her a soda will you?"

"Sure thing, Edie. Hey, kid? You wanna Shirley Temple?"

"No."

"Ah, sure ya do. Gowan siddown over there and I'll make ya something."

I sat and watched. Mom didn't eat anything. She laughed and talked with the stranger and Artie. I watched the stranger stand up and get closer to Mom. His hand rubbed her back. She threw her head back and let out a loud laugh, and then laid her head on his shoulder. His hand wrapped tight around her waist as he pulled her into his chest with a big hug. He kissed her whenever he could sneak one in. She didn't stop him. My insides felt gooky. Maybe it was from the four, or was it five, Shirley Temples I drank. Maybe it was all the maraschino cherries I ate. Artie gave me two in every soda. I didn't like them, but I ate them anyway. The jukebox was playing this stupid song, "I saw Mommy kissing Santa Claus," while I watched my Mommy kissing a drunk.

I turned and stared out the bar window watching people walk

by. I hated Shirley Temple, and Shirley Temple sodas, and I wasn't drinking any more of them, I told myself. What I really, really hated was my snowsuit, along with being here in this bar. But most of all, I really hated Mom's drinking.

The full moon came up in the sky before the sun finished going down. Puddles on the road were icing over. People walking by the window had their coats pulled up to their ears and scarves wrapped around their faces. Cold blasts of air moved around my legs whenever anyone came in or left the bar.

It was after nine o'clock and Artie's was almost empty. Stores were closed. Lights turned off. No one was walking past anymore. I knew Fanny Farmer's was closed, too. I'd have to go to Gilmartin's tomorrow to buy Mickey candy to keep my promise to him. Oh, not again, I thought as I turned and saw Artie pour another drink for Mom. I wanted to leave. Pop was going to hit the frigging ceiling and yell at me for letting her get drunk.

I went over and pulled on her dress. "I'm hungry," I said.

"You just ate."

"That was lunch. It's suppertime. Let's go. Mickey has to be fed."

"Your father can do that."

"Let's go. Pleeze? I want to leave!"

"Inna min-it," she answered. "Inna min-it."

Christmas Pageant

Starlight, star bright . . .
Don't let her drink and come to the pageant tonight.

Judith A. Boggess

We were practicing for the Christmas pageant in the school's basement. Mothers, fathers, and other relatives and friends came to see and hear us kids sing carols and to see who got what part in the Nativity play. I wondered if I'd ever be anything besides someone in the chorus.

Christine said we weren't holy enough or good enough to play Mary or even a shepherd. "Maybe we could get to be cows next year," she laughed, knowing there aren't any in the play. "Besides, singing's easier than rememberin' all them lines."

I looked around at who was playing the speaking parts. She was right. It was the good kids from the good families, like Veronica Muth who got to be Mary. Christine was smart.

How could I get Mom and Pop to come if all I was doing was singing? They'd say they heard the songs before. It wasn't like I had a solo part. Even those went to the teachers' pets. The last day of practice, Sister gave us a mimeographed reminder to give to our parents asking them to come. I gave it to Pop, but he said, "Can't go. Somebody's gotta watch the bar. Ask your mother."

I handed the paper to Mom, and she said, "We'll see."

She never said yes. It's always maybe or we'll see. If something fun was happening at the bar, neither of them would show up.

The night of the pageant, Pete and Nicky's parents came. Even Eleanor's mother came. People piled in, and the lights in the basement were turned off. The stage lights and the exit door light at the back of the room were the only ones left on. We started singing, and Mom walked in with Lina. Mom stood in the back leaning against the wall while Lina went and sat down. A man tried to show Mom to a chair. She refused. She must have driven as she wouldn't risk getting those suede high heels wet from the slush on the sidewalk. I wondered what bar she stopped at on the way. She couldn't pass the Astoria without popping in for a "quick one." Lina waved at me and nodded her head toward Mom as if to say, "She's here." Whoopee! Maybe Mom should have stayed home.

Mom looked pretty in the long black seal fur coat Pop bought for her in Canada on his last fishing trip. No other mothers had a coat like that. I could see her long dangling rhinestone earrings flickering. Her rhinestone necklace and bracelet sparkled whenever they caught the light coming from the back door. She didn't look like the other mothers. She looked more like Lana Turner or Veronica Lake. The other mothers were plain and old-fashioned, except for Timmy's mother, Kay. Did he mind how his mother looked in her tight suit, with a fur wrap around her shoulders, and her long, flaming red hair? I wondered if her color came out of a bottle.

When the show was over Lina said, "You were great. I could hear your voice above the rest of the kids."

"Really?" I said. She embarrassed me but made me happy at the same time.

Mom was standing by the punch bowl talking to Mrs. Banach. "Is the punch spiked?" Mom asked.

"God, no, Edie," Helen Banach said, all flustered.

Mom laughed out loud. The ceiling in the basement was really low, and her laughter bounced off it, up and over all of our heads like a thousand Ping-Pong balls. People stopped talking, turned, and looked at her. I could swear the walls moved and pushed everybody in tighter around me.

"Mom, let's go. My stomach hurts."

"Sure," she said, in a loud voice. "Nothing fun's happening here anyway."

"Where's Bobby Ann?" I asked as the three of us squeezed into the front seat of the car. Lina said she was sick and couldn't come. I wondered if it was true.

"We can stop at Mike's and get you a ginger ale. It's good for your stomach," Mom said. "Maybe you're coming down with what Bobby Ann has."

"She feels warm, Edie," Lina said. "Maybe we should get her home."

I didn't have any fever. I was hot from the stage lights and being stuffed in between them. Still, I didn't want to get trapped at Mike's.

"It's the holidays. I'll have one drink and we'll leave."

And pigs fly, I thought.

Mom drove to the Astoria, parked the car.

"C'mon," she said to Lina and me.

"No," I answered.

"What do you mean, 'no'?" she asked.

"I'm going home."

"Suit yourself," she said, getting out into the street. "You coming, Lina?"

"In a sec, Edie," Lina said.

"Fine," Mom said, shutting the car door. She went up the steps to the bar. Her black fur coat shimmered purple in the streetlight.

"Sorry, kid. What are you gonna do?"

"I'm walking home. I ain't sick anyway."

"Yeah, I know." Lina reached over and gave me a big, long hug. "You did good tonight. I'm real proud of you." I looked up at her face. Her eyes didn't look like they were lying.

"Did Mom say she liked it?" I asked.

"I don't know. She didn't . . . I didn't ask her. But she must've," Lina said.

I was glad I decided to dress real warm to walk to the school pageant. Even with boots on, the slush made my toes cold. I puffed out my hot breath like Pop did with his cigarette smoke, and watched it rise up in the air. It hung there for a while before disappearing. I breathed in real deep and used my belly muscles to blow the air back out. I kept breathing in real deep, holding it for as long as I could, and pushing it out with lots of force. I did it over and over till the pain by my heart stretched out and didn't hurt any more.

1952
Rosendale Theatre

Man seeks to escape himself in myth, and does so by any means at his disposal...
Lies and inaccuracy give him a few moments of comfort.

Jean Cocteau

T̲he theater was crowded. *Singin' in the Rain* was playing, with Gene Kelly and Cyd Charisse, and I was so glad it wasn't another Fred Astaire movie. He's ancient. He's a fossil. I liked the word "fossil." I had wondered how long it'd be before Cyd Charisse had to play opposite Fred.

The movie magazine said Fred was 53 or 54. Mom said that was young. She didn't know what she was talking about. But even at his age, Mom said, Fred was still doing a mix of ballroom and tap dance better than anyone else in Hollywood. Dancing was the one thing he had going for him because he sure ain't handsome and rugged like Burt Lancaster or Kirk Douglas.

Fred was skinny as a toothpick, and Kirk Douglas could snap him in half. And Fred's head was shaped like a Vick's cough drop, a triangle, and he ain't got a lot of hair either. Actually, he was a downright plain paper bag. Any woman with an ounce of brains wouldn't give him a second look, no matter how rich he was. Aunt

Helen said that man could put his shoes under her bed any day. Pop said, "If any man had money, they could put their shoes under her bed."

It bothered me that all these beautiful actresses like Ginger Rogers, Eleanor Powell, Rita Hayworth, and soon, probably, Cyd Charisse, had to pretend Fred was good-looking and charming. If I were an actress, they'd have to pay me double to pucker up to him. Ugh! I'd wash my mouth off with a scrub brush and brown lye laundry soap to get his saliva off me.

The lights dimmed. Everyone stopped talking. There was a crackling static sound at the back of the theater coming from the projection room upstairs. "Shhh! Shhh!" I could hear. Kids squirmed in the two front rows of seats near the screen. No adults sat up close because they'd leave with a crick in their neck from looking up.

Tony Cacchio, the owner, walked with quick steps, flashlight in hand, down the left-hand aisle to the front row. He shined his light in our eyes and snapped at us kids, "Quiet or get out." He meant it for everybody, but he always said it to us. His son, Tony Jr., stood on the opposite end of the row with his flashlight ready. He, too, waited for a giggle or a grumble. He was like his father, or he tried to be.

The theater did away with the newsreels, thank God. They were boring old stuff. Lots of people had television sets now and got their news from them. I couldn't wait for the short subjects to bite the dust, too. They were about, "Where to take your family on your next palm-tree-waving-vacation," as if anyone in Rosendale ever went to places like Hawaii. I wanted the cartoons. If I was lucky, maybe there'd be two or more. Maybe one of them would be Casper the Ghost, my favorite. Pop said for the cost of a quarter I shouldn't complain so much. But I came to the movies every night except Tuesday, when the theater was closed, and I was tired of watching the ho-hum stuff twice in a row.

When the movie short came on the screen even some of the adults groaned a "Oh, no!" Tony and his son, the silent guards at the back of the theater, goose-stepped down the aisles like the Gestapo, and everybody shut up.

Crunched sideways in my seat with my neck bent backward

and the armrest cutting into my back, I stared at the giant screen watching the ocean's breaking waves. Happy faces of a mom and dad and their smiley children as they jumped up and down in the water. Someday when I get big, I'll go to the ocean. I'll go by myself and watch the moon go down at night and the sun come up in the morning. A beam of brilliant light hit my eyes. I couldn't see. I thought for a scary second the sun was blinding me.

"Cherny!" I heard my name called out. "Get your feet outta the seat and on the floor. And pick up the candy wrapper. This isn't your personal dump."

I felt heat rise up my neck. I could hear some snickers behind and alongside of me. It wouldn't do any good to tell Tony it wasn't my wrapper on the floor. He wouldn't care. He was so strict he even trained everyone to raise their seats when the show was over so his job of sweeping up the floor was easier. He wouldn't even sell popcorn or soda. He didn't want the mess.

I dropped my feet to the floor and picked up the paper and shoved it into the lap of the kid next to me. "Here," I whispered. "This is yours. It ain't mine." I slumped down, trying to disappear inside myself. Darn Tony. He'd chain kids to their seats and put tape over their mouths if he could. And if it wasn't for the grownups wanting sweets, I bet he wouldn't even have a candy machine.

Tony stopped me after buying my ticket the other night, and said, "What's in the bag you're carrying in here?"

"Candy," I said.

"Well," he said, "if you didn't buy it here, you can't eat it here." What?

Then he said, "Hand over the bag. Get it when you leave."

He was so freakin' mean. His wife most likely couldn't stand him neither. Bet it was why she never smiled or looked up at you when she sold you your ticket. She was fussy, also. It didn't matter if you were a kid or a grownup, if you gave her Canadian coins, or a ripped bill, or one with writing on it, she'd push it right back at you like it was counterfeit. If you handed her a ten-dollar bill she'd shove it back at you, too, with no explanation. Someone in line would say, "She don't break no big bills." If you didn't have anything smaller, you'd have to leave and get change at Gilmartin's. Then

Gilmartin got smart and said he didn't make change neither unless you bought something. And we tried never to ask Tony's wife for change for the candy machines, because she'd say, "What do I look like, the bank? Bring your own change from home."

Tony's whole family must've sucked sour balls before they opened each night. If there was another movie house in town, I'd go and never come back. And then Cyd Charisse was there in high heels, pirouetting around a dance floor. Her full-circle skirt swirled around and up, showing the tops of her thighs. And there was Gene Kelly, twirling an umbrella, getting soakin' wet from tap dancing in the rain. Too soon the music got louder and "The End" flashed across the screen. Everyone clapped. The house lights came on, the applause stopped, and everybody gathered up their stuff and left, after they raised their seats and picked up their garbage off the floor.

Mickey was curled up in a tight ball like a cat in a seat. He fell asleep after the cartoons were over. This wasn't his kind of movie. He liked cowboy-and-Indian stories.

"C'mon, Mick. Put your arms around my neck." He did what he was told without ever opening his eyes.

"Wrap your legs around me," I said as I hitched him up and hooked my hands under his rear. Aw, crap. He peed his pants. The seat was wet. I kicked it up with my foot and hoped I could sneak out without Tony noticing Mickey's wet pants. Tony said, if Mickey wet the seat once more, he couldn't come back. And if Mickey couldn't come, Pop would make me stay home and take care of him.

I lugged Mickey home and upstairs to our room, undressed him, and put him to bed. I'd bring his blankey next time, and if he peed, I'd wrap him up in it before we left the movie house. Tony wouldn't see his wet britches and I wouldn't get my arms all pissy carrying him home.

The Window Shade

*The farmer takes Jill down the well and all the king's horses
and all the king's men can't put that little girl together again
crooked man, crooked man, pumpkin eater,
childhood stealer.*

Sapphire

It used to be fun to run in the summer rain and splash in puddles, and at Bobby Ann's house, stand underneath the rusted-off metal downspout to wash my hair with rainwater. Now I didn't do that anymore because the lightning might get me killed. When it rained I would close my bedroom window no matter how hot it was inside. Aunt Helen always said lightning can come in, hit the metal springs on my bed, and fry my ass like burnt pork.

I wished there was a curtain on my window. But there wasn't even a shade. Some nights when it was raining I'd tack a sheet up so the lightning wouldn't be so bright, and so no man outside could see me getting undressed for bed. Aunt Helen said men were always looking to find someone to have sex with.

"Judy, you can't put a sheet on the window," Mom said. "It doesn't look good from outside."

"Then buy me curtains like Aunt Helen has."

"No."

"Why can't I have curtains with the rubber on the back?"

"You don't need them," she said.

"But I don't want people seeing me when I get undressed. And the lightning scares me, too. Besides, you got curtains on your windows."

"Get undressed in the bathroom," Mom said, ignoring me. "God, you're acting like your looney-toon aunt with all this lightning crap. Just because it hit her door doesn't mean it's going to hit you." She paused for a minute and stared at me. "Oh, all right. I'll give you money to buy a shade."

Mom measured the inside of the window from edge to edge and wrote a few numbers on a piece of scrap paper. Then she went to her bedroom to her secret stash of money in the metal candy tin hidden under her slips in her dresser. When she came back she handed me a five-dollar bill.

"Go to Rossler's Hardware," she said, "and have him cut you a shade to size, and don't spend the change on candy." She folded the paper instructions around the bill and put it in my hand. "And don't lose this, either."

I raced to the hardware store up past the theater. I liked Mr. Rossler's store. It was dark and cool inside and looked messy, but he knew where everything was. He hadn't changed it much from when Mr. Anderson owned it. It smelled of dust that nobody ever tried to clean up.

Mr. Rossler had everything anyone could ever need. There were hammers, screwdrivers, pliers, and crowbars. He had glazier's tacks and putty knives, metal b-x cable for wiring and black electrician's tape, screws, and tacks. There were curtain rods and wooden dowels, shelf brackets, and window locks. He even had doorknobs, hooks and eyes, nuts and bolts, and bins and bins of nails in all different sizes to make your hands all black and greasy-feeling if you played with them. I don't know why he labeled them one-penny, or three-penny nails – I was pretty sure it ain't what he charged.

If I saw something and didn't know what it was used for, he'd tell me. He asked me if I was going to be a carpenter when I grew up. Didn't he know girls couldn't be carpenters? I had asked.

Pop showed me how to use his hand-cranked wood drill. He taught me how to hammer and use the right screwdrivers for different screws.

"You can't always count on a man to do things for you," he said, "and it won't hurt you to know this stuff." Between him and Mr. Rossler, I learned a lot.

Mr. Rossler looked at the measurements and took a white paper shade from the shelf above his head. He blew away some dust. The shade was too wide for my window. Then he put it into a thing-a-ma-jig and hack-sawed off one end. He put the metal cap back on the end of the shade, wrapped a couple rubber bands around the papery part and handed it over to me. He went to the register to make change and write out a receipt.

"Here ya go, Judy. All done. Yer gonna need two brackets to put this up on the window and four nails. I'll put 'em in this bag. Now don't lose 'em going home. Here. Let me put your change and receipt in there, too. Now, if your Mom don't need them brackets, you bring 'em back and I'll give her a refund. And if you don't need those rubber bands, you bring 'em here and I'll give ya a penny."

He walked over to the old wood-and-glass front door with the dented brass knob. As he pulled the door open he said, "Don't run, now, ya hear? You might fall and mess up your new shade." I galloped down Main Street yelling, "Yippy-kai-yah!"

Mom didn't understand why having a shade would make me feel so happy. She didn't understand being scared of lightning, or of men who might be looking up at my window from our driveway. She made fun of me and called me, "Aunt Helen the Second."

The shade lay on my windowsill for days. Every time I asked when it was going to be put up, Mom said, "Go ask your father. He's the one with the hammer."

Then I'd ask Pop and he'd say, "Go ask your mother, she's the one who swings the hammer." Back and forth, I went between them until I gave up. I sat on the floor and cried and talked to my brown rubber baby doll with the painted black eyes

"Hey, cry-baby. What's the matter?" Eddie asked on his way to the bathroom. He had a hot date with Norma Jean that night, and he was gonna take a shower and get dressed up and put on Pop's

Old Spice after-shave lotion. He gave up on Aqua-Velva, especially since Norma told him she liked the way Pop smelled.

I told him about the shade. Without asking, Eddie went to the kitchen and found an old hammer under the sink. Eddie was six feet tall, and had no problem standing on my windowsill to pound in the nails to hold the brackets in place. He put the shade in the slots and jumped down. He pulled on the shade a couple of times to make sure it worked and to show me how to use it. I loved Eddie. He was the best brother in the whole wide world!

"Now," he said, "you do it." The shade was hard to pull down, it easily pulled free from my hand and flew up the window. *Shit!* It went whap! whap! whap! and wrapped itself around the wooden roller. Eddie laughed so hard I thought he'd pee his pants.

"You should see your face," he said, wiping his eyes with the back of his hand. I was frozen to the spot and couldn't take my eyes off the flapping shade. When he calmed down Eddie told me I didn't break it, and climbed up on the sill and pulled it back to where I could reach it.

"You learned something about shades. Nothing to get upset about," he said. I hugged him and kissed his cheek, and he went to get ready for his date.

After scrounging around in the kitchen junk drawer, I found string and a large, old, yellow plastic belt buckle of Mom's. I stuck the string through the hole in the center of the wooden slat at the bottom of the shade, made sure the string was very long and tied the belt buckle to the string. If this flip, flap, wapping shade thing ever happened again, I could get it back down myself.

It took until the next storm to find out the shade didn't keep the lightning out. My room lit up, but not as bright. Even the streetlight still shined through where the side of the shade curled in and didn't quite meet the edge of the window casing. The streetlight laid a purple-white strip of light on the floor in front of my dresser. I pushed my bed into the darkest corner of my room, up against the wall. I didn't want to ever see lightning again, and made sure by sleeping with my face to the wall.

And then, Bobby Ann told me when my Snow White lamp

was on in my room at night, she could see my shadow on the shade from the driveway.

She's got to be lying.

But the next night, as I carried Mickey home from the movies, I looked at Mrs. Fischer's windows and the rest of the homes on the street. If their curtains weren't closed, but their shades were pulled down, you could see them walking around in their living rooms and even in their bedrooms. I started undressing in my closet at night.

The Night

O comfort-killing night, image of hell,
Dim register and notary of shame,
Black stage for tragedies and murders fell,
Vast sin-concealing chaos, nurse of blame!

William Shakespeare

My room was nice and dark. The hall light, which Pop left on so Mickey could see to go to the bathroom, wasn't even shining in my room. I was sleeping with a thin sheet over me because it was warm out. A hand loosened my cover and rolled me over onto my back away from the wall. The jukebox was playing, "I Believe," and sounds of talking and laughing were sliding in and out of my dream. "No," I said pushing away a big hand. "No. Don't." I tried to turn back to face the wall.

"S-h-h-h," a man's voice whispered. "Keep quiet." He had a sour whiskey breath. I thought his words was steam coming from the heater valve. But it couldn't have been. The heat wasn't on.

His hand was down the front of my underpants. His fingers was digging around in my privates. It hurt and I tried to push him away. I got more awake. It wasn't a dream. A tall dark shadow was standing over me. It was hard to breathe. I knew what he was doing wasn't right because Aunt Helen always said, "Never let a man touch you there." But she never told me how to stop him once he was there.

I begged him to leave me alone. He put his other hand over my mouth. His fingers stunk like a dirty ashtray. "I won't hurt ya," he whispered. "Just do what I tell ya." He took his hand off my mouth.

"It burns," I cried. He wet his finger in his mouth and stuck his hand back down on me. I wanted to puke.

"I'm gonna be sick," I cried. He ignored me, wrapped my hand around his private part and pulled my hand back and forth over it. It felt like Grandma DeWitt's dead finger at the funeral parlor. It felt like Andy's dick the time we were looking at Eddie's girlie magazines. But this felt bigger, like a dead turkey neck, and was way scarier.

"Faster," he said. "Move faster."

I did what he said. I prayed the Hail Marys like Aunt Helen and wished I had said the rosary every day instead of only when it was lightning. After a while, his thing went all rubbery. He moaned and let my hand drop. Then he leaned down real close and whispered in my ear, "Don't tell anyone, or I'll say you kissed my dick." He grabbed me by my hair with one hand, rubbed his slimy, fishy-smelling dick across my lips with his other hand. I twisted my head away. He snickered and backed up. I heard him zip up his pants and leave.

I laid there frozen on my bed as he disappeared into the shadows. He must've turned out the hall light before he came into my room, because I couldn't see him leave. I waited for the apartment door to go "click," before I got out of bed and ran to Eddie's room. My brothers weren't home. I went to the apartment door, listened, and then cracked the door open to see who it was. Maybe I dreamed this. But he had turned off the stairwell light, too. It wasn't a dream, and I was too afraid to go out on the landing to switch the light back on. I saw his back as he went through the dining room door that Pop had said to always keep locked.

I washed off the gooey, sticky stuff he squirted on me and rubbed on my mouth and hand. And I washed myself down there to scrub his stink off me. His smell was up in my nose, making me feel sick to my stomach. I wanted to heave, but couldn't. I sneaked into Mom's bedroom and sprayed myself with her Coty's L'Amant perfume and put some of Pop's Vicks up my nose.

The man's nasty stuff dribbled on my blankets and I had to wash it off the best I could with a wet washcloth. Aunt Helen was right, I thought as I cleaned my blanket and my sheet. It's because I didn't have curtains for my window, and I didn't pray the rosary enough.

I couldn't lie down in my bed, it was too scary. I climbed in bed with Mickey, wrapping myself around him. If Pop hollers about it, I'll tell him Mickey was having bad dreams and needed hugging.

Bad Day at Black Rock

There's one thing to be said for this day:
It was lousy.

Judith A. Boggess

Before I went upstairs I asked Pop for a soda. For once, he said okay. He looked good. He was dressed in his belted khaki slacks, a bleached white T-shirt, and spit-shined cordovan wing tips. Pop was proud of his shoes. They were Florsheims. With steel arches. And cost a lot of money. He bought them special at Yallum's on the Strand in Kingston where he got my shoes.

I took my Coke up to my room, dug out my art supplies, and lay on the floor. I wanted to be alone. I had a fear inside me that other people could see by looking at me what happened the other night.

A strapless gown, I thought, grabbing a pencil and a piece of drawing paper. That's what I'll design. I began to trace around my paper doll. Something Susan Hayward or Eleanor Parker would wear to the Academy Awards. Drawing the fold-over tabs in the right places so the gown wouldn't hang cockeyed on my paper doll was important. The high heels, which were colored to match, had to be part of the hem of the dress. Otherwise, the paper shoes would get lost in the cracks between the floorboards.

This gown would be tangerine. Tangerine taffeta. With a big

bow at the bottom of the zipper. I learned if the crayon was rubbed real hard on paper and scraped off, it'd leave a stain making it look like satin. And when I took two crayons and rubbed them real hard at the same time, and took a piece of scrap paper wrapped around my finger and rubbed that, the heat from rubbing turned the dress into two-toned taffeta. Using a pencil eraser and rubbing away certain spots made the dress seem like a light was shining on it. Another trick I knew was to take a piece of sandpaper and put it under my drawing paper, rub with two or three different crayons and ta-da! I had tweed.

Some of my dresses and gowns were made from glued-together scraps of wrapping paper and ribbon, tinsel from the Christmas tree, labels from tin cans, ripped magazine pages, scraps of material and even gummy rings used to patch torn-out loose-leaf paper holes. They were kept with my paper dolls in the nice cigar box Pop had given to me. My crayons and other supplies were in more cigar boxes. Everything was stashed in a larger cardboard box on the floor of my closet.

Andy came in my room. "Get your ass downstairs, now!" He barked. "Pop's looking for ya."

"Fuck off, Andy." I was coloring, trying to finish the big bow. "Tell him to go whistle for me."

"Hey, thief. You better get downstairs," he said.

"Shut up!" I yelled. "So what if I . . . . You don't gotta keep rubbing it in."

Going to Confession got me called a silly child by Father Mulry. And Andy kept making me feel stupid by calling me thief.

"What's the matter, Aunt Helen?"

"I ain't Aunt Helen." I couldn't stand it when he called me that. "Besides you ain't no angel, either."

"Yeah? Well, you look like her," he said. "Yer her kid and nobody told ya yet."

"Am not!" I wanted to throw my box of crayons at his ugly face.

"Fuckin' uppity like her." He stuck his chin out at me. "Why don't ya go live with the old bitch . . .?"

"Get outta my room, Kirk. I'm telling Pop, Kirk!"

He hated being called Kirk Douglas because of his dimpled chin.

"Kiss my ass, Miss Prim."

Can't help it if I learned to do things right from Aunt Helen. I tried to share stuff with my family, but they didn't want to learn anything new. They want to stay ignorant hicks, I guess.

Andy wasn't going to let up until I cried. And I ain't gonna. Not this time.

"Prima Donna," he called me.

"You don't even know what that is."

"Yeah, I do." Andy danced around on tippy toes with his arms up in the air, waving his hand from a limp wrist.

"Faggot!"

"Call me 'faggot' again and I'll punch your lights out," he said, sounding mean like Pop.

Was he gonna hit me? Let 'em try. After what I'd been through. . . I plain didn't care. It might even feel good.

"Fuck you, Andy!" I stood up to face him and gave him two raised middle fingers in the air. I wasn't afraid to face him and I wanted to punch him. Real bad. I want to smash something, anything.

"Wait till I tell Pop you're cursing again."

"Triple fuck you. Ten times, fuck you. I hope he kills you next time he beats you. See if I ever save your ass again."

Andy stormed out of my room and slammed the door to our apartment. I heard him run down the flight of stairs.

Tears dripped to the floor where I was coloring. Why couldn't he leave me alone!

I blew my nose in the bathroom. Andy never cried if he could help it. Even when Pop beat the pulp outta him. He acted like Cagney. Tough guy. "Girls cry," he said. Not him. Actresses blubber all the time for no reason. Even tough broads like Barbara Stanwyck, Joan Crawford, and Bette Davis. If they could do it, so could I.

Sitting up on the sink and watching myself in the mirror, I let out some wails. Gee, I sounded like a fire siren. With my best saddest face, sobbing into the toilet tissue in my hand, I dabbed at the corners of my eyes like Jennifer Jones. After a few more times at being a crying actress, I gave up and blew my nose into the scratchy toilet paper.

Because of the noise I was making, I didn't hear Eddie come home. He stood by the bathroom doorway and clapped. "Brava, Brat! Encore, encore," he said. He laughed, turned away, and went down the hall toward his bedroom.

Arrgggghhh! My brothers were pissing me off! I bolted out of the bathroom, ran downstairs and out the middle door, and made my way over to the barn. I didn't care if Pop wanted me or not.

Lying on my back in the pile of hay, I kicked my feet and arms and pounded the hay until the dust made me choke. It stuck to the sweat on my face and made my nose itch. Who cared? I watched the dust rise up in the light.

Voices from outside were coming closer to the barn. Peeking out a crack, I saw the Rosenkranse's coming toward the door. I wasn't in any mood to be bothered by them and high-tailed it to the top floor to hide out. It didn't scare me to walk across the open rafters to get to the plank by the open hay window. It'd be hard to notice me there.

Sometime ago the older boys tied a heavy rope to one rafter and it hung down into the front room. We tore apart all the hay bales upstairs once we knew for sure that they'd never be used, and spread the hay on the floor below. We pushed the hay into a mound to jump into. I liked climbing up to the second floor, hanging by my knees from the rafters, and letting myself fall down into the hay.

Bobby Ann said I needed my head examined the first day I hung like a bat with my legs bent over a rafter and then let go. "Ya coulda broke your neck!" she yelled. "Don't ya ever think 'fore ya do something?"

Guess not, because Pop always asked me the same question.

Porky shimmied halfway up the rope and held tight. His brother Georgie grabbed the dangling end and ran back and forth swinging him high. With a whoop and a yell Porky let go, flew through the air, and landed in the haystack.

Lying on his back, Porky saw me upstairs and yelled, "Hey, Judy! Whatcha ya doing up there? C'mon down 'n swing."

"No," I said. "Lemme alone."

"Gotta bug up your rear?"

I moved over and sat on the beam over Porky's head, hooked my foot around the rope, and pulled it up to me.

"Hey, give it back," Porky begged.

"Screw you." I didn't know what I was going to do with the rope. I held it and stared down at them. They told me to drop it. I dangled it out of their reach, then pulled it up and held it near the middle. Standing up, I balanced myself across two open beams. Then I jumped. I wrapped my legs around the rope. It burned the inside of my knees and the palms of my hands as I slid down some. My body flew real close to the wall and I used my feet to keep from crashing into it. Back and forth I swung, kicking off from the wall.

This was great! I was better than Tarzan, and lots better than Jane, because she always needed Tarzan's help to swing. I let go, fell into the haystack, stood, throwing both my hands up, giving everyone two "fuck-you" fingers in the air.

"Jeezus Christ!" Eddie said. "You nuts?"

I didn't see him or Dickey come into the barn.

Before Eddie could say more to me, I was up the ladder and across the beams, and had the rope in my hands again. I was gonna show them I wasn't any flash in the pan. My arms felt like they were getting pulled out of their sockets as the rope jerked and then began to swing toward the far wall. My legs and hands burned twice as bad. Again, I kicked off the wall so I wouldn't smash myself up against it. A part of me didn't even care if I crashed into the wall. I swung back and forth a couple times before letting go. I felt real proud as I pulled myself outta the hay pile, picking straw out of my hair, spitting pieces out of my mouth, and seeing their dumb faces with wide-open mouths.

"Fuck you! Fuck all you pecker-head dick-sucker mother fuckers and see if you can do that!" I screamed and ran out of the barn. Shit, so much for my promise to Father Mulry not to swear anymore.

It was Mickey's nap time. Since Pop had moved the shuffle board to the dining room, Lady and him slept on the dog's blanket in the corner of the bar near the kitchen, under a table. I crawled in behind them and wrapped my arm around Lady, who was wrapped around Mickey, snuggling him up like a puppy in the circle of her body and legs. He sucked his thumb and hung on his baby blanket. Lady wouldn't move till Mickey woke up. Easy as I could, I pulled his blanket from under him and covered him.

Lady nosed my hand. She acted like she knew it was burnt from the rope and started licking it.

The bar door burst open and there stood a wild-eyed Minnie Burhans. Her buggy eyes landed on Pop. This ain't gonna be good for me. I forgot she was coming to see him. Wiping my hand on Lady's head, I made my way further behind her and lay down. Her body hid me but I could still see and hear what was going on. Pop hadn't seen me sneak in, and I sure didn't want him to see me now.

Mrs. Burhans never drank in our bar. She said it was a den of iniquity, whatever that was. I knew Pop was wondering why she was here. She got right to the point.

"I'd appreciate it if you'd keep your little street urchin away from my Donny. She has a mouth like a sewer."

"Now, Minnie, either put up or shut up." Pop said. He was being polite.

"I will not repeat the vile filth spewin' outta her mouth," Mrs. Burhans said. "I heard her with my own ears," she said, pointing to the side of her head. "Just take my word for it!"

Her voice went higher and squeakier. "D'ya know what she said when I told her it was a sin to say bad words?" Pop didn't get a chance to open his mouth. "Well, she said she intends to be the first kid in *Ripley's Believe It or Not* for saying the most curse words in one minute, nonstop, not repeating the same word twice! And she's up to half-minute nonstop already! And she charges the children a nickel apiece to hear her say these disgusting words!"

"She's an enterprising one, for sure." Pop said, shaking his head.

"Takes after her damn old man," Tony Debrosky said, taking a sip of his drink.

"Amen," Bill Kelly added.

If Pop ever asked me what I said, I'd be sorting beer bottles till Jesus came back a second time. Oh, damn me. I shouldn't have felt sorry for the little creep, Donny. But the back of his house was right next to the playground. Mrs. Burhans fenced in their yard so he couldn't get out and we couldn't get in. Donny stood there with sad eyes, peeking through the fence every day, watching us have fun. After the kids went home, I went over and talked to him. Didn't think when I told him to get a nickel, he'd tell Minnie what I was gonna do. And I didn't think she'd hide on her back porch listening to me. By the time she waddled down the steps, I said all the curses I knew and Donny gave me the nickel through the fence. Boy, did she flip her wig! She yelled at me, asking what I thought I was doing. Then I told her about wanting to be in *Ripley's*. Didn't think she'd tell Pop like she said she was gonna.

Mrs. Burhans continued to screech at Pop like a dying opera star, saying, "You'll see to it? Right? You should wash her mouth out with soap and lay a willow switch to her behind."

The vein on Pop's forehead started to bulge and turn dark blue. But in a real sweet voice he said, "Yes, Minnie. I'll see to it. And I'll tell her she should raise her price to a dime." He started laughing loud. Har-de-har-har-har! The men in the bar laughed with him. They laughed Mrs. Burhans right out the front door. She stomped her foot, muttered something about depraved scum of the earth, Satan's handymen and slammed the door as hard as she could behind her.

Crossing my fingers, I inched my way on hands and knees, out from under the table to under the pinball machine and over to the kitchen. From there I could get back outside without being seen. For a moment I squeezed my eyes shut and prayed, just in case. God. Make me invisible for one minute so I can get out of here, and please make Pop forget about Mrs. Burhans. Amen. P. S. Could You have made this a lousier day?

1953

Confession, Again

Confession . . .
The grave soul keeps its own secrets,
and takes its own punishment in silence.

Dorothy Dix

In silence, two by two and evenly spaced apart, the shortest kids led the march over to church. It was Friday, and our fifth and sixth grade classroom had to make Confession. Sister Alma Regina made me walk at the end of the line with John Steely. He had Cerebral Palsy and used special crutches. It was my job to make sure he didn't trip and fall, and help him when he needed it.

After John was seated in church, I went to my pew and knelt with everyone else. The afternoon sun came through the stained-glass windows and made a rainbow on the back of the seat in front of me. I studied the colors for a long time before I buried my face into the palm of my hands.

Confession, again. I was scared enough to wet my pants. If I didn't confess about the man, the priest wouldn't know. But God would.

My knees ached. Why did we have to kneel to think about our

sins? Why couldn't we sit? I didn't have to have hurt knees to know what my sins were.

We had to keep our backs straight or the principal, Sister Francis Rose, would embarrass us by saying, "Do you think Jesus slouched in front of God in the Garden of Gethsemane?" No, I thought, but at least He got to lean against a big rock. Confessing didn't get Him out of being nailed to a cross neither. So, what good did it do Him?

The principal was a tough cookie, and it was how she got the job. Pop said I had to respect her because she'd smack me upside my head with her hand or a wooden ruler, faster than you could blink an eye. She'd probably win in a shootout with Lee Van Cleef from the movie *High Noon*.

Sisters, we were taught, were almost as close to God as a priest, but not quite. More like the Virgin Mary, pure and perfect and real powerful. No one doubted Sister Francis Rose talked with God when no one else was around to hear her, and we knew God answered her. God would always answer her, and later the one who replaced her, Sister Cecelia Catherine, who was nicknamed "Rocky" by Barry Post.

My mind was wandering because I was racking my brain on how to get out of telling Father my "big sin" in Confession. Sister Alma Regina said, "Never, ever receive Communion with a sin on your soul because sin is like cancer." She went on, "It eats at your soul." To make her point crystal-clear, she held up a large poster of a healthy lung and another large one of a cancerous lung.

"This," she said pointing to the healthy lung, "is your soul without sin." She put the poster of the pink-rubber-ball-colored lung on her desk. "And this," she said holding up the other picture, while walking between the rows of desks shoving the picture in our faces, "is your soul with sin on it." It was a scary picture. It was a deformed blob, black, purple, and red. You couldn't tell it was a lung.

My chest itched, real bad. I scratched it. Are my lungs turning black right now? I didn't want to die of cancer like Grandma did. Did she die from cancer because her church didn't have Confession?

How could I tell the priest I touched a man's dick? Or tell him what I let this man do to me? I wished I could tell Bobby Ann, but she couldn't keep secrets.

Sister Alma Regina tapped me on the shoulder. I was so lost in my thoughts about Confession, it made me queasy. God forbid, if the handsome Father Reidy was hearing confessions today, I'd die, after I puked.

I stood on wobbly legs. The sanctuary whirled in front of my eyes. The blood drained out of my face and beads of sweat broke out on my forehead. I never fainted before like Linda Caliendo, but it must feel like this. Sister Alma Regina grabbed my arm as my knees buckled, and told me to sit down. She asked if I was ill.

"I think I'm gonna throw up," I said. She didn't like the word puke and told me never to use it. She pulled me up, yanked me out into the aisle and hurried me outside. Down the steps we flew and over to the nearest patch of green grass.

To save my hide I faked heaving. Jesus? Could I puke just this once, please? I prayed as I sneaked a peek up at Sister's red puffy face with the bushy white eyebrow hairs that looked like sea gulls ready to fly away. She took off her glasses that had fogged over from the heat coming out of her stubby body. She wiped them with a clean white hanky while I tried my best to throw up. Only saliva dripped from my mouth.

Every good actress knew when to stop emoting (a fancy word for acting I got from a movie magazine) and I thought this was a good time. Sister pulled a clean tissue from her pocket and handed it to me to wipe my mouth. An actress like Vivien Leigh, in *A Streetcar Named Desire* could have milked this scene for more, but I had to know when to pull the plug.

Sister walked me to the rectory, which made me feel guilty for tricking her. She asked the housekeeper to call my parents and have one of them pick me up. My father told her to tell Sister Alma Regina to keep me there, or else let me walk home because the fresh air would do me good. "Besides" he said, "she's probably fakin'."

The housekeeper gave Sister the message and Sister looked at me and then looked back at the phone. Shaking her head, the housekeeper said good-bye to Pop and hung up. The two women stood silent and looked at each other. They had this "Tsk, tsk," puckered-up puss on their faces that grownups get, and I hated it because it meant they weren't gonna say what they were thinking.

Sister ordered me to sit on a chair in the rectory foyer, keep my hands in my lap and not touch anything. She said she'd grab an older student from church who lived near me to walk me home.

Jackie Regan appeared at the door with his books in hand ready to go. God, he was so cute with his jet-black hair. He was Irish. He was much more handsome than Tab Hunter and even better looking than Robert Wagner.

"Ya sick, or ya hamming it up?" he asked, as we walked across the bridge.

"I'm sick," I said, which was a half-lie and a half-truth. I was sick from thinking how I'd get out of going to Confession next Friday.

"How come they didn't yank Andy out to go with me?" I asked.

"Yer brother ain't gone to Confession yet. But I did. So I got volunteered," he said. "Just like in the Army."

I had a crush on Jackie forever and never told no one. My whole body was tingling.

Jackie lived with his mother and brother two houses down from the public school lane. Every day, he walked by our bar, to and back from school. He was best friends with Andy.

Jackie interrupted my thoughts, "Well, I don't care if you're sick or not. I'm glad to be outta there. Alcatraz couldn't be worse."

I nodded in agreement.

"Wanna go to the river behind the public school and watch me throw stones?"

"Sure," I said, as calm as I could. Is this the way Debra Kerr felt when Burt Lancaster looked into her eyes on the beach in *From Here To Eternity*? I almost swooned. It's what actresses do. Swoon. They don't faint.

"Ya sure you're okay?" he asked. "Yer face is all red."

"I'm fine. Let's just get off Main Street and walk the towpath before some busybody sees us and tells my father."

"Jackie, you ever see the parrot at the Elms?" I asked. The owners kept a big green parrot in a cage at the end of the bar where they sold the bus commuter tickets.

"Yeah," he said. "Why?"

"It swears." I told him that one day I was in there with Mom when a rider came in to buy a bus ticket. He asked the parrot, "Polly wan-a-cracker?" The bird said, "No wan-a-fuckin' cracker."

Jackie had the greatest laugh and the best smile of anybody.

We followed the towpath behind O'Reilly's liquor store, Moylan's Funeral Home, and Rossler's Hardware. Before we knew it, we were passing behind the Rosendale Theatre, Gilmartin's, and Schryver's Lumberyard. I stopped to eat a few end-of-summer blackcaps, while Jackie lobbed rocks at the big croaking bullfrogs in the marsh. We moved on, getting burdocks stuck in our socks, picking them off, and throwing them at each other. They were next to impossible to get out of my hair and I begged Jackie to stop throwing them at my head.

We made our way behind Pettybone's and few private homes before we left the towpath to cross a field behind Ann Marie's house. We helped ourselves to some of her sour crabapples lying on the ground, walked through her driveway, and came out on Main Street across from the school lane. Jackie and I made our way down the school lane to the crumbling rock wall along the bank that helped to hem in the creek.

We walked the wall until it gave way to a dirt embankment with a narrow path to one side.

"I hate being Catholic," Jackie said, shaking his head. He crunched into the sour apple and spit it right back out. "Damn, these fuckers are sour. And I hate Rosendale, too." He flung the apple across the creek.

"Me, too," I agreed, and handed him my apples to throw.

"And those nuns, they're the worst bitches!"

He was aiming the apples for the far shore.

"Yeah, they are." Mom said men only like it when you agree with them. It made them feel smart.

"Don't ya friggin' want to kill some people in this town? Storeowners. They can't stand kids, ya know? But they like our money."

"Yeah, I know," I said. "You're pretty good at throwing. You could pitch for the Dodgers." And Mom said they eat up compliments about how strong or how talented they are.

"Yeah? Thanks."

Oh, Gawd. He is so gorgeous and we agree on everything! My palms were all sweaty and I had goose bumps inside my chest. Oh, don't let it be cancer, I thought.

"Public school kids are lucky. Why can't St. Peter's have a playground?" he asked.

"We can't have monkey bars and slides because the nuns are afraid you boys'll look up our dresses. Besides, the Apostles never had playgrounds."

"What? Where the hell did ya come up with this . . . this 'Apostles' shit?" He shook his head. "You think crazy, ya know it?"

"No, I don't! Then why can't we wear patent leather shoes? 'Cause you guys can see our underwear if ya look at the toes of our shoes."

"What?"

"I got it straight from the Sister who cut up her arms with a razor blade. See how much you know!"

"Well, smarty-pants, she was bonkers and they put her into a looney-bin. Yer gonna end up there if you keep believin' all the shit these nuns teach ya."

He was laughing at me!

"Don't tell me I'm nuts!" I yelled. "Everybody tells me something's wrong with me! I'm smart enough to know how to get you out of school!"

Jackie threw out his last apple as far as he could across the river. "One day," he said, "I'll be able to throw an apple, a rock, something, and it's gonna hit the other side of the creek. And then I'll go pitch for the Dodgers, or the Yankees in New York City."

"You ain't ever gonna do it," I said.

"I ain't gonna do what, smart aleck?"

"You ain't ever gonna play for the Yankees." I was a Dodger fan.

"How the hell d'ya know? Ya don't know anything. Fuck you." Jackie turned and stormed off.

"I'm sorry," I said. Shit. Damn. Why did I say that? "It's just . . . nobody goes anywhere in this town. Let's go to the barn," I called and ran after him, feeling ashamed, knowing I hurt his feelings.

"Nah. I'm going home. My ma ain't feeling well."

"What's wrong?"

"Dunno for sure. Heard Uncle Roy say to Uncle Joe she's got cancer eating her up or something. Tell Andy I'll see him later." And off he went back the way we came.

Cancer killed Grandma Sarah, but I didn't want to tell him it kills everybody. I was sad his mother was gonna die, too. I wondered what would happen to him and his brother when his mom was gone, because they didn't have a father around.

Would I get all eaten up from cancer, too, if I didn't go to Confession? I worried as I made my way up river to the path to the barn. Gee. Why did I say such dumb things to him? Why did I believe everything the nuns told me? Now Jackie won't ever hold my hand, or ask me to go to the movies, or ask me to hide with him during Hide n'Seek. Bet he thinks I'm stupid.

I wished he would've come to the barn and swung on the rope and jumped in the hay mound. Maybe we could have laid side-by-side in the hay with the sun shining on us and talked. I could see the whole scene in my mind like a part in a movie. Oh, Gawd! What would I do if he tried to kiss me? If he even wanted to kiss me.

From the barn window I watched the path to the public schoolyard alongside the Rosenkranses' house. Tall grasses and reeds waved in the breeze. The reeds were beginning to turn color and get dead spots. A sure sign they'd soon be brown and we could break the pithy stems off and use them for swords again. I heard the public school bell ring. A little later, Bobby Ann and her brothers came running and screaming down the trampled path and charged into their house.

I had to get home. Pop'd think I stayed at school if I came in at my usual time. I picked some burdock pieces from my socks, brushed the hay out of my hair and left the barn.

"Ah, here's the sickly one," Pop said, as I walked through the bar and headed up to my room. "What happened? Did Sister see right through your bad acting job?"

The Con Artist and Vacuum Cleaners

*It was beautiful and simple
as all truly great swindles are.*

O. Henry

The bar door opened and two laughing salesmen walked in. You could tell what they were because they were dressed in suits and ties. One sold Filter Queen vacuums and the other guy sold Electrolux. They stopped in to grab a quick one after a hard day of selling door-to-door. They thought it was funny they met for the first time out front. The men loosed their ties and unbuttoned the top of their starched white shirts. They sat sipping their cool beers and traded stories.

"All that work just to be told to come back after dinner because the husband holds the purse strings," Mr. Filter Queen complained.

"Most husbands are still stuck in the forties," Mr. Electrolux said. "All I hear is 'A broom worked all these years, why fix what ain't broke,' or 'A broom was good enough for my mother, it's good enough for my wife.'"

"Yeah," said Mr. Filter Queen. "How many times ya hear, 'Come back after dinner when my husband is home.' And ya go back and they don't answer the door." He shook his head. "Don't know why I'm in this business."

Pop picked up a towel and began wiping glasses. He listened to the men gripe but stayed out of their conversation. Mr. Filter Queen turned to Pop and asked, "Does your wife have a vacuum?"

"Nope."

"Now don't tell me she uses a broom, etceteras, etceteras . . . ," Mr. Electrolux said.

"Nope."

"What does she use?"

"A dust mop."

"A dust mop? D'ya know how much dirt a dust mop misses? What's your name . . . Ed?" Both salesmen had a look on their faces like someone plopped a chocolate cake in front of them. But they didn't know Pop like I did. In every deal, he has to come out a winner.

"Now, Ed. You don't mind me calling ya Ed, now, do ya?" asked Mr. Electrolux.

Pop was still polishing his drinking glasses. "Nope," he said and looked at the glass he was drying, saw a piece of lint and blew a mouthful of air at it. The piece of lint jumped out of the glass.

Mr. Filter Queen said his machine was quieter. "Mind if I go get it out of my car and show you?"

"Nope," said Pop.

Not to be beat out of a sale, Mr. Electrolux said, "Let me show you my vac too, Ed." And he hopped off the barstool and skedaddled out to his car. They came back and plugged their machines in the socket by the jukebox.

Mr. Filter Queen said his was a canister and Mr. Electrolux said his was a tank, and it looked like it, too.

"You can have a conversation and vacuum at the same time," Mr. Filter Queen said. "See here." He put money in the jukebox and played a song and turned on the vacuum cleaner. "Now ain't it quiet? Purrs quiet as kitten."

It was real quiet.

"Purrs like a kitten?" Mr. Electrolux jumped in. "Ed, what you want is power. You want a tiger, not a kitten. Here. Listen to this power." He turned on his machine and it drowned out the other one.

"How's that for power?" he shouted over the motor's noise. Pop rubbed the Manhattan drink glass until it squeaked. He acted like he couldn't care less about what they were saying.

"Power's what ya want, right, Ed?" Pop nodded his head and kept looking at the drink glass he was rubbing with the towel.

Mr. Filter Queen barged in. "My motor's quieter, has more horsepower and more amps. Noise," he said, looking at Mr. Electrolux, "don't mean power. Even you know that, right, Ed?"

Pop nodded yes, picked up an on-the-rocks glass and held it to the light, looking for water spots.

Mr. Electrolux reached into his carrying case and pulled out several steel ball bearings. This was his best selling gimmick.

"Here," he said, handing the balls over to Pop. "Feel how heavy these are." Pop juggled them in one hand. He nodded his head. Still not saying a word, he handed them back to the salesman, who was sweating a lot. "Now, watch this," he told Pop.

The salesman took a clear plastic tube from his bag. It was special-made so it wouldn't swallow up the balls but keep them hanging in the tube. He attached it to the vacuum hose. Mr. Electrolux put the balls on the floor and sucked up one ball, a second ball, and then a third. "Now ain't that somethin,' Ed?" he chuckled as the balls clanked against each other in the tube.

Pop nodded again and picked up a shot glass. He never polished so many glasses in his life!

"Like to see you try it with a full bag of dirt," Mr. Filter Queen piped in.

He shut off the Electrolux machine and dropped the steel balls into the bag.

Mr. Filter Queen told Pop that, with no bags, his canister machine would outperform a tank model with a bag any day.

"Ya'll have to take my word for it," he said, "because my company don't use tricks with steel balls to sell machines. My company," he said, real proud, "relies on honesty and customer satisfaction."

Pop nodded again. Not taking anybody's side and having run out of glasses to wipe, he began to wash the mahogany bar with seltzer and polish it with a used bar towel.

"What's the bottom line?" Pop asked.

If the price ain't right, he ain't buying anything. The salesmen wrote their figures on slips of paper and shoved them over for Pop to read. Pop hemmed and hawed. They pulled the papers back, made some scribbles and shoved them back to Pop. They dropped their prices but were still almost equal.

"I don't know, guys," Pop said.

"I'll give you this demo and a new machine," Mr. Filter Queen said. "Sell the new one at full price and you keep the demo as a commission."

"Sound's like a good deal, but what's in it for you?" Pop said I should ask that question anytime something seemed like it was too good to be true.

"The company gives me a bonus for selling a certain number of vacs each month," Mr. Filter Queen said. "I gotta make my quota, or I lose money."

Pop said okay to the Filter Queen man. Mr. Electrolux drank up and left in a huff. He went out and sat in his car until he saw Mr. Filter Queen leave.

"I'll sell ya a new machine at my cost," he told Pop, "if ya'll do some word-of-mouth advertisin' and be a reference. Hell, ya can sell it and keep what extra ya make."

"I don't have the extra cash right now," Pop lied.

"Look," Mr. Electrolux said, "if it'll make it easier, I'll take time payments starting the end of the month." Pop said okay. But before the month ended, Mr. Electrolux quit being a salesman, moved out of the area and never came back for his money, or his machine. Pop polished up the Filter Queen demonstrator, sold it to Aunt Helen as a barely used machine, and gave the other two new ones to Mom. And that's how for nothing, Mom got an Electrolux for upstairs, a Filter Queen for downstairs, and Pop came out with money in his pocket and a smile on his face.

Tick-Tick, Tick-Tick

*O night. What holds you
to what was not there at sun's rise?
What demons fly and lurk in bedroom corners unprobed?
What concealed, inhuman brute lies in wait?
What anomaly dare invades private and precious moments?*

Judith A. Boggess

THE GREEN AND CHROME WIND-UP ALARM CLOCK sat on top of my dresser in a clutter of plastic barrettes, bobby pins, and scraps of drawing paper along with bubblegum wrappers, broken crayons, and dust, which was thick enough to write your name in.

Each night I wound the clock tight and set it back down in the exact same clean little footprints its felt feet made under the light of my lamp. The painted-plaster lamp of Snow White, in her princess dress stood with Dopey the dwarf leaning against her leg. A cockeyed lampshade sat above their heads. The hands and numbers of the clock would glow bright green in the dark a long time after the light was turned off.

TICK-TICK, TICK-TICK. I stared at the clock, afraid to go to sleep. I tried to stay awake but couldn't. In school, Sister Alma Regina complained that I looked tired and had black rings under my eyes. She said I had to go to bed earlier. I told her I was in bed by nine each night, and she told me it was a sin to lie. When I walked to school the fresh air perked me up, but my brain got soggy from the heat in the classroom, my eyes would blink, and I couldn't stop yawning. How could I tell her that when I dozed off at night for more than fifteen minutes, I woke up with my heart pounding and my hands shaking? And then I'd lie there wide awake, breathing quiet, listening to the room noises for a long time. I'd hear creaks and groans and I'd look for him in the shadows.

TICK-TICK, TICK-TICK. The kids in my classroom couldn't wait for the weekend, when they could get away from Sister Alma Regina with her white chin hairs and red face that glowed on and off like Rudolph's nose. I don't like the weekends. It's when he comes into my room, when Pop hires a band and it's busy and noisy downstairs.

He must know when I fall asleep because he starts touching me and I wake up scared. Who is he? How does he come out of the dark in my room after the lamp is off? The outside light sneaks around my window shade but never touches his face. I pulled the shade up so I could see him, but it didn't help. He must be tall. His face is always in the shadow. He always stinks like a dirty bar rag and a filthy ashtray all rolled into one.

The dark scares me more than lightning and thunder. Andy hid in my closet one night when I was in the bathroom. When I came into my room, he jumped out and went, "Arrrggggghhhh!" I screamed and screamed till my throat went raw. He tried to shush me by putting his hand over my mouth. I went crazy kicking and clawing and crying all the same time.

Mickey woke up and started crying, and Pop came upstairs, pissed. He had to leave the bar to find out what was wrong.

"We were playing hide-'n-seek and she got all weird and started screaming," Andy said. I didn't want him to get beat and went along with his story.

Pop didn't want to hear it. "Get your asses in bed!" he said. Andy ran to his room. Pop looked at me. "Ya trying to bring the friggin' roof down? Gawd-damn near gave me a heart attack. Ya better be dyin' if ya pull this screamin' shit again!"

I tried to set my alarm to wake me up at midnight. If I was

awake and I heard the man, I could hide or crawl in bed with Mickey and maybe he wouldn't come back again if he couldn't find me. But, Andy got mad because the alarm woke him up. It didn't wake me up. I slept right through it. So did Mickey. Andy shook me awake and threatened me. "Damn you!" He waved the ringing clock in my face. "I'm gonna smash the shit out of this thing." He slapped at the plunger on the back and slammed it down hard. Now the clock sat tilted to one side. He dented it. "You freakin' nut! Nobody sets their alarm when they ain't got school! Jeezus!"

TICK-TICK, TICK-TICK. The ticking was loud in my head like a timer on a bomb in a movie waiting to explode. I tried sleeping with the clock under my pillow, so when it rang it wouldn't wake Andy. But by accident I pushed the plunger in when I rolled over. Besides, the ticking made me sleepier too. Now it sat on the dresser in the dust, cockeyed, dented, ticking till daylight, when my room had no more dark, and I could fall asleep for a little bit.

TICK-TICK, TICK-TICK. I stared at the glowing green hands and wish it to be early in the morning with Mom and Pop in bed snoring. Some nights I crawled under my bed, lay on the bare floor with the fluffy dust balls and covered myself up with my old brown and red plaid baby blanket. Music from a western band like Big Jim Mehan's, or Shorty Idaho's would twang up through the floorboards.

When Pop sang, I could snuggle up in my blanket and pull my knees to my chest. I could listen to "Danny Boy," "I'll See You in my Dreams," "Because," or "Yours is my Heart Alone." I could pretend, when he was singing, "Begin the Beguine" or "Indian Love Call" from the movie *Rose-Marie*, that he was a singing actor, like Ezio Pinza, or Howard Keel singing to Kathryn Grayson. The words of so many songs burned in my brain.

It was hard to stay awake under the bed, but I had to. If Pop had to look for me, he'd have a fit. When the band stopped playing, or Pop stopped singing and the jukebox came on, it was my signal to climb back into my cot.

"Last call. What'll you have?" Pop's voice boomed up through the rafters. This was his way of telling everybody the bar was closing for the night. Drinkers could pay for extra drinks and line them up on the bar, but after last call, not another sale would go through the register. It was the law.

If I was still lying on the floor, I could hear bottles and glasses clinking, and the last tssh-tssh-ding, tssh-tssh-ding of the cash register.

"Put your money in your pockets and no more in the jukebox, please."

I watched him close up the bar when business was bad because of snowy weather or because the next day was a holiday. "Tomorrow's Christmas," he'd say, or Easter, or . Then he'd add, "G'wan home early. Be with your families."

Pop went over and pulled the cotton strings hanging from the neon beer signs in the front windows. He turned off the outdoor hotel sign and he snapped off the green lights shining through glass bricks that framed the two plate glass windows out front. The next switch turned off all the inside lights except for the ones above the whiskey bottles on the back bar. Every night was the same. I followed his footsteps around in my mind.

After the last song played, if people were still hanging around, he flipped the switch off on the jukebox. The next sound I'd hear was the front door opening and closing as the people left, and their car doors squeaking open and clunking shut. The noises echoed up into my bedroom no matter what the season. Same as the voices drifting up and down Main Street when people were walking or talking together on their way home.

Georgie Claus, Uncle Ernie, Uncle Everett, Dad DeWitt, Johnny Plonski, Bill Mills, George Moylan . . . I knew all their voices like words to a song. It bothered me that I didn't know *his* voice because he always whispered. If I knew who *he* was, I could tell Pop. He wouldn't believe me otherwise

TICK-TICK, TICK-TICK. The hands and the numbers were fading. I ran to the living room window. From there, I had a second-story look-see up and down Main Street. Uncle Joe, who looked snockered, weaved his way across the street to his car. Buster Burlanger walked with Fritzie Mertine and his wife Mae till Buster found his car. Gil Kelder and Floyd Swehla stood in the driveway talking. And Eddie "Frog-Eyes" Fogerty staggered up street, walking right past his car. Louie Auchmoody called out to Fogerty to wait up. He probably wanted a ride home, or to tell Fogerty where his car was. There was Joe and Kitty Dutcher, Jackie Regan's uncle and aunt, crossing the road with Bob Hueben. John Boyle held the car door open for his wife, Isabelle. Looking down, I saw Miles Oakley trying to talk to some young women, probably from Kingston, standing by the front door, who were more interested in the young soldiers home on leave from Korea.

I didn't know some people—the gangsters and prostitutes from New York City, friends of Big John Batira—the judges, lawyers, and cops from Kingston coming to play poker and craps, who Pop said I should forget about ever seeing. The man in my room . . . I guess he could be any one of them.

I could smell him. His smell was stuck way up in my nose by my eyes, in my brain, and it wouldn't go away. I tried using Pop's throat spray he used before singing. He said it cleared his sinuses. It didn't work. It tasted salty, and it gagged me.

The man would breathe his rotten cigarette smoke and sour alcohol smell all over me. It sank into my skin. It wouldn't wash off. I'd smell his nicotine fingers he pushed against my lips when he told me to keep quiet. His Vincent Price scary voice was in my head and I hummed to get him out. But he sneaked back in my skull the way he crept into my bedroom–sneaky, never knowing when he'd show up.

The stars were disappearing from the sky. Mom was coming up the stairs. I ran on tip-toes to my bedroom, jumped into bed. The clock ticked. The glowing hands and numbers had faded. Mom went into her bedroom. The man must be a stranger. Strangers do bad things to you. Aunt Helen and Mom said so. They said never trust a stranger, never take money from one and never, ever, get in their car.

Pop came into the apartment and straight to my room. I could smell his after-shave lotion as he bent over me to straighten and tuck in my covers. Pop smelled good.

Bathroom Break

The basis of shame is not some personal mistake of ours but . . . the humiliation we feel that we must be what we are without any choice in the matter, and that this humiliation is seen by everyone.

Milan Kundera

My report cards used to be in the high 90s or 100s till I got into the fifth grade. It wasn't my fault I couldn't concentrate on my work. I was tired. Noises at night scared me awake, and it took a long time to get back to sleep.

Sister Alma Regina called me to the blackboard to add up a column of numbers, divide them, and prove my answer with multiplication. Things multiplied, added, and divided all wrong. I couldn't prove my answers. I even put decimals in the wrong places.

"What's with you?" she asked, breathing down my neck, making my insides tremble. "This is simple arithmetic. You do this, this, and this," she barked, pounding the blackboard so hard with her chalk she snapped it in half.

I didn't know why I kept getting different answers, but the more she corrected me the more confused I got. My head was buzzing like a nest of honeybees. I turned back to the board and the numbers blurred. I rubbed my eyes. It didn't help. Was I going blind? Did I have cancer in my eyes?

Sister called Georgia to the blackboard. "Miss Christadolus," she said, "come up and help Judy do this problem. See if you can get through to her."

It was no good because I was already gone and I wasn't coming back till Sister told me to go sit down. We were taught in catechism class that our souls lived on after our bodies died. They were invisible. I believed it because I could take my soul out of my body and leave whenever I wanted to, and I wasn't even dead yet. When I took my spirit out of the room I went numb and couldn't feel anything, which was good. When bad things happened I left. Sister saw Georgia wasn't having any better luck, and she snapped, "Both of you, go to your seats!"

I moved like a wooden soldier to my desk. Kids were giggling. It didn't bother me. Sister also taught us our bodies were cocoons. The soul inside was waiting for the body to die so it could go to heaven and live with God. This meant my empty shell, and not the real me, was being made fun of. But it still didn't feel good.

As I passed his desk, Pete whispered, "Judy, you okay? You're all white, like a vampire's sucked out all your blood."

Once I tried to teach Bobby Ann how to leave her body but she was too scared to let herself go. She said she worried about how long a body could stay alive without being in it. And if someone was doing what I was doing at the same time, and if they were evil, could they get inside me and take me over?

I never worried because I figured the priest could always do an exorcism to get me back.

Sister was saying she was going to introduce us to algebra a little piece at a time. Then, when we got to seventh grade, we'd know what Sister Cecelia Catherine was talking about in math class. She yammered on, explaining X equals 2 Y and 2 X plus 3Y equals 14. She asked us to tell her what X and Y were. Hands flew up in the air but not mine. Shit! They were letters in the alphabet. How the heck did I know why they stuck them in with numbers? And what good was this stuff anyway? How would I ever use it designing dresses?

Sister looked at me and said, "You're not getting this, are you?"

I shook my head, no. I wanted to be home making paper doll dresses alone in my room. I raised my hand and asked to go to the bathroom. Sister Alma Regina said no. Knowing her, she must've thought I was trying to get out of the lesson. What she didn't know was I'd been holding back from asking for close to a half-hour. I was ready to burst. You could never go when you had to. You had to wait till your classroom took its turn. And the younger grades always went first. Unless it was an emergency, like diarrhea or you were gonna puke all over the floor.

Something's wrong with me. I used to be able to hold it for hours. Bobby Ann said maybe it was a weak bladder, or maybe I hurt it when I fell on the crossbar of Andy's bike. I thought it might be something like cancer because it burned when I peed. Grandma died of cancer down there. I kept waving my hand till it annoyed Sister and she had to ask me again what I wanted.

"Yes, Miss Cherny?"

"May I please be excused?"

Kids chuckled because they knew I stood a snowball's chance in Hades of leaving the room before the lower grades got to go.

"Silence." Sister demanded. "Sit down Miss Cherny. You may go when it is our turn," she looked up at the wall clock, "in forty-five minutes."

"I can't..."

"Sit down!"

I hit the seat with a thud, crossed my legs and squeezed as hard as I could.

"Miss Cherny, young ladies do not cross their legs."

"But I have to go," I said.

More chuckling could be heard. Sister stood up. She whacked her long wooden ruler on a stack of books sitting in a neat pile on her desk and glared at me. I didn't want to get rapped across the back of my head with the ruler. I uncrossed my legs and pushed my thighs as tight together as I could and dribbled in my underpants.

Oh, damn. I wiggled in my seat. With both hands pressed against my belly I bent forward in an attempt to help hold the pee back. But my insides felt like an overfilled water balloon ready to explode. Raising my hand the pee sneaked out.

"Put your hand down," Sister said.

Nuts! You mean old witch. Maybe if I let a little bit out it'd make me feel better. I pulled my dress out from under me. Sister began to write out our homework assignment on the blackboard. She was good at ignoring my squirming. Once the pee started, I couldn't stop it from trickling out until the feeling of fullness went away. Sister's back was turned to the class when someone said loud enough for her to hear, "Phew! I smell pee!"

Could they smell it? The tips of my ears and my cheeks were burning. I tried to hide my face by putting an elbow on the desk and my hand to my forehead while writing down my assignment. My bottom was all wet. I was sitting in a pee-puddle in the hollowed-out seat, indented for our butts' comfort. The backs of my thighs, where they rested on the seat, were wet too. I moved around trying to let air under my dress so the wetness would dry up. I flapped my legs open and closed. Whispered voices came at me in all directions. "Judy peed her pants." There was more tittering.

Sister turned to the class. She glanced at me and at the other students and said, "No talking! Everyone will now wait until all grades have gone to the lavatory. We shall be the last to go today."

Moans and groans rumbled throughout the classroom. The voices came at me again, "It's all your fault, Cherny. Wait till we get you after school."

The half-hour dragged by and, when break time came, I was too embarrassed to stand up. What if the bottom of my dress was wet? What if the seat was still wet? Rows of kids lined up in the aisle next to their desks. They marched single-file out in the hall to wait for their turn in the bathroom. The tightness was back in my chest. I had a hard time breathing. But I had to get up.

My underwear and the back of my legs dried themselves on the wooden seat and were stuck like glue. I had to peel myself loose. I could hear a scritch noise when my panties came loose. The backs of my legs burned and stung and I was sure I stripped off a layer of skin. Warm urine smell greeted me. It reminded me of when I peed in the woods. I wanted to die. Oh, jeez. The seat showed a dark wet round circle in the hollow. I wished I could disappear.

No one seemed to notice. They were more interested in making sure they got their turn. Good. I hoped their bladders were bursting and they'd know how I felt.

It was my turn and I hurried into the girls' room. We only

had a couple of minutes. If you took too long, Sister came looking for you. God forbid you might have to take a dump. She'd beat on your stall door with the side of her fist and demand, "What are you doing in there?" I always waited till I got home to do number two, even if it gave me cramps in my belly.

A girl used the toilet while I ran water in the sink. I wet stiff paper towels, washed the backs of my legs and hoped it'd kill the stink. Could I pull off my panties and rinse them? The toilets flushed. I threw the towels in the garbage and pretended to be washing my hands. For once, I was glad it was forbidden to talk in the bathroom. I went back to the class and found my seat covered by a piece of heavy white drawing paper. I started to pick it up.

"Sit down." Sister Alma Regina said. "Leave it where it is."

Kids laughed. There was no way I could keep from crying but I damn well wasn't gonna let any of these hyenas see me. I sat on the paper, put my hands up to my forehead to hide my face and stared at my desktop. I watched tears plop on my notepaper and spread in circles, making the paper pucker up and the blue writing lines bleed.

My head pounded and my nose stuffed up. Paying attention to the last of the lessons for the day was impossible. Sister called on me and I decided not to hear her. She called my name several times. I wasn't about to answer her. Sister said something about my defiance and I should remain after school. Good. I didn't want to walk home with kids who'd tease me.

The dismissal bell rang. It brought me back from daydreaming. I felt dizzy and not sure of what I was supposed to be doing. I saw kids cleaning up their desks, getting books for doing homework and standing at attention by their places, waiting for permission to leave. Except me. I wasn't standing—not even for the Pope. I slapped my books together and slouched further down in my seat, which was forbidden. Kids filed out in the hallway, and out of the school as fast as they were allowed and made their way home. Sister Alma Regina came over to me.

"Stand up, please, since you've forgotten how to sit up straight. Go to the lavatory and get two batches of towels. One with some soap on it, and another of dry ones. Do you understand me?"

I nodded, yes.

"You'll not leave that," she said pointing to my seat, "for the janitor to clean up."

With a hot face, I left the room. I was glad to do what she said because I had to pee again, real bad. And this time, with no one in the girls' room, I rinsed and wrung out my dried, scratchy, stiff underpants. I sniffed and they smelled better. I put them back on before someone caught me standing there with no drawers on. They were cold against my skin and gave me a chill.

Shame flooded my body as I scurried back past other nuns in the hallway in wet panties carrying the wet towels. They knew I was in trouble or I wouldn't be here after school. I wondered if they told each other about things like kids peeing in their seats. I bet they did. And I bet they laughed about it.

As slow as I could, I scrubbed the pee-soaked seat with Sister standing over me, inspecting the job. She clinked and rattled her black rosary beads wrapped around her waist. She could've hung herself with them, they were so long. I knelt on the floor and pretended I was doing a good job. But I was taking my old sweet time. She couldn't leave till I finished. I hoped I was making her late for something important

Finished, I threw all the dirty towels in the trashcan.

"Now," Sister said, "do you have a problem? You're unkempt, your hem needs fixing and your hair's not neat." She expected an answer after every statement she made. It was safer to say yes or no than to try to explain my parents drinking all night and sleeping late, and there wasn't no one to help me in the morning.

"Is there something you need to talk to me or Father about?"

"No, Sister," I said. My parents said that what went on in our home stayed in our home. It wasn't anybody's business but ours. Besides how could I tell a priest about having to touch a strange man? I couldn't tell Sister or him anything so filthy. Besides the man said to tell no one. It was our secret. He said he'd say I asked to touch him and everyone would believe him and not me. He said he'd say I showed him where my bedroom was and asked him to come to my room. He said nobody believes a kid. Thinking about it made me nervous and made me burn down there. Maybe I got cancer from him touching me. I had to pee again.

It seemed like one sin was piling up on another. Lying to Sister was a sin. Things I couldn't tell in Confession were a sin. Each time the priest asked if I had anything else to tell and I said no, was a sin. I was putting one stain on my soul after another, which got me closer to having to spend all eternity in hell's fire. I tried to make up for it by being quiet in school and better at home. I did whatever the man asked me to do and didn't tell no one. I was trying to be good. I didn't want to live with Satan.

Sister barged in on my thoughts. "When you get home," she said, "take a bath. Eat supper. Someone does make you supper, don't they? Do your homework and go to bed by nine."

"Yes, Sister." It wasn't as easy as she made it sound.

"Good," she said. "And don't have any more accidents or you will get detention from now on. Do you hear?"

"Yes, Sister."

It felt good to get away from Sister, to be out in the sun and have the warm breeze blow against my skin. With no nuns watching, ready to scold me, I ran down the school steps to the sidewalk where I pretended Grandma Sarah waited. She took my hand, smiled at me and walked me home.

Home Sweet Home

In violence, we forget who we are.
Mary McCarthy

So much for going to bed at nine like Sister Alma Regina told me to do. At one o'clock in the morning, I woke up because of yelling voices. The bar must've closed early, because Mom and Pop always waited till everybody left before they started hammering at each other.

I pulled up my shade and lay down in the light shining across the floor. What was it about streetlights and the full moon that could make the colors of my bedroom disappear? Everything in the room looked like props in a black-and-white movie.

Mom had bought me these dumb-looking peach-colored cotton underpants and T-shirts with skinny straps. Old ladies in silent movies wore this kind of stuff, I told her. She laughed and called them snuggies, and said I had to wear them under my dresses because it was cold outside. I wouldn't get caught dead in them, or wear them to school where someone might see them if I bent over. These bloomers came down to my knees, or else rolled up between my legs when I walked. They came in handy for pajamas instead, and Mom would think I wore them to school when found in the dirty clothes pile.

I fidgeted with my twisted undies as I lay on my stomach and dug dirt out of the cracks between the floorboards, with a bobby pin with the chewed off rubber tip. Little piles of hard-packed dirt waited to be scooped up and thrown away as I listened to their arguing.

What the heck? There was a very loud crash. I pushed my ear tight to the floor. Pop was swearing and Mom was screaming. Shit! I ran and woke up Eddie. "C'mon, Eddie. This one's for real. Something crashed. Something big got broke. Maybe the jukebox. Get up."

"Not again," he groaned, sitting up on the side of the bed. "Jeezus Christ! I gotta take a test tomorrow." He cursed under his breath. I handed him his pants and begged him to hurry up. It felt like he was taking forever.

By the time he headed downstairs the fighting was over. Mom was boo-hooing her way up to the apartment, and was holding ice in a bar towel to the side of her face. She ignored us as we went past. We figured if she was walking and talking, she was all right. We didn't ask questions.

Eddie went into the bar with me tagging behind. Holy mackerel! What a freakin' mess. And, boy, did it stink of spilled booze!

"D'ya need help?" Eddie asked Pop.

"Nah."

"What happened?"

"She picked up the fuckin' bench and heaved it 'cross the bar at my head. She's a fuckin' nut case!"

Pop made two-seater wooden benches for the bar to replace all the heavy chrome padded barstools drunks clobbered each other with during a brawl. Mom hauled up one of these benches over her head, and hurled it across the bar at Pop. He caught her reflection in the mirror and ducked as it hit the shelves. It was the loudest crash I ever heard. The only thing that wasn't broken was the mirror. The plate-glass shelves full of whiskey bottles, and glasses had come crashing down on Pop's new shiny electric cash register. Whatever didn't break hitting the cash register, smashed when it hit the floor.

Seeing me kneeling on a bench taking everything in, Pop said to Eddie, "Get her t'hell outta here." He bent over, started picking up broken bottles and throwing them in the trash.

"I belted her not thinkin'," Pop said. "Heard the bottles and glasses breakin' and shit . . . thought it was World War Two all over again."

Mom will be lucky if she had only one black eye and not two in the morning.

"C'mon, Brat," Eddie said. He picked me up, threw me over his shoulder, and carried me up to bed.

Pop ain't ever hit Eddie, Mickey, or me. I guess Eddie was too big, Mickey was too small, and I was a girl. Mom and Andy were Pop's punching bags. Mom said Pop hit Andy because he looked like her, a DeWitt, with blonde hair and blue eyes.

But Andy was always taking Pop's things without asking, or taking things apart, like the chiming mantel clock, and never fixing them. Once he took some of Mom's jewelry and gave it to Donna Baker, who lived up on James Street, who he had a crush on. Mom got the stuff back, and Andy got taken into the dining room and "talked" to. But he got more than a talking. He got the tar beat out of him.

The swinging doors to the dining room had small square glass windows for you to look through so you didn't crash into someone coming at you from the other side. Mom stood by one and watched Pop yelling at Andy. Too short to look through the window, I pushed in and knelt in front of her, opening the door a crack and peeking in.

Pop was getting madder and madder at Andy. He took a swing and punched Andy with his fist and then picked up his leather and canvas razor strap laying on the shuffleboard and started hitting him like the soldiers did to Jesus when He got crucified. Whap! Whap! The leather cracked against Andy's back and anywhere else it hit him when he tried to squirm himself away. He got beat from one end of the shuffleboard to the other.

"Stop him!" I screamed up at Mom.

Mom stood there all teary-eyed and did nothing. I pushed through the swinging doors and charged at Pop. "Stop hitting my brother!" I yelled, and grabbed at the back of Pop's t-shirt with both hands. Somehow, I got a hand hooked over his belt, hung on, and kicked his legs. I made a fist with my right hand and swung like a lunatic, punching his gut, and yelling, "I hate you! You Nazi! You're Hitler, not my father!"

The razor strap dropped to the floor. Andy lay in a heap, his white T-shirt ripped and spattered with blood.

"You rotten bully!" I screamed at Pop, and let go of his shirt. "Hit me! Go ahead! Hit me too, why don't you?"

Pop's eyes were all glassy. He was breathing like a bull in a Yvonne DeCarlo matador movie. He raised his arms up in the air, and for a second, looked around, confused. Then pushing past me, he stamped out of the dining room.

"You okay, Andge?" I asked, walking over to him. My voice was shaky.

"Yeah. Sure. Whadda ya think, stupid? I just got the shit kicked outta me."

He wouldn't let me help him. "Someday I'm gonna kill that fat bastard," he said behind clenched teeth. Tears ran down his bloody face. He wiped his nose on the bottom of his ripped shirt.

We could hear Mom going at Pop. "You proud of yourself?"

"Shaddup, Edith."

"Big Johnny Atlas. Never pick on anybody your own size, do you?"

Why was she getting brave now? Why ain't she helping Andy? Damn her! Why doesn't she shut up?

Andy ran up to his room using the dining room door. Screw it. I locked the door behind him and sneaked into the bar, took ice, and wrapped some in a bar towel. I brought it to Andy, even though he said he didn't need any help.

Mom was threatening to leave Pop for the one-millionth time. I wished she'd go. Get lost. I was sick of her drinking, bitching and bellyaching. She was blaming Pop for all Andy's troubles. "If you took time to do something with us as a family, maybe he would be different," she said.

Without a word, Pop walked out the front door, Mom right on his heels. "Where are you going? I'm supposed to take care of this damn place? What are you going to do when I leave? Who's going to watch the bar for you then?" Pop jumped into his car and drove off.

At least once a week Mom would breath the hot smell of booze in my face, and ask with tears in her eyes, "If I leave your father, do you want to come with me or stay with him?" Sob, sob. Jeezus. I wanted to throw up from the smell of her breath. Of course, I'd go with her I told her. I didn't want to go with her. Where would she go? New York City? Would I still have to drag her out of bars every night? Would she take Mickey? I ain't leaving him here. But he might be too much bother for her. Would I have to take care of him more?

I wish Mickey and I could go live with Millie. I wish we had a grandmother or a Daddy Warbucks who'd come and adopt me like Orphan Annie. And I'd say I couldn't go unless Mickey came too. And Daddy Warbucks would say yes. We'd move far, far away, and live happily ever after.

New York City

Everybody ought to have a lower East Side in their life.
Irving Berlin

Mickey and I came in the kitchen from playing down by the creek. We were hungry and wanted some peanut butter and jelly sandwiches to take back with us.

Pop called me and said, "If you want to say goodbye to your mother, ya better hurry. She's up street at the bus station, leaving for New York City."

Wha . . . ? I ran out the door, leaving Mickey behind. As I charged up the street a burning stitch shot up my right side. I had to slow down and limp along as fast as I could.

She said she'd take me. Why's she leaving without me and Mickey? Why didn't Pop stop her?

Oh, no! The bus was pulling up to the curb. There was Mom . . . with a suitcase. Pop wasn't lying. She was going . . . without me!

"Mommy, Mommy, wait! Don't go! Don't leave, Mommy!" I cried.

She tottered a little and stared in my direction. She didn't look happy. Her eyes were narrow and her lips were squeezed in an angry thin red line.

Mom was with her friend Flo, who was staying at our hotel for the week. Flo said she was taking time off from her job. Pop said she was taking time off her back, and he wouldn't explain what he meant when I asked him. Big John Batira, the guy I thought looked like a Mafia hit man, a pock-faced Edward G. Robinson, brought Flo up to Rosendale and left her "to rest". I asked Pop if Big John was a gangster. He wouldn't say he wasn't, so he must've been. When I asked Flo, she laughed and said, "Whatta kid you have here, Edie."

Flo liked telling Mom stories about the Manhattan nightlife and all the fancy department stores. She bragged about the men who bought her jewels at Tiffany's and about her fur coats she left behind. Flo said her boyfriends took her to Sardi's Restaurant to meet movie stars, and said she went to the Met opera house and Broadway plays. Flo was a hooker. A high-class one, Pop finally said. Too rich for his blood. He claimed men had to pay hundreds to be with her.

One night at the bar, Flo told Mom not to be stupid, and to come with her to the city. "Honey, why give it away free when ya can get paid for it?" she said. Mom laughed and agreed with her.

At the bus stop, Flo was dressed in silky tan slacks and a loose, billowy, almost see-through white blouse. You could see her lacy bra and her melon-sized boobs looking like they'd fall out if she "aw-chooed" too hard. She wore the highest heels I ever saw and carried an alligator pocketbook. She looked hard, like Joan Crawford. Flo had shoe-polish black hair and big fire-engine-red lips. Her eyes were all dolled up with a sky-blue color and her eyebrows were drawn in with black crayon. She had a fake mole near her top lip, like a movie star. She stood on the bus stairs, hanging out the door. "C'mon, Edith. Nuh Yawk Cit-ee's waiting."

Bill Russell, the bus driver, put Flo's suitcase in the storage compartment on the outside of the bus. He was familiar with Mom's "antics," as Pop called them. He looked at Mom and shook his head.

"Hey, Edie," he said. "Gotta make up your mind, kid. Haven't got all day."

"No, Mommy. Don't! Please?" I pulled on her suitcase.

Mom waved Mr. Russell off, and kissed her friend goodbye. The bus door closed with a swish. Grey smoke belched at us from the exhaust pipe as it pulled away from the curb.

Mom handed me her suitcase, flipped her fingers through her hair and licked her lips, making them shine. She tugged on her suit jacket, threw her head up and stuck out her chin. The muscles in her jaw twitched as she strutted back to the hotel on her platform high heels.

Mom reminded me of Bette Davis, playing the part of a queen. But she looked more like a drunk and overweight Grace Kelly, if Grace Kelly would ever be either.

Mom's toe caught the raised edge of the slate sidewalk and stumbled. "Why don't they fix these damn things before someone twists an ankle?" Taking a moment, she glared down at me and said, "Today, I could've been out of Rosendale. Free! And I could've become a very rich lady. But no, because of you I'm stuck here. You happy now?"

Halloween Prank

There is nothing funny about Halloween. This sarcastic festival reflects, rather, an infernal demand for revenge by children on the adult world.
Jean Baudrillard

THE SONG ON THE JUKEBOX, "Crying in the Chapel" by the Orioles, ended. I watched the needle rise up and out of the way as a metal half-circle arm scooped up the 45-rpm record, tilted it sideways and returned it to its empty slot. Life had gone back to usual these couple of months since Mom decided not to leave.

The bar was quiet for a change. Eddie Fogerty sat slouched over his Dobler beer with one leg crossed over the other. His faded baseball cap was twisted to the left so it wouldn't bump into his glass when he tipped his head to drink. He took a long drag on his cigarette, and before he exhaled he took a big swig of beer. Fogerty's bottom lip curled up and over his top one, wiping away the foam on his upper lip. He smacked his lips and burped, and cigarette smoke came out of his mouth. I giggled. He was fun to watch.

Fogerty put his glass back onto the wet cardboard coaster and stared into it like a fortune teller looking into a crystal ball, and his eyes blinked shut. The cigarette between his fingers grew a long ash as it burned down to his stained fingers. He didn't seem to feel it burning his skin. Eddie's nickname was "Frog-Eyes," because, his eyes bugged out like the actor, Peter Lorre's.

Bob Hueben came in. Mom said she thought he was handsome and funny, and everything a woman could want. He was tall, had dark hair, and was well-dressed. He was the opposite of Fogerty, who wore a scroungy white T-shirt, rumpled pants, and untied work boots.

Bob walked over and slapped him on the back. The long ash from Fogerty's cigarette fell on the bar. "Hey, Fogerty. How t'hell are ya?" Bob asked. Fogerty, scared awake, looked up. He smelled a free drink coming. He smiled and held out his hand for a shake.

Mom wiped the ashes from the bar. She stubbed out the cigarette butt now smoldering in the plastic ashtray. She didn't like the plastic ashtrays with all their burn marks, but they were safer around drunks than the heavy glass ones.

"What'll it be, Bob, the usual?" Mom smiled and looked into his eyes for a long time. She knew how to flirt and Pop didn't care. He said it was good for business.

Mom said a guy would give you anything if he could believe, even for a second, that he could get to first base with you. She liked to rub it in Pop's face that more money came in while she was tending bar than when he did. Her smiling brought the guys in, which made women come in, which made guys spend lots of money trying to "loosen up the girls" with drinks. Pop told Mom not to get carried away with her fluttery eyelashes because he might not always be there to protect her from grabby hands.

Pop attracted women with his singing. But these women expected him to buy their drinks. They weren't interested in the guy sitting next to them. Mom said all men were horny jerks, and when they were drunk, you better lock up your dog. It was probably a joke, but to be safe, I made sure Lady was upstairs with me at night when I went to bed.

"Edie? You having a Halloween party this year?" Bob wanted to know.

"Sure thing. You coming as Lancelot?"

He laughed and they talked about other parties and costumes people wore.

"Is Ed having pumpkin beer again?" John Plonski asked, catching the conversation as he came in and sat down next to Fogerty.

"Shit, yeah," Fogerty replied. "Gotta have orange beer coming outta your hollow weenie." He laughed himself silly at his own joke. He was drunk as a skunk.

Pop put orange food coloring into pitchers of beer in the early part of the evening and told people it was pumpkin beer. Some swore they could taste the pumpkin. It sold as fast as the green-dyed beer on Saint Paddy's Day. Pop said you could sell anybody anything so long as you could keep a straight face. I believed him.

Most times, I only half-listened to the talk at the bar. But my ears perked up when the talk turned to tricks played on Halloween when they were kids. I needed a good gag to play on the old bag, Mary Conlin. Everyone hated her. The big kids called her "The Cat." I don't know why unless it was because she was always sneaking around butting into people's business. Pop said since she stopped drinking and got religion she was driving everybody nuts, including her poor husband. Pop said she was gonna drive John to an early grave. John said he drank so when he went home he could pass out and not have to listen to her, and, if he got lucky enough, he might one day up and die. And, sure enough, one day he just did that and everybody said it was his only way to get away from Mary's nagging.

Mary lived near the middle of James Street. She went to St. Peter's Church. Her favorite place to sit was in the last pew, at eleven o'clock Mass, where she took it upon herself to read you the riot act if you came in late. She also got to those who left early. The following Sunday, Mary would ask what was so important it couldn't wait till after Mass. Those who didn't show up at all got a phone call from her asking if they were sick, or if someone died, the only two excuses she accepted for not being in church on Sunday. For some reason people felt they had to explain to her what was none of her business.

Mary haunted the place where the teenagers liked to park and make out, up by the electric dynamo plant on Lawrenceville Road, which happened to be across the street from her sister's house.

Mary's sister, Miss Susie Hornacher, was the opposite of her. Miss Hornacher was a tall, thin, brown-haired woman who never got married. She taught at the public school in Rosendale, and was kind and sweet. On my days off from Catholic school, I'd go sit in her class. Miss Hornacher never raised her voice and she let you go to the bathroom whenever you had to go. I begged to go to the public school, but Pop said, "Absolutely not! You're a Catholic."

Mary must've been someone's mistake left on her mother's doorstep in the middle of winter. She was gray, cold, and hard. A peanut-brittle old lady and not shy on the nuts, neither.

Eddie got pissed at her the night she walked over to the parking area and caught him and Norma Jean smooching. He was usually polite. But Mary stood there shining a flashlight on Eddie till he started up his car. Eddie cranked down the window and asked her why she didn't have anything better to do than minding everybody else's business. They let go some heated words at each other. Eddie drove off telling her she was a jealous old hag and she should go screw herself with a broom handle because no one would ever touch her.

Mary hopped in her car and drove straight to the bar to tell Pop what Eddie said to her.

"Pull down the shade when you're at your sister's if it bothers ya," Pop said. "Besides who asked ya to police the parking lot anyway?"

"Well, Ed Cherny," she said, "if you don't want to be a grandfather before your son gets married, then you better teach him some morals other than those of a jackrabbit."

"Mary," Pop said, leaning over and bringing his huge forearms to rest on the bar top, "I wish ya was a man for one minute." He rolled his hand into a fist and stuck it under her nose. "It'd give me great pleasure to pop ya in the kisser. Get outta here and stick ya nose up somebody else's ass because it ain't wanted here." He slapped the palm of his hand hard on the bar, making men jump.

You gotta give Mary credit. She didn't flinch. She stood tall, every gray-haired, scrawny, ugly inch of her and shot back at Pop, "You can't intimidate me, you gawd-damn overbearing, obnoxious, ignoramus, asshole!"

O boy! Pop's forehead vein was pumping. "Know what ya need, Mary?" he said. "Ya need a good stiff one and I don't mean a drink. And, before ya get any ideas, I don't mean to oblige ya. I'd rather fuck a dead Billy goat. It'd be a whole hell of a lot better looking, and whole hell of lot livelier!"

"Speaking from experience?" Mary asked as she grabbed a full glass of beer from the bar and flung it at Pop's face.

Oh, oh. She did it! Woman or not, Pop vaulted over the bar one-handed, surprising everybody he could swing his weight up so high and land on both feet in front of her. Mary backed up and made for the door as he reached for her. Men jumped from their seats and held Pop back till Mary could hop in her red-and-black Pontiac convertible and take off down Main Street.

Lost in daydreaming, I didn't catch who Mom played her worst Halloween trick on. But I heard what I needed for the nastiest gag ever.

I'd have to get some fresh cow flop from Dad DeWitt's, a paper bag, and some matches from the kitchen. I smiled at how Bobby Ann would knock on Mary's door while I hid behind her, Porky, Georgie, and Myron. I'd put the bag of manure on her porch. And as soon as Mary opened her door to chase us all away, I'd light the bag on fire and we'd run like hell and watch from the street as she stomped out the fire. I couldn't wait to tell Porky and Bobby Ann. Five more days to Halloween!

The Halloween prank went off without a hitch. Norma and Eddie came with us to watch and make sure we didn't get in any serious trouble, like Mary shooting a shotgun at us. It was the best fun I had in a long time. Mary cursed at us.

"Yer a gawd-damn Cherny! I can tell!" she screamed, looking out at me as we taunted her. "Ya fuckin' little bastards!" She was dancing up on one foot, trying to shake the cow shit off her shoe. "And Rosenkranses', you fuckin' heathens, you're out there, too. Wait till I get my hands on you, ya little mother-fuckers!" Boy, for a Catholic, this woman could swear. She could give Pop lessons!

We laughed all the way to Gilmartin's, where we took off our masks, pooled our pennies from our Halloween bags, and shared soda's. Even Jack and Mae Gilmartin tried not to smile when Eddie told him what we did. We were having so much fun I hated to go home.

Mickey was already in bed. I took him trick-or-treating earlier. He didn't want to stay out too long because all he was interested in was eating the candy he already had. I washed him, put him to bed, and told him he could keep his bag of candy by his pillow, but he had to promise he wouldn't eat it all up. He was a good kid. There were only a few candy wrappers on the floor by his bed when I came home.

Later, during the night, the man woke me up by tugging on my shoulder. I was awake but I pretended to be asleep and mumbled at him to leave me alone. I kept pulling away and rolling back onto my stomach. He gave up, but not for long. He slipped his hand down the back of my underwear and forced his fingers in between my legs from behind.

After he left, I felt the burning when I went pee in the toilet. I didn't know what he did, and it was okay, because I didn't want to think about it or remember it.

Maybe If I . . .

O shadow, freed at sun's set,
pleasure seeking aberration,
hide seek player of the night . . .
O creature of the dark.

Judith A. Boggess

It wasn't a good idea, but I had do something to keep the man away from me. Pop would have a hissy fit if he caught me, but I was going to sleep under my bed tonight. Maybe the man would think I wasn't home. I grabbed a pillow and my Aunt Jemima doll, lay on the floor on my stomach, and crawled under my cot. It was dark under there and the dust balls made me sneeze. I took a deep breath and blew them over into the corner out of my way.

The jukebox blared a new Patti Page song, "How Much is that Doggie in the Window," a dumb song for grownups to sing "arf, arf" to. I fell asleep to people downstairs laughing, singing, and barking to the song.

In a distance, I heard Pop saying, "Where t'hell is she?" He sounded upset. Was he looking for Lady? She was sleeping in Andy's room.

Rubbing my eyes, I squirmed out from under the bed as Pop flipped up my bedcovers. The look on his face scared me. "What in blue-blazes ya doing under there?" he said. He grabbed my arm and pulled me up. The light in the room hurt my eyes and I squinted. "Get ta' hell in bed," he said, giving me a rough shove. Nuts. I forgot to bring the alarm clock when I crawled under the bed.

Pop was shaking mad. I leaned over the edge of the bed and grabbed my pillow from the floor.

"Look at the dust! Gimme it!" Pop growled, and pounded my pillow. I lay like a board, too afraid to move. Pop put the pillow under my head, fixed my covers and tucked me in with strict orders to never do such a dumb-jackass thing again. He flicked off the light, and stomped to his room, cursing under his breath.

I lay in the dark and listened to my heart pounding in my chest. I was scared. But at least the bar was closed and I was safe. The man didn't find me tonight. But I have to find another place to hide.

Maybe if I sleep in my closet . . .

I could wait until nine, after Pop checked on me. This time I'd remember to set the clock for two and get back in bed before he came upstairs.

Late afternoon I started to clean out the far corner of the closet under the clothes pole. I put boxes around the back to keep anyone from seeing me after I crawled behind them. To make sure, I spread out the clothes on the hangers above me.

Mickey came in. "Whadda ya doin'?"

"Making a secret place to hide," I answered.

"Can I play?"

"No. It's my secret spot. Stay out of here."

He started sniffling.

"Oh, why are you crying? Jeez, Louise."

"Ya don't like me."

"Yes I do."

"No ya don't. Ya won't lemme play."

"Oh, for crying out loud. Climb in here. There, nobody can see you. Okay?'

Mickey grinned at me from under the rack of clothes. I put boxes in front of him and arranged the hangers. He was hidden from a quick look.

"Here's your blankey and teddy bear. You stay in there as long as you want. But you got to keep your mouth shut. This is our secret place," I said.

Mickey shook his head and stuck his thumb in his mouth. He fell asleep. I forgot about him as I played moving the furniture around in my doll house. Bored after a while, I went to Bobby Ann's to see what she was doing. We hung out together until Pop whistled for me to come home for dinner. I could see he wasn't in a good mood when I came into the kitchen.

"Sit down," he demanded. "Where's Mickey?"

I shrugged my shoulders.

"When did ya see him last?"

"In our room."

"Where in your room?"

I shrugged my shoulders again.

"How about the closet?" he asked.

Oh, fuck me. I forgot about Mickey in there. I got scared and slid down on my chair.

"Sit up straight!" Pop yelled. He looked into my face. "Why'd ya lock him in the closet?"

"I didn't lock him . . . ."

"Then why the hell was he in there with the door locked?" Pop's voice got meaner.

"We were playing and he wanted me to lock the door so he could hide and so nobody could find him and he must have fell asleep and I guess I forgot him and I went over to Bobby Ann's and . . ."

"And Mickey woke up alone in the dark, screamed like he was being killed because he was scared shitless. We thought he was with you all this time. He could've died in there. Suffocated to death, died of fright!" He shouted. "He could be dead and ya'd be going to his funeral tomorrow. Is that what you wanted?"

I shook my head, no. I felt so bad, I started to tear-up.

"And, don't start snottin'. It ain't gonna bail ya out this time," he said. "You set the table, clean it, and do all the dishes by yourself tonight. Wash, dry, and put away."

"But that ain't fair," I started to complain. "I just forgot."

"'Ya forgot' ain't no excuse," he said. "Maybe now you'll use your head for something besides a hat rack."

Freaking grouch. It's all Mickey's fault. He's the jerk for falling asleep. See if I ever let him play with me again, stinking Brat.

Pop told me to get washed for supper and set the table. Without a word, I went about my job. I was going to give everybody the silent treatment. Mom looked at the place settings and told me to put two more down.

Great. Just great. On the night I have to do everything, she gets the bug to cook . Invite extra people, too. I'm gonna do the dishes so slow I won't have time to do my stinking homework. I don't care if I get zeros.

Finished with chores, I raced upstairs before Pop could corner me about homework. Could I still use my closet as a hiding place tonight? If I did, I better not let Pop catch me or he'd more than kill me. I'll be sure to set the alarm to wake me at twelve so I can get up and go into the closet. Then I'll set it again for 2 a.m., before Pop and Mom come upstairs. I won't care if it awakens Andy. I ain't afraid of him.

Later in my dream, I was sitting on a porch swing, rocking back and forth. And the heel of my foot was pressing against my privates. All kinds of tingling things were happening down there and going through my body. The strange feelings felt good. Then they left my body as I got wide-awake and realized I had to go to the bathroom. What a strange dream, I thought as I opened my eyes. And there he was. His dark shadow was walking out of my room. His footsteps sneaked down the hallway to the apartment door. Shit! What happened to my alarm clock? It was supposed to go off at twelve. It was gone. The apartment door closed very quiet. Did the man steal my clock? I jumped out of bed and looked around in the dark and listened for the sound of its ticking. I couldn't hear it.

I searched for the glow-in-the-dark hands. The clock wasn't in my room. I tiptoed out to the hall, turned on the hall light the man switched off, and followed a ticking sound to Eddie and Andy's room. My brothers were both asleep. Eddie was snoring. On his dresser was his clock set for five-thirty and along side of it was mine set for six. He must've taken it, afraid he'd oversleep. He had to be to work by seven in the morning to load beer trucks.

I stood in their doorway listening to my brothers breathing

and snoring. I was mad Eddie took my clock, and I was shivering. A chill ran through my body and all the hairs stood up on my arms and legs. Every plan I made got messed up. I didn't know what else to do.

Lady was sleeping on the bed between my brothers, under the blankets with her head on the pillow. She picked up her head and looked at me.

"Why didn't you bark? You stupid, good-for-nothing freakin' fleabag."

Some Days Are Lousier Than Others

Now and then, there is a person born who is so unlucky that he runs into accidents, which started out to happen to somebody else.

Don Marquis

IN WESTERN MOVIES, when cowboys wanted to blow something up, they laid out long, thin lines of gunpowder that sizzled and sparked when it was lit with a cigarette butt. If they were scaredy-cats, they'd drop a match on the black powder and run for cover. It was great watching the smoky black line go across the movie screen, and *blam!* Whole mountainsides came down, blocking getaway passes, even blowing Indians to smithereens.

In war movies, Army men laid fuse lines rolled off hand-held spools. They untwisted the line after cutting it and hooked it to posts on a detonator box. The other end of the fuse line was stuck in dynamite, at least ten sticks, all taped together. Then they strapped the dynamite to bridges and waited for Nazi tanks and their soldiers to get to the center of the span, and *blam!* Soldiers were blown sky-high, and the bridge and everything on it would fall into the river. I wanted to do that. I wanted to explode something into a zillion pieces.

Not having any gunpowder, long burning fuses, or dynamite, I settled for toilet paper. I didn't want to use firecrackers because one went off in my hand once, and my fingers went dead all day and I couldn't hear for a long time. It was like my head was packed with cotton and everybody was mumbling.

I took the roll of paper from the holder and wrapped it around the toilet bowl, up and over the shower curtain rod, back down around the tub faucet, and around the sink. Back and forth I went, making my fuse line. I really wanted to hear something go *blam!* But I guess I'd have to pretend.

I pulled out the matches from my jeans pocket that I sneaked from the bar. Did cowboys and soldiers feel this excited? Standing in the bathroom doorway, I lit a match and held it to the end of the paper. Holy shit! The paper lit up and fire jumped like crazy around the bathroom, but it didn't follow the path I laid out. Poof! It went up in flames and smoke all at once. One minute the room was fiery red and then it became a gray cloud with black papery ash floating down to the floor. God, there was a lot of smoke!

Maybe I should've used butcher string dipped in turpentine instead. Crap! Pop's going to smell this. His nose was a smoke-finder ever since Don Burnett fell asleep with a cigarette in his hand and started the mattress on fire in room seven.

"Mickey, get up." I coughed. He was taking a nap. I had to get him out of the smoke creeping in our bedroom. Oh, no. I heard pounding footsteps.

Is Pop coming? I got to get out of here.

I ran to my brothers' room, opened the window and climbed out onto the fire escape. The door to the apartment opened. I shut the window and took off down the stairs, and jumped from the ladder as if the Nazis were hot on my tail.

The bathroom didn't catch on fire, but smoke and black pieces of tissue must've still been floating through the air when Pop came down the hallway. I dropped the matches by the bathroom door. He found them and must've figured Mickey started the fire. I could hear him yelling and Mickey crying. Shit. Damn. I didn't mean Mickey to get in trouble, but no way would I tell I started the fire. Pop would make me his slave till hell froze over.

On the patio under the fire escape, Andy was hammering nails through upturned bottle caps and fastening them onto a board.

"Hey Andy, whatcha doing?"

"Not you again. What's the old man bellowing about up there?"

"Ain't gotta clue. You nailing bottle caps to a board?"

"Duh! What a bright light bulb ya are," he said. "Ya smell like smoke."

I ignored him and changed the subject. "I just asked you a question. You don't have to get snotty."

Mocking me, he said, "I just asked ya a question . . . make like a friggin' bee and buzz off."

"Why can't I help?"

He didn't answer me.

"Can I watch?"

"No."

"Why can't I . . . ."

"'Cause . . . ."

"I'll zip my lip, promise, cross my heart, hope to die."

"Hah! With my luck, ya'll live forever," he said, pounding a nail into the center of a cap.

I watched without saying another word as he worked.

"Okay, pain in the ass," he said. "Hand me a cap and get a short nail outta the jar. Not that one, jerk; that's a finishing nail. I want one with a head. See that's a head, dumb dildo."

"What's a dildo?"

"You, ya dummy! Hand me those caps with the edges up."

"But you can't tell what they say when you nail them to the board."

"Don't want to know what they say," Andy said. "This is gonna be a boot scraper. It's a present for Mom to put by the back door. And ya better keep your trap shut about it."

"Jeez! Why you always have a bug up your ass? I'm going to the playground. You can fix your own damn boot scraper," I threw the bottle cap and nail at him.

"Go suck your thumb," he teased.

"Fuck you, Andy, and Mom will hate your ugly, stupid-looking boot-scraper. She never uses anything we make and she won't use this neither, because it's dumb, just like you. She'll throw it in the fire barrel and burn it when you're not looking."

Andy got so angry he threw the hammer at me as I turned and ran away from him. It bounced on the ground, missing me by an inch. I screamed, "Asshole!"

"Bitch!" he yelled.

A safe distance away, I stopped and looked to see if he was going to chase me. He couldn't catch me. Nobody could. Instead, Andy raised the half-finished boot scraper up and over his head and flung it to the ground. He yelled as he bent, picked up the board, stood up, and smashed it over and over again till it split into pieces. His face went red and his blond hair got all messed up. He stood there in his black-and-white plaid flannel shirt and jeans with rolled-up cuffs, his fists clenched tight and shoved down by his sides. He looked at the pieces of his work he turned to splinters, picked them up and threw them in the rusty fire barrel. Then he turned, walked out the driveway toward Main Street, leaving the hammer, jar of nails, and can of bottle caps lying on the ground.

Pissed off, but scared of Andy, I headed to the schoolyard, it was best to leave him alone and not remind him to put Pop's stuff away. At the schoolyard I grabbed the swing highest from the ground. The metal links bit into my hands as I ran backwards fast as I could, jumped up and plopped down. My butt hung off of the seat as I leant back with arms stretched out. I pushed with my legs, pulled my chest up, and pressed my elbows down, forcing myself higher and higher in the air. My hair whipped my neck and slapped my face and eyes. I flew so high my butt rose up off the seat. The chains buckled and clanked, warning I could flip right over the top bar and be thrown off the swing. It happened to a kid once.

Straight out, lying back, I pushed my luck. I could touch the sky with my feet. My sneakers pointed to the heavens. One day I'm going to put my feet right through a big, white cloud.

On the back-swing, I looked down over my knees and was amazed at how far away the ground looked. Fly! I want to fly away. If I could fly, I wouldn't care nobody ever wanted to play with me. If I could fly like a bird, it wouldn't matter no one listened to me. I'd talk to the birds and make their sounds. I could zoom right off this swing, stretch my arms out, and fly like the falcons and eagles by the train trestle. I could touch the sky, if I wanted to. If I wanted, all I had to do was let go . . . if I wanted to . . . .

"Hey, Cherny! Get off that swing!" DeFiore yelled as she came around the side of the schoolhouse.

What's her problem? There were five other swings with no one on them. I ignored her. Mary's mother died a few days ago and she was acting weird since. She was three years older than me, but played with me sometimes because she didn't have many friends either. Her father, Mr. DeFiore, cooked Chinese food at "The Well," the bar across from the movie theater. He slept days and worked nights, leaving his girls home alone. They had a small house in John Delay's housing park out by the Elms.

"Hey, Cherny! Ya deaf? I said get t'hell off that swing! It's mine!"

Oh, well. I was tired anyway, dragged my feet in the furrow of loose dirt, and before I came to a stop, Mary grabbed the swing by the chain and jerked it toward her. The seat pulled out from under me and I tumbled off.

"What t'hell? I was getting off. What's a matter with you?" I asked, getting up from the ground, brushing the dirt off my pants.

"Yer what's a matta' with me, ya li'l bitch."

Mary shoved the swing at me, hit me in the hip and knocked me off-balance. She lunged, pushed me down. The back of my head smashed in the dirt from Mary landing on top of me. My hip hurt where the swing smacked me.

Before I knew it, she was pounding me with her fists. My nose crunched and I tasted blood, scaring me. Mary cursed me and called me names. "Yer glad my mother's dead!" she screamed. "Yer glad she's dead!" Covering my face like boxers do in a fight movie, I tried to protect what I thought was my broken nose, and became afraid Mary was gonna leave me for dead, like Eddie did to that kid in Kingston.

"Stop!" I cried. She grabbed two fistfuls of my hair and bashed my head into the ground.

"That guinea friend of yers, Ann Marie, told me ya was glad my Ma was dead. I hate you!" She bashed my head some more and beat on my arms covering my face.

"What's going on over there? Do I gotta call the cops?" Mrs. Burhans hollered.

Mary stood, kicked me in the ribs, and said, "Ya better hide if ya see me coming. I'll kill ya the next time I get my hands on ya, bitch." She walked away crying.

Mrs. Burhans was standing in her backyard. "Hoodlums!" she yelled. She grabbed her Donny and pulled him into the house. Mary was gone and there was no one here to help me. No one here to tease me about getting the crap kicked out of me either.

Sobbing and shaking like a leaf in a hurricane, I couldn't stand. Every part of my face, my head, and even the roots of my hair hurt. If I couldn't walk on shaky legs, I'd crawl. Pretend, as I crawled on my belly, pulling my body with my arms and hands. Pretend you're with Audie Murphy and dynamite just went blam! Pretend you're dying. You can make it to the weeds by the path. Com'on, I kept telling myself. You can do it.

I puked in the weeds and wiped my mouth on my shirt. Christ, I couldn't stop shaking. Now I knew what Great-Grandpa Struber felt like with Parkinson's disease. I will make it to the barn. Can't tell Pop, he'd say, "You'll live. Go wash up." Besides Pop might have figured it was me who started the fire. And he'd say God was getting even with me by having Mary beat the hell outta me instead of him. Can't tell Mom. She'd ask what I did to piss Mary off. Won't tell Andy. He'll just laugh. I'll tell Eddie tonight. Maybe he could get Peggy Russell to kick Mary's ass. Peggy's tough and Mary's age.

THE SUN CAME OUT AND SNEAKED THROUGH THE CRACKS in the barn siding and the breeze coming through had the cobwebs with dust, dangle-dancing. If Mary came looking, she wouldn't know where to find me. Sitting hunched over, pushed way back into a dark corner, I tried sucking my thumb. My face hurt. It really hurt. But I was safe.

In the barn no one would call me skinny, or a bow-legged banty chicken. Here no one would be pointing a finger, calling me baby. And, just because I was in fifth grade didn't mean I had to quit sucking my thumb, neither. I wasn't a baby! I was sick of Pop saying, "Where's the butcher knife? I'll cut it off. Ya want buckteeth?", or,

"Yer gonna swallow it and choke t'death." Mom embarrassed me whenever she got the chance. "She's getting bigger, but . . .", or, "She's pretty, but . . ." After the buts, came the loud whisper, "She still sucks her thumb no matter what we do to break her of the filthy habit, blah, blah, blah . . ."

I only do it where no one could see me, like at night or at rest-time in school. But I'd forget and get caught sometimes. Why can't they leave me alone? I don't care if I get buckteeth!

Sniffing back more tears, I pulled my skinned knees tight to my chest. I could hear it now when I got home, "How did ya rip your pants? Why can't ya act like a girl? Stay out of the trees. No climbin'. . . Keep off the . . . If you didn't . . . Why don't ya ever listen . . . I told ya not to . . . Ya won't be happy till ya kill ya'self, break a leg, have it amputated, crack your skull, be a Denny Dimwit . . . ." Aggghhhaaa! I stuffed my shirt-covered fist in my mouth and screamed "Aggghh-haaa!" over and over again, as loud and as hard as I could, for as long as I could.

Exhausted, I lay on my side, curled into a tight ball, like a wounded soldier in enemy territory in a barn in France, all covered over with loose hay. I squinted at my pale, wrinkled, flattened thumb and shoved it back in my mouth. Wait till I get big. Nobody is ever going to hurt me ever again. You just wait and see.

Answer The Phone, Will You, Lou?

No, Sir; there is nothing which has yet been contrived by man by which so much happiness is produced as by a good tavern or inn.

Samuel Johnson

"Say, watch your mouth, fish-breath. Kid's sitting over there," Catherine Foertsh said to Tony Debrosky.

"Whadda I say? Whadda I say?" Tony slurred.

"Don't worry. She don't hear a thing when she's got her nose buried in a comic book, goes all deaf and dumb, in one ear and out the other," Pop said. "Talk to her. She won't even answer ya."

The men and the ladies at the bar laughed.

So much for what Pop knew. I wasn't deaf. I heard and saw everything going on, and I remember it, too! If he was forcing me to sit here, I'd pretend I didn't hear him.

Earlier, Pop had been looking for me to do chores, and found me outside sitting by the chimney. He got his tail in a twist because I was cutting the legs off the daddy-long-legs so they looked more like spiders.

Don't know which pissed him off more, me cutting their legs off, or me using his nose-hair scissors to do the job. It didn't seem to bother the daddy-long-legs any. They only limped if I didn't cut the legs off straight.

"How'd you like me to cut your legs off? He bellowed. "Would you want to go around walking on your knees and elbows for the rest of your life?" Pop yanked the scissors out of my hand. "Where ta' hell are your friggin' brains, up your ass?"

Pop said I had to plop my butt on a barstool till he told me I could leave. If I asked to get down, he'd say, "Now sit there longer just for asking."

So I sat pretending to read, but I was really getting new curse words to add to my growing list I was collecting. Also, I got to practice being a spy by peeking out the corner of my eye, or looking up at my eyebrows, without moving my head away from my comic book.

This was as good as being a federal agent for Robert Taylor in the movie *Bribe*, although that movie stunk. I learned who got fired from work, who got new cars, and who couldn't get one because he was having a kid. I knew who beat his wife, and which husbands and wives were cheating on each other, including my relatives. I liked knowing things my brothers didn't know. Secrets weren't hard to keep because there wasn't anybody to tell them to.

Brr-ring, brr-ring. The telephone rang and snapped me out of daydreaming.

"Answer the phone, will ya, Lou?" Pop called to Louie Auchmoody.

"Sure, Ed." Brr-ring, brr-ring.

Louie picked up the handset and spoke loud for everyone to hear, "Reid's Hotel an' brickyard. We lay anythin'. You call. We haul. Day or Night. Black or White."

Brr-ring, brr-ring.

"Wha' t'hell?" Louie said.

Brr-ring, brr-ring.

Louie looked at the handset. It was ripped from the pay phone. He jiggled the receiver. It kept ringing. A cigarette dangled from the corner of his mouth and his fedora was tipped back and to one side. Looking like Humphrey Bogart, he grinned and walked to the bar and handed the phone to Pop.

"Here, Ed. Must be for you," Louie said.

The phone stopped ringing. Pop put it to his ear. "Reid's Hotel," he barked into the dead handset. Its frayed cord swung in the breeze. Customers stared at Pop and Louie in silence like they were watching a scene between Orson Welles and Bogart.

"Yeah, sure, he's here," Pop said to the make-believe caller. "Here Hill, phone's for you." Joe Hill took the phone.

"Joe, here," he said. "Who t'hell's callin' me an' disturbin' me from my most serious drinking time?" He waited a minute like he was listening to someone on the other end. "Yes, dear. Yes, dear. I will, dear. See you shortly, dear," he said, in a softer tone.

Joe gave the phone back to Pop. "For cryin' out loud, Ed. Anyone else calls for me, I ain't here."

"Here, Louie," Pop said. Laughing, he handed him the receiver.

Louie went to place the handset back in the phone booth and it rang again.

I giggled. This was better than the movies.

"Damn," Louie said. "Who ta' hell is it this time? Hello, Reid's Watering Hole."

Louie called out to George Craft, the taxi driver, "Hey, Craft, someone up at the Valley Inn wants a cab."

George belted down his shot of whiskey, and said, "Tell 'em I'm a'coming." He took a swig of beer, staggered out the front door, and said, "Don't throw out my glass, Ed. I'll b'right back."

Everyone cracked up laughing as George got into his cab and drove off. I giggled with my head down.

"What t'hell happened to the phone, Ed?" Louie asked.

"Aw, shit," Pop said, and shook his head. "Ya wouldn't believe it."

"You miss last night, ya you did," Veikko Jalante, the masseur from Williams Lake Hotel piped in. "Ed have bi-i-g fight in bar, ya?

"Young whippersnappers from Kingston come. Tough guys. All muscles, no brains, looking ta' kick ass," Veikko said. "Bottle goes 'crack' over Frog Eye Fogerty's head. He drops to floor; bleed bad. Ed gets pissed. Fists come from nowhere."

Veikko went on. "Smitty, ya know, Owen back from Korea, go crazy, knocks heads together. Him and Ed pound piss out of young studs. Young asshole goes to call cops. Ha! Ed, never move so fast, ya? Asshole in phone booth puts foot against door so Ed can't open. Ha! Jackass gets big surprise! Ed rips door off hinges."

All eyes turned from Veikko and look at the wood-and-glass door leaning cockeyed against the phone booth. They looked back to Veikko.

"Ya. Yust don't close door. It fall and break foot bones. Ha! Ed like King Kong gorilla. Throws door on floor, rips phone from asshole's hand, breaks wire, grabs shirtfront and asshole fly out of phone booth like Superman.

"Ed grabs him up." Veikko takes a fistful of his own shirt. "Feet no touch floor." Veikko dances around on tiptoes. "Push him through screen door. No open. Right through," he said. "See pretty new screen door now, ya? Ed step through front door with asshole. Hang him on telephone pole. Lift him right up and hang him on foot peg, all drippin' vet. Funny thin' I ever sawed. Ed scared piss outta him. Ha! Ha! Run right into shoes and drips on ground. Ha! Ha!

"Ed and Smitty," Veikko continued, "throw friends of asshole out ripped screen door. Swish, right out. Ed tell 'em not come back, or not be so lucky next time."

"Good Kee-rist! Whadda you gonna tell the phone company?" John Crookstan asked, laughing with the rest.

Pop shrugged his shoulders. "Tell 'em a drunk passed out against the door, had no choice, had to get him out some way. Who wants another drink? Round's on me." Heads tipped back, draining their glasses. Pop didn't buy drinks often, but a free drink now would get customers' minds off the fight and back to spending money.

Ha! Now I knew what all the noise was at 1:30 this morning, and why there was a guy hanging from the telephone pole kicking like a broken puppet, and screaming he was choking to death. I thought someone put him there as a joke. His friends pulled their car up to the telephone pole, stood on the hood, and helped him down. Then they took off like a bat out of hell. Never knew what I'd see next.

King Charming

*There are glances of hatred that stab,
and raise no cry of murder.*

George Eliot

Pop was still angry about those damn daddy-long-legs. He told me I couldn't go out to play for a week. "It's no fair keeping me cooped up like the *Prisoner of Zenda*," I said.

"Ya keep your mouth shut. When I want your two cents, I'll ask for it. D'ya unnerstan'?" he said, looking up from his newspaper.

I nodded.

"Answer me! Can't hear your head shakin'. D'ya know what 'Answer me!' means, or ya stupid?"

"Yes!" I snapped at him.

"Yes, what? Yes you unnerstan' what I'm sayin', or yes ya too stupid to know what I'm sayin'?"

"Yes, I know what you're saying."

"Take the snotty tone outta your voice, young lady, or I'll give ya something to be snottin' about."

I pressed my lips together, squooshed them into a tight circle and bit the side of my cheek, Yeah sure, try and hit me.

"D'ya know anything about the missing Coke bottles?" he asked.

Oh, screw me! No wonder he's a crab-ass today and got me sitting here. I took some Coke bottles from the basement a couple a days ago, sneaked uptown and cashed them in at Roosa's grocery for the deposit. I knew I wasn't supposed to, but I wanted a box of chocolate cookies with the scalloped edge and white sugar sprinkles on top, and I didn't have enough money.

"And don't lie, I already talked to Mr. Roosa."

I'm never gonna buy anything from Roosa's again, that dirty rat fink.

Pop said I had to work off my theft. He wanted the stairs to the hotel rooms swept down and he wanted it done now.

"But I did them yesterday," I said. "Besides it's worth more than what I got for those stinking Coke bottles. And I gotta go to the Grange for dance. I'll do them later. Cross my heart and hope to die," I said.

"Bullshit!" he bellowed. "With you, later never comes."

"But...."

Blossom and Blanche taught tap-dancing, ballet and acrobatics next door on Saturdays at the Grange. They let Mickey take tap dancing classes for free. He was good at it. I did ballet and tap and begged to go to classes.

"No buts about it," Pop said.

Angry thoughts were tumbling in my mind like a rockslide down Joppenberg Mountain. Right. Do what you're told. No crying. Don't you dare.

"Ya better learn to do what you're told, when you're told or ya'll never work for nobody. D'ya think I got this far thinking I know it all?"

Yup. Sure do.

"I gotta get a drink," I said, jumping down and going into the kitchen. I poured a glass of milk and stood staring at my sneakers. Knowing it'd piss him off, I twisted my foot on the linoleum floor, making annoying squeaking sounds. Maybe he'd give up and let me the heck outta here. Maybe I wouldn't miss much of the class.

"Stop the damn shit with your foot," he snapped. "Get out here and look at me, Miss Priss, so I know you're hearing me."

I'd have to be deaf not to hear, I thought.

"Wipe the smirk off your face, or I'll wipe it off," he threatened.

I crossed my arms in front of my chest, stuck one hip out to the side and glared at him.

"Don't look at me with that tone of voice. I know what ya thinkin'."

If he did, I'd be dead right now.

"Uncross those arms."

I dropped my arms by my side and hooked my thumbs in the slash of my pockets.

"Now," he said, "get the dustpan an' brush an' get those steps done. Pronto!"

I clicked the heels of my sneakers together, saluted him the way Nazis and Veikko Jalante did when he played Hitler at the bar. "Aye-Aye, Herr-Kap-pe-tan," I said.

"For being such a smart ass," he added, "you can wash the stairs too." He followed me as I picked up the dustpan and brush. "And if you stomp, pout, or whine, I'll find more jobs for you."

I wanted to stamp my feet till they stung but didn't dare. Instead, I shot him my squint-eyed look that said, "Drop dead!"

"Who t'hell do ya think ya are, looking at me like that!" he bellowed.

Maybe he could read my thoughts. I told myself, Don't let the enemy see how you feel. If you shake or cry, you die, pushed past him, and walked through the bar.

"Where ya going? I'm not through talking, young lady!"

Oh yes you are. Fuck you! Double fuck you!

"I'm gonna do your stupid stairs!" I said. It came out as a shout. Louder and nastier than what I would've liked, but he ignored it.

"Well, ya better do 'em right. And lose the gawd damn sarcastic attitude while you're at it!"

Opening the door to the stairwell I thought, don't stomp or he'll have you walk up and down the stairs a million times without making a sound, like he did to you last week. If I banged a door shut, he tells me to open and close it twenty-five times quiet, or to start over. If I complained about not liking supper, he made me do dishes every night for a week without help for being ungrateful. And if one piece of silverware had a fleck of food on it, he'd dump the whole batch back in the sink and make me wash them again.

"If one's dirty, they're all dirty," he'd say. "Do things right the first time, and ya won't have to do 'em over again. I'm teachin' ya lessons ya'll need the rest of your life. Some day ya'll thank me," he said.

Yeah, when pigs fly!

"When are you going to learn?" Mom's voice came echoing in my head. "It's not the right way, not the wrong way, not the Navy's way but Ed's way. That's how things have to be done around here."

Yeah. Pop never let us kids do anything without saying, "Here let me show ya the right way." Then he'd do the job himself. But not the stairs. He'd never cleaned them.

"Here," he said one day, "A present for ya. Somethin' to make your life easier." The present was a new dustpan and brush he bought from the Fuller Brush salesman. It didn't make me happy.

The twenty-four stairs were divided in half by a landing and it all had to be washed in the direction it got swept. No gray water streaks or wet spots were allowed, and the banisters had to be wiped down, also.

Pop was always finding something I wasn't doing right. He checked on me when I was halfway done. He walked to the top and back down inspecting each step, lifting the rubber treads, looking under them for tiny specks of grit.

"There's dirt here," he said. "If one's dirty . . ." *Blah, blah blah.* "do 'em all over again."

I wanted to push or trip him. But, with my luck, he wouldn't get hurt. He'd get up and come back and kill me. He went in the bar and I climbed the stairs. Stomp, stomp, stomp and stomp. What the heck, I missed my chance to be at the dance class. I didn't care what he'd do to me now. At the top of the stairs, I jumped up and down about five times and ran in our apartment to refill the water bucket. I wouldn't sweep the stairs again. I'd just wash them and dry them.

These couldn't be my real parents. I was adopted. My real Pop had to be Uncle Howard. He was my King Charming. If that was true, then Aunt Helen would have to be my Mom. Yuck!

I felt worse than Cinderella, because I was too young to have a Prince Charming come rescue me. But, I could dream of having a King Charming father. Like the song in the movie " . . . a dream is a wish your heart makes. . ." I could dream of not living in this bar and not having a Pop who shoved Mom around, making her hit her head on the kitchen grill and have stitches in her eyebrow. And I could dream that my mother only drank tea. Silent tears ran down my face.

My real folks wouldn't fight or drink. They'd come find me someday. Someday . . . , I thought, as I worked my way down the stairs. I hummed words from "When You Wish upon a Star." I thought if I kept believing in my wish it would come true just like the song said.

Someday I'll have a real pretty home, and my father, King Charming, will have a maid. And I won't have to clean anything, especially the stairs.

Swearing

*Take not God's name in vain; select
a time when it will have effect.*

Ambrose Bierce

The clothes were finished rinsing. The water drained out of the washer into the kitchen sink. At the same time being careful not to get my fingers caught in the wringers, I put wet dresses and blouses through the rollers and watched them plop into the wicker laundry basket. When done, I popped the wringers loose, "so they don't glue themselves together when they dry," as Pop had warned, and shoved the washer in the corner of the kitchen.

Dragging the laundry basket over to a window in my brothers' room, I opened it, and tugged on the clothesline. Mike Rosenkranse wasn't home with his tractor trailer and that was good because our clothesline ran out to a pole right next to where he parked. That meant I didn't have to hang short stuff first and I wouldn't get screamed at because the sheets got wiped across the top of his trailer.

As I stood by the window about to pin my dress on the line, I heard voices down below.

"C'mon guys," Myron said to Georgie and Porky. "Judy's gonna do it again."

"Wha' she doing now?" Porky asked.

"She's gonna curse."

"Yeah? Where?" George asked.

"Down front of Schmidt's."

"Why there?"

"It's for the new kids livin' there. They ain't ever heard her and she got some new cusses."

I ducked down below the window and listened to the Rosenkranse boys.

"Who're the new kids?" Georgie asked.

"Dunno. Relatives, I guess. Ask Judy," Myron said.

"We gotta pay her?" Georgie asked.

"Course not. We're friends," Myron said. "The others pay."

"How she 'member all them words?" Porky asked.

"Beats the shit outta me. She's got a mem'ry like an elephant."

"What time do we gotta be there?" Georgie wanted to know. "I got errands for Ma."

"When the fire siren goes off. So get going. We'll wait for ya at home."

I peeked over the sill and watched as Georgie raced out of the driveway, and Porky and Myron went home. I looked at Eddie's clock and saw that I had fifteen minutes to put the clothes out to dry and get down to the Schmidts' house.

I SAT ON THE FENCE THAT RAN BETWEEN THE SHRUBS meant to keep kids off Grace and Al Schmidt's property. The Rosenkranse boys, Bobby Ann, and I waited for the fire siren to go off. Stevie Robbins and Carole Connelly were the Schmidts' nephew and niece from different families who came to visit for the summer. Stevie was gonna live with them and go to Saint Peter's school. He had a metal plate in his head. Pop said he heard Stevie's head was dented in the brain department and he was giving his parents hell, so they shipped him off to Grace and Al.

Stevie said he'd pay a whole dollar if he and Carole could hear me swear for one minute without saying the same word twice. He didn't think I could do it.

The fire siren blew at twelve noon. Everyone up and down Main Street, plugged their ears and froze as if the siren screeched out, "Simon says, 'Halt'!" People cursed and dogs howled until the noise died down.

Kids came and gathered in front of the Schmidts'.

"Looks like we're gonna make some money today," Bobby Ann said, rubbing the palms of her hands together. She took charge of the kids and the money.

"Aw-right!" she said. "Gather around and listen up! Anybody ain't got money, get lost! This ain't no freakin' free show. How old are ya, kid?" Bobby Ann asked. "We don't want anybody here under seven."

"He's my cuz'n and I gots to watch him. If he goes, I go. Then you ain't getting my nickel."

"Ah, for Pete's sake, aw-right. But put your hands over his ears. Everybody else, ante up now or git." Bobby Ann held out her hand. "What's this?" she said, looking down at the palm of her hand. "Three cents, two double bubble gums and three wax soda bottles for the two of you?"

"It's all I got, Bobby Ann. Honest."

"Okay," she said, pocketing the payment. "Now where the heck is this Stevie kid with his dollar?"

"Here he comes!" Porky shouted. "He's by hisself! Where's the girl?"

"She ain't coming," Stevie said.

"Okay, buster, where's the dollar?" Bobby Ann asked.

Stevie gave her a large silver coin.

"Wha … ? A silver dollar?"

"Yeah. I'm saving them. I got two with the same date, so you can have this one."

Bobby Ann bit down on the silver dollar like the cowboys did in the movies to see if gold coins were really gold. "You gotta watch?" she asked.

Stevie held out his wrist.

"Shit, a secon' hand an' all. It's one of them glow-in-the-dark Timex's." she said.

I gave her a look and said, "Can we get going here? Day's a-wasting."

Bobby Ann called out, "Everybody anted up? Then, gather

around because we ain't gonna repeat anything, and Judy ain't gonna be screaming!"

Six or so kids, plus the Rosenkranses, sidled up around me. I sat like a movie queen on the fence. Bobby Ann dropped the coins and candy in her pocket to be divvied up between us later. I'd let her keep the gum as part of her pay for being my business manager.

"Lemme know when you want to start," Stevie said looking at his watch.

"Count backward from ten to one," Bobby Ann said.

Eddie, walking by with Norma Jean, Dickey and Lina, stopped to see what was happening. They stood on the sidelines. I closed my eyes for a second, and then stared into space.

Bobby Ann looked over at Stevie. He began to count backwards, " . . . five, four, three, two, one, zero.

I started:
"Four-Eyed-Birdbrain
Cootie Head
Bedbug Eater
Fink
Idiot
Ass
Asshole
Ass Kisser
Lard Ass
Stupid Ass
Jackass
Pervert
Jerk
Nincompoop
Fool
Imbecile
Simpleton
Ninny
Dunce
Dimwit
Nitwit
Moron

Blockhead
Knucklehead
Dunderhead
Ignoramus
Queer
Faggot
Lezzee
Freak
Fart
Fart Face
Fart Ass
Fart Head
Nigger
Nigger Lover
Guinea Wop
Kraut
Kike
Spick
Mick
Canuck
Limey
Gook
Chink
Fuck
Shit
Piss
Crap
Poop
Poop Head
Shit Head
Shit Eater
Stupid Shit
Booger Nose
Snot Nose
Snot Eater
Booger Eater
Bull Shitter

Twat
Pussy
Pussy Face
Pussy Breath
Pussy Eater
Cunt
Cunt Breath
Hussy
Harlot
Hooker
Tramp
Trollop
Slut
Strumpet
Street Walker
Jezebel
Prostitute
Whore
Whoremaster
Prick
Dick
Dick Face
Limp Dick
Dick Breath
Sucker
Dick Sucker
Prick Sucker
Snot Sucker
Cock Sucker
Mother Fucker
Butt Fucker
Cum Sucker
Cunt Lapper
Muff diver
Muff burger
Tit
Tit Brain

Tit, Titty Sucker
Scum Head
Scumbag
Scrotum
Son of a Bitch
Bastard
Jesus, Mary and Joseph, and
Goddamn!"

"One minute!" Bobby Ann yelled.

"Hot shit! She did it!" Porky screamed, jumping up and down and clapping his hands.

"Fuck, damn, man, she did it!" Dickey said to Eddie, Norma Jean, and Lina as they walked up street laughing and shaking their heads.

Stevie started to disagree. "Now, waitta minute. They weren't all curse words."

"What?" I said, and jumped down from the fence, putting my hands on my hips. I stood on tip-toes, brought myself nose to nose with Stevie and stared him in the eyes. He backed off the curb and into the street, while the rest of the kids scattered.

"Which one of them words can you say in front of your aunt and not get your face slapped! Huh? Huh?"

"Sh-sh-it-it. Sh-sh-it-it," he stuttered as his face turned white as Casper's sheet.

Bobby Ann grabbed my hand and pulled, whispering in pig Latin, "Etslay amscray. Ownay!"

Seeing Stevie's pale face and the stammering as fear, I shook Bobby Ann's hand off.

"Shit?" I said, poking him in the chest with my finger and making him back up more. "You can say shit?"

From behind me came, "No, he cannot, young lady! What in God's name is going on out here? Get in the house, Stephen, and you vagabonds get away from my property! Go home where you belong!"

The hair stood up on the back of my neck as I turned, looked wide-eyed and saw Grace Schmidt looming large and menacing in her yard.

"Olyhay itshay! Ets-lay o-gay, Bobby Ann!"

Bobby Ann and I made a beeline up street to the barn to count the money. We rolled around in the hay, laughing till we almost peed our pants, thinking about Stevie explaining to his aunt what we were doing. I didn't tell Bobby Ann, but I said a little prayer that Stevie wouldn't rat me out. His Uncle Al drank at our bar and I didn't need Mr. Schmidt telling Pop I was doing this swearing thing again.

My Brother Eddie

*"He followed in his father's footsteps,
but his gait was somewhat erratic."*

Nicolas Bentley

Even if Eddie was my brother, he was a knockdown, lip-smacking, gorgeous guy. He should've been a movie actor like Robert Taylor, who the movie magazines said had a perfect profile like Eddie's.

Eddie always had a smile on his face like Mom. She said she read smiling took fewer muscles than frowning and that meant less wrinkles. But I couldn't help wondering if Eddie was pretending to be happy like her.

Eddie had great teeth. They were straight and large. Not pure white, more like the color white of ivory keys on a piano. Us kids got our teeth from Pop's side of the family. Mom's were soft and got lots of cavities. Pop joked saying her teeth were like stars, they came out at night. She didn't think that was funny.

Eddie's jaw was square as Victor Mature's. And he stood six feet tall, with big shoulders and a hairy chest and back. High school girls had crushes on him and they did stupid things to get his attention.

Pop was yelling at Eddie in the dining room, and I spied to see what was happening because Eddie never got into trouble. I pretended to use the ladies room, and stood behind the bathroom door listening and peeking around the edge. What I heard scared me. It was better to pretend I didn't know anything, because Eddie couldn't have done what Pop was asking him about.

Eddie said this girl started saying smart-ass things to him at school. He said she got mad because he called her a dog. She raked her fingernails down his cheek, leaving four bloody scratches on his face. I wondered about those.

Eddie turned his head to the side for Pop to see his face messed up like in a scene in a B movie.

"Sorry, Pop. It was a reflex action. I swung the baseball bat I had in my hand. I didn't mean to hit her."

Holy shit! Only in the movies did Al Capone or Legs Diamond beat up guys with bats. No movie star ever hit a woman like that on the wide screen. They smooshed a grapefruit into her face, or gave her a smack on the cheek if she asked for it.

"Ya just innocently happen to swing the bat and hit her in the mouth!" Pop roared. "Jeezus-H-Christ! Ya knocked out her friggin' teeth, and you're sorry? D'ya know how much this is gonna cost ya? Ya'll be lucky her old man doesn't press charges and throw ya in Sing-Sing!" Pop slammed his hand on the dining room table. Eddie jumped. I jumped.

"Ya gonna be eighteen in September! Yer supposed to graduate next June and be an adult. Ya damn fool! This could mean jail." Pop shook his head. "D'ya know what guys will do to ya in jail? How stupid can ya be?"

It was probably important to Pop that Eddie graduate because Pop only made it to eighth grade and always felt dumb around people his age.

"Don't be like me," he told us. "Get an education."

Pop mumbled under his breath, cursed and said, "It's gotta be that thick-headed Dutch blood of your mother's."

He ranted on till he sputtered out like a dud stick of dynamite at the end of a short fuse. Eddie hung his head and did his best to look sorry. He looked up at Pop with sad beagle-brown eyes and said, "I'll get my summer job again and pay ya back, Pa. Honest." This summer he spent his vacation loading beer trucks at the Ballantine Beer warehouse. Guess he'd be going back there again next summer.

"Yeah! Ya'll shit, too, if you eat reg'lar," Pop said. It didn't sound like he had trust in Eddie. Pop only liked to spend money on stuff important to him, like fishing or hunting gear, or things for Mom, like flowers, candies, and cards, which kept him out of the doghouse. He's going to hate shelling out money for a lawyer and medical bills.

Eddie wanted to go to college and had saved money from the years he worked tending bar and recently, from loading beer trucks. He said he'd give it all to Pop.

Pop told Eddie he'd talk to the principal at the high school and speak to the girl's parents. He'd offer to get the girl's front teeth replaced and do whatever else had to be done if no charges were placed.

"I'll try my damnedest to keep you outta jail. But if I can't, you'll have to take your lumps like a man."

Eddie looked frightened and nodded.

"Look, Pa, after graduation I'll go up to Ballantine's and load trucks fulltime. Maybe I can get to be a driver. I'll pay you back."

Pop put an arm around Eddie's shoulder and said in a lower, calmer voice, "Okay. Don't worry. I'll take care of everything."

The girl's smashed-in teeth required surgery to remove the stumps. After her gums healed, she had teeth made. By the time Pop finished paying the dental bill and gave the girl "a little something for her pain and suffering," like his lawyer suggested, Pop said Eddie could have gone to two colleges. After high school graduation, Eddie became a truck driver and repaid Pop. He never went to college and this wasn't the last of his troubles.

Eddie came in the apartment around one in the morning, a few months later. He went straight to the bathroom. He threw up in the toilet and flushed. He was drinking like Mom, too much. I was used to waking up to her upchucking from switching from beer to Wild Turkey to scotch and back during the night. Now Eddie was in there puking. The water in the sink was running and I figured he was washing up. Was he crying? Sounded like it.

I tiptoed to the bathroom door and pressed my ear against

the door, heard the water turn off, and then these strange growling sounds. I knocked and called out, "Eddie, I gotta go pee. Can I come in?"

"Go 'way, Brat. Lemme 'lone."

"C'mon Eddie. I gotta go pee real bad."

Eddie opened the door but didn't look at me. He was holding onto the sink, straight-armed, head hanging down between his hunched shoulders. He was looking into the sink like he dropped something.

His knuckles were raw and bleeding on both hands. I saw his face in the mirror as I moved behind him. His top lip was puffy on one side. His eyes were red and swollen. And he was stripped to the waist. A bloody, ripped T-shirt laid on the tiled floor. His dungarees were dirty.

"Jeez Eddie, what the heck happened to you?" I asked. "You in an accident or something?"

He looked like George Raft got the best of him in one of his gangster movies. Eddie burst into sobs. Bloody snot ran out of his nose and dripped in the sink. I closed the door so Mickey or Andy wouldn't wake up, pulled a yard of toilet paper off the roll and handed it to him. "Here, Eddie. Blow your nose."

Eddie sat on the side of the tub, wiped his eyes and blew his nose. The tears didn't stop. I climbed up onto the sink and opened the medicine cabinet. Lauren Bacall must've done this for Bogie, or maybe it was Katharine Hepburn for Spencer Tracy, I thought. I rummaged through the cabinet for peroxide, salve, gauze, and adhesive tape. "Give me your hands." Gently, I placed his hands palm down on a folded towel on his lap. I poured peroxide over his wounds and waited. I sopped up the foamy, bubbling blood from his skinless knuckles with a clean washcloth. Eddie winced. The scissors were never in a handy spot in the bathroom when you needed them. I was forced to use my teeth to rip adhesive tape into pieces and stick them dangling from the bottom edge of the sink. This tape was tough. It pulled at my teeth like cold taffy. This never happened in the movies. Darn it, I needed scissors to cut the gauze.

"How did you get so wrecked? Tell me. I won't tell anybody. Cross my heart and hope to die." I turned on my biggest smile.

"Yer a good kid, Brat. Dunno know what I'd do wi'out you." He smiled a lopsided, puffy lip smile.

Gosh, his breath smelled worse than Rosenkranses' old kerosene space heater. "Gee, Eddie. If you lit a match we'd both explode." I wrinkled my nose and waved my hand in front of my face.

Eddie grinned. "Dun make me laugh. It hurts." Slowly his smile faded and he looked at me real serious. "I did somethin' stupid, Brat. Got inna fistfight tonight at school."

"At the high school?" I asked, thinking, Not again.

"No. George's school on Washington." He meant George Washington School on Washington Avenue, only his tongue and mouth weren't working together.

"Who…?" I asked.

"Don't matter. I killed 'em."

"Wha!"

"I killed 'em!" he cried.

He couldn't be saying that. I looked at my brother's face and wondered if he was turning into a bad guy – the kind Elliot Ness came after in the middle of the night, busting down doors with a Tommy gun blazing, arresting the criminal.

Eddie and I were seven years apart and didn't have much in common besides our parents, and that I loved him and believed he loved me, too. But first he cracked a girl in the mouth with a bat and now he beat up some kid and thought he killed him? The bathroom started to feel real small.

Pretend you're the priest in the confessional, I thought and grabbed the scissors I saw laying on the back of the toilet. Think. What would the priest say? I know! The priest would forgive him and make him say, under the pain of going to hell, to never do this again.

Wrapping gauze around both his fists like a prizefighter, I asked, scared of the answer. "Why do you think he's dead?"

Still crying, Eddie gritted his teeth and pulled his puffy lips into a grimace. His eyes narrowed as he pulled up his bandaged and taped hand, made a fist and pounded a make-believe enemy into the floor tiles. "I hit 'em and I hit 'em and hit 'em! He went down. I grabbed 'em by his T-shirt and I pounded the piss outta him! I pounded 'em and pounded 'em till his face looked like hamburger!" he said, with a hoarse voice.

"The guys pulled me off and the kid just laid there, sprawled out on the stairs like ... shit dropped outta the ass of a bird." After a long moment, he whispered, "He's dead, Brat. I know it. He's dead." Looking at the floor, he went on. "Your big brother's a killer." His voice went up in pitch as he said, "I'm worse than the old man. He never killed nobody. Not even in the war."

Eddie put his elbows on his knees and pushed the heel of his hands into his eyes, rubbing hard. He sobbed some more.

"All I wanted to do was go to college an' get outta Rosendale," he cried. "This is such a fuckin' dead-end scumbag town."

"Look at me, Eddie," I said. "The kid'll be okay. Really, he will. You pray to Jesus. Say you're sorry and you won't ever fight again. He'll fix it. You'll see. Everything will be better tomorrow. The kid will be all right."

I didn't sleep well. I prayed to Jesus because everybody around me said it's what you do when nothing else looks like it's working. I didn't really believe that anybody heard me when I prayed. Nothing ever got better around here, it only got worse. I guess it helped some people to think there was somebody up above who listened, who grants wishes. Maybe it'd help Eddie if he thought Jesus was up there pulling some heavenly strings for him. Me? I'll keep my fingers crossed instead.

Anyone with brains knows Jesus prayed to save His skin and it didn't keep Him from getting crucified. We were taught in school His death had a reason, a purpose. It was bad for Jesus, but good for us. This didn't make much sense to me, killing Your only Son before You'd forgive sins not even committed yet, like Eddie's. But nothing much in the Catholic religion made sense. The nuns kept saying I think too much. There were some things I had to take on faith, they said. Pop said it was good I was going to Catholic school or I'd be a heathen like Mom, or worse, an atheist. Prayers or no prayers, maybe almost killing, or killing somebody, would turn out good for Eddie in some way.

From Eddie's bedroom I heard the springs of his iron bed squeak to his flip-flopping around. I don't think he slept much better than me. He took a solemn oath in the bathroom that he would go to Confession, and if the kid lived or died, he'd never fight again.

For days afterwards Eddie read the daily newspaper and whoever he was looking for in the papers must not have died, or went to the police. And Eddie kept his word and refused to argue or fight any more, especially when he was drinking. He soon got put to a test.

Eddie was working on a slow night for Pop, and Norma Jean, his girlfriend, was sitting by the bar next to me. A drunk at the other end sat falling asleep over his drink, when he suddenly bolted upright and went to the men's room. Coming back out, he decided to sit on the barstool next to Norma to flirt with her.

Eddie ignored the guy, but warned him. "If ya mess with her, she's liable to get ticked off, and I won't be responsible for what she does to ya." Eddie began to wash some glasses.

"Ha!" The guy laughed loud. "I ain't never met no yellow-bellied-sapsucker like ya, leavin' your girl to defend herself. Now ain't you some man."

Norma Jean and Eddie both ignored him. I wondered if I might have to duck and run for cover, because this guy was spoiling for a fight. He leaned over in front of Norma and grabbed her left tit and squeezed it hard. I gasped and looked at Eddie.

Eddie sipped his beer and nodded to Norma. Her face went red and she spit in the face of the drinker. "You bastard!" Without warning, her left fist flew up from under the edge of the bar and hit the guy with an uppercut to the chin. It drove him up off the barstool and he fell on his butt on the floor.

"Son-of-a-bitch! She hit me!" he whined, in a startled voice.

I thought he was going to cry.

The drunk got up and staggered toward the front door.

"I tried to warn you." Eddie laughed.

I was so proud of Norma Jean! But most of all, proud of Eddie for keeping the promise he made to me in the bathroom that night. He was a good guy again, like Robert Taylor, or Tyrone Power.

Sled Riding

. . . . If you wound the tree in its youth, the bark will quickly cover the gash; but when the tree is very old, peeling the bark off, and looking carefully, you will see the scar there still. All that is buried is not dead.

Olive Schreiner

The old town dump truck doubled as a plow in the winter, and it creaked and moaned like an old lady stiff with arthritis. The old-timers called the truck, "She."

"She" wheezed and puffed choking-black fumes as she rattled past the bar, pushing snow off the road. Two men looking like Eskimos in a blizzard, stood in the dump body with shovels, throwing a mix of sand and salt down to the street.

People in the bar stared out the window and watched as "She" struggled by.

"Keeps up the state will have to come dig us out in the Spring," George Fisher laughed. 'She' sounds like she's gonna die right in her tracks."

"Yup! "She's" about had it." Johnny Plonski agreed.

"Yup! Think so, too," Rudy Beyersdorfer said. He and his wife looked at each other and nodded. "Best we get going home, Mary. Or we'll end up rentin' a room from Ed for the night."

The Beyersdorfers finished their drinks and left.

I sat watching the snow fall and listened as talk picked up again about the run-down truck. It's funny how men always said women could talk for hours about nothing and here they're doing the same thing.

"'Bout time the town gets themselves a new truck." Tony Debrosky said.

"Can't afford it," George Fisher answered.

"Hell! And why not?"

"'Cause of cheap bastards like you who don't want to pay no more taxes." George and the others laughed.

"Ah, stuff it up your ass," Tony replied.

Pop looked at Eddie Fogerty and flipped him a quarter. He nodded his head toward the jukebox.

"Hey, Frog-Eyes, play 'Mommy Kissing Santa Claus,'" said Fritzie Mertine, who was sitting with his wife, Mae.

"Kiss this," Fogerty said, and grabbed at his crotch.

The talk changed to betting on how many inches of snow we'd get, when it would end, and how many drinks the loser would have to buy.

"Won't last long," Jerry DeFelicis said. "Flakes are too big. Besides the *Farmer's Almanac* says we're not in for bad storms this year."

The falling snow was the size of cornflakes, but they turned smaller. Two hours later snow made a blanket up and over the parked cars across the street. They looked like humps on the back of a sleeping dragon.

All bundled up, I went outside and stood under the streetlight while the flakes were still big, trying to catch them on my tongue. They turned pale purple as they floated past the light on the utility pole. The snow became a scarf wrapped around the village. The only sound I heard was the chain-covered tires of "She" as she clanked her way up past Roosa's grocery store.

All winter my sled sat propped against the chimney, ready and waiting for a snow like this. From my coat pocket I took a piece of Ivory soap and rubbed the runners of the sled to slick them up. My tow rope was too short from constant breaking and retying and I couldn't find a way to walk without the sled banging the heels of my boots. I cussed and swore I'd find a longer piece of rope even if I had to cut some off our clothesline, or take some that Pop kept in the cellar with his fishing supplies.

I listened as I slogged my way up the half-cleaned, half-snow-clogged sidewalks, and stopped to check for other kids. No one was in earshot. My heart was pumping hard in my chest under the heavy layers of clothing Pop insisted I had to wear. He always thought the worst. If it were up to him, I'd live in a birdcage and do nothing with the word "fun" in it.

I was hot, and could see my breath puffing out of my mouth. My head was sweaty and itchy under my striped stocking cap that I kept leaving places, hoping to lose it. I plain hated all hats, except for the wide-brim ones the movie stars wore and I swore I would buy one day.

Off it came, the hat got stuffed in my pocket. When I reached Emcee Lewis's Jewelry Store, I bit off my wool mittens, undid the plastic buttons of my coat, and as I passed Roosa's I yanked my scarf loose. The heat gushed out away from my body, as I sucked in a breath of cold air. Ahhh! Maybe I should've worn that horrible hot dog brown colored snowsuit that was still stuffed in the back of my closet, it might've been cooler than this wool one. "*Say-la-vee*," as Aunt Helen would say.

Voices and laughing came on a cold gust of wind that bit the tips of my ears. I saw dark shapes, two blurry kids pushing through the snowflakes. "Hey Georgie! Hey Porky! It's me, Judy. Where's Bobby Ann?" I shouted and waved.

"Home, washin' dishes!" Georgie shouted back. "She ain't coming. Why didn't ya come get us?" he asked.

"Thought you were already gone," I said.

Georgie and Porky pulled a sled big enough to hold four people. I could squeeze two on mine if I laid on top of Bobby Ann while she steered. Bobby Ann and I agreed to take turns going alone because I liked going fast and another body slowed me down. As we passed the Astoria, we climbed up and over the snow piled against the front porch of the bar to walk in the street. It was a lot easier going in the road.

"Did ya wax your runners?" Porky asked.

"My mom never makes jelly and I had to use Ivory soap I swiped out of the ladies' room," I said. "Need some?"

"Nope. Got wax from my Ma's jelly."

We walked past the front of the church and I blessed myself with the sign of the cross.

"Why ya always do that?" Porky asked, taking his hand and making zigzag lines down the front of his face and chest.

"I don't know."

"What's it for?" he asked.

"Don't know that either."

"Then, why'd ya do it?"

"'Cause my teacher says I have to whenever I go past a church."

"Okay," he said with a shrug.

No one was sledding yet and the snow wasn't plowed off the driveway around the rectory, or in front of the convent that sat behind and above the rectory. At the top of the hill behind the convent was a huge headstone with a cross on top, marking the grave of Father John Gleason, from Montreal. His brother Patrick put up the headstone in 1895 when Father John died. It was all up there on that stone. Every time I went sledding, I said a prayer for him. It felt like bad luck not to, but I didn't tell anyone that. Besides I liked headstones. They told whose bones were in the ground under your feet.

We had to tamp down a path to ride on. Georgie and I turned our sleighs over and pounded the snow to a flat track. Then Eddie showed up with Norma Jean and she brought her toboggan, which would help make the trail quicker. Soon all the Post kids were there and others began to show up. If I was lucky, Eddie might let me have a ride on the toboggan.

Eddie and his older friends livened up the run. They packed snow in two places to make a jump that made your stomach say hello to your tonsils. The trip over the first jump threw Kenny Post off the back of the toboggan. He rolled head over heels and almost smacked a tree with his head. The toboggan slid sideways and more bodies fell off and rolled downhill past the convent.

Diane Post and her sister Judy were rolling and falling down laughing. They looked like walking, talking polar bears with the snow stuck to their coats. They brushed themselves off and trudged back up the hill, giggling.

The idea here was to see how far you could go sledding before going off-track and crashing. Starting from the grave marker, you had to make it between two large trees that grew up almost side-by-side, go over two jumps, past more trees, and fly past the nuns' convent. If you made it below the convent, you had to lean hard left without dumping your sled over, zip across the driveway, across the lawn of the rectory, across the second part of the driveway, and go down the next slope toward the school. Then you had to dig your toes in the snow and bring yourself to a quick stop before you flew off the rock wall that ran along the side of the school below. You prayed that if you did fly off the wall that you would land in the snowbank made by the maintenance man who shoveled the school sidewalk.

It was the ride of your life if you could make it all the way to the wall, missing fallen-off riders and slow-going sleds. I flew off the jumps and my stomach did flip-flops. It worried me that I might puke as my body slapped hard against the sled when I landed. My stiff fingers eased the steering bar of the sled into the tight turn before the driveway. My nose dripped and it froze on my face. My eyes blurred and dripped water onto my chapped cheeks. Cracked, peeling lips bled each time I hollered out, "Outta my way, you jerk! Comin' through!" remembering to keep it clean because the nuns could hear me. I broke over the last downward slope and started digging in my toes to keep from shooting off the wall. Yeah! I made it all the way to the edge! Most kids, afraid of going off the wall, turned around on the rectory lawn.

The snow stopped and turned into a freezing mist. It made a crust of ice on areas we weren't using for sledding. Around nine o'clock, Sister Cecelia Catherine, the principal, came out on the porch and rang a hand bell, which meant it was time to pack it in for the night.

Andy hollered, "Hey, Sister! We got school t'morrow?"

"Yes!" she called back. "Only for those who came here tonight to go sledding. No excuses, Mr. Cherny. I expect to see you and everyone else tomorrow morning."

"Ha, ha! What a joker ya are, Sister!" Andy laughed. The kids threw snowballs at him and booed him.

Sister wasn't joking. She knew every one of us and probably wrote down all our names. I could choke Andy for opening up his big mouth. We could have had a day off.

Everyone, including me, who took off a jacket, hat, snow pants, and gloves picked through the pile to find their belongings, and then trekked back up the hill for one last ride down across the rectory lawn.

I found all my stuff and the hat that was way too ugly for anyone to steal. I yelled out, "Hey! Anyone leave a hat?" There were no takers. I tried again, "Hey! Anybody want a hat?" Still no takers. This stinks. I couldn't even give this freakin' Pippi Longstocking hat away.

I decided to take my last ride all the way to the wall. From there I could jump down to the road instead of walking from the church like everyone else was doing. Some kids were all ready crossing the bridge to Main Street, a few went to their homes on James Street, while others stopped to talk on the rectory lawn and light up cigarettes.

Up at the headstone, I ran and leaped onto my sled, lying on top of my snow pants and coat. At the end of the hill by the convent, I was flying faster than I ever went before and I shot like a bullet across the driveway, rectory lawn, and across the other half of the driveway. My heart was racing as I went flying down the last incline, whizzing toward the edge of the wall. Shit! I realized I was riding on top of one big ice sheet! And I couldn't break through, no matter how hard I pounded with my toes!

"Oh shit!" I shouted, cramping the steering bar hard to the right and leaning with all my weight trying to dump the sled over. Instead, it began spinning around in circles. There wasn't enough time or space left to do anything else. Oh, fuck me! I'm dead, I thought, as my sled and I went flying off the wall backwards. Holding tight to the handgrips, I closed my eyes and screamed, "Ahhhhhhhhhhh!"

For a second, I laid out flat, hanging in air like the cartoon character Wile E. Coyote who realized the cliff he was lying on had broken off. My feet and sled turned downward in slow-motion, and then wham! I was on my butt in a mound of ice-crusted snow with a runner of the sled sticking itself into my leg above my left kneecap. I lay back wounded thanking Jesus I wasn't dead. Ow-ing, I lifted the sled off my leg. It had made a hole in my jeans. I could hear Mom say, "Do you have to destroy everything you wear?"

Eddie and Norma Jean came running when they heard me scream. They stood in the street smoking cigarettes and laughing. I heard, "Holy shit! Did ya see that?" But no one helped me. The Rosenkranses didn't give me no sympathy. Andy and Jackie Regan laughed, and Andy called me dumb. I told them I was bleeding. "Oh, quit your fakin'! Ya not gonna die! Go put a Band-Aid on it. Ya shoulda known it was all ice." He sounded like Pop!

"How t'hell was I supposed to know!" I yelled at him. "None of you jerks told me it was iced over. You gonna help me or not?" I was on the verge of real big tears--angry tears. I was embarrassed with Jackie standing there laughing, too. "It's not funny, Regan!" I snapped.

"Why'd ya think we all stopped up on the lawn?" Andy asked. "Yer a piece of work! C'mon, Jack. Let's go. Wouldn't want to watch the baby bleed ta death. Might give us the heebie-jeebies."

Why doesn't someone rescue me like in the movies? Where's the dogsled? Where's the Saint Bernard? Aw, nuts! I picked myself up from the snow pile, pulled on my coat and looked at my knee. Everyone who lived on Main Street was crossing the bridge and the rest of the kids who lived up James Street already disappeared. I needed to get moving or walk home alone.

"Hey! Wait!" I yelled, as I packed snow into my hat and tied it along with my scarf against my knee.

They ignored me and kept on walking. Wish Bobby Ann had come tonight. Didn't know how bad I was hurt but I knew blood was running down my leg. Now I wish I didn't take off my snow pants. They would've protected my knee. Pop would've called me a jackass with 20/20 hindsight.

My wet jeans became frozen boards strapped to my legs. They scraped against my skin. I kept blowing on my fingers to get them warm. Jesus don't let me fall down and freeze to death and get frostbite. And gangrene. And then get amputated. I couldn't feel my toes anymore and got scared. I wondered if I'd end up like Jerry Mertine and have to have my leg cut off.

My neck was raw where the damp wool collar was rubbing. I walked faster and blew harder on my fingers, but couldn't catch up to the others. Why couldn't I lie on a sled and have someone pull me home? Gee, our bar never felt so far away.

The wind started up. Snow and ice pelted my face. Oh, great. A freaking blizzard. Don't let me wander off in the storm, I thought as I pulled my arm up to my face to block the stinging ice. Dumb ass me! I couldn't get lost. If I kept walking straight down the sidewalk, I'd end up at our bar.

The Valley Inn and the Well's lights were off. Mike from the Astoria turned off his outside lights. But he and Andy Ellsworth, our truant officer, who used to be a policeman in Rosendale, were still in the bar drinking and talking. As I got closer to home, I saw our sign light was turned off, too. Probably a few die-hards were still sitting at the bar talking and drinking with Pop.

"She" had dumped piles of snow on the sidewalks and homeowners gave up shoveling for the night. It was a losing battle. The only place to walk was in the road and I thought I heard "She" coming up behind me. Just as I climbed over the snow blocking our driveway, "She" went rumbling by and plowed us in some more. Lot's of shoveling tomorrow, I thought. When I reached the kitchen door, it felt like I was coming back from the Arctic with Robert Peary's expedition. In school we watched a movie of him trudging through the tundra. Like him ice covered my hair, stuck to my eyelashes, and made a glaze over my coat, which I had finally put on. The insides of my boots were packed with snow. I was shivering and shaking as I leaned my sled by the kitchen door. My stiff fingers had a hard time turning the doorknob.

"Don't make a mess!" Pop called from the bar.

Throwing my snow pants and coat on the floor, I slammed the outside door shut and mumbled, "Think he'd ask if I need help? Nope. Get told, 'don't make a mess.' Can't you see I'm wounded?"

Finding a fork in the sink, I stuck a tine into the icy clasp of my galoshes and pulled up, yanked on the next one and the next, till all the clasps were loosened. I should have worn my ugly pull-on boots. Small balls of snow clung to me and spilled on the kitchen floor as I kicked off my shoes and boots.

Damn. I was making a mess. My coat lay in a puddle. I picked up the snow from the floor and took my boots over to the sink, rinsed them out, turned their tops down, and stuck them over the top of two empty milk bottles under the sink. The warm water hurt my hands. I grabbed the dry mop and swished it around the floor. It didn't pick up the water off the slate floor. But at least it spread it out so it'd dry up faster and look as if I tried to clean up.

Picking up my clothes and shoes, I hobbled barefoot upstairs to my room. Maybe I had become invisible. Pop, Mom, and the customers acted like they didn't see me as I walked through the bar. No one even noticed my limp, and I did my best Academy Award limp ever.

My knee needed to be looked at and I needed to get out of my wet jeans. In the bathroom I took out the red mercurochrome – the fire-water made in hell by Satan – the gauze, the metal tin of adhesive tape, and I looked for the freaking scissors. I could feel the cold air coming off my body and I wanted to jump in bed and feel warm again. My eyes fought to stay open, I was so tired.

Pulling the wet jeans off, I thought, Holy mackerel! My leg was streaked with blood down to my foot, and look at that gouge above my kneecap! I thawed out in the shower and learned getting warm with water could hurt, a lot. My knee throbbed and didn't look any better either. Not wanting to hear the sermon that would come with asking for help, I didn't ask.

I dried my wound with wads of toilet paper and doused the cut with the red medicine. It burned, and I gritted my teeth. It wouldn't stop oozing. Nuts. I rested my heel on the edge of the tub, bent over my leg and squeezed the cut shut. I put a small piece of tape across it like Pop did once to the gash I put in my head. Then, I put a thick pad of gauze on top and taped it down. In my dry, peachy-pink, godforsaken granny underwear, I limped my way to the radiator and hung my wet coat and clothes on it.

Mickey was snoring. I tucked the covers in around him and crawled in my bed and pulled the tangle of blankets up and over my wet head.

Boy! Did I ever sail off that wall! I hugged my pillow. Wheeeeee! The thought of it filled me with a tingling feeling like I had when I was hanging up in the air before I crashed to the ground. Wait till I show Bobby Ann my knee! Bet I get a neat scar.

Painting Christmas

*When your dreams tire, they go underground
and out of kindness that's where they stay.*

Libby Houston

THE FUN OF SHOPPING IN KINGSTON at Christmas time was to see the green garland stretched across the streets, wrapped with colored lights. In the middle of each garland was a brightly lit large plastic Santa face, or a snowman, or a reindeer. The other fun thing was looking at the decorated shop windows. Kingston held a contest for the best holiday theme. Shoppers voted to choose the winner by placing a ballot in a box inside the stores. A few days before Christmas, the ballots were collected and counted. A photo of the winning window, and its artist was put in *The Kingston Daily Freeman.*

"It's a gimmick to get people inside to buy," Pop said. "Folks'll feel guilty votin' and not buying something, even if it's a pack of gum." Pop was good at spotting crafty business schemes. "A buck's a buck," he said.

After Mom decided to decorate the bar windows, other businesses in Rosendale did their's too, but they hired someone. Unlike Kingston, in Rosendale there wasn't anything to win because the businesses couldn't agree on a prize, or who'd donate what, or who'd run the contest.

Mom said she painted Christmas on our windows for the fun of it. Every year after, Rosendale storeowners decorated for the holidays, but Mom never took her paints out again after that one Christmas. "Once was enough," she said. "If I started this fad of brightening up this drab little town, so be it."

Mickey and I came stamping in from outside. It was snowing again, but the snow was too fine and dry and wouldn't pack. Building a snowman would have to wait.

Mom was at the kitchen sink filling two glass jars with water. On the kitchen table lay a Christmas card with three choirboys on the front, each holding a large candle. Their mouths were open in big Os and the words "Noel, Noel" floated above their heads. Along side of the card were paintbrushes of different sizes and jars of poster paints.

"Whatcha doing?" I asked, as I helped Mickey take off his boots and snowsuit.

Mickey ran into the bar to find Lady, while I stayed and watched Mom.

"I'm going to paint the front windows for Christmas."

"Like in Kingston?"

"Uh-huh."

"Can I help?"

"I don't think so."

"Why?"

"Because you can't. And don't touch the paint," she scolded.

I set the pot of green paint back where I found it. "Some of these are hard as a brick." I said pointing to the little jars.

"Hot water softens them," she said as she took a paintbrush, dipped it into hot water, and drizzled some into each of the paint pots.

Mom gathered up her supplies, had me carry what she couldn't, and set up on a table by the front window of the bar. She had Pop take down the neon beer signs, and we washed and dried the windows.

Picking up a paintbrush, Mom drew a thin black outline, making the window look like an untouched page in my coloring book. Then she began putting in colors.

Her face got all soft and dreamy as she painted. The only time a hard look crossed her face was when I asked a question. She started the windows right after lunch and kept going through dinner. Pop made a sandwich for himself and I made peanut butter and jelly for Mickey and me. When Pop finished eating, he made a sandwich for Mom, brought it out and set it on her table. He didn't speak. She didn't say thank you. She kept right on painting . She acted like she was off to her place in the clouds where she went when she was drinking and didn't want to be bothered.

Like a magician, Mom twirled her brushes in and out of the pots of paints and created Christmas on the four large windows, two in the bar and two in the dining room. She brushed in green holly leaves with red berries and ornaments with stripes. She painted three-foot-tall choirboys in red robes and white surplices, holding song sheets instead of candles. With her brush dipped in black, she wrote the word "Hallelujah" backwards over their heads and hung musical notes in the air in place of "Noel." My eyes stayed glued to her every move.

Mom called what she was doing, "reverse painting on glass". She had to paint the foreground first, she said, and the background last, so it looked right from the outside. From the backside the paints were dull. But from the street, the glass made the paintings glossy. The trick, she said, was all the highlights had to go on first and then the rest of the colors. "You keep the picture of what you want in your mind," she said. "You have to focus. Now keep quiet and stop distracting me."

I zipped my lip. When her eyes would squint, I squinted mine. When she took a step backwards, I stepped backwards. When she cocked her head and studied her work from outside, I tailed behind and did the same.

"Who do you think you are, Marçel Marçeau?" she asked. I thought I was a silent shadow. But all I did was annoy her more.

"Get out from under my feet!" she said, "You're making me nervous and I can't concentrate." Back inside, she took a rag, swiped out an area of color and reapplied the paint. I slumped down in a chair and tried not to fiddle with her art supplies.

"Can I do a dining room window? One on the back?" I asked.

"No!"

She glared at me and I shut my mouth.

But why couldn't I? I bet I could paint as good as her. I stayed in the lines in my coloring book, and knew how to shade and highlight things. Didn't I have a certificate saying I was exceptional in art? Didn't I win second place for the pumpkin picture I colored?

It was a real good pumpkin and I should've got first, but Barry Post won it for his landscape picture. But, even still, it was the first time two kids from the same school won in the county coloring contest.

People from the village stood out in the cold on the sidewalk watching Mom paint. They moved from one window to the next with her.

"Ya'd think Rembrandt was painting the Sistine Chapel the way they're lining up out there," Pop said.

"Wasn't it da Vinci, Ed?" Owen Smith asked.

"Whoever . . ."

They were wrong. Both of them. It was Michelangelo. I knew, because I studied art in school.

"Nobody in this town has Edie's talent," Owen said.

"Yeah? That and a dime will get-cha a cup of coffee. What good is it if ya can't make money at it?" Pop replied.

"Maybe ya can sell 'em gawkers a spiked hot toddy and charge'm for watching," Owen joked. "Set up a concession on the sidewalk."

"Yeah," Pop laughed. "And sell 'em pizza, too."

Mom ignored them. Maybe she didn't hear them. She didn't act like she did.

When the windows were done, Pop asked her, "What's gonna happen when ya get condensation running down the glass?"

"I'll retouch them," Mom answered, "same if someone rubs up against them."

They decided to put greens around the inside edge of the windows and then string lights through the boughs to keep people away. Pop seemed to like helping her.

Mom went into the foyer of the dining room. The foyer was a small room with a huge mirror on the wall facing the outside door.

There were big brass hooks around the frame for people to hang up their coats. Mom looked and looked at the mirror. She ran her hand across the shelf under it, which was a place for ladies to set their pocketbooks while taking off their coats or touching up their makeup. I could tell she wasn't looking at herself. She was planning something. It showed in the way she went over to the table and rummaged through a box of old and new greeting cards sitting by her art supplies. She picked up one card after the other saying, "No. No. No."

"Ah!" She said when she found a silver-embossed Christmas seal about the size of a half-dollar stuck to the back of an old envelope. "Yes. This is it."

Stamped into the foil was the image of the Madonna holding the Infant Jesus in her hands. Mom got her paints, picked up a large paintbrush and began to paint on the mirror.

I kept looking over my shoulder afraid Pop would have a hissy fit if he saw what she was doing. She turned her brush sideways and sketched an outline of the figures like before. But this time, she began applying middle-tone flesh color to the face and hand areas. Then she blocked in shades of blue for Mary's robe. Next came Mary's brown hair and white veil. Jesus was wrapped in a white cloth, but not all white. It had shadows of lavender and pale pink and highlights of pale yellow. Fine-line details were added last with a tiny brush with no more than a dozen hairs. Mary's face looked peachy and peaceful as she smiled at the baby in her hands. Mom put shades of yellow and white around Jesus' head making it look like He was glowing. She worked at the painting fast, but careful. I changed her rinse water without her asking whenever I saw it was getting all mud-colored.

I never saw Mom like this before. She wasn't even drinking and she had a calm look on her face as she kept looking at the seal and back at the painting. When she put the seal down, I saw she caught the image almost perfect on the mirror. But it was so much bigger and in such pretty colors!

Mom finished the painting and Pop came in to see what she was doing. And he didn't get mad. Instead, he put greens trimmed off the Christmas tree around the mirror to cover up the hooks.

Then he put colored lights on like he did on the front windows. I think Pop was proud of her. He said, "It's beautiful." He went and got his camera.

He couldn't stand in the foyer to take the photo and opened the door and stepped out on the patio. People came out of the bar to see the painting. Pop snapped a few pictures, looked at the faces of his customers standing there in awe and said to Mom, "Let's leave this door open so people can see the painting from the street."

"But the heat?" she said.

"I'll block off the inside doorway."

Mom put candles on the shelf in between the boughs in front of Mary and Jesus. Pop made her put them in glass jars because he was afraid of fire. Pop said, "People will be dropping in to see this. It looks real great."

Mom beamed bright as Baby Jesus's head.

And people came from Kingston and High Falls and even New Paltz to see our windows, but especially to see the life-size Mary and Jesus. The newspaper from Kingston sent out a photographer. Mom was famous now. She got a picture of her and her paintings in the newspaper.

After the article, a steady stream of cars came and went by in the early evening for about three weeks. Whole families with their kids drove by, pointing and saying, "Stop! Look!" They parked their cars, got out, came over, stood outside the doorway and stared at Mary. Some blessed themselves with the sign of the cross and prayed. Some people even came in the bar to find out who the artist was and bought Mom a drink, which made her happy.

Pop had left a wicker wastebasket in the foyer for trash, but people started putting money in it, mistaking it for a collection basket. He later donated the money to the church for food for the poor.

The parade of people stopped after January sixth, the Epiphany, when the Wise Men found Jesus. And by then Pop wanted to close the door and take down all the decorations. Mom didn't seem to mind washing the paint off the front windows because the paintings were now water-streaked and they got smeared from people brushing up against them.

Mom used old dishtowels to wipe the windows clean and sop

up the water dripping to the floor. The hardest thing I think she had to do was take the soapy rag to the face of Mary. She stood in front of it a long time and looked like she was gonna cry, but didn't.

"How'd you get so good at painting," I asked, feeling sorry for her.

"Don't know. I just am."

Mom picked up the wet rag and sloshed it around on Mary's face, turning it to a peachy-blue smear. As she cleaned the mirror she said, "I got an art scholarship once when I was in high school."

"What's that?"

"Something you get when you're good at what you do."

"What do you do with it?"

"Doesn't matter now." Mom was rubbing the mirror hard with a bar towel. Her face turned sour. She looked at me and said, "Your grandmother burned my scholarship in the wood stove."

"Wha'? Why? I don't understand."

"Your grandmother didn't want me to become an artist. She said, 'no daughter of mine is going to stare at naked bodies and make pictures of them. If that's what you want to do, become a nurse.' And I will never forgive her for burning up my chances. Never," Mom said, her lips pulling into a tight, thin line. "Not as long as I live."

She grabbed up her cleaning supplies and went to the kitchen to put them away. I followed behind carrying the wet towels. "But can't you paint pictures and sell them now," I said.

"Too late," she said, and walked out to the bar.

"But you're so good, even the newspaper said if your painting was in Kingston, you would've won first prize."

She reached up to the second shelf of the back bar and took down her bottle, poured herself a drink.

"That's all water under the bridge now," she said. "Salute." She raised her glass and took a big swallow. Smiling a half-smile, she added, "First today, Babe, but definitely not the last."

Don't Look A Gift Horse . . .

*Trust not the horse, O Trojans. Be it what it may,
I fear the Grecians even when they offer gifts.*

Virgil

"What dress do you want?" Aunt Helen asked, as she picked through the sale rack of girls' clothes at Ward's. Each year, Uncle Andrew, not because he had to, but because he wanted to, treated Mickey and me, and my cousins Colleen and Nancy, to new clothes for the holidays. He left the doling out of the holiday money to Aunt Helen. Other times, he let family use his discount at Wards.

There was never anything I liked on sale at Wards and it was the only place Aunt Helen, like Mom, ever took me to buy clothes. Mom wanted the extra money to drink. Aunt Helen had other reasons.

Sliding the clothes hangers back and forth on the rack, she said, "I'm trying to find something not too plain." She lied. She was trying to find me something cheap.

Each time I pointed to a dress with a color or pattern I liked, she looked at the price tag and said no. From the sale rack, she pulled a couple plaid dresses with white collars and white trim on the sleeves. Nobody wanted them, which was why they were on sale. I didn't want them either.

"These won't show dirt or stains," she said, smiling at me. "They're very practical for you."

"I don't like plaid," I said. Red-haired, freckled-faced Peggy McGlocklin wore plaid to school because she was Irish, or maybe it was Scottish. And I wasn't either one.

Aunt Helen continued, "Here, a nice green plaid. It'll go with your blonde hair and brown eyes. Oh, and here's a brown, and it has blue in it. You like blue, don't you?"

"I like blue, but I hate plaid."

Aunt Moncie, who always came along with Colleen and Nancy, looked at Aunt Helen and started talking low in Slovak. It was about the dresses. I couldn't speak it but I understood Slovak, and they would've had a hairy-canary if they knew. It didn't take long to catch on Aunt Helen planned to use part of my money to pay for my cousins clothes. And Aunt Moncie, who didn't seem too happy about it, went along with it. They must've thought I was stupid or something and would never know. For a couple a years, I didn't say anything. But I was older now and knew that less money spent on me, meant more they could spend on my cousins. If I could help it, it wasn't going to happen again. Colleen didn't know what was going on, and Nancy was too little to understand. I thought about telling Colleen, but then she might say something to Aunt Moncie, and I didn't want to start Hiroshima all over again.

Aunt Helen must've figured Aunt Moncie needed clothes for my cousins, and I had a father at home, they didn't. Aunt Moncie worked as a waitress after divorcing Uncle Ray, "the philanderer," as Aunt Helen called him.

Aunt Moncie rented a room to Uncle Andrew for $15 a week. After work, no matter how tired she was, she washed Uncle Andrew's clothes, starched and ironed his shirts and pants and cooked for him, usually a steak he got on his way home. Aunt Moncie and my cousins ate franks and beans. It made her mad he never shared, but she didn't say anything. I think she was afraid he might move out, or yell at her. Pop said his brother was a nasty s.o.b. if he didn't get his own way, and sometimes even if he did. Pop said when he was eight, right after their father died, Uncle Andrew smacked him and Aunt Moncie around because he was now the boss because he was the oldest.

Aunt Moncie pointed to a blue dress on a different rack and then to the plaid dresses Aunt Helen still had in her hand. They talked like rapid-fire machine guns with foreign bullets. Their hands whipped through the air and Aunt Helen's voice became meaner. It sounded like Aunt Moncie was trying to get the blue dress for me, along with a couple a plaid ones.

Not smiling anymore, Aunt Helen looked at me and said, "All right, damn it. If you take two of these plaid dresses, and you can get the blue one." She shoved the plaids in my face. "Choose!"

"I don't like plaid . . . ."

I was drowned out by a very irritated hiss. "Fine. Then you'll get nothing."

Aunt Helen and Aunt Moncie went at it again, hands shaking the dresses till they threatened to fall off the hangers, fingers pointing to the clothes rack, fingers pointing at each other, voices getting louder. The salesclerk was watching, while pretending to be busy. I wandered over to the dress rack where my cousins were looking. There were flowered dresses, a bright yellow one, and another in my favorite color turquoise, made of taffeta with a lace collar.

Aunt Helen, grabbed me by the wrist and dragged me out of Ward's with Aunt Moncie and my cousins tagging behind. We went to Nugent's and to London's department store where they carried better clothes than Ward's. Aunt Helen said it's where the upper crust shopped, and you could see the difference. Not a plaid dress in sight.

Aunt Moncie and Aunt Helen had Nancy and Colleen trying on dresses in both stores till they had four each. Then the aunts picked out a sweater and a slip for each cousin along with some nice underwear and pretty socks.

At each store, Aunt Helen asked the saleslady where the discounted clothes were and she left me there to look for my size while she helped Aunt Moncie. What I liked was neither in my size, or it was an ugly color. I sat on a chair, waiting and pouting.

Aunt Helen said, "Well, since nothing suits you, it's either back to Ward's or you get nothing. What do you want to do?"

I didn't want anything. But if I came home empty-handed Mom would pitch a fit and say, "Why did you turn down free clothes? Free is better than nothing."

I said okay to the two plaid dresses and the blue cotton one, a plain white slip, plain white cotton underwear and plain white socks with no fancy stitching or lace. There was no money left for a fourth dress, or a sweater, or else they forgot I still needed them. I didn't care. Sweater or dress, I know it would've been a crummy orange, or a puke-green color, anyway. These ugly dresses will rot in my closet till Mom forces me to wear them or I outgrow them. She can give them to the orphanage, except for the blue one.

On the way to Rosendale, after dropping off Aunt Moncie and my cousins at their house, I asked Aunt Helen, "How come I don't get the same kind of clothes Colleen gets?"

"What are you talking about?"

"Her clothes are nicer."

"It's your imagination. She got four dresses and you got four dresses."

"I only got three . . . ."

"What, you want more? You're lucky you're getting anything. Don't look a gift horse in the mouth. Uncle Andrew doesn't have to buy you anything, you know."

"It's just . . . ."

"Just what?"

"Colleen's stuff is prettier. Even her underwear. Even Nancy gets prettier clothes than me," I blurted out.

"You don't like what you got? You want me to take everything back? Not good enough for you, Miss High and Mighty?"

"No. It's not . . . . It's just . . . ."

"You're never satisfied, are you? Instead of being grateful, you're very selfish. It's not your money you're spending. Besides, where do you go that you need fancy clothes?"

I slouched in the car seat and turned my face to the window, fighting back the urge to scream or cry, or both. I'll tell Mom you cheated me. Gave some of my money to Aunt Moncie.

A couple of weeks went by, and Mom invited Uncle Andrew and his girlfriend, Marie, to come for Sunday dinner so he could see the clothes Helen bought. She made me thank him with a hug and a kiss, which, ugh, I didn't like doing. Why did I get to pretend I was glad I got these clothes?

Uncle Andrew, Marie, and Mom sat in the dining room while I went in the ladies' room, changed and paraded out the dresses I got. Each time I took off a dress, I rolled it in a ball, threw it on the floor and stomped on it, except for the blue one. Mom knew Aunt Moncie would've had Colleen and Nancy do the same so Uncle Andrew could see where his money went.

Uncle Andrew asked me how I liked my dresses after I changed back into my jeans and T-shirt. I stared up at Mom who had told me to be honest if he asked.

"I hate plaid," I said, in a quiet voice

"Why did you get them?" he asked.

"'Cause Aunt Helen made me, because they were cheap on sale, and because then Colleen and Nancy could get better stuff at London's."

From then on, Uncle Andrew gave money to Mom for my Christmas clothes.

1954
MARY, MOTHER...

You might as well fall flat on your face as lean over too far backward.
James Thurber

THE STATUE OF MARY, Mother of Jesus and Queen of the month of May, stood on the classroom windowsill. Her dainty plaster toes stuck out from the hem of her gown. Under her feet is a green-painted snake with a red forked tongue. Dead. The dead snake lay stretched out over the top half of the earth.

Beautiful Mary stood on top of the world, crushing out evil with her bare feet. I looked at her soft blue robe, the white veil and gown, all trimmed with gold leaf, and wondered what it would've been like to have her for my Mom. I wondered how it'd feel to be a nun wearing a veil and a long dress.

The words of a hymn slid through my brain that asked the Virgin Mother to protect me and smile on me with love. I wished my class seat were closer to her. I loved the smell of the flowers we brought in and put on her windowsill-altar. Big bouquets of lilacs, daffodils, narcissuses and violets were stuffed in colored paper-covered cans. They sat with the foil-covered jars holding yellow and red tulips.

It was hard to understand how Mary could've been so good

that God would give her His only Son to raise and love. There was so little to do, no place to go way back then, it was probably a heap easier to be holy.

"In respect of Mary," Sister Alma Regina said, "nuns wear long dresses and veils and never marry. We are God's Vestal Virgins and can only be married to Him. And being married to God, we can't have children of our own. This is why we become missionaries or teachers. We are given the duty of instructing children, who belong to others, in ways that please God. It is an honorable profession. One you girls should all think about."

Sister was always drumming into us the merits of becoming a nun or priest. And she even sneaked it in between instructions on how to make scalloped edges on crepe paper panels for the window behind Mary.

"Like Mary," Sister reminded us, "if you ever thought about being God's servant, you need to be perfected in His eyes." Which I thought meant to be perfect, without sin, to give up all the bad stuff I thought was fun. It was hard being perfect, and I failed at it a lot. But I tried, when I remembered.

"Hard work, doing more than what is expected of you and without complaining," Sister said, "will make God and Mary very proud of you. Doing for others, without thoughts of rewards, is what God expects of you. God," she insisted, "will heap rewards on you, greater than you can imagine when you go to Heaven. Especially, if He didn't do it here on earth. Maybe," she said, "if your life isn't going right, you aren't praying enough, or going to Mass on weekdays, or you just aren't trying hard enough."

Sister continued drilling and filling our brains with religious stuff. "The month of May is not only the month of Mary," she reminded us. "Next Sunday is Mother's Day, for your earthly mothers. What can you do to make your mother proud, happy or pleased with you? Knowing," she said," whatever you do for your earthly mother, you are doing for Mary, who intercedes for us with Jesus, who takes your prayers and good deeds directly to the attention of our Heavenly Father."

Of course, Jesus always did what His mother asked of Him. So it was like having a one-hundred-percent guarantee that all the good stuff we did would be appreciated by God the Father. This was a direct pipeline only Catholics had with God, because other religions didn't pray to Mary.

On the way home from school, my head was buzzing with ideas. Going upstairs to our apartment, I thought, I'm nine months shy of being twelve. I can think of something to make Mom proud, happy or pleased. In our apartment, I turned the knob of the living room door and looked in. Maybe if I cleaned this room, we could use it for something else besides storage. This could be my Mother's Day gift to Mom. In four years, Mom never seemed to want to clean it and Pop didn't do this kind of work, so it stayed like a storage room after the gambling went into the basement.

I set my schoolbooks on the floor and pushed my way through the junk to get to the couch. Heavy cardboard boxes had to be shoved out of the way. I lifted and toted boxes to one side of the room. With a path cleared to and around the couch, I pushed it across the wooden floor over against another wall. I did this without a lot of noise because I was over the bar and I wanted this to be a surprise. I played the radio to cover up the sounds. After an hour I was tired, but I was happy with my first day's attempt.

It took four days after school to clean, clear, and stack boxes out of the way and to find things to decorate the room. On the fourth day, all the wood got lemon-oiled and polished. Lamps sat on top of Grandma DeWitt's tatted doilies on end tables. On the mahogany coffee table I put the polished chrome, open-mouthed pelican ashtray and silver-embossed table lighter used for cigarettes. On one end table, I put Pop's pipes around the rim of the humidor. I unpacked the encyclopedias and some storybooks, dusted them and arranged them according to size in the pine corner bookcase Eddie made in wood shop. I stood back and looked. I was proud of what I did. In three more days it'd be Mother's Day and I could hardly wait to see the look on Mom's face when I showed her the room.

Saturday morning I cleaned my room, swept and washed down the hotel staircase, and even sorted beer bottles in the cellar, all without being told and without grumbling. I was trying harder to get myself "perfected." Then I went out to play at the playground.

Sunday morning, I awoke earlier than usual and got dressed for church. To make sure everything was still neat, I peeked into the living room to see if it needed any touch-ups. Tiptoeing past Mom and Pop's bedroom, I opened the living room door and stared in stunned silence. Someone tore up the room! The mess jumped up and laughed at me. All my hard work was undone.

The lamps from the end tables were on the floor. The coffee table upside-down on the couch. The end tables were on top of the coffee table. Open boxes were around the floor with crumpled pieces of newspaper for wrapping and protecting breakable items. Everything was wrecked, except for the bookcase, which was pulled out of the corner and shoved closer to the doorway.

There was a poisonous quiet in the room. I felt if I breathed in too deep I'd die. Hairs rose up on the back of my neck as I felt someone behind me, turned to see Mom staring at me from her bedroom doorway.

"What are you doing?" she asked. "Are you the one who has been rearranging everything?"

I shook my head yes. The look on he face scared me. She could be nasty if she woke up with a bad hangover.

"Get the hell out of there!" she growled, keeping her voice low so she wouldn't wake up Pop. I backed out of her way as she walked in the room and waved her hand in the air over the jumble of boxes. "This is not your personal playground, young lady. Nothing in here belongs to you. Stay out!

It never dawned on me that none of these things belonged to me. I always thought they were ours. But I guess it wasn't true. It was clear from the look on her face and her angry voice, that I had messed with her belonging's. Everything was hers, or Pop's. I didn't own or buy one thing in this room. How stupid could I be?

"I was packing for when we have to move in three months," she said. "Now, thanks to you, I get to do it all over again. Don't play in here again!"

Oh, damn me! I forgot! If I couldn't make Mom happy, how could I ever please Mary, let alone, God? Marching on wooden legs, I went down the hall to my room. She shut the living room door with a bang, and scuffed along behind me to go to the bathroom.

Closing my door, I leaned my back up against it. Pop said if someone made me feel bad, to think of them on the toilet. He said everybody has to go to the john. Even the Pope. When I thought about the Pope taking a poop, sitting there with his tall cap on, it made me giggle. And giggling kept me from crying. I turned, stuck out my tongue to the door, and blew Mom a raspberry.

At my dresser, I opened the top drawer and dug under the pile of underwear for the Mother's Day card I made the night before. It was folded blue construction paper, trimmed with pieces of white lace paper doily Sister had given us at school.

The bathroom door opened. Jesus don't let her come in here, I prayed. I listened for her bed to squeak, and scrounged around in my cigar box for a black crayon.

After making a quick change to the card, I tucked it under my dress into the top edge of my undies with the word Sunday printed on them. Sneaking into my brothers' room, I went out the window onto the fire escape, down the steel stairs and jumped the short distance to the ground. Pulling out the handmade card from its hiding place, I made straight for Rosenkranses'.

Millie was up and dressed. Everyone else was sleeping, which made me glad. I didn't want to bump into Bobby Ann and have her ask what I was doing here again. Millie was slipping a flower print bib-apron over her head, tying the strings around her waist. She filled her aluminum coffeepot with water, popped her head around, and gave me a big smile.

"Good mornin'! Whatcha ya doing up and about? Ya want some breakfast?" she asked, as she put the stem and the basket with the ground coffee into the pot of water.

"No, thank you," I answered. "I didn't go to church yet. I have to receive Communion and can't eat. Here," I said, sticking my hand out to her.

She put the coffeepot on the burner of the stove and lit the gas. Wiping her hands on her apron, she took the card.

"For me? Oh, this is beautiful," she said, turning it over in her hand. "And in blue, my favorite color. Did you make it all by yourself?"

She made me feel proud. I shook my head, yes. I wondered

if making Millie, my almost-mother, happy with a card meant for my real mother, would make God feel pleased with me. Or would He be angry because I didn't give it to Mom? Did I need to go to Confession, or could I go to Communion today? Was this a venial sin or .... My mind rambled as Millie read aloud.

"Happy Mother's Day." Real careful, she turned the page and read, "To Mom Rosenkranse." The letters in Rosenkranse were kind of squished in after the word Mom. The last few letters got smaller and curved around the top edge of the card. The next line read, "I love you." Millie smiled and said, "Ah, come here, sweetie. Let me give you a hug. She gave me a big squeeze, and said, "I love your card." My heart thunked hard against my chest. I smiled so big it hurt my cheeks. Millie finished reading before she kissed me on top of my head, "Hugs and kisses, from your daughter, Judy. X O X O X O ...."

Safe

*O night. What holds you
in the darkness of my mind?*

Judith A. Boggess

Even though I turned off my lamp, undressed in my closet, prayed my rosary, and promised to become a nun, the man kept coming to my room. I couldn't sleep with Andy, or under my bed, or in the closet, because Pop got too upset when he found my bed empty. I ran out of ideas, and tried to sleep at Bobby Ann's house as much as Millie would allow.

But Bobby Ann said she was getting flak about me being there all the time. So, I asked her to stay over some weekend nights. She said my room was too noisy with the bar right under it. But I kept at her and she gave in. The man didn't come when she was there until one night.

We were lying in my bed talking and listening to Shorty Idaho and his country band playing downstairs. Bobby Ann slept at the head of the cot with me at the other end. Pop came in at nine and tucked us both in for the night and we dozed off. But I was a light sleeper and woke up around 1:30 in the morning. I lay there listening to Bobby Ann snoring when I heard the apartment door open, a loud splash of music come in from downstairs, and then the hall light turned off. He's here again. I held my breath. The floorboards squeaked. It wasn't Eddie's way of walking, and Andy was already in bed. And it wasn't Mickey sleepwalking, because he was snoring away.

A dark shape stood in my doorway and moved in the shadows. He wasn't halfway to my bed and I could already smell his cigarette stink. Soon I knew I would be breathing in his sour whiskey breath. Squeezing myself tight to the wall, I covered up most of my face, hoping he couldn't see me. He went to the end of the bed where Bobby Ann was sleeping. Careful about moving around too much, I peeked over the top of my covers to see his face. The shade blocked most of the light coming in and I couldn't make out who he was. But I saw a cowboy shirt. Bobby Ann said, "Get 'way from me." She sounded still asleep.

Then she got up on one elbow, looked my way and shouted, "Judy, leave me alone!" The man now knew I was at the foot of the bed and walked over to me. He slid his hand under my covers.

"Leave me alone," I said. "Go bother my sister." I didn't know why I said that except Bobby Ann and I always pretended we were sisters.

He went back and started touching her.

"No," Bobby Ann said in a groggy voice.

He kept trying to stick his hand down our underpants. He was doing it to Bobby Ann when finally she came wide-awake and yelled, "Get outta here! You scummy pervert!" and he dashed out of the room.

"Who ta'hell was that?" she asked, looking down at me.

"I don't know," I answered, and crawled over to her, shaking.

We huddled together in the dark. The band stopped playing and "That's Amore" played on the jukebox.

Bobby Ann didn't understand if this happened before, why I didn't tell my mom or pop, or lock the apartment door.

"I'd get killed if I locked the door. And then I'd have to tell why I did it and they wouldn't believe me. They'd say I was making it all up. Besides the man told me he'd say I wanted to touch his dick. And they'd believe him. Please, Bobby Ann. You can't tell no one. Please."

She promised, crossed her heart and said, "Let's go to sleep.

We'll figure it out in the morning. C'mon. Lay down by me. I'll take care of you," she said. "He won't be back. If he does, I'll bust his balls."

Bobby Ann pulled the covers up around us and we snuggled up like two spoons. With her arms wrapped around me, I got the best night's sleep in months. I didn't even get up to go to the bathroom, which was good, because when I did, I was afraid he was hiding behind the door, or the shower curtain.

Bobby Ann sneaked out early next morning leaving me sleeping. She couldn't wait to go home and tell her mom what happened. I should've known better when she crossed her heart but didn't say, "hope to die," that she wouldn't keep her promise to me.

Millie was afraid of Pop, she once said. She thought he was mean to Mom. But she pulled all five feet of herself up, marched over to the bar with Bobby Ann, and told him everything. He kept calm even when she asked, "Well, what are you going to do?"

Pop told Bobby Ann to go get me.

"Why, Bobby Ann? Why'd you rat me out?" I cried, "He's gonna kill me."

"The pervert?"

"No. My Pop!"

"No, he won't. Besides Lina said never let nobody touch me, and to tell her or Ma if somebody did. So I told Ma. No freak should be touching you either. It's wrong," she said.

I bawled. I knew I was going to be in big trouble.

Bobby Ann got me a cold wet washcloth. "Here," she said. "Wipe your face. It'll stop ya from crying. C'mon. Get dressed. Your Pop's waiting for you.

Pop was sitting on a chair by a table in the bar. I stood in front of him and he leaned forward and held both of my hands in his. I felt like a coon caught in a trap.

"Is what Bobby Ann told Millie the truth?" he asked.

I couldn't speak. I was trying to keep the puke in my throat from coming up and shooting out all over him. I swallowed and nodded.

"D'ya know who this man is?

I shook my head no.

"Couldn't see 'em," Bobby Ann said, "he was in the dark. He was tall and thin, and wore maroon color cowboy shirt with white pearl snap buttons.

"If you could see all that, why couldn't you see his face?" Pop asked.

"It was higher up in the real dark," Bobby Ann said.

"So ya didn't see his face?" He asked. "Ever?"

"Nope," she said. "He stunk like booze and cigarettes. That's all."

"Everybody comes in here wears a cowboy shirt," Pop said to Millie. "It could've been anybody."

"From now on lock the apartment door when ya go to bed," he said. "He won't be back. And if he does, ya scream bloody murder like I know you know how. Ya hear me?"

I still couldn't talk. I bobbed my head up and down.

"And if you recognize him, ya let me know, and I'll fix him. Bet your ass I will."

Pop never asked how many times the man was in my room. He probably knew from Millie's talk with Bobby Ann. I wanted to go hide in the barn, to get away from Bobby Ann, Millie, and from Pop. They kept staring at me like they could see what the man had done to me. Pop stood up, patted my head, and said, "Gowan. Get some breakfast."

If I ate breakfast I'd throw up. Instead, I bee-lined out the kitchen door, across the driveway, past the barn and down to the creek, leaving Bobby Ann behind. I didn't want her around. If I went to the barn, she would've found me. I wanted to be by myself, wade across the creek to one of the islands, and hide there for the rest of the day. Bobby Ann made me mad and glad that she told.

BEFORE GOING TO BED, I turned the lock on the door. But first I checked under my bed, in my closet, and in the bathroom. Then I checked the rest of the rooms. He was nowhere to be found. But I was afraid he could be.

Pop had an extra door key made and hid it in the registration desk on the landing at the top of the stairs. He put a dab of red finger nail polish on it, blew it dry and then put it in a dish of old keys in the drawer. Pop told my brothers and me not to go into the desk, or take the key out if a guest or anyone else was standing in the hall. "It won't be a secret key if anybody knows about it," he said.

The dark still scared me and I still spooked real easy when someone sneaked up behind me and tapped me on the shoulder, like damn Andy was always doing just to hear me scream. The creaks and squeaks in the night made me hold my breath and wonder if it was the man. Sometimes the shadows in my room looked alive—moving and breathing.

Did he find the key? Was he hiding around the corner by the guest rooms when I took the key out, even though I checked? Did I leave the door open? Did Andy or Eddie leave it unlocked? I must've checked five times or more each night before I fell asleep exhausted.

Even though it felt better with the door locked, I didn't sleep the whole night without waking up at least once, startled, breathing hard, and looking into the shadows. It wasn't till after the bar closed and Pop came upstairs to bed that I felt safe.

The man never came back. And I said prayers of thanks. I just wished he'd stop running through my mind like our muddy river whenever he wanted to.

The Skate Key

Friendships, in general, are suddenly contracted; and therefore it is no wonder they are easily dissolved.

Joseph Addison

"Judy . . . Judy . . . Ju-d-i-t-h A-n-n . . .!" Bobby Ann leaned over and shouted in my ear. I was lying on my stomach on my bedroom floor.

"Wha-a-a t?" I asked, pulling away from her kneeling down on all fours next to me.

"Wanna play jacks?"

"Na-h-h-h." I rolled over on my side and laid my head down on my arm.

"Hopscotch?"

"Na-h-h-h." I danced my clothespin doll around in the air.

"How about we see if anybody wants to jump rope? How about double-dutch?" Bobby Ann stood up.

"Don't feel like jumping rope."

"How about we get some empty 'vaporated milk cans from my garbage? We can crunch 'em on our heels and run up and down the sidewalk pretending we're riding horses."

"That's for babies," I said. "We're too old for that."

"Kidding. Just trying to get you to do something. Ya want to dress up and dance?"

"Don't feel like it."

"Well, whadda ya want to do besides sitting here playing with those stupid clothespin dolls?" she asked.

"What's wrong with them? You helped paint their faces and make clothes for them."

"Maybe I'm getting too old for dolls." Bobby Ann stood up and shoved her fists onto her hips and added, "And maybe I'm getting too old for you, too."

"We're best friends," I said. "We took a blood oath."

"Then let's do something. Play jacks. Bounce a ball. You know, one-zees, two-zees, ..."

"I always beat you, then you get mad."

"Jesus-H-Christ. You been strange ever since he . . . ."

"I'm not strange!"

"I'm leavin'. You never want to do anything except stay in your room, roller skate, or suck your thumb. I'm gonna find somebody else to play with. Maybe I'll make a new best friend, a better one," she said.

"Fine. Go ahead. See if I care. Leave!" I shouted, jumping up and pointing to the door.

Bobby Ann stared at me. "You better snap outta it or they're gonna take you off to the nuthouse, and then you can play with your stupid clothespin dolls all day. By yourself. Forever!" she yelled. She stamped out of my room, slammed the apartment door behind her and stomped down the flight of stairs.

Snap out of what? So what if I like being alone. Don't care if she's mad at me. Let her go make another friend.

The clothespin dolls were scattered over the floor. Picking them up one at a time, I looked at them. Stupid-looking face. Look how sloppy your mouth is painted on. Look at this lousy dress. You look like crap!

"Plain dumb fucking ugly, you are!" I shouted at the fistful of dolls and threw them, one at a time across the room at the wall, calling them each a dirty name: faggot, jackass, piece of shit . . . .

Right away, I felt bad for them and picked them up, and put them in their cookie tin, slapped the lid on and hit it hard, again and again, squashing down their grinning wood faces. My hand stung from slapping the lid of the tin.

"A-g-g-g-h-h-h!" I screamed stuffing my pillow in my mouth, and then sat down on the floor, falling over on my back, and looked up at the ceiling. Bobby Ann wouldn't understand, I thought. I lost my skate key! I can't believe I lost my damn skate key!

Tears burned my eyes. I grabbed my pillow and yelled in it at the top of my lungs to keep from blubbering. And I didn't want Pop to hear and come see what was wrong.

"Give me back my skate key," I moaned in my pillow. Maybe God had cotton in His ears, or a wax buildup. He knew how important skating was to me. I prayed, "Dear Saint Anthony, please come around. Something is lost and cannot be found. Please find my skate key." He sure takes his old sweet time finding stuff. I must've said this prayer fifty-hundred times since yesterday.

What would I do if I couldn't skate anymore? Skating was almost as good as swinging your highest on the playground swing. Or zipping down the slide, sitting on a piece of wax paper. It was good as sticking your face out the car window going 50 mph. I could go anywhere on my skates and get back home before anyone knew I was gone. When I lay flat out, pumping my arms and stretching out my legs as far as they'd go, I almost did a split! But I was fast. Nobody could catch me. I even passed cars on Main Street, and made better time than they did. Bobby Ann said I took too many chances out in the road and should stick to the sidewalk. I didn't care. The cars could watch out for me.

I asked Pop this morning for money to buy a new key from the hardware store, and he said, "Why did you lose it?"

Why did I lose it? It's just lost! Do you think I did it on purpose? I must be crazy to talk to myself like this. Maybe men in white coats would come get me someday.

"This'll teach ya to be careful with your stuff," Pop said. "Put it in a safe place next time, a place where ya can find it again when ya want it."

How to hell was that going to help me right now? I was sorry I asked him for money.

Mom said her usual when I asked her. "Go ask your father." I explained I did. "Well," she said, "then you've got your answer."

Lately I was starting to hate both of them.

Now what could I do? Eddie was loading beer trucks at Ballantine's. I couldn't tell Andy. He'd find my key, tease me, and wouldn't give it back. But I could get Mickey to help me look for it again. He helped me look upstairs and downstairs yesterday. He was only five but it was an extra pair of eyes.

Mickey was playing with his trucks on the back patio. "Hey, Mick! Help me look for my skate key and I'll take ya to Gilmartin's for an ice cream after dinner." I lied. I didn't have money or I would have bought a key. But Mickey would do anything for candy or ice cream. And it was better than him going inside the bar, drinking shots of beer and getting paid nickels to say, "Fuck you!" to a total stranger. He was treated like the parrot at the Elm's Bar.

Mickey and I searched all over our driveway and around the grass edge. We went up one side and down the other side of Main Street. We looked in the gutters, storm drains, and even in downspouts. No luck.

What I found was some long cigarette butts, which I stuck in my pocket for later when us kids got together in the barn after supper.

Later at home, I stared at the skates with their leather straps sitting in the corner of the kitchen where I dropped them yesterday with my key, I thought. Whenever I got home from roller-skating, the skates had worked their way loose enough to just kick 'em off. The skates and the key were always side-by-side, waiting for me the next morning. Maybe I was getting forgetful because I had a brain tumor from falling and hitting my head too much. I wished I could remember where I could've lost it.

"Don't cry, Judy. We find it 'morrow," Mickey said, and put his arm around my shoulder as I slumped back on the kitchen floor.

"You don't understand, Mickey. I'm never gonna be able to skate again, never."

Andy came in from fishing and popped his head in the screen door. "What's the matter with you?"

"She los' her ska' key," Mickey said.

"Tighten 'em with a pair of pliers," Andy said. "Get your skates. C'mon, I'll show ya. Put my pliers back in my fishing box when you're done with 'em. Don't lose 'em."

Out front on the patio, Andy tightened the toe clamps with the pliers. "Here. Shove your foot under the clamps. They tight enough?"

They were so tight I thought I'd rip the soles loose from my shoes, but I wasn't complaining. "Thanks, Andy. You're terrific!"

"When ya take 'em off, loose the strap and bang your heel on the ground an' the skates'll pop off."

"Okay." Away I flew, skating down the walk in front of the bar, jumping a crack in the slate sidewalk and missing other ones that could trip me and land me on my hands and knees.

"Thanks, Andy." I waved back at him and Mickey. I left the sidewalk for the road. A car behind me honked its horn and zigzagged around me.

"Get up on the sidewalk where ya belong, ya crazy kid!" the driver yelled.

Screw you, I thought and raised both my middle fingers high up in the air to him as he drove by.

Bobby Ann

Life without a friend is death without a witness.
Spanish Proverb

"Hiya, Ma! Whatcha cooking?" I called to Millie, as I walked into her kitchen.

"Mike's hankies," she said.

She's gotta be kiddin'. No oatmeal? I looked into the pot on the gas stove and wrinkled up my nose. Yuck! Guess I won't be eating breakfast here today.

Millie had a long-handle wooden spoon and was stirring her husband's dirty handkerchiefs around in a pot of bleach and Rinso Blue, the detergent advertised in *Look* magazine saying it had Solium, the Sunshine Ingredient, in it.

"Where's everybody? I asked. "Ain't Bobby Ann up yet?"

"You're here real early," Millie said, smiling at me. "Everyone's still in bed. Go wake her."

"Okay, Ma!"

I bounded up the stairs to Bobby Ann's room. We hadn't seen each other for two weeks. At first I was avoiding her, and now she was avoiding me. She didn't even come to the barn, or to the playground anymore.

Wait till she saw the new old crinoline and poodle skirt I got from Norma. We could be Marge and Gower Champion now. And

I'd let Bobby Ann wear the new outfit to make up for ignoring her. I was anxious for her to get up and get her chores done so we could play. We had been best friends ever since Porky and me stared at each other across the driveway almost five years ago.

Millie didn't care if Bobby Ann came to my house to play with me or stay overnight, even after the man thing happened. No one else, not even my cousins ever slept over and they didn't even know about the man. I stopped asking to stay overnight at other kids houses after hearing a parent say, "Oh no! It's her again." And being told I could only play for an hour because they had something else to do. It was okay because I had Millie and Bobby Ann. Millie was the only person in all of Rosendale who loved me like one of her own kids. And Bobby Ann was the sister I never had.

Bobby Ann and I would play for hours, dressing up in long, worn-out skirts and crinolines that dragged on the floor that we begged from Lina or Norma. We even had an old pink lipstick from Mom. We weren't supposed to, but we put on her mascara, often poking ourselves in the eye with the bristles of the brush. Our eyes teared-up and the mascara smeared. Pop said not to go outside because we could get shot for raccoons.

Sometimes we pretended to be Betty Grable, Ginger Rogers, or Cyd Charisse. We twirled around in circles across the dining room floor. Pop didn't care if we played inside as long as we kept the dining room closed and the music turned down.

Bobby Ann didn't like playing the male dancer, but she was bigger and taller than me. And I was the one who went to the movies every night and watched Fred and Ginger, and then arranged our dance routines. It was my record player and collection of records from the jukebox that we danced to. Besides, she was too big for me to hold over in a dip. I tried, and almost dropped her on her head.

Saturdays, after chores and rainy after-school days, we got dressed up, danced, and shared our dreams of leaving Rosendale becoming a star, or maybe even a ballerina like Leslie Caron. We were going to be a "somebody."

When Bobby Ann couldn't play I designed beautiful gowns I knew actresses would wear someday. If I wasn't drawing I was picking out melodies on the upright piano.

Gill Kelder played the piano. Sometimes he put thumbtacks on the felt hammers, which made the music sound like it was coming from an old rinky-tink piano. Gill showed me where middle C was and how to play chopsticks. He told Pop I had a nat'ral ear for music. Soon I was begging for piano lessons. Pop hired Mr. Sweeney, the choir director at Saint Peter's to teach me, but playing piano was too much like arithmetic. There was three-quarter time, and one-quarter notes, with so many beats to a measure. It got screwed up in my head and made my eyes blurry and my brain buzz.

Mom and Pop couldn't help because they didn't know how. They also didn't know I always heard fancy music in my head, stuff not on the jukebox. It came out of nowhere and fell in my brain, then itched to get out. And they didn't know how hard I tried to match what I heard with the sound the piano keys made. Mr. Sweeney quit because he couldn't explain in a way I could understand, the counting, the flats and sharps. Instead of playing piano, I began putting words to this music I heard in my head and saved the song lyrics along with my dress designs in a cigar box under my bed.

"Bobby Ann! C'mon, get up!" I said, shaking her awake.

"Don't touch me! And don't call me that no more. My name is Barbara."

I could see she was in a shitty mood. Must be cramps, which made her real bitchy the first few days.

I didn't think too much of it when she said, "I don't want to play with you no more," and rolled over in bed, turning her back to me. She never liked being waked up early.

But something was different in her voice.

"Got your friend, right? Got cramps? You're fooling, right?" I asked.

"No, to all three."

"Whadda I do?"

"Nothing." She looked over her shoulder, stared at me for a second and said, "It's, oh boy . . . being friends with you is a big problem. No one wants to be friends with me."

"Why?" I pulled at her shoulder till she turned over to face me.

"Look," she said. "I'm older than you. I'm interested in boys and you're not. I don't want to play no stupid dress-up anymore because we ain't going nowhere. We ain't never gonna be famous. We're just a couple of stupid hicks living in this stupid redneck town. Ain't no movie-man ever gonna come into Doc's drugstore, discover us and want us in his movie."

I felt scared, right down to my socks.

"You coming over tonight? George the Indian is playing and we...."

"Oh, gawd!" she groaned, and pulled the pillow over her face.

"You like being George's drummer."

"No! I don't," she said, pulling the pillow away from her face. "Not anymore. Get it? No!"

George the Indian played guitar and harmonica at the same time. He wore an Indian headdress. Bobby Ann got to beat on the tom-tom he brought along and sometimes put on his headdress. When he told me to, I'd pass his cowboy hat around and collect his tips. George always gave us a quarter, which we spent the next day on candy. He played and drank at all the bars in Rosendale, but on different nights of the week.

"Look," Bobby Ann said. "I like George, but I can't be hanging out in your bar."

"Why? Your ma doesn't care."

"Shit!" she said, sitting up in bed. She pushed a long blonde strand of hair from her face. "Look, no kids want to hang around me if I'm hanging in your bar. Their moms won't let them. So, if I'm seen with you, I can't be with them. D'ya get it now?"

"I think so," I said. My mind was jelling up. My head went all fuzzy like it did when I tried to understand Mr. Sweeney's piano lessons, or when I was at the blackboard in school doing algebra. My knees started shaking and my insides flip-flopped like an eel out of water.

"But can't we ... ah, ah ..." I stammered.

"For crying out loud! Do I hafta spell it out for you!" Her voice raised and her face flushed. She put her bare feet on the floor, stood up and trudged to the bathroom. I followed close behind. She shut the door in my face.

"Can't I even pee without you sniffing it?"

We always sat in the bathroom together and waited for each

other to get done even if we were taking a poop. If it smelled bad, we'd open the window.

I was hurting all over. But I'd show her I was growing up, too. I wasn't going to bawl because she was hurting my feelings. I could pretend what she said doesn't matter.

Bobby Ann opened the bathroom door and ignored me as she shuffled her way back to her bedroom. She sat on the bed and looked at me for a long time with sad blue eyes. My stomach lurched.

"Okay," she said. "Shit. First, I like you but . . . by not hanging around with you the last couple weeks, I learned I'm getting too old to play kid games. Two, I want a boyfriend and no one will date me if I hang out at your place, because, three, the bar . . . your parents . . . . They got the worse reputations in town. Nobody nice goes in there."

"Nice people come in our bar all the time."

"Yeah, well did you ever see . . ." she asked, and ran down names of people who'd never been in our bar. People I never gave any thought to, except when they didn't want me in their house. Crap. Maybe these people didn't want anything to do with us because we're no good.

"Maybe they don't drink," I said, not believing myself. "Or maybe they're old farts. Or maybe they're too damn uppity."

"No, Judy. They're decent people who don't swear like your whole damn family does, except your mother. But she's got her own shit, like hanging her tits out her bedroom window at the crack of dawn for some man down in your driveway to see."

"Bullshit! Not true! Never happened!"

"Yeah, it did. I heard it up street. And even if it didn't happen, people say it did. Folks don't talk crap about you less you give'm reason to. And decent folks don't let their kids run the streets, or hang out in the bars babysitting their mother, while she gets ossified, and then have to help her stagger home. They care for their kids."

"My parents take good care of me!"

"No they don't, stupid! Look what happened to you. Look what almost happened to me!"

"Pop makes me lock the door now. He takes care of me," I said.

"Like so much happy-horse-shit!" she yelled in my face. "My mother takes care of you better'n they do. You practically live here! You eat here. You sleep here. You just ain't moved your clothes in yet!"

"We're blood sisters. We cut our fingers and held them together. We got the same blood," I reminded her.

"No we don't! That's some dumb freakin' shit you got out of some freakin' gawd damn cowboy and Indian movie. That shit ain't real. When are you gonna wise up? I can't believe I went along with all your crap."

"I hate you!" I screamed at her. "I don't want you for a sister anymore! I don't need a sister! 'specially don't need you, Miss Barbra-An-n!"

I grabbed the pillow she was holding in her lap, took a wild swing and smacked her solid across the chest. She fell backwards on her bed, clutching her pillow. I fast-tracked out of her room, half-jumping down her stairs with tears streaming down my face. The screen door slammed behind me as I tore across the lawn to the safety of the barn.

Sitting in the corner of the hayloft, I thought about what she said. I stared at the scar on my pointer finger; the one I sliced with a razor blade the day we became blood sisters. Bobby Ann only nicked hers with a straight pin. Ouch! A large splinter stuck itself in my fingertip as I rubbed it on the rough wood floor, hoping to sandpaper off all traces of our friendship. The wound started to bleed. Good, I thought, as I squeezed my finger, removed the splinter, and watched the blood drip into the dust on the floor. I'll squeeze your blood right out of me, I thought. I don't need a sister, or a friend. I don't need anybody, not anyone in this whole rotten town!

Besides I got the movies, the playground, the barn, the creek, and the piano. Who needs Bobby Ann? I could dance by myself. Maybe Mom would let me take tap and ballet again next year at the Grange. I'd become famous and I'd ignore Rosendale, say I never lived here; make up being from some ritzy place. Maybe I'd change my name. I could be Judith Evans, or Judith Howard. Someday these so-called decent people would want to say they knew me, and want my autograph. Well, when that day came . . . .

Then I remembered. We're moving next month! I'm leaving this stinking town, getting away from Bobby Ann and all these so-called decent folks.

Maybe I am slow. Maybe I am some kinda idiot. Slowly it seeped into my brain that next month I'm not only losing my friend, I'm losing the barn, the movies, the piano and dancing lessons. Ohmygawd! Even the creek and the woods . . . the playground . . . everything. I'd be losing it all! Millie . . . my other Mother . . . . I can't breathe!

A pain hit me like Dad's billy goat had butted me full-force in the gut. I doubled over, hugging my knees to my chest and rocked. I opened my mouth wide to yell. No sound came out. I wanted the world to hear me scream, and I couldn't make a sound.

Leaving

It's interesting to leave a place, interesting even to think about it. Leaving reminds us of what we can part with and what we can't, . . .

Richard Ford

It was August, pack up and move time. Mom was emptying the upstairs kitchen cabinets of cleaners and rags.

"How'll I get to school in September?" I asked.

"Schoolbus."

I wondered if I'd know anybody on it.

"Of course you'll know them," Mom said. "You're going to school with some of them right now."

"Why can't I walk?" I wanted to be able to stop at Gilmartin's or Vaughn's for candy or a comic book.

"Don't be silly," Mom said. "What will you do when it rains or snows? It's over a mile, you know."

I didn't think about bad weather.

This was lousy. I wouldn't get to go to the movies much anymore. Pop said I could go to Sunday matinees, but that was when the babies went.

"Why can't I go at night?"

"'Cause," Pop said, "I ain't your chauffeur, and I ain't making two trips a night to town so you can see some dumb-ass movie."

"Moving outta the village stinks! There's nothing up where

we're going. Nothing. No stores. No kids. I might as well be living in exile," I wailed.

Porky still hung out with me almost every day. We had to play on the playground or by the river now, because some jerk burned the barn down.

Schryver's Lumber Company, over by Pettybone's, bought the barn and used it for storing wood. Mr. Schryver padlocked the barn door at night, but didn't know one of the hinges was busted. We could yank it loose from the door jamb on the bottom. It made a gap wide enough for us to squeeze in.

Late one night I woke up to sirens and flashing lights in our driveway. I smelled smoke and thought the hotel was on fire again, like when Don Burnett fell asleep in bed with a cigarette in his hand. But this time, there was a yellow-orange glow on my shade. I opened the window, smelled smoke and saw flames leaping up out of the barn roof. I went to Andy's room, out his window and sat on the fire escape with him watching the barn burn to the ground. I cried. But this felt right that it wouldn't be here anymore. I imagined the barn was speaking to me, saying it was sad to see me go too, and it didn't want to be here anymore. Goodbye barn. Thank you for being my friend.

The next day Porky and I sat throwing stones in the creek when he said, "I'm gonna miss you." He was the only one to say that.

"I'm gonna miss you too." A lump stuck in my throat.

He reached over and touched the top of my hand. "I ain't never gonna forget ya punchin' me and giving me a black eye. You didn't fight fair. You had a roll of pennies in your fist."

"Sorry," I said. "Eddie taught me that trick. He said you were stronger, and I had to even up things if I wanted to beat your ass."

"What did I do?" he asked.

"Don't remember." I giggled. The fight was a while ago.

We laughed and fell back against the sand embankment.

Porky leaned over me and gave me a kiss on the lips.

"Yuck! Shit!" I yelled. "Phoooo!" I spit and sat up. "Whadda you doing?" I took the back of my hand and scrubbed my mouth.

"I . . . I like ya." He stuttered and blushed.

We play-kissed when he played the daddy coming home from work. But this was different.

"Yeah, well, I like you, too. But cut that shit out because you scared me." I was afraid Porky might touch me like the man did.

"C'mon," he said, changing the subject. "Before ya leave, I gotta teach ya how to skip a stone. You're the only girl I know who can't do it." He stood up and reached out his hand for me to take.

LATER IN THE DAY Mom and I drove boxes up to the house we were moving into. The area was called Maple Hill. Other than it being up on a hill, all the trees on our property were all sap-dripping pines. Maybe that's why they changed the name later to Rosendale Heights.

With the land came a two-bedroom bungalow with no insulation, and a diner with a small bar attached. It was owned by an old Negro lady who wanted to retire. Pop didn't ask Mom about buying this place, just like he didn't ask her about leasing Reid's. He'd just plunked down his money and expected her to be happy with his decision. She wasn't.

The house was an asphalt-side bungalow with a tin roof almost touching the ground in the backyard. Inside was a kitchen, two small bedrooms and a long, skinny living room. This place wasn't much to look at. In fact, it was freakin' ugly.

"Where's my bedroom?" I asked.

"Your father is turning the kitchen into a bedroom for Andy and Eddie. Your's and Mickey's is in the back.

"Where's the kitchen gonna be?"

"At the end of the living room," she said. "We'll divide the room in half. It's long enough."

When I asked if I could help paint, Mom said she'd wallpaper and paint after we moved in. "Getting out of Reid's," she said, "is all I can think about right now."

Pop had big plans. He was gonna turn the small bar and diner into a large diner with a big back room and have a bar on the side big as Reid's.

"Please, Ed," Mom begged, "open the little joint for now." But he wouldn't listen. Even Dad DeWitt told Pop, "Expand after you got your business built up and you got money in the bank. Open now and build later."

"He has champagne taste and a Coca-Cola pocketbook," Mom said. She crabbed Pop was wasting money hiring this guy, Sutt, who lived all winter at Riker's Island prison for not paying child support.

"Sutt only lifts a hammer when you're around watching him," Mom told Pop. "You're paying him to sit on his ass and get drunk." She also tried to get Pop to transfer his liquor license before it had to be renewed so he wouldn't lose it. Once it expired it would be hard to get back. The madder Mom got, the more stubborn Pop got.

All this talk was going in one ear and out the other. Even I knew you have to make Pop think it was his idea or he'd turn a deaf ear to you. If Mom said, "Do you think it'd be good thing to open the little place as is?" he probably would have said yes because it was his idea then, not hers.

Their fighting was bad for several weeks. "You're going to run out of money," Mom said. "And then what are we going to do?"

"Lemme do the worryin'," he said.

"Famous last words," she mumbled.

Pop sold off whatever he didn't need and borrowed lots of money from his brother.

"Get packing up your room," Mom ordered. Meaning if I didn't, she would. Each time I asked Mom the date we were leaving, she answered, "Soon" or "Whenever your father gets his ass in gear." I didn't want to pack my stuff till the last minute. Otherwise, I wouldn't have anything to play with.

Instead of packing, Pop was planning a farewell party, and that's when the crap hit the fan.

"Are you crazy?" Mom screamed. "We're supposed to be out that night by midnight!"

"What's Reid gonna do?" Pop said. "Throw us out in the street?"

Sleeping At The Astoria

Bed is the poor man's opera.
Italian Proverb

Yup! That's exactly what he did. Mr. Reid got the sheriff and his men to throw us out at midnight. Pop refused to leave and went back to tending to his party, while Mom stood in the street sobbing on Mike Wazelewski's shoulder.

Mike had said we could stay at his place, the Astoria Hotel. I took him at his word and lugged my suitcase, Mickey, and myself up Main Street in my p.j.'s at midnight.

Mickey weighed a ton. I couldn't have carried him another step when I opened the screen door of the bar.

"Hi, Ma," I said.

Ma Wazelewski looked at us, got off her barstool from behind the bar, and came clucking over.

"What is this?" she said. "You in your pajamies."

Betty Auchmoody turned from her drink and looked at me. I babysat her four boys when she and Lou went out drinking. Most times, Lou was at Reid's and Betty was here. "Hiya, kid," she said. "Whassup? Ya leaving town? Am I losing my sitter?"

She knew we were moving. I didn't answer her, and told Ma Wazelewski that Mike said we could stay here tonight.

"Of course," Ma said and took my suitcase and me out of the bar to the stairs that led up to her rooms.

"Ya watcha the bar, Betty. I be right back," Ma said.

Upstairs, she took a key ring from her apron pocket and opened a door. The room was clean and smelled fresh. The walls had pink cabbage roses and stripes on them. The windows had drapes over shades with white crocheted pull rings. On the bureau was a starch white dresser scarf. The iron double bed was made up with a white nubby spread and two feather pillows. I was afraid to touch anything and didn't know what to do with Mickey. My arms were numb and felt like lead after carrying him upstairs.

Ma put my suitcase on the floor by the closet and turned on an imitation hurricane lamp with a green shade and painted-on pink flowers. She flicked off the overhead light and pulled the drapes closed, blocking out the streetlights and car headlights. The room was so pretty. The wood floor was polished and shiny. She had a braided rug by the side of the bed to put your feet on in the morning. I stood froze to a spot in the doorway, still clinging to Mickey, listening to him snore in my ear. Was she really letting us sleep in that bed?

Ma smiled. "Put 'im on da bed," she said, like she was reading my mind. "He's too big for such a little girl to carry."

She came over and took him from my arms.

"Uff," she said, "such a big boy."

"Ma, ya want us to take a bath before we get in bed?" I asked.

I knew we both could use a bath and I didn't want to dirty up her sheets.

"Nah, nah. Ya hop in. Okay?" she said.

"Okay."

"Dun be scared. You stay here long as you like. Everybody stay here, ya mather, ya fatha. We all one big family. Okay?"

"Okay."

"I be right downstairs if youse need me. Ya wan' help with Meekey?"

"No, thank you."

"Okay, 'night now." She bent down and kissed the top of my head.

"Night," I answered. She left and closed the door

It was so quiet. The noise from the barroom stayed in the barroom because the hotel rooms were not over the bar.

Were Mom and Pop still arguing with Mr. Reid? Did the cops go? Was Pop in jail? I was glad to be at the other end of town, away from it all. I was glad Mike said we could stay here.

Mickey had to be waked up enough to sleepwalk to the hall bathroom so he wouldn't pee the bed. I aimed his toodle for him or he would've peed on the floor.

In bed, I made Mickey sleep on a towel and told him to wake me up if he had to go. I don't think he heard me. He rolled over on his stomach, pulled his knees up to his chest, stuck his butt in the air like a frog, and shoved his thumb in his mouth.

I couldn't sleep. I didn't feel tired. It was too quiet in this room. I went to the window and pulled back the curtains. Remembering to hold tight to the shade, I gave it a jerk and it pulled itself up around the roller. Sitting on the hard chair, I looked up and down Main Street.

There wasn't much to see – a few parked cars, Whitey's Valley Inn, Betty and Lou Auchmoody's and Sylvia Sicarri's houses, O'Reilly's Liquor Store and Hermance's Grocery Store. If I craned my neck far enough, I could see Moylan's Funeral Parlor.

I couldn't see the stars. The streetlights, the tall buildings and the overhang of the Astoria's roof blocked them. It was okay because I'd given up wishing on stars. I'd still ask for sick people to be healed and poor people to get food, because I'd never know if they got anything or not. It's easier to ask for other people, but I ain't asking for anything for myself, because nothing ever came through. I knew Easter and Christmas came even if I didn't believe in the Bunny or Santa or ask them for anything. And I knew I could still be a somebody without ever wishing on a star, or praying to Jesus, or without Bobby Ann.

The room was cool when we first came in, but it was now taking on a damp, stuffy, summer smell. I pushed up the window and stuck in the screen that leaned against the wall under it. I heard music coming from the bar and laughing and the screen door opening and banging closed.

Turning off the lamp, I went back to bed, and waited for my eyes to get used to the dark. In the streetlight spreading around the room, I studied the shapes and shadows. They didn't seem so dark as in my room at Reid's.

The cool sheets were wonderful to feel. I could smell the sunshine in them. And I didn't even have to brush sand off of them before climbing in. I rolled over and rubbed Mickey's back. He started to snore.

I was dozing off when a thought startled me wide-awake, and I went stiff in the bed. I didn't check the closet or under the bed. No, he's not here, I told myself. Ma Wazelewski would know. But I should look anyway, I thought.

The closet door was open a crack. I pretended to be asleep in case someone was watching me from there. Was it closed when we came in? I couldn't remember. What if someone was in there?

Oh, hell, I thought and jumped off the bed, ran over and flicked on the overhead light, raced to the closet and yanked open the door where wire coat hangers clanked together. I shoved the door closed and banged against it with my rear-end till I heard the latch click.

Then I checked the bedroom door making sure it was locked, got down on all fours and looked under the bed. The closet door popped open. I stuffed a scream and pulled my head up so fast, I clunked it on the underside of the bed. Oh, damn, damn, damn. I rubbed my head.

It took a moment to realize the closet door was warped and wouldn't stay latched. I turned off the light and climbed back in bed talking to my pounding heart, telling it to slow down. "Everything's all right. We're getting out of Rosendale," I whispered, and threw my arm over Mickey, snuggling up close to him.

"Mom's not gonna drink because we won't have another bar right away," I said in his ear. "And Pop and her won't fight no more. And we're gonna have friends, if we can find some, because we have a separate house away from the business."

And the man . . . he'll be gone too.

"And guess what? Mom'll make us breakfast and lunch and supper. And we'll have rooms with shades and curtains and papered walls and . . . ."

BE GRATEFUL

The one thing to do is to do nothing. Wait . . .
You will find that you survive humiliation.
And that's an experience of incalculable value.

T. S. Eliot

SHE COULDN'T MAKE ME DO IT. Why did I have to go to Aunt Helen's? No!

"Just go until the end of August," Mom said. "When you get back, your room will be done and the diner will be open."

"You're trying to get rid of me," I cried.

After moving, I thought I was free from ever having to go to Aunt Helen's again. I wanted to see our house getting fixed up and to help Pop some more. He let me mix and spread concrete to build the walk and the brick stairs to the diner.

"I ain't going! You can't make me!" I yelled at my mother. "You can't send me to that witch's dungeon!"

"Look," Mom said, with a smirk, "I'll ask Aunt Helen to take you over to Colleen's as much as she can. You'll be helping me more by going. We don't have a lot of money right now, and Aunt Helen will take you clothes shopping for school. Besides, you get out of eating potatoes. Just do it!"

"Okay!" I snapped back at her. I was sick of potatoes.

Pop fired Sutt, but not before he put a serious dent in Pop's wallet. And, when we left the bar, Mr. Reid didn't want anything belonging to us. He refused to buy the leftover liquor like Pop did when he took over the lease. And he refused to buy the bulk food, like the 50-pound sack of potatoes we used for French fries.

Pop was big into "life teaching you lessons." About Mr. Reid, he said, "Just because ya treat people like ya want to be treated, don't mean they'll do the same." Pop took the sack of potatoes, flung it over his shoulders, and said, "This is a lesson that's gonna get eaten, 'stead of letting it eat at us. These'll be the best damn potatoes in the whole world."

Mom could've written a cookbook on a thousand ways to make potatoes. We ate them in fritters, scalloped, mashed, baked, French-fried, pan fried, and pancaked. Mom stuck them in soups, stews, and casseroles. I was potatoed out, and learned that I should be nice because I'm a nice person, not because I want someone to be nice back to me.

Cousin Colleen and I were both skinny with blonde hair. We pretended to be sisters even though she had a little sister. Nancy was short with dark brown hair, like Aunt Moncie, and a royal pain. We could never play by ourselves unless she was taking a nap. And she never wanted to, and we got stuck having to watch her. Colleen and I would hide and jump out from the side of the house and scare Nancy to hear her scream, trying to make her pee her pants. We'd say, "Did we scare you? Oh! We're sorry." We didn't want her telling on us. If we teased her just enough, she'd go back in the house and tell Aunt Moncie she didn't want to play outside anymore.

Colleen wore Western clothes when she wasn't forced to wear fancy dresses. She wanted to grow up to be a cowboy, or a general in the Army. When she wasn't being a general, she talked like a cowboy, saying things like "Y'all" and "Howdy pardner," and she walked bowlegged, rocking side to side like she just got off a horse. Colleen had a cap gun and wore a fringe vest with a metal sheriff's badge shaped like a star on it. And she had this cowboy hat she pulled down so far on her head her ears stuck out, making her look like Dinny the Dimwit in the newspaper cartoons. She even wanted to smoke cigarettes like a cowboy around a campfire, and stole a cigarette butt once from Uncle Andrew. I liked Colleen because she didn't always want to play dolls.

"Hey Judy. Wanna smoke?"

"Nah."

"Why not?"

"Did it already," I said.

"Well I want to."

"Got a butt?"

"Yeah. I pinched a big one from Uncle Andrew's ashtray."

"Got matches?" I asked.

"There's some by the stove. I'll get them." She slipped into her house and sneaked out a book of matches.

"Can't do it here. Your Ma will catch us."

"I know," Colleen said. "Let's go upstairs in the garage."

The two-bay garage sat behind the house. We went in and climbed the ladder to the storage area. Nancy was playing in the backyard. It took her a while to realize we were nowhere in sight. She called and called for us to come back. When we didn't answer her, she began to sniffle.

Colleen struck a match and took a drag on the butt. She swallowed the smoke, which set her coughing and choking. Nancy stood in the yard looking at the garage, crying, "Come play wif me. Waaaahhh!"

"Ignore the little twerp," Colleen said. "She'll shut up."

But Nancy wailed even louder.

"Shit, Colleen. She can wake the dead with that mouth. She sounds like a friggin' fire alarm."

"Here," Colleen handed the butt toward me, "take a puff while I holler at her."

I took the butt.

"Shut up, ya little jerk!" Colleen called out. As I took a long drag on the cigarette, she asked me, "Hey, how come you don't choke?"

"Told you. Done this before," I said. I knew not to swallow the smoke and to hold it in my mouth, pretending I did.

Colleen took another drag, hacked and sputtered again.

"Damn," she said, wiping tears from her eyes. "I can't see and it's burning my fingers."

We heard the screen door slam.

"Oh, crap," I said. "It's your mom."

Colleen stubbed what was left of the cigarette out on the floor. Aunt Moncie yelled for us.

"Here, hide the matches." Colleen brushed at the remains of the tobacco on the floor. Her face turned the color of a dead steer's sun-bleached bones in a desert.

Aunt Moncie looked mad. When we got close to her, she got even more upset. She could smell cigarette smoke on us.

"What were you two doing in there?" She sniffed the air around Colleen. "Were you smoking? Don't you lie to me, Colleen Rae Mitchell!" she said. "Where did you get a cigarette? And where did you get matches?" She stared at me and asked, "Where are the matches?"

I ignored her. Aunt Moncie began patting Colleen's pockets.

Figuring I was next to be frisked, I stuck my hand in my pocket, pulled them out and handed them over to her, avoiding her eyes by looking down.

"These are from my kitchen! How dare you steal from my house!" she yelled at me. "How dare you come here and teach my daughter your filthy habits! You could have burned my garage down! All I asked was for the two of you to play with Nancy and instead you," she said, pointing her finger at my nose, "are teaching my Colleen to smoke!" Her voice was getting higher. "I don't need your kind here! How dare you!"

Colleen wouldn't look at her mom. Sometimes being yelled at so many times and accused of so many things I wasn't guilty of, made my aunt almost funny. Her whole family, including my father, could rant and rave forever without coming up for air. I knew if I kept silent she'd soon run out of steam. I also knew that, in this side of the family, you couldn't stick up for yourself; it only made things worse. If you told the truth, they'd say you were lying. If you lied, they'd say you were lying. So I kept my mouth shut and let her believe what she wanted. I knew I was screwed blue and tattooed. Once Aunt Moncie was convinced I was guilty, I'd be sentenced to be hung like a cattle rustler before you could blink an eye.

Aunt Moncie leaned in, looked me square in the eye, wagged

her finger in my face and said, with a rattlesnake hiss, "You should be grateful to be here with a decent family. Your parents don't love you. They never loved you. If they did, they'd take better care of you, teach you what's right and what's wrong. They don't love you at all!"

I didn't think she was funny anymore. I brought up all the hate I could muster in my eyes and stared back.

"Who are you to look at me like that?" Aunt Moncie said, and stormed back to the house, dragging Nancy with her.

"Colleen! Get in the house!"

"Yes'm," Colleen muttered.

"And you," she said, pointing her finger at me, "stay outside. I don't want you in my house. I'm calling Aunt Helen to come get you." The screen door slammed with a bang.

Getting home was what I was going to do even if I had to call a cab. I went inside and said I had to use the bathroom, but went in the foyer to use the phone to call the cab and see how much it would cost from Kingston to Rosendale. There was a lot of loose change and dollar bills in my pants pocket from doing chores for Aunt Helen. I'd use them all.

Colleen heard me talking on the phone. She snitched to Aunt Moncie who canceled the cab. Aunt Moncie then began talking nice to me. I wouldn't answer her and went back outside and sat on the stoop to wait for Aunt Helen. Colleen sat down next to me.

"Sorry you had to take the blame. But she'd kill me if she knew."

"Don't care," I said. "I just want to go home"

"But you can't go by yourself in a taxi."

"Why not?" I asked. "Leave me alone."

Aunt Moncie came to the door and asked me to come inside to have something to eat. The oven smells drifted out the door. I didn't have any appetite, not even for my favorites, chicken and corn. It pissed me off that grownups got away with hurting your feelings; tromp all over you and forget they did it. And you're supposed to say "It's okay," especially if they got all icky-nice. Well, I would never forget what she said.

Having what Pop called a memory like a camera wasn't always good, according to him. He once said I better learn to forget;

because bad memories can eat at ya, and it don't do a damn thing to the person you're pissed off at. But not even Drano the drain cleaner was going to eat these words from my brain.

Aunt Helen pulled up in the driveway. "Hey, whadda you doing out here? What's going on?" she asked, as she got out of her car.

"I want to go home." I sniffed. "Take me home."

"We'll go after I talk with Aunt Moncie."

"I want to go back to *Rosendale!*"

"Why?"

"Cause . . . ." I started crying.

"What t'hell went on here? Moncie!" she shouted.

Aunt Moncie met Aunt Helen at the screen door and started talking in damn Slovak again. Why didn't they speak English?

"I know you're talking about me and I know what you're saying," I said.

"We're not talking about you," Aunt Helen insisted.

"Yes, you are. She said she wanted me out of here," I said, pointing my finger at Aunt Moncie.

"Let's talk inside," Aunt Helen said to Aunt Moncie.

As we drove away from Aunt Moncie's house, Aunt Helen tried to find out why I was being so stubborn about going back to Rosendale that night.

"Look, you want to go home, then talk to me. Aunt Moncie said you were teaching Colleen to smoke in her garage."

"Was not!" I folded my arms across my chest.

"She said you had matches."

"Wasn't mine."

"Where did you get them from?"

"Colleen."

"Where did Colleen get them?"

"The kitchen."

"Where did the cigarette come from?"

"Colleen got it from Uncle Andrew's ashtray."

"You sure you didn't bring it?"

I looked at her hard and said, "It was Colleen! But nobody believes me. I want to go home!" If wailing worked for Nancy, maybe it'd work for me too. "Waaaahhh! Waaaahhh!" I could crank this out all night if I had to.

We pulled into her driveway, and she shouted, "Okay! Okay! Get out and get your gawd damn crap. I'll take you the hell home. Fuckin' H-Christ. Anything to shut your gawd damn trap. You're not coming back here, ever. Even if you change your mind. Even if you beg me. Once you're gone, you're history. I'll get someone else to stay with me. They'll get all the nice stuff I was going to buy you."

I didn't give a shit. She never bought me anything till the last day of my visit. "You'd take what you can get from me and leave right away if I bought you stuff sooner," she had said. So what if I was going home without anything. I don't care. Mom would get over it.

"What am I gonna tell your father? Why do you have to leave tonight?" She could see whatever she said wasn't working. "It's getting dark out. I don't like to drive in the dark and you know it. You could go tomorrow in the daylight. Aunt Moncie didn't mean to yell at you." She yammered at me all the way into the house and while I packed my clothes.

"You don't know what she said to me."

"What did she say?" she asked, as she rifled through my suitcase. "You're not taking anything that doesn't belong to you, are you?"

"Take me home. I want to see my Ma and Pa," I said and puckered up my face, like I was gonna start howling again.

"Okay. All right, already. Ma and Pa. Jeezus Christ, you sound like you're some retarded hillbilly from the Ozarks. Can't you say Mom and Pop like I taught you? Son-of-a-bitch. Why do I put up with such an illiterate little shit like you? Gawd damn kids. I'm glad I didn't have any of my own. Fuck it. You got your shit packed? Let's go. Gawd damn it. And make sure you don't take anything belonging to me, because you're never coming back. You hear me? Get your ass in the damn car."

I picked up the baby doll with the green eyes and cracked head Aunt Helen had bought for me at the Salvation Army. Her eyes blinked open and closed as I stuffed her under my arm. She was real pretty and I didn't care that she was used. She had tiny white teeth and a red felt tongue. Her head was a little cracked, but Aunt Helen said it was because she was a composition doll and probably got wet. Aunt Helen knitted her a sweater and a hat to hide her damaged head. I slept with her every night.

"Where are you going with her?" Aunt Helen asked, pointing to the doll.

"Home. You bought it for me."

"It's staying here. It was for you to play with while you're here. I never said you could take it home." She pulled the doll out from under my arm and threw it on the couch.

I stared up at her till she couldn't look at me anymore. She brushed past me to grab her coat and flashlight from her bedroom. I petted Penny the dog goodbye, picked up my bags and ran to the car. I'm never coming back here again. Not ever!

JUSTICE

Justice ... limps along, but it gets there all the same.
Gabriel Garcia Marquez

The diner was lit up and cars were parked in front of it. A sign in the window said, "Grand Opening." Pop and Eddie were behind the counter waiting on people. The place was full. No sooner did Aunt Helen pull in a parking spot and turn off the engine, I reached in front of her and started blowing her horn and bouncing up and down on the car seat. She slapped at my hand and yelled, "Stop that, you damn fool! You've got everybody looking at me!"

Pop waved from behind the window, Eddie shook his head side to side, and Aunt Helen blew out a puff of air.

I loaded up my arms with my things so I wouldn't have to make a second trip back to her car. Kicking open the car door and using my butt to close it, I dashed off to the house without saying, "Thank you," or "Goodbye." I left Aunt Helen standing in the parking lot, staring after me.

"Well, thank you, too!" she called out, and slammed her car door shut and strutted over to the diner.

Who knew what she'd tell Pop about me coming home tonight. Who cared? I was home.

Mom met me at the front door of the house and took the paper bag full of dirty clothes from my arms. I dropped my suitcase on the porch, hugged her around her waist with all my might.

"What's this?" she said. "I thought you were staying until the end of the month."

"Change of plans," I said and made for my room.

My room was painted and papered. The window had a shade and curtains. Mickey had the cot now and I had a real twin bed, with round metal bars in the footboard and headboard where I could stick my bubble gum. It was a shiny, dark-brown paint and felt slick like a car's fender. Burrowing my face in my pillow, I thought, "It smells like Ma Wazelewski's, all fresh air and bleach."

After putting my clothes away, I went to the living room and curled up on the couch by Mom, who was watching television. Mickey was lying on the floor, coloring in his Hopalong Cassidy coloring book, Andy sat at the kitchen table drawing. Mom put her arm around my shoulder. Aunt Moncie's wrong. Everything will be better now.

The Diner, School, Friends and Dreams

". . . being alive is so much work at something
you don't always want to do...
The machinery is always going.
Even when you sleep.

Andy Warhol

Pop put me to work in the diner the day after I came back from Aunt Helen's.

"Ya hafta start learnin' the business because when you're older ya gotta work here after school," he said. "Andy and Eddie won't be around forever."

We were open twenty-four hours a day. Mom, Pop, and Eddie each did eight-hour shifts. Andy filled in when Eddie wanted time off and would have to work full-time if Eddie got married. And when Andy was gone, *whahla!* that left only me.

"Who's going to cover for me when they're gone?" I asked.

"We'll cross that bridge when we get to it," Pop said. And, when I asked again, he said, "Stop counting your chickens before they hatch," which was like getting no answer at all.

Pop said I had to use boiling hot water, soap, and lots'a bleach to kill germs from people's saliva on the dishes and silverware because he couldn't stand spoons or cups with tea or coffee stains on 'em.

"That's why they make bleach," he insisted. "If ya use some every time you do the dishes, there won't never be a stain on them." A little bit to him was half a cup to a sink of water, which I said burned out my nose hairs. He laughed and said it didn't.

Pop cranked the water heater up to scalding. "Dishes and glasses," he said, "have to be very hot to drain-dry." He refused to use a towel because it left lint on them. "And," he said, "don't even ask. If it has a crack, throw it in the garbage. All kinds of diseases live in cracks – TB, maybe even cancer. Toss 'em out."

Pop also had ideas about flies, too. They carried germs from sitting on and eating horse manure. He killed every fly coming into the diner looking for a free meal with a whack so hard, it was a wonder there was anything left to wipe up.

"Flies," he said, "take a bite of your food, chew it up, spit it out, and then stamp on it with their feet. Then they slurp it up and finish eating it. And," as if that ain't bad enough, he went on, "they lay their eggs in your food. And ya know what they turn into? Maggots! Think about it when a fly sits on your food." He learned all this stuff from the Board of Health in Kingston. A friend of his who worked there got me into a special class for restaurant people. I learned there were flu-like food poisons you could give to people if you handled food without washing your hands after taking a dump. The man teaching the class said the "twenty-four-hour flu bug" was just that--someone's dirty hands touching your food. Yuck!

My hands got fiery red from sterilizing dishes. They stank from bleach. Rubber gloves didn't help because hot water ran down inside them when I rinsed the dishes under the faucet. The gloves also kept the heat in and made my hands feel even more burnt. Eventually, I got used to it.

Other jobs Pop gave me were cleaning bathrooms, sweeping floors, and filling napkin holders, salt and pepper shakers, and sugar bowls.

Before school each morning Pop took time to show me how to cook eggs on the grill. Later, I graduated to hamburgers. Eggs were hard to flip with the long, flat-bladed flipper, and I got to eat a lot of fried egg sandwiches before I learned how not to break the yolks. He taught me when to push the bread down in the toaster so it'd pop up right when the eggs were finished. He said I would make an excellent short-order cook.

I liked bacon. But he wouldn't let me touch the slicing machine. "Bacon's expensive and we have to save it for the customers," he said. "Besides ya'd end up takin' a finger off."

Sometimes he let me serve soup or drinks. I liked making sodas. We had a real soda fountain like Doc Vaughn's, with a seltzer spigot, and syrup canisters with hand pumps that had to be refilled once a week from gallon jugs. And there was hard ice cream to scoop out of five-gallon containers – vanilla, chocolate, and strawberry. We had chocolate syrup, sliced strawberries, and walnut pieces swimming in thick syrup to put on ice cream sundaes. And whipped cream and cherries on top. I couldn't have any of this, either.

"Ya'll eat up my profits," Pop said. He was always worried about his profits. He didn't know I squirted whipped cream in my mouth, or took a spoon to scoop out ice cream when he left to go over to the house for something.

Pop let me have the day-old Danish pastries. He sliced them in half, put butter on them, and toasted them on the grill. Till customers saw him cooking them and asked to have theirs heated up, too. Then they weren't mine anymore.

When the pie was down to the last gooey piece that no customers wanted, I asked for it before my brothers got to it. After scarfing down all this pastry for half a year, I got sick of them. All I ate from a pie was the filling and, when I left the crust, Pop gave me his spiel about starving refugees eating from garbage cans.

"Don't know what's worse," Pop said, "running a bar and watching people get drunk or owning a diner and having to sober them up."

Either one. It didn't matter. On the weekend, drunks made a mess of the bathroom. Men were the worst. They couldn't aim straight and missed the urinal. The next day, I got to wash the walls and the floors where they sprayed. Sometimes they puked in there, too – in the urinal, the sink, the garbage pail, or the toilet. But most of it was on the floor. I was glad somebody invented rubber gloves and Clorox, because no way would I touch that stuff with my bare hands. Pop had a sign on the wall that read: "In case of atomic attack, hide under our urinal. It hasn't been hit yet."

He had another sign alongside that one: "If you don't eat here, don't shit here. We don't want the ass-end of your business." If a person came in the diner and used the bathroom and headed out without buying anything, he'd say, "Leave your dime on the counter, or y'all come back again. We're here for your convenience – a twenty-four hour roadside shit house." It'd crack everyone up.

A HALF-YEAR WENT BY and I settled into a routine of school, work, and seeing my two new friends. At school it was like Sister Cecelia "Rocky" Catherine, the principal, had it in for me. She had me sitting near the front of the class where she could always watch me. I wondered if Sister Alma Regina filled her head with a bunch of garbage, or if it was because she had Andy in her class first. He was always doing something to tick the nuns off.

Sister Cecelia Catherine had a nasty streak. She never lost her temper and yelled. She was just plain mean. If there was any whispering she told me to be quiet even when I wasn't doing the talking. She liked grabbing Eleanor Post and me by the hair and yanking us out of our seats and into her office to scold us.

We weren't the only ones on her hit list. Tommy Graham got hell because he was left handed and she tried to make him right handed, and Bobby Bailey got caught making spitballs and she made him make a zillion of them. She dressed him up in a yellow choir robe, tied green bows in his hair, and dragged him around to all the rooms, where she threw the spitballs on the floor. He had to get down on his hands and knees and pick them all up. The kids laughed at him. I didn't think it was funny and felt sorry for him. When I told Mom about it she said, "No, it's not funny. Sister is sadistic. She's teaching you to laugh at someone being humiliated. Don't you ever do that."

When I got finished with school or work in the diner, I hung out with Alice Crispell. She was older than me. Andy had the hots for her. Later I met the girl who lived across the street from us. Her name was Erika Weber. She came straight from Germany. We met when she came over to see if her brother Walter could play with

Mickey. At first, Alice and I made fun of her, saying "Heil Hitler," and crap like that. Then she cried and explained her family came to America to get away from the Nazis. It made me feel like a jerk, and I apologized.

Alice and Erika were the only girls close to my age and in walking distance of our diner. They had older thoughts than I did. They also had their periods and tits. My boobs were late starting and I was still waiting to get my friend. They talked to me about boys, fucking, and having babies. Some of it I knew, some of it was gross, and some stuff I pretended to know so they wouldn't think I was ignorant. Even Bobby Ann didn't know all of what they told me.

It was a real pain when Andy started being at Alice's house more than I was. He visited her when her parents were working. If I was there he told me to get lost and not come back or he'd break my skinny freaking neck. Erika said they wanted to get it on without us watching. Maybe she was right. We got to be better friends then. I liked it when I got to sleep over at Erika's house and listen to her family talk German. Their house was spotless, with no extra junk around. And Mrs. Weber made the greatest food. My favorite was her plum soup with a cinnamon-and-sugar kind of puff pastry.

Except for a few curse words Erika taught me, I couldn't speak German. But I got good at getting the gist of what was being said, like I understood the Slovak my aunts spoke. Some words sounded alike.

Tonight at the dinner table, while I was waiting for Mrs. Weber to sit down before I ate, Alida, Erika's older sister, asked in German, "Who said she could eat here? She's here all the time. Tell her to go home where she belongs." I got up from the table and left in tears. Everyone, including Erika, was surprised that I knew what Alida said.

At home, I sat pouting and watching television. Why did Alida want me gone? What's it to her anyway? I'll never eat dinner there again, unless she's not there. I thought it'd be different, not living in the village. Why didn't people want me around?

Pop came into the living room and switched the station because he wanted to see some guy playing a violin. His name was

Yehudi Menuhin. If I had a name like his, I'd change it. But he sure could play. He was doing, "The Flight of the Bumble Bee." Pop liked stuff like that. Mom went for Perry Como or Andy Williams on the Steve Allen show. Pop said he'd rather watch Lawrence Welk with his fake champagne bubbles than those "crooners" who couldn't sing to save their lives. I liked Pop's big tenor voice. It was like thick pea soup and the "crooners" were like chicken broth, thin and drippy.

IN BED THAT NIGHT the ticking sounds of the alarm clock drummed in my ears. The numbers glowed. The clock sat under the chipped plaster lamp of Snow White and Dopey with the yellowed, torn shade.

"When you gonna throw that ugly thing away?" Erika asked.

"When my mother gets around to buying me a new lamp," I lied. I liked my lamp.

I wound the clock before going to bed. Like always, I set it back in the little footprints it made in the dust. The clean circles from the pads on the bottom of the clock gave it a space in the comic books, handmade paper dolls, and the White Owl cigar box filled with crayons.

"How long you gonna play with kid stuff?" Erika asked. "Aren't you too old for paper dolls?"

I never tried to explain they were my creations, or my dream of going to Hollywood to be a dress designer to the stars. But after that, I put all my dolls, my designs, my songs and my toys in a cardboard box and shoved them under my bed so she wouldn't know I had them. What was so great about growing up, anyway? I didn't want a body boys would want to touch. I wasn't looking forward to turning thirteen.

Lying in bed, I did my search of the dark, looking for strange shapes in the shadows. There was only the sounds of Mickey snoring and sucking his thumb across the room. He still slept like a frog, with his legs tucked under and his butt sticking up in the air.

Rolling onto my back, I let one arm dangle over the edge of my bed, and dozed off to a place where I wasn't asleep but I wasn't really awake either. The clock's tick-tick was all I heard.

My eyes snapped open. I sucked air in through my nostrils and held my breath to squelch a scream. What just touched my hand? I was afraid to move, afraid to make a sound. I listened and waited, too scared to lift my arm up onto the bed.

"Meow." Tommy, Mom's orange tabby, jumped up on my bed and pushed his face in mine. I let out a deep sigh and looked into the shadows. Nothing moved. Tommy. It must've been him touching my hand. He rubbed up against me, forcing his body into my armpit where he curled up for the night to sleep. I wrapped my arm around him. "Damn cat! You scared me," I whispered to him.

Moving out of the village didn't get rid of the bad memories and dreams. This wasn't the first time that I woke up afraid to move or breathe. Would I ever stop being afraid of a man that I wouldn't know even if he was sitting right next to me? Maybe with time I'd get used to the sounds and shadows of this house.

1955
THE AUGUST FLOODS

In the world there is nothing more submissive and weak than water. Yet for attacking that which is hard and strong nothing can surpass it.

Lao-Tzu

July and August '55, a year after moving out of the village, was one of the hottest summers ever for our area. It was so nasty out, the birds wouldn't sing. The temperature went into the high 90s and stayed there. The humidity was making whatever I touched in the diner feel damp. The electric fan sitting on top of the refrigerator, turned its motor-head left and right, and blew hot air around like an old man with asthma who had a creaky neck from arthritis. I sat at the end of the counter, sweating, reading the comics in the newspaper, and eating lunch.

"Ya'll break a sweat just standing still," Leo Trandle said, as he came in the diner. He swiped his brow with a clean hanky he took from his pants pocket. He sat on a stool next to me. Leo must've been the tenth person to complain about the weather. Pop agreed with all of 'em.

"Gimme an iced tea, kid," Leo said.

Taking up my newspaper, Leo pointed to the forecast saying the temperature would rise to over a hundred degrees tomorrow.

"If I was a bettin' man, I'd lay odds it's gonna hit 102 tomorrow." He grinned.

That was funny coming from Leo who played the numbers or the ponies every day.

"Yer on," Pop said. "Five bucks on 105 tomorrow."

"Ya crazy, Cherny? 105? Boy, this'll be like takin' candy from a baby."

Later, Hank Wenzel, our mailman-bookie, came in for ice coffee and a hamburger. He was a short, slight man with a face that looked like it had been run over by football cleats.

"Hey, what ta' hell's happening in Boston, Ed?" Hank asked. "Ya see the *Freeman* t'day? Thousand cases of that polio shit there. Christ. Hope it stays there."

"Ya can say that again," Pop answered. "I'm more worried about Hurricane Connie hitting us. After last year with Hazel killing a hundred seventy people."

"Ah, ya worry too much, Ed. It'll prob'bly spin out to sea, like the last two did. The weather people are always trying to scare the shit outta us."

"I don't know, Hank. Gotta bad feeling. Knees are aching something awful. They say Connie will hit harder than Hazel. And that bitch took down the pines next to my house and all my electric lines with 'em."

Pop should've bet on this hunch, too. The temperature went to 105 the next day, and smiling, he took Leo's five bucks. Connie hit six days later, killing fourteen people in New York, twenty-five total. Hurricane Diane came in right on Connie's heels five days later with 100-mph winds and lots of rain. Diane took one hundred eighty-four lives by the time she blew out. The Rondout Creek went over its banks and over Main Street twice in less than a week. Connie's water just stopped pouring outta houses when Diane drowned them again, but worse. The creek rose up twenty-four feet.

Houses upstream got torn loose from their foundations and went bobbing down the river, crashing against bridges that got ripped loose from their moorings. Ten bridges from Ellenville to Rosendale were smashed to smithereens or were badly damaged. Whole trees, two and three feet around, came down the river like bouncing buoys with their roots waving hello in the air. The trees tangled up with other junk and created logjams. The jams raised the river higher than it ever was in the village and kept it high. Two-story homes on the lower Main filled up like giant fishbowls. Their whole first levels were underwater from floor to ceiling. People thought they could stay in their houses and ride out the storm. But volunteers in rowboats had to rescue adults and children in their pajamas. The creek was so deep on Main it went up and over Doc Vaughn's stairs and through the doors of the Rosendale Theatre. They didn't have a dry seat in the place.

Every day I read more about the damage the flood was doing. It didn't seem real because we were up high and dry outside the village. It got more real when I heard about the crazy stunt Eddie pulled off.

Boy Scouts were camping on one of several islands in the creek behind Villa Bianco, on Creeklocks Road. Their leader didn't seem to know a hurricane was coming. They got stranded as the creek started to rise. Rowboats couldn't cross the creek. It had turned into a raging river.

Eddie volunteered to swim out to the island. The story we got from Eddie, and several of his friends, was that he said, "Tie a rope to a tree here and I'll tie the other end around my waist. You guys hold onto it. I'll swim across and tie my end to a tree. Once we get a line strung across the river, you get in the rowboat and use the rope to pull yourselves hand-over-hand to get to them."

Everyone knew Eddie had won medals for swimming non-stop across Williams Lake and back, which was a good half mile. But some doubted he could do this.

"Ya sure ya want to try this?" Ray Temple said he asked.

"Got a better idea?" Eddie wanted to know. "If we don't get 'em soon the creek'll crest, and we won't have to worry about getting 'em at all."

Eddie stripped down to his skivvies, tied the rope to his waist, and dove in the water. Twice he was hit with large tree branches and went under, and the guys on shore hauled him back. Eddie rested till he caught his breath. He blessed himself with the sign of the cross and kissed his miraculous medal hanging on a chain around his neck and said, "Okay, Jesus. You and me. Here we go. Third time's the charm."

Ray Temple said the Boy Scouts cheered Eddie as he came near the island. They grabbed his arms and helped drag him up on shore where he lay down exhausted. The boys and their leader tied the rope around a tree, and the rowboat crossed the creek and rescued everybody. Eddie was the last one to leave the island. It made me mad he never got his name in the paper like other people did! He laughed at the special award I made him. I put "HERO" on it. "I love you, Eddie," I told him. "You are my hero." What would I have done if he had drowned?

Volunteers hung out at the Chalet Bowling Alley parking lot. Pop yelled at the Red Cross in their van for having the nerve to charge for coffee and doughnuts. "Where does my donated money go that ya can't give a man a cup of coffee for free? Sons of bitches!" he said. Pop never donated another dime to the Red Cross ever again.

Back to the restaurant Pop went and loaded his car up with free hot coffee, free hot booze, free pastries and rolls he bought that morning. He told every wet, tired, hungry person he met, "If you ain't got money, go to my diner. Dry out and get something to eat."

"Ed," Mom said, when she heard about it, "we can't keep this up. We're barely feeding ourselves."

Pop had run out of money before he could get his bar open. He let his liquor license run out, also. When he started making ends meet in the diner, the Rockefeller Thruway opened and took the long-distance tractor-trailers off Route 32 that ran in front of our diner. We needed that truck trade. Now it was all but gone. With 32 being flooded over four weeks, and local traffic not getting through, Mom said this would "kill us". She was afraid it would put us in a money pit so deep, we wouldn't be able to climb out.

"You give the shirt off your back," Mom said. "Who's going to pay your bills when this is over? The church? Charity begins at home!"

"There's people out there that's got gawd damn less 'an we do right now, and they need help," Pop said.

"Yeah? And some magnificent un-see-able something is going

to reward you for your generosity? Where in heaven? That isn't going to help us here and now!"

"Shut up, Edith. Stop thinking about yourself."

"No! Because you never think about tomorrow!"

Pop grabbed up the pot of hot booze, the coffee urn, and other supplies, and stomped out. Each time he came back from town, he told me what was going on and ignored Mom. He had buckets of dirty coffee cups for me to wash. I was getting tired, but I was helping.

Walk To Town

*He maketh his sun to rise on the evil and on the good,
and sendeth rain on the just and on the unjust.*

Bible: New Testament. *Matthew* 5:45

Customers at our diner were telling about houses washing downstream and bridges pulled down from twenty miles away to here. In Rosendale, bullshit could be manufactured in the blink of an eye, but just in case, I wanted to see what happened and how bad the theater got hit. Skipping and humming, I set off for town.

Five minutes away from our diner, I stopped and stared bug-eyed. I was still a half-mile from the village and small waves were lapping at the tips of my sneakers. The creek never got this high! Sure, the lowest end of Main Street always flooded in a heavy rain. But you could drive or walk right through the ten or twelve inches of water. I looked at Tratarios' new grocery store where it sat at the base of the hill. It was so deep in dirty creek water I knew all the food inside was ruined. I looked around and saw telephone poles and route signs stuck up here and there. It was the only way I could guess where the highway split and went through town. No wonder Pop laughed and said, "If ya want to see anything, ya better borrow a rowboat."

Louie Mastro, a blaster, had to dynamite a logjam at LeFevre Falls before the creek would go down enough to open the main roads to emergency traffic. That's when I knew I had to check out the theater. It was bad enough I couldn't go to the movies every night of the week like before we moved, but if Tony closed for good I'd curl up and die.

When I asked Pop if it was okay to go back down a second time, he said I better not come home covered head-to-toe in mud.

"Put boots on your feet," he growled.

I opened my mouth to gripe, but he read my mind.

"I don't care how hot it is outside. Ya going down there, ya gonna put something on your feet, young lady. Yer not ruinin' 'nother pair of sneakers."

Obeying with a sour puss, I took off again. No one was guarding the road into the village. When I came around the bend I saw the Bridge View Inn that sat on the riverbank next to the bridge for years. The front door and parking lot faced route 32. A screened-in porch that was a dining room, hung out over the creek. I think it was before building inspectors. At best, the porch looked like a swayback mare. It was two stories up in the air, no land under it. To keep from sagging down to the water, it was braced up with two-by-fours against the foundation. The porch jiggled when you walked across the floor to your table, making you feel like you were stepping on a wet sponge. And that was before the flood. Pop always said, "One day, a porch full of people are gonna find themselves eatin' with the eels and the crappies." Well, after this flood, with trees crashing into it, the whole building would have to go.

On the next bend in the road was All Saints Episcopal Church, with a view of the creek. Lying on the ground was a whole lot of smelly, slimy gray-green muck, and clay-covered dead fish. Yucky clothes, a battered cooking pot, a beat-up garbage pail, broken tree branches, and busted-up boards from houses were all over the place. A big tree was on its side. It was decorated with scraps of fabric, maybe from a blouse or a dress. Lying near it was a mud-packed head of a Tiny Tears doll with clouded-over eyes, a ripped Keds high-top sneaker, and – Holy Moley! – a soggy Captain Marvel comic book.

I stood on the low rock wall that held in the lawn of the church next to the sidewalk, and looked back at the Bridge View Inn where it sat swaying like a drunk. I stared at the junk lying around me. This wasn't B.S. This was sad.

Pee-eww! This town sure does stink! My insides felt funny. Kind of glad and sad all at once. Like how it'd be watching a bully go sailing off a cliff wearing my brand-new roller skates he just stole from me.

A man in dirty jeans and muddy boots called out to me, "Hey, kid!"

I stopped in my tracks, almost pissing my pants. Who's that? Ah, it's only old Fritzie Mertine.

"Whatcha ya doing here?" he said. "G'wan, git home 'fore ya git run ov'r or som'."

"Ah, c'mon, Fritzie. It's me, Judy Cherny. I'm going to help the Rosenkranses' clean out their house."

I lied. Well, I'd help them if they needed it, even if Bobby Ann and I weren't speaking.

"Awright. Watch out on da' mud. Don't fall an' break ya freakin' neck," he warned.

Fritzie and his wife, Mae, used to drink at Reid's. He was a boxer, a Golden Gloves champ. After his wife died he became a drooly drunk that sat on the stairs in front of his apartment talking to himself. Some jerks beat the crap out of him on his way home from a bar one night. They robbed him of his government money. They found him next morning sprawled out on the sidewalk right where the hoodlums left him. He ain't been right since. Fritzie is Jerry Mertine's brother.

Fritzie was helping the volunteer fire department hose off the road and the sidewalks with the same dingy creek water that flooded them. They shoved the crap from the sidewalk into the road with push brooms, shoveled it into the dump truck, which plopped the whole mess back in the river.

Whistling, "Hi ho, hi ho, it's off . . . ," I tromped on. I liked listening to my feet locked in Andy's black, hand-me-down buckle-up galoshes, make these great squishing sounds in the muck.

People dragged their belongings out in the sun to dry. Furniture sat on gray clay-covered lawns. A tingle ran up my spine and over the back of my head. I scolded myself with a picture of Sister

Cecilia Catherine's squinty eyes and wagging white finger, saying, "It's not right to take pleasure in others' misfortunes. Put yourself in their place. What if this had happened to you?"

But I couldn't. 'Cause it didn't. And I was feeling mighty glad for me.

Christine was the first kid I saw who was home. "What happened to your things?" I asked. Nothing was sitting outside.

"My Paw put everythin' upstairs " she said, as she pushed a shovel of soggy plaster out her front door. "It didn't get wet."

Standing in her living room, I saw a brown water stain on the wallpaper near the ceiling. Floodwater filled the whole first floor. The houses on this end of town were only a stone-throw away from the creek. It was hard to think of her living room turning into a giant fish tank for nasty needle-teeth eels, crap-eating carp, and long-whiskered bullheads.

Later on, the Army Corps of Engineers would come, dig out all the islands in the creek, hack down the three large sycamores across from the Church, and put ugly giant gray-and-white-streaked boulders on the bank. There would be nowhere to sit in the shade and watch the river after a rain. They would make the creek crawl and never flood its banks again.

Christine's father turned from ripping wet plaster off the wall.

"Either help or git," he said, in a snotty voice.

I stared at him and remembered when I asked to use her bathroom and wasn't allowed to. I had to run all the way home to be able to go and just made it in time.

He can clean up his own mess. I hope he gets a sore back. I left without saying goodbye.

I walked past the public school lane where Eddie's friend Gwendolyn LoBello lived and thought it wasn't fair to flood her house. She had CP or MS or some such initials. And Barbara Plonski who lived across the lane from Gwendolyn, it wasn't fair to flood her family's house, either. Barb was older than me. Her brother Johnny was in my grade at Saint Peter's. We were friends. Their father, John Sr., hung out at our bar and said I could come to his house whenever I wanted because I never picked on Barb because she was chubby.

When Barb went to high school she got real skinny from not eating right. Then she went swimming, I think it was May Day. She caught pneumonia. I visited her in the hospital. Later that night she died.

Across the street from the school lane lived Ann Marie. I stood in front of her empty house. The memory of her mother calling me "white trash" was as fresh as it was when I was nine.

I turned away and made my way up Main Street to the driveway alongside Reids expecting to see the Rosenkranses' outside cleaning up their yard. But the creek shifted their house right off its foundation. It looked like it was so tired it wanted to fall down. It was empty. Please, Jesus, let them all be safe.

The land went up from here on out of town. If it weren't for high water marks on buildings, you'd never see the gradual rise. Being farther away from the creek, the flood didn't hit these houses and businesses as hard.

I looked at a broken window with torn curtains hanging in brown-stained strips and couldn't feel sorry for them. Good, I thought. God made you as dirty as you made me feel when I lived here.

Mr. Reid came out from his bar and saw me standing in his driveway. He scrunched up his face like he'd just smelled a pile of dog poop. I crossed the street and stood with arms folded in front of my chest and my feet spread apart, facing the bar. I glared at him while he shoveled ca-ca's out the barroom door.

Bet the upright piano got ruined. I wished Pop stole it when we left. The shuffleboard must be ruined too. No way Reid could pick that sucker up to save it. The picture of him trying to lift it made me laugh. Out loud.

"G'wan! Get outta here!" Reid yelled.

I was good at giving the "evil eye" and standing forever without twitching a muscle. Catholic school had taught me good. I wasn't moving. Not for him, not for nobody. It was a free country and he don't own this side of the street.

Thinking about Reids made me feel yukey. Watching Mr. Reid got boring, and was glad when he stomped back in and didn't come out again. It was getting late and I needed to get to church for confession. I'd check the theater on the way. I felt like one of them good guys in the Bible, where Moses parted the Red Sea. And I got to leave before the raging waters washed over the bad guys. Thank you, Sweet Jesus!

Maybe the Sisters were right, and God did work in mysterious ways, and we weren't supposed to question Him. This idea was like a wool blanket on a cold night, warm, but itchy. Again, I felt glad and bad at the same time. I didn't know what feelings were the right ones to be having. For years I worried God forgot about me. Now I wasn't sure. I wish Ma Rosenkranse was here to talk to. She was full of common sense.

The Rosendale Theatre didn't get too trashed. When it opened again there'd be new seats, new rug runners, new candy machines, and it'd smell cleaner than ever, Tony said. He wouldn't let me in to see the mess, but he promised he wouldn't be closed for good.

The dingy village would be gone, because everything is being bleach-wiped and washed down. Windows getting fixed, and paint making the buildings look better than before the hurricanes. It'd be a different looking town, like I never lived here, except for the people. They'd be the same. Small towns have big memories. Can't paint over them, I thought and headed to Saint Peter's.

The Catholic school sat a driveway's width from the bank of the creek. It looked like the basement community room took on water. A maintenance man in rubber boots was going in and out carrying soggy boxes. The Sisters were sorting through the mess.

Every Saturday since moving and riding the school bus home, I had to trek up to church for Confession. One priest heard all the confessions, unless a big holy day was coming up and Catholics would get religious, then two were needed. There was no sure way of knowing who'd be on duty. We weren't supposed to ask, but if I could find out I did. No way would I tell Father Reidy, who looked like Gordon MacRae, the movie actor, what my mortal sin was. And I got him all the time lately. Not confessing and worrying if I died I'd go to hell was starting to get to me.

Kneeling, I waited for the window in the confessional to open. When it did, it was with a bang and startled me. I blurted out, "Bless me Father, for I have sinned . . . ." I hated having to tell any priest the bad things I'd done or said, or had thought about doing or saying. I guessed at the number of my wrongdoings and wished I could lie and say "I didn't do anything wrong." But that wouldn't fly, because only Jesus was perfect. And I was a sinner, so I had to come up with numbers. Next year when I got to high school – depending on whether I went to Saint Ursula's or Kingston High – maybe I'd quit going.

There must be a way to get the priest to ask a question so I knew who was behind that black cloth screen. "I had immoral thoughts about people in Rosendale . . . ."

He said nothing. Was he listening to me, or was he bored and not paying attention?

"I was glad some people's houses got flooded . . . ."

I waited.

He didn't ask why. He doesn't care. He was there to punish me, to hand out Hail Mary's and Our Fathers for me to pray, and make me promise not to do the same stuff over again. I jumped when the priest asked if I had anything else to confess. Damn! It was Father Reidy.

"Nope!" I said, and crossed my fingers. Crossing your fingers turned a lie into a fib, which was a venial sin, not a mortal one. I don't know who told me that, but it worked for me.

It was hard to keep my mind on my final prayer, the Act of Contrition.

"Oh, my God, I am heartily sorry . . ." I wanted out, and raced through the prayer

Home. I wanted to get home, out of these muddy clothes and boots. I wanted hot water, a brush, and scouring powder to scrub my hands. And food! Mom maybe made a pot roast with gravy and potatoes. Maybe she even made up my bed with clean sheets, if she washed clothes today.

"For these and all my sins I am heartily sorry . . . Amen." Done. Bang! Father Reidy slapped the window closed. I stood up and pushed back the velvet drape and breathed in the cool air of the sanctuary. I held the curtain open for the next person in line. She looked at me and down at the floor. She hesitated, lowered her eyes, and went in the confessional. I dropped the curtain closed, looked at my feet and saw dried mud on the floor.

It was Mrs. Mathews. She looked so perfect, dressed in black and white. She reminded me of Jane Wyman starring in a black-and-white movie I saw once. What could her sins be? Did she lie, or say bad words?

Kneeling at the altar before the beautiful statue of Mary, I prayed the prayers to wash away all my sins . . . except "the one" I kept promising God I'd soon tell. I just didn't know what part was the sin. The not telling about it? Or the feelings? Or because I let it happen?

I practiced telling in front of my mirror. Each time I sounded like an idiot, tripping and stuttering over my words. How much did the priest have to know? Thinking about it made my face get hot and my brain get fuzzy, till I couldn't think straight. My head ached, and I got sharp pains in my stomach. I can't keep this secret anymore. I gotta get rid of it.

The Problem of Confession

*I have yet to see any problem, however complicated,
which, when you looked at it in the right way,
did not become still more complicated.*

Poul Anderson

WHY DID FATHER REIDY have to hear confessions today? Why couldn't Father Mulry? I would've told. I would've. Jesus, why can't you ever give me a freakin' break? My mind raced as I walked away from the church.

When I got to the bridge, I stopped, leaned over the railing and watched the swollen river do its roller-coaster ride with the bobbing tree branches and trash. Too bad this muddy river can't wash away the garbage I'm keeping inside me. If I wasn't afraid of going t'hell, I'd jump. No matter how many confessions I went to, or how hard I scoured my hands with scrub brush and bleach, this muddy river of memories kept coming back in my dreams. It brought pictures of a dirty me, a drowning me, a me I hate. The dreams of the man scared me awake. I lay in bed; eyes wide open, looking in the dark, struggling for air, blood pounding in my ears till it drowned out the tick-tick of my lopsided clock.

My imagination floated with the current, I saw myself falling off the side of the bridge, and like in my dream, going underwater into the blackness, not knowing which way was up or down. I felt logs crashing into my body, the wind being knocked out of me, gasping for air, and clawing at the water. It'd be easier than telling about the man. I read that drowning was like falling asleep, once you couldn't hold your breath anymore. How bad could it be? Memories swirled in my head, flooded my mind, and threatened to pull me under.

I snapped out of my daydream and wondered why, even after moving, these feelings of being dirty chewing gum on the bottom of someone's shoe wouldn't leave me. Why am I crying again? I'm such a lily-livered chicken. Jump or Confess. One or the other. But what about hell? Just put the man in the same place where setting the bathroom fire is, where Mickey got blamed, or cutting off the daddy long leg's legs. Put it all . . . put it where I won't remember and feel bad anymore. I guess I should tell. I looked back up at the church. There were no more cars outside.

Okay, Jesus, next Saturday, come hell or high water, ha-ha, I'll take whatever punishment comes. Even if I have to pray a million rosaries, how bad could it be? I have the rest of my life to pray them, I thought and hightailed it home.

"Nice of you to join us," Mom said. Pop, Mickey, Andy, and her were already eating dinner. I grabbed a plate and sat down.

"Did you wash your hands?" Pop asked, without looking up from his pot roast, gravy and dumplings.

Why did he ask questions he knew the answer to? I went to the sink and washed up. Was this the right time to ask him? I wondered.

"Did ya hang the towel up?" Pop asked.

"Yes," I answered, trying not to sound snotty when I stuffed the towel over the bar on the wall.

Mom went to the stove to get more meat from the pot.

"I want to go to Saint Ursula's High School," I blurted out.

Pop kept shoveling food in his mouth like I didn't say anything.

Mom turned from the stove. "That's the all-girls' Catholic high school in Kingston, on the Strand?" she asked. "When did you come up with this hare-brained idea?"

"On the way home from Confession."

"This isn't something the nuns talked you into?" she asked.

"No. Well, Sister Cecelia Catherine keeps asking who's going to go. She needs to know before September. But, I have been thinking about it for a long time."

Mom sat down. Pop looked up and said, "There's tuition, ain't there?"

"Yeah, I have to let Sister know so she can find out if there are enough openings. Plus, she has to get information about uniforms, and how much it's gonna cost."

"Why d'ya want to go?" he asked.

"I think . . . I want to become a nun."

"Haaaaaaaaahhhh!" Mom shrieked and slapped her thighs. "Your brains really did get rattled when I had the whooping cough." She laughed some more. "I thought you wanted to be a dress designer, another Edith Head. What happened to that idea, and where do you think we'll get the money from, the money tree?"

I still wanted to be a dress designer since I couldn't be a dancer, but whoever heard of anyone famous coming from Rosendale except A. J. Snyder and the Rosendale Cement Company, and his business is all but dead now?

"You? A nun?" Andy put his hand on his mouth and pretended to stifle a laugh.

"Get me a cup'a coffee," Pop said to Mom. "And you," he said to Andy, "shut up!"

"I just sat down, Ed," Mom griped.

Pop's lips pulled into a thin line and his forehead vein pulsed. He pulled the napkin out from under his chin and slapped it on the table. She hopped up and got his coffee.

"If you're sure it's what ya really want to do, we'll figure it out," he said. " Ya ain't backin' out halfway through. Ya hear me?" he said, giving me a stern look. "Ya go, you're gonna graduate from there. I can't afford to waste no money on whims."

"Thanks, Pop." I jumped up from my chair, ran over, gave him a hug around his neck and kissed his cheek. I can't wait till I tell Sister Cecelia Catherine. She's gonna be so surprised!

"Yeah, yeah. Gowan, siddown," he said, pointing to my seat with his fork. "Finish your supper. Ya got dishes to do."

"By the way, Ed," Mom said, changing the subject, "Millie

Rosenkranse called earlier and said everybody is all right. They're staying up in Tillson with her mother until they can find a place to rent."

Pop nodded his head and kept eating. I was glad to know they were okay.

1956
GOING TO SAINT URSULA'S

Hope is a bad thing. It means that you are not what you want to be.
It means that part of you is dead, if not all of you.
It means that you entertain illusions.
It's a sort of spiritual clap, I should say.

Henry Miller

IN THE SPRING OF '56 Sister Cecilia Catherine began preparing eighth grade students for graduation in June. She arranged a day trip to Auriesville, a Catholic retreat center farther north in New York State, thinking it might further influence the graduating students to become nuns or priests. But none of the boys took the bait, and only Linda Caliendo and I raised our hands when Sister asked the girls who'd be attending Saint Ursula's in September.

Hoping she'd be surprised and pleased, I waved my hand at her, grinning from ear to ear. It was tough keeping it to myself till today. I thought I'd bust with excitement.

Sister looked around the classroom, wrote down Linda's name and looked over at me.

"You!" she said. "You're going to Saint Ursula's?"

"Yes," I stammered.

Kids snickered. The look on Sister's face, the tone of her voice, made me feel like I was breaking up into a million pieces. It took all my might to hold myself together.

"You're sure?"

"Yes," I whispered wishing and wondering how I could take back my "yes."

1970
Epilogue

The last word is never all there is.
You take a breath and someone interrupts with his or her story.
And you wait patiently, until you get your chance to speak again.

Judith A. Boggess

My art show opening was more successful than I ever thought it could be. You couldn't wipe the grin from my face. The landscapes, floral arrangements, and portraitures painted in oil were well received, with sales exceeding expectations. Who would have thought that this Rosendale street-urchin, this hapless child called white trash would ever rise to this kind of celebrity? Had a fortune teller predicted I would end up with a one-woman art show at the prestigious IBM Country Club gallery in Poughkeepsie, New York, or would have my oil paintings tour across the USA in an All Women's Traveling Art Show—I would have laughed until tears ran out of my eyes, and asked, "Who are you kidding?" But yet, here I am like a Phoenix, having risen from the ashes of abuse, neglect and contempt, to stand among family, friends, fellow artists, art critics, art collectors, and gallery owners checking their calendars for open dates to show my work. No longer am I, Judy the Bar Brat, defiled and distrusted. Now I'm known as Judith. Judith the Artist, and I say this without conceit, a very good one.

Despite having to give up the childhood dreams of becoming a dancer like Ginger Rogers, or being a famous dress designer to the stars like Edith Head, memories that make me smile to this day, I made it out of and off the streets of Rosendale. Damn it! I made it out!

Telling Pop that I wanted to quit Saint Ursula's after being there one month was very difficult. The fact was, I knew within the first week, this was not going to work out for me. Less difficult was sharing my upset with Mother Superior that had I known Saint Ursula's curriculum didn't offer any art classes, I wouldn't have enrolled. When you graduated from here, you came out ready to be a nurse, secretary or nun. I sure wasn't cut out to be a nurse, as I have an aversion to bedpans, or a secretary, because I have two left hands on a typewriter, or a nun, unless I could maybe be an art teacher. Telling Pop my heart was really set on going to art school in New York City after graduating, met with derision. "You'll only get married and have kids. It'll be a waste of money, just like ya going to Saint Ursula's," he said. "I don't care if ya think ya don't wanna become a nun. Maybe you'll change your mind. You begged to go there, you're gonna graduate from there."

Faced with that edict, I did what any emerging defiant thirteen-year-old would do. I got myself kicked out. Before the first year was over, Mother Superior sent a letter home with the directive that I attend Kingston's public high school the following year and the years thereafter. She said deliberately failing all my classes except for Science, (I still don't know how I passed that), showed I did not have the discipline or the temperament required of students attending Saint Ursula. The only good thing to come from that year was to finally go to confession and to hear the priest say, "Oh my child, you should have told sooner. You didn't do anything wrong, my dear, dear child. I'm so sorry. Remember, Jesus loves you." And bang! He closed the window between us. I knelt in the darkened confessional stunned, confused, and feeling like I did when I was told Jimmy Cagney didn't really die in the movies. Something died in me though. The banging closed of the window became a door slamming shut on all the dogma I had struggled with in grade school. I remember thinking, "I wonder what came before Catholicism, and what came before that?" Somehow I thought if I could get back to the beginning of believing, I would get answers instead of all the questions I had that were never answered. This set me on an exploration that led me into Hindu meditation, Buddhism and Native American teachings, where I reside today.

Coming from a small elementary school with eight grades in four classrooms, Kingston High School was a major adjustment from changing rooms several times a day and even some buildings, to using lockers and the cafeteria, which the later I didn't know how to use, was too embarrassed to ask, and never did learn. PB and jelly from home was my staple. I majored in art and dress design, and was on the high honor roll every year. In my final year, once again I had to put aside my dreams as there was no way to finance art school, or the cost of living in New York City. Just the thought of going to the city was intimidating and frightening to this hick kid with the wild dreams of making it big and had never been anywhere. Embarrassing also, because I didn't know who to ask for help, or even what questions to ask. No one, not the guidance counselor, the art teacher who thought my dress designs were before their time, and not even my mother ever suggested trying for a scholarship—a word I'd only heard once at age 12 from my mother who had made it feel like a dirty word, not to be uttered in her presence, and best quickly forgotten about.

My father's prediction of marriage and children came to fruition. Determined to find my way in the art field, I took private art classes when and where I could afford them, utilized many library and how-to art books, participated in outdoor and indoor art exhibits, belonged to three Artists Associations, and for a few years, was President of the New Paltz Arts Association. I worked in watercolor and oils, with brush and painting knife, and drawing in pencil; tried many styles from abstract to realistic to finally find my niche in oil painting. Need I say my art was a great morale booster? Living in a bad marriage that was doomed from the start, ended in divorce in year 13 (my lucky number). Being a single parent with four children, and working to pay a mortgage makes today, despite the many obstacles, a day to revel in the joy of my accomplishments. I'm here sipping wine and smiling, watching red sticky dots go on titles of paintings, indicating they are sold.

    Unlike the Hollywood movies, there was no "kissing my horse an' ridin' off into the sunset" with Rory Calhoun. No, "living happily ever after," with Dick Powell. There are times I still have to remind myself to keep putting one foot in front of the other, to breathe deeply, exhale fully. Pick up that paintbrush. Smile.

PHOTOGRAPHS

Cherny's Grocery Store, Kingston, NY
(L-R) Eddie, Ed Sr., Judy, Mickey, Edith, Andy

St. Peter's school 8th grade graduation (Top step L-R) Nicky Dittmar, Judy Cherny, Msg. Mulry, Eleanor Post, Pete Stein (2nd step L-R) Linda Caliendo, Veronica Muth, Johnny Blake (3rd step, L-R) Richie Giorgi, Lenny LaFera, Tommy Graham, John Bianach, (4th step L-R) Georgia Christodolas, Lydia LaFera, (Top row L-R) Larry McKay, Barbara Barbato, Herbie Hohmann (LaFera's cousins front row)

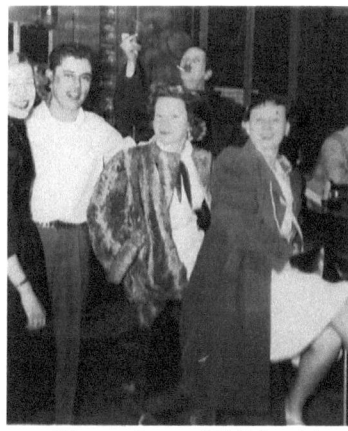

Cherny sisters: (R) 'Moncie' (L) Helen

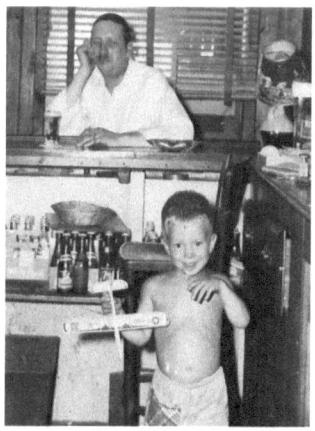

(Top) Frenchie (B) Mickey Cherny

Mickey Cherny & Lady Kerry

(L) Judy Cherny (R) Edith Cherny (B) Mickey Cherny

Best Friends: (L) Geo. Claus & (R) Ernie DeWitt

PHOTOGRAPHS | 401

(L) Edith Cherny & her father, (R) Morris DeWitt

(L) Edith Cherny (R) Lina Rosenkranse

(L) Everett DeWitt (R) Jerry Mertine

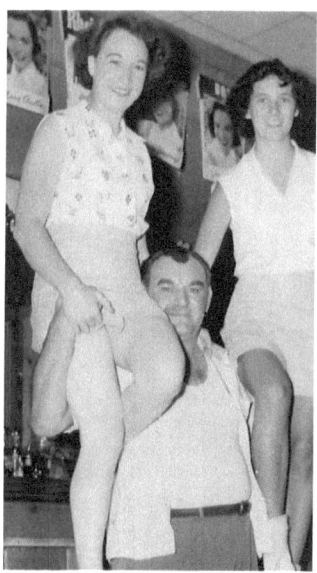

Steve Katona

George Moylan, Funeral Director

(R-L) Rudy Beyersdorfer (Cider maker), Mae & Jack Gilmartin, (unknown)

Jerry Mertine

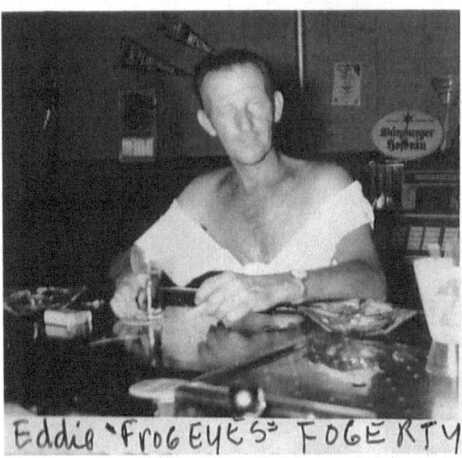
Eddie "Frog Eyes" Fogerty after a bar fight

Photographs | 403

Louie Auchmoody

Roy Dutcher

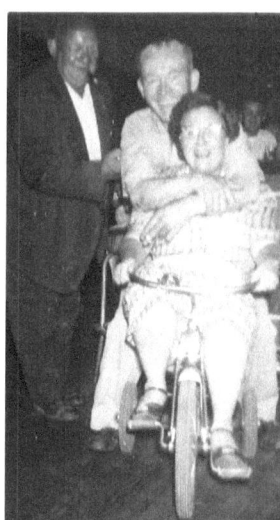
Joe Cherny (in the middle)

Ed Cherny & Mike Wazelewski

Bob Hueben & Son

Johnny Polanski & sister, Anna, (L) unknown

Gil Kelder

The Quicks

Joe & Kitty Dutcher

Millie Gersback & friend

Bill & Marge Russell

(L) Unknown (R) Big Jim Mehan

Unknown

Unknown

PHOTOGRAPHS | 407

Unknown

*(L) Sisters: Helen Evans &
"Moncie" Mitchell, New Years Eve*

Unknown

(L) Big Jim, Unknown, (R) "Tiny" Ray Williams

(L) Bill Mills, (R) Unknown

(R) Geo. Craft, Rosendale Taxi

(R) Geo. Craft

PHOTOGRAPHS | 409

(R-L) Ed & Edith Cherny, Unknown patrons

(L-R) Gert Howe, George Craft, Judy Cherny

Fritzie Mertine

Main St. view from St. Peter's

Roxy's Barber Shop - Main St. Rosendale
Pete LoBello's Barber Shop next to Vaughn's drugstore

PHOTOGRAPHS | 411

Main Street, Rosendale, NY

Narrow Main Street, (R) Mr. Roosa, (Far L) Geo. Moylan, son Moose, Roy Dutcher

Astoria Hotel

Edge/Obit

Edge/Obit

Photographs | 413

Reid's Hotel burning to the ground

Flood of '55, Main St., Rosendale in front of the Red Brick Tavern aka Schryver's Lumber Co. Inc.

St. Peter's Church, James Street, Rosendale, NY

www.ingramcontent.com/pod-product-compliance
Lightning Source LLC
Chambersburg PA
CBHW031749220426
43662CB00007B/338